To my dear & valued friend Ed Ames, יהי' "ד
With Love & Respect for
your committment, your courage, your
values, & your eveready willingness to
fight for your people.
Morton A. Klein ZOA

The Indictment

By Sabina Citron

gefen
publishing house
JERUSALEM ◆ NEW YORK

Layout: Marzel A.S. — Jerusalem

Cover Design: S. Kim Glassman

ISBN: 965–229-373-3

Edition   2 4 6 8 9 7 5 3 1

Gefen Publishing House Ltd.
6 Hatzvi St.
Jerusalem 94386, Israel
972–2–538–0247
orders@gefenpublishing.com

Gefen Books
600 Broadway
Lynbrook, NY 11563, USA
1–516–593–1234
orders@gefenpublishing.com

www.israelbooks.com

Printed in Israel   Send for our free catalogue

To my mother
A lady of uncommon dignity, humanity and wisdom

Remember, when you and I, alone in a forest
In the dying days of War,
On a chilly, drizzly April night
Tried to cross a highway — to the other side
Away from pursuing Nazis and dogs
Searching for survivors
Of our bombed-out train
In vain…

Remember, how our deep despair turned to joy
As we watched the "mighty" German army now in full retreat!
Down below at our feet
And then, as if by miracle
The traffic stopped… for a while
We crossed to safety and yet
Not safe…

Remember, how in Auschwitz
In a night *Selektion*
Your presence of mind
Saved both our lives?
Remember how we quarreled over crumbs of bread
You tried to force on me, from your meager ration?

Remember how on the train to Auschwitz, Steve was wounded
By our "guards"
Remember the orgy of violence
How our "guards" raped some women
Killed their men…

Remember how we lost hope of ever seeing Steve again?
Miraculously Steve survived.
Your firstborn Adas did not…
How you mourned him…
How it broke your heart
How amnesia blissfully overtook your mind
And at least for a while
Helped heal your heart…

But you were strong,
Your mind intact,
Lived, surrounded by our love
Beyond the age of ninety-three.
Oh, what a triumph
Over adversity!

Note to the reader

Many chapters in this book have literally been written as individual essays, and therefore the reader may find some repetitions on some issues.

Contents

Foreword

It's late, time is ticking away…

And I am, as it were, the last of the Mohicans…

My children have always urged me to write, perhaps not this book, but a book about my life, including the Holocaust, I suppose. They also urged me to write about my activities following the war and the Holocaust.

Those activities will be briefly described in the chapter dealing with the aftermath, although volumes could be written about the struggle of survivors of the Holocaust, myself included — a struggle for justice and equality, a struggle that lasted almost half of my life…

I did not want to relive the horrors of the Holocaust by writing about it, or my experience during those awful, difficult days and years. I felt a pressing need to write about the problems of the world we face today; the difficulties Israel faces every day — ever since its rebirth — and how indifference is, once again, threatening a return to the bad old days.

The survivors of the Holocaust know all there is to know about indifference! We were persecuted, humiliated beyond description and eventually put to death while the world remained indifferent. Most of us still find it impossible to understand how a civilized world could close its eyes and ears, and pretend not to see or hear the voices of the doomed victims.

As I said earlier, I do not wish to relive those horrors, but I also find it impossible to say nothing about those horrible times. So the following, brief description of only the most basic things we were subjected to and lived through forms an introduction to what guides my life and actions today.

I am probably one of the youngest Holocaust survivors, since all children under fourteen years of age were taken — nay, torn away from — their parents, never to be seen again! I was three months short of fourteen at the time of that horrific *Selektion* in May 1942 which was only the beginning of horrors to come.

We were herded like cattle to the "small ghetto" that replaced the first ghetto in Kielce, Poland — one room per family. The Nazis were not only brutal and sadistic, but also arrogant in their supreme belief that they were

1

the "Master Race." We were forced into slave labor, and shunted from one slave labor camp to another.

We were starved deliberately; we were forced into horrible living conditions where hygiene was difficult or impossible. Yet every effort was made by our people to preserve dignity and maintain basic hygiene.

We were forced to work in ammunition factories where death from explosions was a frequent visitor. And so during these horrible days, if one didn't die of starvation or typhus due to the terrible hygienic conditions, if caught attempting to escape, one could die on the gallows.

In the first slave labor camp, in Pionki, Poland, where I was still together with my brothers and parents for about two years, my eldest brother attempted to build a tunnel under the barbwire fence to create an escape route. I don't know of anyone who escaped successfully, however. If they were not caught by the Nazis, often the escapees were beheaded by local Polish anti-Semites! The Nazi guards, primarily young Ukrainians recruited to the Nazi S.S., brought caught prisoners back to camp and they were hanged on the gallows, while the rest of the camp was forced to watch. This was clearly intended to prevent further escape attempts.

In July 1944, when the front came closer to where we were, we were loaded on cattle cars, not knowing where we were being taken. At this point we were separated from my father. As soon as the train began to move, the doors of the car were opened, two Ukrainian guards appeared at the door and started shooting at random, killing at least one man and wounding my brother Steve, among several others. They then proceeded to rape a number of women, right in front of their husbands, right in front of us! The horror was indescribable.

We eventually arrived somewhere — we did not know where. It turned out to be Auschwitz, although we had no idea yet what Auschwitz was. There we were separated from my brothers during a *Selektion*, not knowing what would happen to my younger brother Steve, who was wounded in the knee. We were led away, again having no idea where to.

We were taken to Auschwitz (as opposed to Birkenau, as we discovered later). We were given striped clothing like criminals and some wooden shoes, and then taken to the showers. We were told to strip naked and leave all our belongings behind; we would pick them up later, the guards claimed. As it turned out there was nothing left when we returned; all that we had — the precious few belongings, including family pictures — was gone.

We were taken to huge wooden barracks with "shelves" for beds stacked on top of another on each side with little space between the shelves. In the center of each barrack ran a narrow platform used by the capos (and later others) to strut and shout orders at us. We felt trapped, humiliated and above all, anxious about my brothers, not knowing what would happen to them, or ourselves, for that matter.

The next day, I met another girl outside the barracks. She looked at me and asked pointing to some smokestacks, "Do you know what these are?" I had no idea and told her so. She said, "that's where the crematoria are; that's where they are burning people." In total disbelief, I looked — now I could indeed detect the smell of burning flesh!

After a *Selektion* in Auschwitz we were sent to several more camps, among them, two slave labor camps (one near Hanover — Bomblitz — the other, Elsnig, near Leipzig, both I.G. Farben factories) and Bergen-Belsen, but not in that order.

Bergen-Belsen seemed like a deliberate attempt to kill people with typhus. No sanitary conditions. Winter setting in. It was late October. Starved emaciated women that we were, we were herded into large tents, holding more than a hundred women, perhaps as many as two hundred. We were forced to lie on straw on the ground, one next to the other, like sardines. In fact, predictably, typhus did break out. We now know that Anne Frank and her mother and sister, along with so many others, died of typhus that horrible winter of 1944.

My mother and I, together with several hundred other women, were "selected" for slave labor once again, some two weeks after our arrival in Bergen-Belsen. Another slave labor camp — another ammunitions factory. Again, starvation, hard work and minimal hygienic conditions and rest. We worked twelve-hour shifts and stood for hours for *Appels*, roll calls during which they counted us before departure for work, and after arrival.

After several months of this, we heard rumors that the Russian front was getting near…and that the war was going badly for the Nazis. We wondered if these were not yet more rumors and false hopes. But early one morning, we were forced to board cattle cars, once again taking us…where?

After some days of stops and starts, we found ourselves sitting in the middle of what seemed like a very large railway siding. Through the small windows on one side, we could see gasoline cisterns; on the other side were what appeared to be trainloads of ammunition. We were told — I no longer remember how and by whom — that we were close to Potsdam, near Berlin. We presumed our captors (I have always considered it ironic that they are referred to as "guards"; they certainly weren't protecting us from anyone!) were either hoping that Berlin would not fall or that they would not be captured by the Russians as opposed to the British or US forces.

In the first few days, our guards were strangely nice to us. They brought us water and some bread, and even took us out of the cattle cars for short periods to the little forest across the railway. But that only happened twice. After that, it seemed like an interminable, endless waiting; one knew not for what. After a while, bread and water were only rarely brought to us, and the refuse was removed from the cars only at long intervals.

We were getting more and more desperate with each day and each hour. I remember one particular morning. I was "fortunate" to sit under one of the train's tiny windows; I remember getting up, looking towards the sky, towards heaven, and uttering a plea, a prayer: dear G-d, may this end — one way or another, for we have no more strength…

As if from nowhere, we suddenly heard the roar of aircraft, and before we knew it, bombs started falling on our train cars! They were not aimed at the gasoline cisterns, nor at the ammunition cars, but at us!

I must have lost consciousness, but I remember thinking before I opened my eyes that if this is death, it is not so terrible. But then I had another thought: if I can think, maybe I am not dead… I cried out to my mother, who had apparently also lost consciousness. Thankfully she quickly came to, and answered me.

We realized that our cattle car was lying on its side from the impact of the explosion. We later discovered that the bombs, which were British, hit every second car; ours was not hit.

None of the women in our car seemed seriously injured; we only had scratches and bruises. Due to the impact, the wood of what had been the wall — and was now the floor — was splintered. With strength we didn't know we still possessed, we chipped away at the splintered wood creating a larger opening, and one by one we lowered ourselves to the ground. Again with unknown strength, we "ran" (it might be more accurate to say "hobbled") toward the little forest on the other side of the railway, away from where our captors were now hiding. We were surprised to find little huts there, in that forest, as if hidden from view.

A man approached my mother and me, as we were nearing the forest. He didn't need any explanations; he knew exactly what had happened and who we were. He tried to help us; he wanted to bring us food and blankets. He told us to go into the forest and hide in trenches until he was able to come. We later found out that he was Polish, forcibly brought to work in Germany by the Nazis, but he and the others were not in concentration camps.

He did come back, bringing us some food, but also bad news. He heard that the Nazis — our "guards," were going to search for us with dogs and told us that we must cross the *Autobahn* — the nearby highway — away from our pursuers. We managed to hide for the next few days in a school on the other side of the highway, where we found ourselves among other refugees. The next few days were filled with fear of being discovered.

Our train had been bombed on April 20, 1945, Hitler's birthday. We were liberated when the Russians entered the area, some nine days later. There were nearly a thousand women in those cattle cars; apparently more than half perished in the bombing that day...

This book is dedicated to them and to the one and a half million children and all victims of Nazi barbarity who didn't live to see the true liberation of their Homeland — Israel.

Introduction

The world we live in is once again in turmoil. The entire world faces a new age, and a new enemy — an enemy unknown before. An enemy who knows no borders. An enemy who seems to strike at will, anywhere in the world. An enemy brutal and savage. An enemy against whom retaliation is often difficult and sometimes impossible.

What makes it even more difficult to defeat this enemy, and defeated it must be, is the worldview of the new generation. This is a generation that grew up in safety and security in the West; a generation that knew not the atrocities of WWII; a generation that does not believe that any war is justified, against any enemy, regardless of the heinous atrocities it commits. This generation fashions itself as "humanitarian-pacifist"; it has ready-made slogans and rallies against anything that does not fit with its way of life.

This generation, which claims to abhor the violence of war, nevertheless appears to have unending patience and understanding for the new enemy the world is facing, regardless of the horrible, brutal, and savage violence it employs in pursuit of its goals. The clever, if malicious, propaganda the enemy has employed over the past three decades to justify its atrocities has managed to brainwash and condition and to inoculate this new generation against the worst horrors the world has ever known.

Clearly, this use of human bombs as a method of warfare, to inflict the greatest possible suffering on the greatest possible number of innocents, most often deliberately aiming at civilians — and especially children — is nothing short of savagery. Those who escape horrible deaths in these attacks are maimed for life. After the news headlines have faded, countless men, women and children still lie in rehabilitation hospitals or in their own homes, their arms and legs twisted or gone, their wholeness shattered forever.

Can this new generation be so brainwashed and so conditioned, that human suffering means nothing to them; or are they really using the enemy's propaganda as a fig leaf to justify their indifference? For it is impossible to imagine that a majority of this "new generation" is totally oblivious or ignorant of facts, in this age of instant communication, where nearly every individual has access to computers, which provide alternative information on any conceivable subject.

And while it is true that Arab-Muslim propaganda has permeated much of Western society through institutions of higher learning and the like over the last three decades, it is difficult nonetheless to imagine that young scholars are incapable of independent thinking. True, political correctness often gets in the way, but still…

It is galling how informed people, who should know better, still claim — or at least go along with the claim — that somehow the human bombs the terrorists are employing are an aberration, a small violent minority within Islam, not representative of Islam, and that Islam is a "peaceful" religion despite all the evidence to the contrary.

Has anyone heard or read any condemnation by Islamic scholars, religious leaders, academics or even lay Islamic/Arab leaders of suicide-terrorist bombers? Has anyone heard a clear, unequivocal condemnation by Arab leaders of terrorism as immoral? Or has anyone heard a clear unequivocal statement against global jihad by Arab-Muslim leaders?

Quite the contrary. The hate propaganda emanating from Arab-Muslim preachers and "scholars," the hatred and violence imbued in their propaganda, praises terrorists as heroes and "martyrs"! In fact, the UN finds itself in the strange situation of not being able even to define terrorism, because of Arab-Muslim obstructionism.

There have been many books written in the past decade about the true face of Islam, and of course for the skeptics, there is always the Qur'an (you can read it straight from the source).

Israel has endured many years of Arab wars of aggression, terrorism, boycotts and the like, having to fight this lonely battle while at the same time being subjected to unwarranted criticism, and even condemnations!

The world is only beginning to wake up to the fact that it is facing a global jihad, while most of the young population appears to be living in denial. How then can they succeed in fighting a cunning enemy, when their own people prevent defensive measures?

Israel's situation is even more complex, as in addition to the above, it is also facing not so subtle anti-Semitism.

The following pages will attempt to show some of the complex issues Israel is facing vis-à-vis terrorism: the global jihad and its beginnings, as well as other issues concerning simple justice denied following the mass slaughter of European Jewry.

These pages will attempt to show the indifference Jewish people were faced with, during and after the Holocaust. During the most horror-filled years, the indifference of the world to the plight of the intended victims of Nazism, when many could still have been saved from certain death — the indifference displayed by nations who have arrogated to themselves the mantle of "humanitarianism" — defies belief! But then again, these are the very same nations who have themselves persecuted the Jewish people over millennia.

This book is a form of indictment of the leaders of these nations, who to this very day subject the Jewish state and its people to "special treatment." This book is intended to lay bare some facts which may not be generally known.

This writer also still hopes that if only good people refuse to remain silent and indifferent, the world could be a better place. For, as the popular quote has it, "All it takes for evil to triumph is for good people to do nothing."

Chapter I

The Aftermath

In the aftermath of the Holocaust, most survivors, if not all, attempted to reestablish normalcy in their lives. For the very many whose entire families were wiped out it was inevitably more difficult than for those who were fortunate to have some members of their families survive.

I was very fortunate, indeed; I was together with my mother the entire time. Eventually, after the war, we were reunited first with my father and soon thereafter with my brother Steve. Neither Steve nor my father knew that either one of them or that my mother and I had survived. My eldest brother Adas did not survive. The reunion happened in the strangest of circumstances, in places we least expected to meet...

None of this was easy. Even in Auschwitz, my mother and I were almost torn apart.

During a *Selektion* where the Nazis were taking younger women for work, my mother and I clung together. She was only forty-four in Auschwitz, but she was so badly emaciated that she looked like a ninety-year-old woman. I knew that she had no chance of being selected for work, so I gradually moved with her to the end of the line, hoping that we would be left be. But no! The Nazi officer, with an entourage of capos, came towards the end of the line, pointed to me, and said, "*Noch diese* (This one, too)." I pulled my mother by her hand, and he said, "No, only you." What happened next was in no way premeditated: I defiantly stood there and said, "No — you can shoot me right here, but I won't go without my mother!"

The Nazi seemed to stare at me, but walked away without a word. It is of course impossible to know what he thought. Perhaps he thought that since there were at least three hundred of us standing there on the *Appelplatz*, we might all rush towards him and overwhelm him. He was after all one, whereas we were several hundred, mostly mothers and daughters. I guess we will never know...

As I said earlier, survivors of the Holocaust (many of whom I knew and lived with, in close proximity) reestablished their lives, many very successfully. There were many weddings as young men and women, more often than not all alone in the world, tried to build families. We celebrated effusively the birth of children. We worked and built homes for our families. Some people began to engage in commerce, most very successfully. Wherever our people lived they helped build communities, often providing work for other newcomers.

Toronto, Canada, the sprawling town-like city where my family and I lived, turned into a metropolis within a few short decades. The Jewish population, including Holocaust survivors, played a disproportionate role in contributing to the growth and the welfare of this community.

I guess some of us, myself included, lived in blissful ignorance for some two decades, for one day, we woke up to discover that Nazism was not dead — but in fact had attempted to legitimize itself in various ways. The first we saw of this was when a Nazi "leader" announced his intention to speak in a public park in the center of the city, no less! Of course, outrage erupted in the Jewish community, and Jewish war veterans, survivors of the Holocaust and others came out in force. The Nazi was prevented from speaking as the police stepped in, quelling a major confrontation between the Nazis and the war vets, as well as some survivors.

Soon thereafter, we were shocked to discover that there were more than a thousand Nazi war criminals — a thousand members of the Ukrainian Galiczyna "SS" Division alone — living apparently undisturbed lives in our midst, most even under their own names! There was also another disturbing incident when a Nazi party — "The Nationalist Party of Canada" — attempted to put forward candidates for municipal elections.

All these events were shocking beyond belief to survivors, who reacted with anger and incredulity; how in the aftermath of the Holocaust was all this possible? I, along with others, attempted to pressure the local Jewish community leaders and later lobbied both the provincial and federal governments, to do something abut these issues.

We were told that freedom of speech, enshrined in Canadian tradition, prevented various government bodies from taking action against Nazi groups! We were told that Canada had no legal means to deal with the "alleged" Nazi war criminals. Needless to say, those explanations brought nothing but a sense of disbelief and outrage among survivors particularly, but also to some in the Jewish community in general; unfortunately, however, not in the "establishment."

We attempted to lobby our Members of Parliament, where we found more sympathetic ears in James Walker M.P., a gentile, a truly wonderful person. A group of survivors in Montreal, Survivors of Nazi Oppression, whom I met while at a national conference of delegates from all over Canada in Montreal, were equally involved in lobbying their M.P.s and other government officials.

What happened after several years of these efforts was that a "Private Members Bill" was introduced in Parliament by two dedicated Members of Parliament, Milton Klein from Montreal and James Walker from Toronto. The "Private Members Bill" was passed, which is a rarity. A special commission on hate propaganda was established, made up of high-level lawyers. One of them eventually became the prime minister of Canada, another a minister of justice, while the chair of the commission was the dean of the faculty of law at McGill University.

The commission presented its recommendations in a lengthy report, within a year, in 1970. Their chief recommendation was that since Nazi hate propaganda led to the mass murder of the Jewish people — the Holocaust — it therefore must not be allowed to become legitimized. They pointed out that Canada was a signatory to the UN Genocide Convention (1948) and the Human Rights Convention (also 1948). Both of these oblige the signatories to bring about appropriate legislation in their respective countries, dealing with incitement to hatred and violence against identifiable groups based on religion, race, color or ethnic origin. The result was hate propaganda legislation that criminalized incitement to hatred and violence against identifiable groups as above. The commission also pointed out that most of Europe had similar legislation, especially Germany, Austria and Italy. Italy had very onerous legal provisions dealing with the revival of a Nazi or Fascist party — some European countries have even imposed the death penalty on those attempting to revive a Nazi or Fascist party.

The Canadian legislation, however, had a major built-in flaw. One of the exemptions provided in the legislation is religious belief. In other words, if a Nazi "believed," based on his or her religion, "that Jews are evil," his propaganda would be exempt! Thus the Canadian government relieved itself of its burden on one hand, but made the law inoperable on the other.

Meanwhile the "Nazi Party of Canada," which I referred to earlier, was denied status as a legitimate party, since most of their supporters' signatures turned out to be fraudulent.

At the same time, another Nazi came to our attention, toward the end of the 1970s. This was a man who had a legitimate printing shop in the heart of Toronto and at the same time produced massive amounts of Nazi hate propaganda, boasting of sending it to forty-five countries, in several languages, including English, German, French and Arabic.

His name was Zündel, not that it matters. What matters is what he stood for; he was involved in the most vicious and poisonous anti-Jewish, anti-Israel Nazi propaganda. I only refer to his name because this man was involved in Nazi hate propaganda and incitement for nearly three decades, and this issue continues to this day — although I allowed myself to disengage from it more than five years ago.

But going back to the early 1980s, we had to engage lawyers (some of whom have since become judges and are still good friends). But it was a long struggle, almost half of my life, from 1965 to 2000.

During that period we had to utilize whatever laws were available in the criminal code, since we could not apply the hate propaganda provisions; the provincial attorney general simply would not provide his consent, which was required.

I will not describe the long saga; suffice it to say that Zündel was taken to court under another section of the criminal code, the False News section. After a lengthy court process, we won. We — that is, the Canadian Holocaust Remembrance Association (C.H.R.A.) — but I swore the affidavit which led to the charges.

The C.H.R.A. was the main force in all these endeavors. Zündel and his lawyer appealed. He lost the appeal and eventually appealed to the Supreme Court of Canada.

Meanwhile we — the C.H.R.A. — were also involved in another court case against a Nazi war criminal, a Hungarian gendarme captain who was responsible for the deportation to Auschwitz and to other concentration camps of more than eight thousand Jewish people — the entire population of Szeged in Hungary! Even prior to the deportation, he, together with a German Nazi officer, stripped Jews of their personal jewelry including wedding bands and watches, all this after they were forced to leave their homes and all their belongings. He then forced them into various humiliating and degrading situations.

One group was to spend the last days prior to deportation in a brick factory, amid dirt and dust. Another was made to spend days in the open on a football field during rain, without shelter. A third group he forced to stay in pigsties. Words fail me to describe the predicament of these people.

There was massive evidence against this man. He was tried in absentia and convicted in Hungary. There was witness evidence from the trial, as well as transcripts.

Because of Canadian government inaction, I believed we should force the government's hand by publicly naming him in a press conference at our lawyers' offices. We gave the journalists copies of evidence, as well as other background information which proved that Canada not only had the necessary legal tools to bring to justice Nazi war criminals, but was in fact obliged to do so. It was also obliged to search for such criminals if they resided on Canadian territory.

In fact several such trials occurred following World War II, involving crimes committed against the military. We had experts in international law, both Canadian and US, providing us with the necessary material information. Despite all this, the day following the press briefing, one tabloid accused us — that is the survivors of the Holocaust, the C.H.R.A. and me personally as the spokesperson — of telling "awful lies about an innocent man." How did the newspaper manage to "ascertain" the "innocence" of this man in such a short time? There was also a nasty editorial in the same paper accusing survivors of "taking on the colors of the perpetrators." Needless to say, we asked for an apology in a meeting with the publisher; he was pleasant enough, but — no apology!

We looked for a good libel lawyer, with little success. No one really wanted to take on the case, for a variety of reasons of their own. We finally approached a very large legal firm, with whom we have contact to this day, and they handled this case as well as the Zündel case for us, to its very conclusion.

We managed to gather witnesses and additional evidence. The day before the trial, the tabloid contacted us through their lawyer and offered to settle out of court. We were suing the editor, the newspaper and the publisher personally. Some months prior to the trial the editor was replaced, interestingly enough.

We settled for our legal fees, which were substantial at this point, and first and foremost, an apology. Since the defendant did not appear, nor send lawyers in his defense, the judge ruled in our favor.

But it didn't end there. Our lawyers were approached by lawyers for the federal government to provide them with our documents. The government was now prepared to bring this case to the federal criminal court.

After a long, protracted period which included a special court session in Hungary to take additional evidence, and a poorly represented case by the government in Toronto, the case was lost! This time, the lawyer for the defense was one Douglas Christie, who defended Zündel during his trial as well, and became known as the lawyer for all the Nazis.

The name of the Hungarian gendarme was Finta; again, the name means nothing to me. What mattered was what he did, how in his supreme arrogance he treated the Jewish people of Szeged before sending them to their deaths.

His trial was extremely difficult to watch, as his lawyer, an obvious sympathizer with the Nazis, attempted to make a mockery of the entire proceedings. The lawyer for the prosecution, did not — to all appearances — understand the full weight of the evidence against the accused, and the most damning evidence was passed over with hardly any weight given to it. Christie, the lawyer for the accused, recognized this and had a field day; he made the most outrageous statements and got away with it. The judge seemed to be almost totally preoccupied with his computer — a novelty in courts in 1985 — and hardly paid any attention to what was going on in the courtroom itself, as Christie flirted with one of the female members of the jury, making a mockery of the propriety of the court.

There were many disturbing incidents of this kind during the weeks of the court proceedings, but none to remedy the situation. We could see that there would be no justice because no proper emphasis was placed on the evidence and practically nothing said about the seriousness of the war crimes or the crimes perpetrated by the accused and his government, which not only cheerfully collaborated with the Nazis but in fact instituted anti-Jewish laws of its own long before the Nazis marched into Hungary in March 1944.

The accused himself was far from being an ordinary captain; he served as head of the "Jewish Section" as a special "detective" in the Investigation Unit. This special "section" made it easier for the Nazis to implement their nefarious program. He was also a special instructor of the Gendarme Academy. All this put him in a unique position to carry out the uprooting and deportation of the Jewish people of Szeged. Most of the valuable evidence with which I personally was familiar — because of my research — as well as the transcript from the trial in Hungary, with all the witness evidence, etc., was not made proper use of at the trial. The jury of quite ordinary-looking Canadians was not made familiar with much of the evidence, and they themselves knew little or nothing about war crimes perpetrated against the Jewish people of Hungary.

The war crimes provisions in Canadian law, in this case in particular, were for court martial, since the accused was an officer. But that was not to be, and the civilian jury was hardly qualified to judge this case, nor indeed any case dealing with Nazi war crimes.

This case, too, eventually went to the Supreme Court of Canada, where the accused was acquitted, claiming he merely followed orders. Of course there were no such provisions in Canadian or international law. He also claimed that he relied on an anti-Semitic Hungarian propaganda sheet which claimed that Jews were a danger to the state, although no such evidence existed in support of this outrageous claim.

And so another miscarriage of justice was committed. Now the Canadian government could claim, and did, that no case against Nazi war crimes could be brought to trial, because there was "no hope" for success.

After the Supreme Court decision there was an outcry in the Jewish community, even from those individuals who had not previously been involved. Petitions and briefs were put forward by several Jewish organizations including B'nai B'rith, the Canadian Jewish Congress and two or three others, and of course ourselves, the C.H.R.A., pointing out the flaws in the Supreme Court judgment, and imploring it to reverse its decision.

The Supreme Court decision was a narrow one, 4–3. We thought we had a chance; all it would take was for one justice to reverse his or her decision. Unfortunately for justice, and for Canada, and for the victims of Finta and of the Holocaust in general, this did not happen.

A similar miscarriage of justice occurred in the case of Zündel, the Nazi propagandist hate-monger. Also in a narrow 4–3 decision, the Supreme Court found that the "wrong law" was applied at his trial. They found that the Canadian hate crime provisions should have been applied. The section dealing with False News was then nullified by the Supreme Court claiming it was no longer operative since it was designed for a different period, dealing with aristocracy.

The descending justices thought the law was eminently appropriate since it dealt with False News, and Nazi hate propaganda was indeed false news!

So we could not get the provincial government to utilize the hate propaganda legislation which was so relevant to the case, and the Supreme Court of Canada ruled in its wisdom against us. Our lawyers were almost as disappointed as we were. They suggested one more attempt at the Human Rights Commission. Here again Christie, the lawyer for the Nazis, represented Zündel. He used every argument, logical or not, including challenging the impartiality and jurisdiction of the Human Rights Tribunal. The case dragged on for years. Here too, I was asked to swear out the affidavit. Before long other organizations in the Jewish community asked if they could join us, which of course only prolonged the proceedings. The mayor's committee also decided to join the effort.

It took several years. Eventually Zündel could no longer afford his lawyer — Christie — or at least that was what we were meant to believe. Perhaps Christie didn't want to spoil his "unblemished record" as he saw the writing on the wall. Zündel skipped town shortly thereafter. The case dragged on for several months after that, but eventually Zündel lost his case. The Tribunal of the Human Rights Commission ruled that Zündel must cease producing and distributing his propaganda, even on the Internet. The Internet ruling particularly was precedent-setting.

Zündel in the meantime was living in the US with his new wife. A year or so later, the US deported Zündel to the Canadian border for some immigration violation.

The Canadian authorities were not eager to allow Zündel into Canada, since he was not even a Canadian citizen. Zündel ended up spending the next two years in jail on the border on the Canadian side. A recent extradition request filed by Germany saw the deportation of Zündel to that country, where he is still in detention pending trial, on many charges dealing with Nazi hate propaganda as well as Holocaust denial which is a crime in Germany. I neglected to mention that Zündel is a German citizen, where he traveled frequently, distributing his poisonous stuff and encouraging local Nazis. He was wanted in Germany on these various charges but it is a bit incongruous that German authorities could not apprehend him during his many visits to Germany...

But as the old saying goes, "The more things change, the more they remain the same"!

A recent newspaper item (*Jerusalem Post*, October 27, 2005) informed us that:

Anti-Semitic tracts are on sale at the Frankfurt Book Fair again this year. English language copies of *The Protocols of the Elders of Zion* and Henry Ford's *The International Jew* were displayed on the shelves of one of the Iranian book sellers at the fair, according to German political scientist Matthias Kuentzel [an author and educator specializing in anti-Semitism and Islam, Kuentzel wrote *Djihad und Judenhass*, Jihad and Jew-hatred] who purchased the book there.

Last year, the book fair, one of the world's largest gatherings of publishers, was criticized for allowing Arabic book publishers to display Arabic versions of Holocaust denial and other anti-Semitic texts.

One has to wonder, if Holocaust denial is a criminal offense in Germany, how was it possible that Arabic books containing such propaganda could be displayed and sold with impunity? Worse still, one version of Iranian anti-Semitic propaganda, by one Mohammed Taqi Taqipour, states that "a global Islamic movement will soon destroy Israel"!

A spokesman for the book fair explained that in order to take legal action, someone has to complain to the police, but apparently the previous year a complaint was lodged, and nothing was done. In Germany especially, things of this sort should not be tolerated!

But here again Germany is not alone. In the late 1980s, I was invited to speak by a group of students at York University — one of the largest universities in Toronto — and was amazed to see how Middle-Eastern students were dispensing anti-Israel, anti-Semitic propaganda with impunity in broad daylight. Jewish students registered their protest with the administration but nothing at all was done.

Now it is no longer a rarity. Some two decades later Arab-Muslim propaganda is entrenched at nearly every university in both Canada and the US to say nothing of Europe; according to Islamic scholar and author Bat Ye'or, Europe has now become Eurabia.

How any country in the world can permit open advocacy of genocide is beyond comprehension. A dedicated effort is needed to combat this phenomenon, but "freedom of speech" and political correctness gets in the way!

The C.H.R.A.'s fight for equal rights under and before the law was long and arduous, but we have at least prevented Nazism from becoming re-established or legitimized, at least in Canada. Canada opted out of depriving some Nazi war criminals of their fraudulently obtained citizenship, and some are facing deportation. Still, how does any of this represent justice?! Not a fair outcome, but at least their lives are no longer peaceful.

Advocacy of genocide, whether by Nazis, Fascists or Muslims, must not remain unchallenged ever!

The additional danger is of course that Iran had for years — without detection — attempted to develop nuclear weapons, a disturbing turn of events that came to light only fairly recently. Of course Iran has the temerity to claim that the nuclear program is for "peaceful use" only! For nearly two years the Europeans have been negotiating with them to give up their uranium enrichment program, providing them with all sort of incentives — read: bribes! The Iranians are successfully stalling, while all but certainly continuing their efforts to attain nuclear capability. They already have long-range delivery systems, including long-range missiles, that could easily reach Israel and Europe and possibly the US. How long is the world going to wait before taking action?

The Russians and the Chinese are ready to veto any attempt to impose sanctions on Iran at the UN Security Council. The Russians themselves, after all, were instrumental in helping Iran develop its nuclear program.

When poisonous hate propaganda can continue with impunity for years, how long can it be before poisonous words turn into horrible deeds?

Chapter II

Anti-Semitism Old and New

Immediately following WWII and the tragedy of the Holocaust, there existed the hope — not entirely unjustified — that perhaps, just perhaps, the world was inoculated against the virus of Jew hatred (anti Semitism).

To a large extent, there were signs of that at least in Europe, where the genocide against the Jews had been implemented and witnessed. The extent of the horror of the crimes the Nazis committed against the Jewish people was filtering out daily. People were wondering if the sheer magnitude of the crime could really be comprehended not only in terms of the numbers — six million — but also the utter bestiality and premeditation.

The ongoing debate of man's inhumanity to man — based on blind race hatred against a peaceful and defenseless minority by a "civilized" well-educated society — seemed to defy all previously-held beliefs. But now, having witnessed the power of single-minded hatred based on propaganda, and the resulting horrific crimes, there seemed to be some hope based on a new understanding that such crimes could never again be perpetrated.

The old Nazis were certainly demoralized after the defeat of their "Thousand-Year Reich" promised by Hitler. In Germany soon after the war, 1946–1947, you would hardly guess that this was the place where large rallies of tens and even hundreds of thousands of Nazis marched, paraded or listened, transfixed by their Führer as he declaimed the evils of the Jews!

Now all was quiet. Almost every German you spoke to would tell you of his friends, the Jews... What a "transformation"! What causes a people indoctrinated to hate so ferociously that they either participate in the crime or at the very least turn a blind eye to it to suddenly turn meek and docile?

If ever there was a need for psychologists to analyze such a response, this must be it. Would this be common to defeated people elsewhere, or was it just a feature of this particular movement, at a particular time in history?

Not that one can ever generalize about people. This question is directed at the Nazi ideology as a mass movement, with a mass following. Certainly not a few Germans — who actually opposed Hitler and his Nazis — suffered in various degrees themselves. But one must realize that Hitler came to power in a legitimate election on March 6, 1933. We must seriously question how a civilized and well-educated people would consider voting for a man who openly led bands of hooligans — a man who was not seen as particularly bright or capable, nor an economist — to help lift Germany out of a recession. What did Hitler have to offer an apparently intelligent nation besides appealing to their base instincts?

Today, some fifty-three years after the defeat of Nazism, and sixty-five years after Hitler's coming to power in Germany, we still don't understand how rational human beings became irrational, or at least behaved in an irrational manner in the climate created by hate propaganda.

Instead of studying this phenomenon, some psychiatrists studied the victims of Nazism and even their offspring, ascribing to them certain attributes that amount to blaming the victims and their children.

Perhaps Western society itself — having done little (or to put it more accurately practically nothing) to help save the victimized Jews — felt more comfortable "analyzing" the survivors than themselves, or even the perpetrators.

Western society — particularly the Americas, both North and South — demonstrated their unwillingness to even save a thousand Jews who managed to escape the Nazi grasp. The 1938 tragedy of the thousand or so ill-fated passengers of the steam ship *St. Louis* — whose passengers had apparently obtained visas from the Cuban Embassy in Germany — is well documented as it attempted to unload its unfortunate human cargo in every Western port after being refused entry to Cuba, its original destination.

How Hitler must have relished this failure to rescue Jews. How must he have felt, knowing that he was being given carte blanche to do with the Jews as he pleased.

The Nuremberg Laws, which deprived Jews of many rights, were followed by "Kristallnacht," a pogrom German style, where Nazi hoodlums were let loose on the Jewish population throughout Germany. Every Jewish business or home was ransacked and vandalized, most synagogues set on fire, the holy books desecrated and burned. Jews were beaten, several were murdered, and many were carted off to the first concentration camp, Dachau.

Another test was passed. Now it was clear that neither the outside world nor the local population in general was any obstacle to Hitler's plan for the

Jews. In hindsight, the Kristallnacht of November 9–10, 1938, was the "dress rehearsal" for the Final Solution.

But what about now?

The old generation that remembers the Holocaust and its aftermath, in Britain and the US, even today still refuses to acknowledge the danger inherent in anti-Semitic Nazi propaganda.

The excuse that curbing race hatred is somehow an interference with legitimate freedom of speech is nothing more than an acquiescence to age-old anti-Semitism, which, over the centuries, has caused untold suffering and hundreds of thousands of deaths in a multitude of religious persecutions — from Crusaders up to the Inquisition and after — in all manner of pogroms and massacres, all officially sanctioned by the then governments and the Church.

A most telling analysis by a scholar of German origin, Professor Frederick M. Schweitzer, Ph.D. (who was himself enrolled in the Nazi Hitler Youth at an early age), describes the danger of Internet anti-Semitism:

> [It is] a lethal mode of hatred, which ebbed and flowed in intensity, but had a continuous existence from approximately the twelfth to thirteenth centuries, which marked its decisive stage until the genocidal climax in the German Shoah of European Jewry.

Professor Schweitzer, who was recently asked to testify as an expert witness before the Human Rights Tribunal in the case against Nazi propagandist Ernst Zündel, referred to the Zündel documents produced for the proceedings as typical anti-Semitic diatribe. He described the material as not any different from age-old anti-Semitism, repeating the same libels.

Chapter III

Yom Hashoah 1998

Yom Hashoah, 1998: fifty-three years since the tragedy of the Holocaust ended. Or did it?

My mind races. The feeling of overwhelming sadness seems to permeate my whole being. I am on the verge of tears but I know I won't cry. I did this morning, just listening to a speech by one of the Israeli leaders referring to the situation then and now. He said that then, we were dispersed and helpless; now we are in our own country again, our Jewish state, with an army to protect the state and its people…

He continued in Hebrew, and I only caught the drift of what he was saying, but tears ran down my cheeks.

There are some programs about the Holocaust on television. Two young people in their teens speak about their experiences attending the "March of the Living" to Auschwitz, Poland, a year earlier and what they drew from it.

I could never quite understand why people felt a need to revisit that G-d-forsaken land that still brims with anti-Semitism, despite all that happened, despite the fact that there are practically no Jews left in Poland except for a very few elderly men and women. (G-d only knows what prompted them to stay…)

But, of course, the young people attending the march, and others like them, are not revisiting. They are perhaps driven by a need to know, to remember, to witness…to understand… Is it possible to understand? Even those who lived it and survived do not understand. It is not possible to understand Hitler's genocidal policies in a vacuum.

Hitler had many helpers. Not only the well-known culprits who participated and diligently carried out the genocidal policies of the Nazi regime, with bureaucratic punctuality and conviction. Hitler also had quite a few less well-known partners, whose participation was less obvious to the casual observer.

Only now, more and more, are some of these facts coming to light, or rather, to the attention of the general public.

Strangely enough, some of these issues and their significance to the tragedy in general appeared to surface with the "Nazi gold" issue. But it turns out the "Nazi gold" is but the tip of the proverbial iceberg.

The Swiss government at the time not only bought and helped to launder "Nazi gold," they not only sold the Nazis all sort of goods including precision instruments in short supply in Germany, but they helped the Nazis in an even more direct way to murder Jews!

Notwithstanding the fact that some Jews found refuge in Switzerland, having first obtained valid visas from relatives, etc., many more thousands — the exact number may never be known — were turned over to the Nazis when they tried to reach the Swiss border. Curiously, when the Swiss role in purchasing the "Nazi gold" plundered from the Jews and extracted from the murdered victims' teeth became public it was a *cause célèbre*. Very few, if any, speak of the much greater crime of handing Jews over to their murderers.

The Swiss — while claiming "neutrality" — participated in strengthening the Nazi regime, thereby prolonging WWII. They claim that they simply acted in order to survive as a nation, but the bogus claim of Swiss neutrality pales in the face of the reality of the extent of their cooperation with the Nazis — cooperation that was not even demanded as far as it is known.

The fact that the Swiss handed over Jews to be murdered was neither required by the Nazis nor can it be justified in any way whatsoever. The Jews were simply a nuisance to the Swiss, and they had "no more room" for them!

But, here again, the Swiss were not alone. The *St. Louis* referred to earlier — a ship of some 915 men, women and children — sailed from Hamburg, Germany, to Cuba when the tragedy of the Jews was already well apparent and certainly known to governments the world over; again, the Jews could find no place of refuge.

Cuba refused to accept them. The entire eastern coast of the Western hemisphere, including all the South American states and North America (including the United States and Canada), had no place for 915 Jewish men, women and children, most of whom were subsequently killed in Auschwitz.

There were other ships similarly trying to escape Nazi tyranny, all in vain, among them the *Struma*, which sunk off the coast of Turkey after being forbidden to dock at the insistence of the British. These hapless victims were hoping to make their way to what was then known as Palestine — *Eretz Yisrael*!

There are records of many similar tragedies of escaping Jewish people, who could find no place of refuge, not even in their own homeland — *Eretz Yisrael*!

Chapter IV

Remembrance and Resolve...

Much has been written about the Holocaust and remembrance; one often despairs at what is remembered, and what is forgotten...

Barely fifty-three years have passed since the defeat of the Nazis by the Allies in 1945, and yet, that horrible war barely changed the attitude of the Allied nations. True, a great deal of lip service is paid to such lofty principles as justice, nonaggression, human rights and the like, but the changes in reality are few and far between, and often misplaced.

In the United States, the populace generally remains uninvolved, indifferent as ever to problems elsewhere. Whether we choose to call it isolationism, pacifism or simply self-absorption is irrelevant.

In Britain, France and Germany, too, the people care only about their own immediate problems. It is clear that the successive governments of these countries, as always, act only out of what they perceive to be their national (usually short-term) self-interest in the global arena.

Who then will act for the best interest of those who have nothing but goodwill to offer global powers? Who then will act on behalf of the truly endangered minorities or small countries such as Israel?

The United Nations — following the genocide and the aggression committed by the Nazis — is serving nothing more today than the self-interest of those countries which can wield the greatest influence over the largest number of member states. More often than not, this influence is actually coercion.

Since 1973, the Arab oil states — OPEC — have openly exhibited their will to use oil as a weapon. The UN has simply accommodated itself to this new means of wielding power and coercion, carrying on as if nothing had happened. Even the press and other media after an initial shock reaction went on spouting the line of the cartel. The Arab oil states, instead of being condemned — or at least censured — were in fact supported by other oil-producing states including Canada, which saw a windfall profit for its own oil-producing industry. Who ever said cartels were illegal?

Japan and other oil-dependent countries simply toed the line imposed by OPEC. And so it is not justice and nonaggression dominating the workings of the United Nations, but just the opposite!

Member states defend the current UN claim that some forum for international relations is better than none, but who is it really better for? For those states which do not see themselves as the target, or are not directly threatened by the goings-on at the UN. A cursory glance at the number of UN resolutions directed against Israel tells the whole story. Why is Israel singled out?

Thankfully, every now and then there appears on the international scene an individual who has the courage to say it as it is, with no care for his personal ambitions. Regretfully, such individuals are few and far between, but they do make an enormous difference, at least to those who have a need for the truth to be told. At times Richard Butler, the UN Representative for UNSCOM, has been one such individual. In the late 1990s he was in charge of inspecting Iraqi sites for weapons of mass destruction, including deadly mustard gas and equally deadly biological agents such as anthrax.

Richard Butler appears to have been the only individual inside the UN willing to state the ugly truth about Iraq's Saddam Hussein, with his propaganda campaign and his goal to obliterate Israel from the face of the earth. Yet Richard Butler too appears now to have changed totally in regard to Israel — what happened?

There were other voices — particularly Republicans, then the minority party in the US Congress — who, thanks to Butler, raised similar questions and even questioned the motives of other Arab leaders who came out in support of Saddam Hussein. But has the Republican party's clear vision really been borne out? One cannot help but remember the Republican administration under then-President George H. W. Bush during the first Gulf War, a response to Iraq's aggression and occupation of the neighboring Arab state of Kuwait, in 1991. Iraq's attack on Israel in that conflict was a totally unjustified naked aggression against the Jewish state, yet Israel was forced by the US to forego legitimate self-defense, when Iraq was raining down scud missiles — which the Iraqi government threatened to fill with poison gas — on Israeli cities.

Why was Israel forced into this untenable situation by the US? Apparently in order to keep together a shaky coalition of Arab states. And why would

Arab states forbid Israel's legitimate right to self-defense? That is the most disturbing question of the second half of the twentieth century, and one that much of this book is concerned with.

This book is also about the injustices committed against the Jewish people even in the aftermath of the Holocaust by the very nations now doing the bidding of the Arabs.

Is it all narrow self-interest? Is it anti-Semitism deeply imbedded in the psyche of some world leaders? Is it a policy blindly followed by successive governments, initiated by anti-Semites decades earlier? Or is it a combination of all of the above?

Perhaps this book will raise more questions than it answers, but it will be an attempt to lay bare these perplexing issues and hopefully engage the involvement of those who still choose to remain on the sidelines. If it succeeds in provoking debate, and an honest examination of historical facts, then this book will have fulfilled its mission of remembrance and resolve.

Chapter V

Israel and the Arab Nation

In dealing with a conflict — any conflict — there must be a willingness to go beyond propaganda. In order to be understood (let alone resolved), the Arab-Israeli conflict must be viewed in the context of history as well as the existing culture of the region. There is, of course (and even primarily) the issue of religion, which may prove to pose the most significant obstacle to any resolution of the Arab-Israeli conflict.

The Muslim claim that Islam has superseded both Christianity and Judaism, and that Mohammed is the last prophet (as they see it, superseding both Jesus and Moses) may take centuries and many new generations to change, if change is indeed possible.

Change itself is vigorously opposed not only by the religious mullahs, but also the regional leaders. The mostly despotic dictatorial regimes can only exist in a culture like the present one, which opposes religious pluralism and tolerance as well as economic change. However, so long as religious exclusivism is practiced in the region, economic change itself will make little or no difference.

A case in point is the Muslim Arabs residing in *Eretz Yisrael*. They are well educated for the most part, contrary to massive illiteracy among their counterparts in Arab states in the region. Education has not in any way changed their culture or their belief in religious exclusivism. Economic growth in Judea, Samaria and Gaza is prevented by an age-old culture of backward practices, which keep old despots, including the likes of Arafat, in power.

Israel is anathema to the Muslims as a whole, since way back in the seventh century Jews, among whom Mohammed desperately sought acceptance, rejected his new religion. Israel also represents a threat to the despotic, dictatorial regimes because of its very modernity. The modern State of Israel, because of the relatively high standard of living, the freedoms Israeli citizens enjoy, and the way the country has developed as a whole since independence in 1948, represents a tremendous contrast to the Arab states where development is stagnant, and betterment for the average citizen is still a far-off dream.

Unfortunately, their dreams do not include striving for better education of the masses, or improvement to their economies; the dream for most Muslims continually incited by their mullahs and their leaders is the elimination of the Jewish state!

Tremendous financial resources are continually devoted to that single-minded effort. For Western countries to turn a blind eye to this reality is tantamount to acquiescence to Arab-Muslim belligerence and aggression. Worse still, the Western media is not much help. For whatever reason; whether it is to curry favor with the despotic regimes, or due to simple fear of reprisals, the media has become nothing more than a platform for Arab-Muslim propaganda. The few worthy exceptions do not always reach the masses even in Western countries.

Chapter VI

Arab Propaganda

Arab propaganda has remained a powerful tool in attempting to subvert Israel's very legitimacy. Particularly since the Yom Kippur War of 1973, using the oil weapon against Israel has had coercive influence and power over oil-dependent nations.

Every Arab war waged against Israel seems to be followed by additional terrorist acts and infiltration. Contrary to international law and rules of war, the aggressor Arab states — instead of being punished by the United Nations — are being mollified because of the oil weapon and Western dependence on it. Japan too is a large consumer of Arab oil, as are numerous other countries in Asia and Africa which are also subject to pressure and coercion by OPEC, the Arab oil cartel. And so, the United Nations — created following WWII as a result of Nazi aggression and the horrific crimes of the Holocaust with the intention of safeguarding against aggression and providing protection for minorities — has now become subverted to serve the very nations who commit such aggression.

The Arab-Muslim states have managed over time to create an automatic majority at the UN General Assembly, imposing their will on the rest of the world. The Western world — to say nothing of the "rest of the world" — having learned nothing from history and the Second World War in particular, continues as ever to follow the path of least resistance.

Following several unsuccessful wars against Israel, Arab states continue their practice of boycotting Israel, including secondary and tertiary boycotts aimed against Jews everywhere, and countries whose companies do business with them. The obvious aim is to isolate Israel, as well as hurt its economy.

The boycotts' intensity has subsided somewhat since the so-called "Oslo Peace Process" started on September 13, 1993. Terrorism against Israel and countries allegedly sympathetic to Israel was rampant following both the 1967 War and the 1973 Yom Kippur War. Following September 1993, terrorism subsided for a while, but was not entirely eliminated. How could it be, when Arafat on the very eve of the signing ceremony on September 13, 1993, announced for all the world to hear that sooner or later the PLO flag would fly over Jerusalem? Not "East Jerusalem" (which, by the way, is where some of the holiest sites in the Jewish religion are located), but Jerusalem!

Contrary to popular belief, Arafat continued his campaign of incitement against the Jewish state and continued to call for jihad — holy war — to liberate "Palestine"! This campaign continued despite the Oslo Peace Accords and throughout the time the Labor regime was in power in Israel — the very government that signed the peace accords with Arafat. The belief of some that Arafat or the Arab nations in general could be mollified by sharing a tiny piece of land, representing a fifth of Palestine, flies in the face of reality.

That so many Arab states — in fact all — should be so agitated by the very existence of the Jewish state should speak volumes. Why doesn't it? In an age when communication is so widespread that ignorance of facts cannot be an excuse, what is it that drives Western powers to support the Arab "cause" against Israel? Can it be more than Arab coercion?

Why is the world not involved to the same extent in ongoing conflicts elsewhere in the world — far bloodier, with many more victims — in Asia, Africa, South America and even in Europe?

How can a tiny state, having miraculously survived numerous wars of Arab aggression to say nothing of the still ongoing terrorism, be such a "sore," such a "threat" to the Arabs — and why would the world accept such an outrageous claim?

Whether or not Israel has nuclear capability is beside the point. Israel has never attacked a neighboring state, except in self-defense.

One of the great ironies of the twentieth century was the passing of the UN resolution — introduced of course by the Arabs — that "Zionism equals racism." The fact that the very Arab states which threatened — and still do — to eliminate the Jewish people and the Jewish state from the face of the earth should issue such a proclamation, and that the UN world body should vote on it and accept it, defies logic and any sense of morality.

Here we have racists, bent on genocide, calling their intended target "racists"! The resolution, initiated in 1975 — two years after the Yom Kippur War — was rescinded around the time of the Israel-PLO Oslo Peace Accords. Rescinding the UN resolution was the work of US Ambassador to the UN John Bolton, who was then the assistant to the secretary of state, and Senator

Daniel Patrick Moynihan, former US Ambassador to the UN. The Arab states predictably voted against rescinding the offending resolution.

One of the more telling pieces of Arab propaganda was retrieved from the Internet, July 24, 1996, allegedly quoting from the Muslim holy book the Qur'an, as follows:

> Ibrahim (Abraham) was not a Jew nor a Christian but he was [an] upright [man] a Muslim, and he was not one of the polytheists. Most surely the nearest of people to Ibrahim, are those who followed him and this Prophet [Mohammed] and those who believe and Allah is the guardian of the believers." (Qur'an 3:67, 3:68)
>
> Al-Ibrahimi Mosque is the third Islamic holiest place in Palestine, located in the city of Khalil al-Rahman (Hebron). Since 1967, the occupation authorities have changed its structure. Its drinking well, eastern door and steps, and one of the towers were demolished. Currently, more than half of the Mosque has been transformed into a synagogue…

The fact that Islam as a religion did not exist at the time of Abraham (indeed not for another two and a half millennia) does not seem to get in the way of Arab propaganda. Neither does the fact that the burial cave of the Jewish Patriarchs referred to above as a "mosque" holds the graves of Abraham and Sara, Isaac and Rebecca, and Jacob and Leah, and is not only a historic site but one of the most important religious sites to the Jews. Moslems apparently relish putting up mosques atop other people's holy places.

The greatest desecration committed by the Muslims is of course in Jerusalem on the Temple Mount, where both the First and the Second Temples stood. This is the holiest site for the Jewish people; and it was here that the Muslims erected a mosque, called the al-Aqsa (one of a number of sites variously claimed to be the "third holiest site for Muslims").

Elsewhere the claim was made and then repeated by Arab-Israeli MK Dahamshe that:

> The Western Wall is not a Jewish holy site and part of the ancient Holy Temple, but part of the al-Aqsa complex.

The claim goes on to say that:

> Mohammed when he flew to heaven on his special horse
> — Burack — tied the horse to the Western Wall.

There is no end to fictitious Arab claims. There is no evidence that Mohammed was ever in Jerusalem in his lifetime, and there is no mention of Jerusalem in the Qur'an. Certainly the al-Aqsa did not even exist in Mohammed's lifetime. Here again, facts do not get in the way of Arab propaganda.

The Mosque of Omar, also known as the Dome of the Rock, was built in 691, almost six decades after Mohammed's death and over five decades after the Arab conquest. The al-Aqsa was built in 701 CE and Mohammed is said to have died in 632 CE, almost seven decades earlier. Al-Aqsa supposedly means the "furthest mosque," but what about Turkey, which is even further?

What has been historically established is that the Temple Mount is the holiest site to Judaism and has been for three millennia, since long before Islam came into being; in fact, some sixteen centuries before.

There is no historical equivocation to the fact that both the First and Second Jewish Temples stood on the holy ground of the Temple Mount. (That is where the name of the Temple Mount originates.)

To the Jewish people, the Temple Mount represents not only Jewish history in Jerusalem and *Eretz Yisrael*, but even more importantly, it is also Judaism's most sacred religious place and symbol.

To the Arabs, the Temple Mount represents conquest. Conquest over the "infidels," both Jewish and Christian. As we shall see, it is also part of their "supersession" myth.

Yet the propaganda states that the Temple Mount is a historical Arab holy site. Not all Arab propaganda is that easily discernible, however, by the average individual, who may have little or no knowledge of either the history or geography of the region.[1] But most Arab propaganda does not stop at distorting or misrepresenting history. Such misrepresentations are merely a vehicle for anti-Jewish, anti-Israel incitement leading to violence and an attempt to delegitimize Jewish history and Jewish rights in our own Land.

An example of the vicious and unscrupulous Arab-Muslim propaganda is the long discredited *The Protocols of the Elders of Zion*, still officially distributed in most Arab countries, including "moderate" Saudi Arabia and Egypt. The peace accords signed between Egypt and Israel in 1979–80 forbid such

---

1. See appendix 2.

incitement and were supposed to usher in an era of peace, coexistence, and better understanding. Israel is still waiting. The existing situation is often described as a cold peace. Egypt, however, gained back the Sinai Peninsula (to which its claim, incidentally, is unclear except that the British somehow bestowed it, and which it lost in two wars of aggression) simply by signing a piece of paper, which proved worthless.

The "peace accords" with the PLO went in the same direction, except that Arafat didn't even have the good sense to wait with incitement and propaganda until after all the negotiations were concluded. There will be more about this in the following chapters.

Chapter VII

The PLO Trojan Horse;
an Offspring of the Arab League

Few people remember or seem to care about the origins of the PLO as a terrorist organization.

The PLO was created at a general meeting of the Arab League, in Cairo in 1964. This event and the date are critical to understanding what is behind the Arab-Israeli conflict. The PLO, or the "Palestine Liberation Organization," was clearly not created to "liberate" the "West Bank" from the Israelis for the "poor, homeless Palestinians." The so-called West Bank — Judea and Samaria — were still under Arab-Jordanian rule at the time, following the 1948 War, when Jordan illegally annexed Judea and Samaria and parts of Jerusalem.

(To the Arab League and to Arab-Muslims generally, the "West Bank" comprises all of Israel including Judea and Samaria in their euphemistic description of the area. Somehow, the description stuck even though the West Bank does not denote a geographical area historically).

The PLO was the monster that wreaked havoc not only in Israel and on its borders, but also targeted Jews on hijacked planes and ships during an era spanning more than two decades. Many planes were hijacked to neighboring Arab countries, but Jews were not the only victims. PLO terrorism became a fact of life, and travelers all over the world, particularly by air, had to consider that they too might become hostages to terrorism.

But the monster the Arab League created did not spare even Jordan and Lebanon (both members). In Lebanon, the PLO became virtually a state within a state, except that it was a terrorist state, and ruled by terror. The local inhabitants — particularly the local Christians — were targets of robbery, murder, and all sorts of indignities by the marauding terrorists, who could rob people at will without fear of reprisal. In Jordan too, the PLO created so much havoc that they were banished in September 1968 by the king in a drive that practically amounted to a massacre, later referred to by the PLO as "Black September."

Whether all of this was intended by the Arab League is not the issue here. The real issue is the fact that the Arab League created a terrorist organization to "liberate Palestine," that is the Land of Israel.

The Arabs in their ongoing campaign to destroy the young state and its people waged war against Israel again and again. In addition to the three major wars and the Arab economic boycott, there were the ongoing terrorist incursions and the closing of the international waterways to Israeli shipping, both of which clearly represented acts of war under international law.

In 1967, after months of preparation and threats to push the Jews into the sea, Egypt removed the United Nations Peace-Keeping Forces from its borders with Israel. The world held its breath as it "prepared" for a slaughter of the Jewish people, but did nothing!

At the eleventh hour Israel prepared a preemptive strike against Egyptian military installations, particularly airfields and runways, thereby preventing Egypt's military from attacking Israel by air. Having secured its western border, Israel turned to Jordan, asking if it would consider remaining neutral. Jordan refused. The Jordanian leadership — misled by reports from the Egyptians claiming to have the upper hand over Israel, when in fact that was no longer the case — induced the Jordanians to attack Israel from the "West Bank." The rest as they say is history. In a stunning victory, unprecedented in the history of military warfare, Israel managed to defeat several Arab armies on all its fronts.

It is important to point out here that from 1948 to 1967, during the nearly twenty-year illegal Jordanian occupation of Judea and Samaria — the "West Bank" (which, incidentally, did not create an outcry in the UN) — the Arabs of the area did not need or make any attempt to create the "Palestinian" state they are now calling for.

A Palestinian Arab state, of course, has no precedent in recorded history. Considering that the Arab nations already control territory comprising some 5.3 million square miles, consisting of twenty states, it is important for people to understand how Arab propaganda and international coercion is changing reality.

The Jewish state was and continues to be an irritant to the Arabs and other Muslims. Israel's defeat of the aggressor states in every war so far (thank G-d) has only added to their discomfort.

It has been said by Israeli leaders, including Golda Meir, that if the Arabs lose a war, they will live to fight another war. If Israel were to lose any war, the bloodshed would be horrendous. The hatred of the Arabs towards the Jews, and their declared genocidal aim, tells it all.

Why Israel would be pushed by so-called "friendly" states to give up land — historically Jewish — to an Arab enemy dedicated to Israel's destruction is beyond comprehension.

The Western countries, including Europe and the United States of America, have no moral or legal rights to make such demands of Israel. Apart from Israel's historic rights to the land, including Judea and Samaria, and given also that the land is so small and narrow and very vulnerable to aggressions, Israel's rights under international law in the aftermath of Arab aggression are unimpeachable.

The claim that the Arabs, with a majority population in several towns of Judea and Samaria (the "West Bank"), need a state of their own is a transparent hypocrisy not supported by the facts cited above. The real aim of the Arabs is to weaken the Jewish state and make it again vulnerable. The fact that Arabs have over the last several decades acquired more weapons than any other country should give us all pause.

They are still aiming to get what they call the Islamic Bomb — in fact, they may already have it. Egypt has at least two atomic reactors, as does Pakistan (which has become an atomic power since this was written), and Iran is now well on its way with the help of the Russians.

The West too, including Canada — who sold atomic reactors to Pakistan — are doing their best to improve the Arab armament. The claim always is if we won't do it, someone else will.

The West, and Canada and Britain in particular, have gone a long way in encouraging the "Palestinian" Arabs to create a state of their own on historically Jewish land. Nation building within Israel's vital borders is OK, while the separation of Quebec is not, despite the huge territory Canada possesses. Surely the Western powers must know that such a state, if it ever comes, will be nothing but an outpost for Arab aggression, a Trojan horse!

But the Arabs have played a clever game. What they could not gain through several wars of aggression against Israel, terrorism and economic warfare, they were hoping to achieve through the PLO turned "peacemaker." Once the territory is handed over, all bets are off. But you cannot change a leopard's spots — Arafat was until his dying day who Arafat always was — a hater of Jews, a terrorist who always incited his followers to terrorism and holy war against the Jewish state.

Thankfully, our enemies always seem to shoot themselves in the foot and betray their own true plans before they come to fruition. If we needed even more proof of the "peaceful intent" of the Arabs in Judea, Samaria and Gaza, their behavior during the 1991 Gulf War spoke volumes. If anyone needed convincing, all they had to do was watch hour after hour of televised images of Arabs chanting, "Dear Saddam, you Habib, please bomb Tel-Aviv!"

The well-known US conservative William F. Buckley Jr., in a column that appeared in the *Jerusalem Post* on February 26, 1998, offered, as always, some keen observations on what he called the "Baghdad Pact." He analyzed the political situation in the aftermath of the premature American military pullout from Iraq, discussing Iraqi non-compliance with the UN weapons inspection program and the prospect of peace given Saddam's predilection not only to possess, but to use chemical weapons against his own population (the Kurds), to prove his "superiority in the region." He concluded however that:

> Unlike Hitler, Saddam was not suicidal; given the US military power ready to be deployed, Saddam would not have committed suicide, but might have been deprived of his splendid palaces which would have made him feel less "regal."

Buckley felt that the concessions Saddam made to UN Secretary-General Kofi Annan were merely a notch on Saddam's belt of military power, given that mere possession of weapons of mass destruction gave him the power to terrorize and be "hoisted onto the commanding geopolitical heights he want[ed] to occupy" in the region.

Buckley concluded his column by stating:

> [Saddam] invaded Kuwait and was chased out in an ignominious military encounter with the US. He tried to destroy the oil reserves of Kuwait by setting fire to several hundred oil wells and contaminating the seas for hundreds of miles around. He has tortured and killed inmates and sub-inmates by the hundreds and thousands.... And for this man's country they are cheering in Egypt and Jordan and Syria. [Buckley left out the "Palestinians."] Can the hatred of Israel so obsess a people as

to derange all their faculties…. On this one your servant sur-
renders: One does not know what to say.

It is a rare instant indeed when William Buckley is at a loss for words, but
what in fact can one say?

So long as terrorism is considered legitimate in the Middle East, suicide
bombers will be encouraged by their leaders — religious leaders in particular
— to commit these outrageous acts against Israel and its people in order "to
achieve rewards in heaven." This region, where Muslim clerics think nothing of
offending Israel by calling Judaism a "gutter religion," still remains immersed
in the Dark Ages. So long as the Arab Muslims consider accommodation
with others impossible, the "peace process" is nothing but a euphemism for
surrender and a sham.

The Muslims retain a sense of "superiority" over other religions, which
they claim Islam has superseded. This explains why, when the Israeli army
in 1967 finally regained access to Jewish holy sites in Jerusalem's Old City, it
found desecration and ruin everywhere. Jewish synagogues, including the
holy books within them, were destroyed. Jewish cemeteries, including the
ancient Mount of Olives, were desecrated, many headstones overturned or
even removed and used as latrines for Jordanian soldiers!

Dictators and despots have always needed a war and an external enemy
in order to subdue the masses and make their basic needs subservient to the
war effort. So long as this reality continues, nothing will change in the region.
The masses will remain impoverished; kings and dictators alike will maintain
their palaces as a mantle of power. So-called liberal thinkers in the West will
keep stressing the deprivation of the masses, but put the finger of blame on
the alleged "enemies" instead of where it belongs.

The hypocrisy of the Western powers and Europe in particular will continue to prod Israel to make sacrifices and concessions for a nonexistent peace.
That these countries crave to do business with these dictators is one thing; to
prod Israel to commit national suicide is another.

Chapter VIII

The Failure of the Oslo Peace Accords

Did Oslo ever have a chance? The Oslo Peace Accords — as initially presented to the nation and the world at large — spoke only of "limited autonomy" for the Arabs in Judea, Samaria and Gaza. The accords referred to a gradual process, which was to build mutual confidence between Arabs and Jews. Hence the process was spread over a period of years. At the end of the process, Israel was to retain the present security borders along the Jordan River in the east and the existing borders with Egypt in the west.

While the Arabs were to enjoy the freedom of deciding how to run their day-to-day lives, issues dealing with international relations were to be left in Israeli hands. Again, no sovereignty, but limited autonomy, was what the peace negotiations were to be about. (Even if there was a silent agreement to the contrary by Shimon Peres, then foreign minister, that would have represented subterfuge, misrepresentation and above all, a misleading of the nation.)

Israel very simply wanted to restore normal life, to grant the Arabs some self-government, but retain the security of its borders and sovereignty over the areas in question.

Prior to the signing of the peace accords, there were those in Israel who would have cheerfully given up Gaza to Egyptian control, but it appears even Egypt was not too keen on controlling an area which, as those who knew it agreed, was almost impossible to control. (Gaza was known as a hell hole even when it was under Egyptian control). But then again, there are those who still remember the heavy casualties inflicted by the Egyptians on Israel in the areas adjacent to Gaza in the early days of statehood, in 1948, and all the wars and terrorist attacks in between.

It seems Israel tried to do the only thing it could do: give the Arabs a sense of dignity through self-government, and interfere as little as possible in the day-to-day activities of the Arabs in the designated autonomous areas, while preserving national security. But things began to unravel almost immediately, and the tragic mistake was that the Israeli government ignored (to its detriment) what soon appeared to be major violations by the Arabs under the leadership of the PLO, newly legitimized by the name "Palestinian" Authority. Why any Israeli government would agree for the Arabs to continue to call themselves "Palestinians" when there is no historic reason for it was probably seen as a meaningless concession at the time, but one that they would live to regret given all the propaganda which sprang from it.

The "Authority" was supposed to create its own police force, with the outside limit of eighteen thousand (already a high number). Eventually the force was illegally doubled, and, in appearance and demeanor represented more an army than a police force, at times wearing camouflage fatigue and uniforms, in many cases, with all the trappings of a military. Some police force!

Yasser Arafat, whose official title was chairman, was referred to as "President" Arafat. He started entertaining foreign dignitaries in his headquarters, all of which was in clear violation of the peace accords, which clearly forbade such direct foreign contacts.

As already referred to elsewhere, on the very eve after signing the "peace" agreement, Arafat declared to the world that "sooner or later the 'Palestinian' flag will fly over Jerusalem!" Vintage Arafat! No sooner did he sign the peace accords, than he was out on the warpath again, proclaiming to the whole world that he would rule over Jerusalem.

This incident and the other violations were dismissed, not only by the world at large, but by the Israeli government of the time. Then the terrorist attacks started in earnest again. The world and Israelis were told that the victims of these terrorist attacks were "victims of peace," and that Arafat's hands were tied — that he could not really reign in the terror because that would cause a "split" in the "Palestinian" population!

What about his solemn promise, along with then Prime Minister Yitzchak Rabin, that "there will be no more blood, no more violence," on the White House lawn on September 13, 1993, televised to the whole world?

Soon the various chieftains of the PLO began to call themselves "ministers" — "minister of justice"(!), minister of this, minister of that. They began official contacts with foreign officials in Jerusalem at the "Orient House," again in total defiance and violation of the accords, which stated that Jerusalem was to be off-limits to PA functionaries. Clearly, that was not the intention of the peace process, or the limited autonomy provisions.

Various PA offices were functioning in Jerusalem illegally and some clandestinely, but apparently in full knowledge of all concerned, further establishing "facts on the ground," bolstering the PLO's claim to the city. Needless to say, this was again in defiance of all agreements signed by Arafat. After some temporary closures of these offices, they were opened again under different names, doing basically the same thing. The cat and mouse game continued.

Violations piled up on top of violations. Instances of PLO "police" challenging Israeli soldiers were seen again and again. The issue that really broke the proverbial camel's back was a tape introduced in the Knesset (the Israeli parliament) by then opposition Member of Knesset (MK) Benjamin Zev Begin. The tape revealed PLO Chief Yasser Arafat praising suicide bombers as "martyrs" and calling for jihad — holy war — in front of a large crowd somewhere outdoors, and leading the chant "with blood and tears we'll liberate Palestine, to Jerusalem, to Jerusalem."

This was in January 1995, when the Labor government was still in power, the government of Rabin, whom Arafat called his "friend" (with friends like these…!). This incident was not a one-time occurrence, either. Much of this was actually shown on "Palestinian" television, and continued well into March of 1996.

As the Labor government was preparing for elections to be held on May 31, 1996, these events seemed to subside somewhat, although Arafat was seen on tape surrounded by Hamas chieftains more than once, giving the same message — jihad! Shimon Peres was even repeating what Arafat allegedly told him: that jihad meant a "peaceful jihad"!

Just prior to the elections, Arafat promised yet again to amend or rescind the PLO covenant calling for Israel's destruction. The covenant has yet to be amended! Some may say Israel is a strong nation, and perhaps a "minor issue" such as the PLO covenant shouldn't be regarded as more than an irritant. But we have no business signing peace accords with people whose declared goal still remains the destruction of the Jewish state.[1]

Clearly, the peace accords signed by Prime Minister Rabin and Yasser Arafat were supposed to usher in peace and security to both Arabs and Jews. The peace process was supposed to build confidence on both sides, and over

---

1. See Appendix 10.

time usher in a truly peaceful coexistence. It is equally clear that that did not occur, and is not likely to happen any time soon.

Arafat not only violated all relevant parts of the peace accords and made a mockery of the peace process, he barefacedly demanded that Israel live up to its commitments. To that end he enlisted the Europeans[1] and individual countries everywhere to pressure Israel into further concessions, which were never part of the Oslo Accords.

Arafat proclaimed his intention of unilaterally declaring a "Palestinian state" as soon as was feasible, which would have been a further violation of Oslo, and a grievous one. The territory under Arafat's control at the time was where 96 percent of the Arab population of Judea and Samaria and Gaza live, yet he sought additional territorial concessions.

Eretz Yisrael (Palestine) was already once divided by the British when they assigned four-fifths of the land to Jordan, a country that had no historical precedent.[2] This left an area now under Israeli control consisting of barely 10,800 square miles, including Judea and Samaria. Israel, surrounded by an Arab-controlled landmass some five hundred times its size, is one of the smallest countries in the world.[3]

But the failure of Oslo cannot be blamed entirely on the Arabs. Every now and then, the world produces leaders such as Chamberlain who believe — even honestly believe — that peace is possible when it is not. They conjure up plans and ideas they believe will lead to successful conclusions; they insist on the delusion that peace is native to all leaders, to all people. And so, just as the 1930s gave us Chamberlain and Munich, the 1990s gave us Shimon Peres and Oslo.

Both agreements were predicated on peaceful coexistence and compromise, but neither produced the dreamt-of results. Chamberlain's "compromise" was giving to Hitler land that was not his country's, and Czechoslovakia became the scapegoat. But not even that "grand gesture" by a Britain reluctant to confront reality could prevent the coming conflict and WWII. Quite the contrary, Hitler, realizing Britain had no stomach to challenge him, became

---

1. See *Eurabia* by Bat Ye'or; in the pact between the Arab League and Europe, the Arabs demanded that the PLO and Arafat be regarded as legitimate representatives of the "Palestinians."
2. See Appendix 6.
3. See Appendix 8.

even bolder and after the occupation of Poland in 1939 and the blitzkrieg, one country after another in Europe fell like dominos. Oslo, on the other hand, was not a compromise over other people's land.

Shimon Peres's "grand design" envisaged a peaceful Middle East with all the adherent benefits to all the peoples of the region; those would include a free exchange of culture and ideas, commerce and tourism, and the like. Certainly, if such an outcome were possible, the sacrifice Israel was about to make could have made some sense, at least to a part of the population inevitably tired of conflict and the ongoing bloodshed. But reality intervened. The bloodshed continued, suicide bombers continued their ghoulish assignment, and Arafat continued praising them in Arabic as "martyrs." If this is peace — what is war?

Peres's willingness to give up land — which was not historically Arab and which still bears historically Jewish names — to an enemy bent on the destruction of the Jewish state, based on an unrealistic fantasy, eventually led to his downfall. Peres not only lost the elections in 1996, but soon thereafter was routed as head of the Labor Party — an ignominious end to a dreamer of impossible dreams in a very dangerous part of the world.

Chamberlain is reported to have said on his deathbed, "Oh, but I believed Herr Hitler…" One can only wonder what Shimon Peres will say in his defense… if he ever wakes up from his dream… The damage done by the unrealistic assumptions of Oslo continues to plague Israel, its people, and leaders, to this day.

The intractable problem of what to do when peaceful coexistence does not appear to be realistic has always been a major issue for all Israeli governments since Ben Gurion. The ongoing belligerence, bellicosity and warfare by the Arabs, including those who are not Israel's immediate neighbors, and their religious leaders clearly calling for the eradication of the Jewish people and the State of Israel, is not a prescription for peace.

While some Arab leaders still referred to as "more moderate" keep calling on Israel to make concessions (and sacrifices) to advance the "peace process," none of them ever appeared to be leaning on Arafat to live up to the agreements he signed.

As already referred to elsewhere, Arafat kept none of the major conditions he had signed to. He violated all of them, including the agreement to rescind or amend the PLO covenant calling for Israel's destruction.

That any Jewish leader could have continued with this charade, and that world leaders could have continued to pressure Israel despite these barefaced violations of the agreements, is nothing but hypocrisy.

How can leaders of states who continue to refer to themselves as "even-handed facilitators" of peace look at themselves in the mirror in the face of realities which are so obvious, or should be, to all?

Chapter IX

UN Resolution 242

Resolution 242, along with the UN-brokered ceasefire and armistice following the Arab-Israel Six Day War, called on the parties to arrive at peaceful arrangements without coercion, among other things. The resolution also implied that Israel could return some land after satisfactory peace had been achieved.[1]

The key words in the resolution were: (1) that only the parties to the conflict will agree among themselves on a peaceful resolution of the conflict, and (2) this was to be done without coercion by either party (and certainly without coercion by third parties). The other key issue in the resolution was that no land would be transferred without a lasting and durable peace and secure and recognized borders.

Even more importantly, the resolution called for permanent and defensible borders and nowhere did it say "all the land" conquered in the defensive war of 1967. The US Joint Chiefs of Staff recommended defensible borders for Israel in 1967, which included Judea, Samaria and Gaza plus parts of Sinai bordering the Negev Desert, as well as the tip of the southern Sinai to ensure safe navigation for Israel at the Straits of Tiran. The recommendations were presented to President Lyndon Johnson but were subsequently buried.[2]

Clearly there was plenty of coercion in the negotiations between Israel and Egypt at Camp David by then US President Carter following Egyptian President Sadat's "grand gesture" of a visit to Israel in 1977 and a peace offer that came on the heels of further aggression against Israel.

International law never rewarded aggression by returning land to the aggressor nation. Yet the Sinai Desert across which Egypt launched the 1973

---

1. See Appendix 9.
2. See also Dore Gold's "defensible Borders," published by the Jerusalem Center for Public Affairs, June 15-July 1, 2003, and Professor Paul Eidelberg's piece for the *Jewish Press* referenced in chapter 36.

aggression against Israel was handed to Egypt following the conclusion of the peace negotiations.[1]

The people of Israel — overwhelmed by Sadat's gesture of peace — had no difficulty in handing Egypt the entire area of the Sinai, even after they had to dismantle a number of small settlements along the postwar border. The Israeli government of then Prime Minister Menachem Begin, in his generosity of spirit, even gave away the newly-created airport and an oil field, despite Israel's desperate need for oil and the existing Arab states' use of oil as an economic weapon against the Jewish state.

When all the *t*s were crossed and all the *i*s dotted, Egypt's negotiator, Boutros Boutros-Ghali (the future UN secretary-general), demanded on behalf of his government that Egypt retain its right to join other Arab states (against Israel) if a future war were to erupt. So much for the permanence of peace treaties in the Middle East.

This last effort of coercion against Israel by US President Jimmy Carter is remembered with great bitterness in Samuel Katz's new edition of his *Battleground: Fact and Fantasy in Palestine*. It also raises yet again the inevitable question of what became of the UN after selecting Boutros Boutros-Ghali as its secretary-general. In its brief history so far, the UN has ostensibly been dedicated to promoting peace and human rights everywhere as a reaction to WWII; its secretary-general and its ambassadors — it was envisaged — would serve humanity first and foremost, and always would be selected on the basis of their particular credentials to follow these lofty concepts.

The most obvious individual who did not fit this category was Kurt Waldheim, whose connection to the Nazis was apparently well known before he assumed office as UN Secretary-General.

And what of Boutros Boutros-Ghali? While there is no attempt here to equate him with Waldheim, his particular role in the negotiations between Egypt and Israel and the last-minute "non-peaceful" addition to the peace agreement hardly fit with the original lofty credentials required for a secretary-general of the United Nations.

The still uneasy peace that exists between Egypt and Israel hardly lived up to expectations. The first Israeli ambassador to Egypt described how he was

---

1. Apart from international law, the question of whether the Sinai Peninsula is really Egypt's is not quite clear. See Samuel Katz, *Battleground: Fact and Fantasy in Palestine* (NY: Bantam Books, 1977).

isolated and singled out for "special treatment" during his stay in Cairo. The vile propaganda against Israel and Jews in general is still officially circulated in Egypt in violation of its agreement. Not only are such long discredited propaganda pamphlets as *The Protocols of the Elders of Zion* officially circulated, but the official press — with the apparent approval of the Egyptian government — still publishes vitriolic incitement to hatred of Israel and Jews.

Clearly this is not the peace hoped for by Israel and envisaged by UN Resolution 242 nor then Prime Minister Menachem Begin, after he agreed to hand over the entire Sinai Peninsula to Egypt. UN Resolution 242 clearly allowed for adjusting borders and there was no requirement for Israel to return all the land; furthermore, land was to be returned only for a true, durable and lasting peace.

Menachem Begin, every inch a gentleman, wanted to show the world that Israel does not covet the land belonging to any other nation. And Israel had no real claim to the Sinai except under the international law pertaining to Egypt's continued aggression.

The situation in Judea and Samaria — the "West Bank" — is very, very different. First and foremost, it is the Arabs who have no historical rights to the land. The aggression committed against Israel again and again by the Arabs in that territory further nullifies any Arab claim. But even more importantly, the Mandate for Palestine created by the League of Nations — the predecessor to the United Nations — never envisaged any Arab state in the area. The Jewish leadership of the Diaspora agreed to Britain being the Mandatory power in the mistaken belief that Britain would, in fact, carry out its promise both to the Jewish people and the League of Nations. The Preamble to the League of Nations mandate — which received royal assent by the king of England — promulgated the establishment of the Jewish homeland in Palestine, recognizing the Jewish people's "historic connection" to the land.[1]

The League of Nations document refers to the then residents. This includes the Arab population which is seen as residents with no particular rights, historic or otherwise, but merely rights accorded to the existing population.

The current claim that the Arab population of Judea, Samaria and Gaza is anything else but Arab, and part of the "Great Arab Nation" — as the Arabs refer to themselves — is nothing but a fantasy and a hoax perpetrated by the

---

1. See Appendix 1.

Arab nations on the world, designed to question and undermine Israel's right to its land.

The Balfour Declaration never envisaged any additional Arab states. The Arab nation was already well looked-after following WWI with some twenty separate Arab states comprising approximately 5.3 million square miles.

The creation of Jordan by the British was not envisaged in the Balfour Declaration, let alone yet another Arab state on what was left of the Mandate after the creation of Jordan! As already stated, the Arab residents of what was "Palestine" never required a state of their own, while Judea and Samaria were under the illegal control of an Arab state, Jordan. They never referred to themselves as "Palestinians" until relatively recently, after Israel took possession of the territory of Judea and Samaria in its defensive war in 1967.

No one ever referred to the Arabs in the area as "Palestinians," connoting a particular peoplehood. The fact remains that the roots of the Arabs in this area lie elsewhere in the Arab world. Emblematically, Arafat himself, longtime symbol of the "Palestinian" cause, was himself a native of Cairo.

The whole notion of referring to themselves as "Palestinians" was to create the impression or the belief that they were "dispossessed," "indigenous" people going back to Canaanites! There are of course several problems with that piece of propaganda; one is that in Arabic, Palestine is "Philistine," disregarding for a moment the fact that the name of "Palestine" was imposed by the Romans in the aftermath of the Roman conquest of *Eretz Yisrael* in an attempt to eradicate the name of the Jewish state for all time.

The "Palestinians" cannot claim to be both Canaanites and Philistines since the Philistines were not indigenous people either. And if they were either Canaanites or Philistines, they cannot also claim to be descendants of Abraham! Yet the Arab propaganda war against Israel continues unabated, as they claim former "Palestine" as their land in a barefaced lie flying in the face of history.

That propaganda, however, in no way obliges Israel to cave in to either European or even US pressure to create a Trojan horse in the midst of its soft underbelly, its heartland in Judea and Samaria. UN Resolution 242 does not require that Israel either return to unstable indefensible borders, or that it give up land to a nonexistent entity which has no precedent in the history of the area.

The attempt by the previous government of Israel to mollify the Arabs of the area has created nothing but further demands, with absolutely no peace in sight. The Oslo Accords did not provide for an independent Arab state, but simply limited autonomy.

UN Resolution 242 refers to the conflict between the Arab states and Israel and the armistice following the 1967 and 1973 wars of Arab aggression. "The Palestinians" were not a recognized party to either the conflict or its aftermath. The "Palestinian cause," (read "Arab cause") too was a creation of Arab propaganda with the hypocritical collaboration of Western powers.

The claim by Arafat to declare an independent "State of Palestine" flies in the face of the Oslo agreements. The attempt by the Europeans to coerce Israel to sign on to such a suicide pact is not only inconceivable, but defies Resolution 242 as well. Clearly, the "Palestinians" were not party to Resolution 242!

Israel must insist on defensible borders in spite of the pressure from all sources. Coercion is not a way to make peace; it is the tool of gangsters and terrorists. While Arafat had no problem using coercion, Israel should remind the Western world what UN Resolution 242 states.

Chapter X

The Perfidy of Leaders during WWII

The perfidy of Western world leaders during WWII, and even before, should never be forgotten. Hundreds of thousands of innocent lives could have been saved — if only. But most perfidious of all were Britain and her underling Canada.

The League of Nations Mandate for Palestine — designed to re-establish the Jewish homeland in *Eretz Yisrael*, and entrusted to the British to settle the land "closely," with full support of the Jewish communities in *Eretz Yisrael* and the Diaspora due to the Balfour Declaration — turned out to be a betrayal and a great disaster for the Jewish people.

Jewish leaders (both in the homeland and the Diaspora), perceiving the British as being sympathetic to the Jewish return after the Balfour Declaration favored the return of the Jewish people to their homeland, supported British intentions of carrying out the League of Nations Mandate. But it soon became apparent that the British — for reasons of their own interest vis-à-vis the Arabs in general — perfidiously perverted the Mandate, standing it on its head. Instead of helping the ingathering of the exiles, Britain issued one "White Paper" after another, putting roadblocks in the path of Jewish people wanting to immigrate to *Eretz Yisrael*, thus whitewashing and reneging on its obligation. Particularly odious, if not barbaric, was the curtailing and outright prohibition of Jewish people entering Palestine — *Eretz Yisrael* — during the Nazi era.

Even before the mass slaughter had begun, Nazi persecution of Jewish people made life in Germany and in various European countries all but impossible. At that time, escape and even some legal emigration was still possible. If not for the British, hundreds of thousands of innocent lives could have been spared.

Rickety fishing boats barely afloat, carrying hopeful immigrants to *Eretz Yisrael*, were mercilessly turned away from its very shores by the British.

Some, like the *Struma*, and many other less well known boats sunk, full of innocent human beings. All they wanted was to finally go home, to escape the persecution and save their families' lives. What on earth were the British thinking? Surely they must have known they were condemning countless thousands of human beings to death!

Canada — a lesser player in this horrific human tragedy — refused to grant temporary refuge to any Jewish people even when it was known that the Jewish people were being murdered daily by the tens of thousands in Auschwitz, Treblinka and elsewhere; even when their stay in Canada was guaranteed by the local Jewish community not to be a burden on the state.

In the words of the Canadian official responsible for refugees and immigration: "even one is too many."[1]

As I write these words my heart breaks. How can a people be so hateful, so cruel as to turn their backs on the lives of innocent human beings being slaughtered, and not lift a finger — knowing full well they could have saved them! And today Canada, the British and the European states dare to preach to Israel how not to defend its people against terrorism.

But coming back to the League of Nations Mandate for Palestine, just a few facts of the history of that period:

1. The Land was sparsely populated and badly neglected prior to the re-establishment of the State of Israel.
2. At that time the local Arabs, who wandered in over time from neighboring Arab states, did not refer to themselves as "Palestinians"; they were simply Arabs, part of the Arab nation, nor did anyone else regard them as anything else but Arabs.
3. The Balfour Declaration called for the re-establishment of the Jewish Homeland — it did not call for creating yet another Arab state. It merely provided that the existing population, be it Muslim or Christian, have its rights preserved.
4. There was a continuous presence of Jewish people in the Land of Israel. Even after the expulsion, small communities managed to survive, and continued their religious practices even after the destruction of the Second Temple in 70 CE, and the subsequent Jewish revolt in 139 CE.

---

1. Irving Abella and Harold Troper, *None Is Too Many: Canada and the Jews of Europe, 1933–48* (Toronto: Lester and Orpen Dennys, 1982).

5. Throughout the period of dispersion, Jewish people longed to return to *Eretz Yisrael* and *Yerushalayim*, never, ever giving up. Some were lucky and did manage to settle in the Land despite restrictions and prohibitions of every unimaginable kind; others less fortunate were turned away, again and again.

The country suffered many invasions both because of its geographical location and its religious significance. But the invaders, some great empires, came and went; some vanished from history entirely, but we, the Jewish people, are here — again, thank G-d!

We are a resilient people. We have survived many tragedies and we will survive the current challenges with the help of the Almighty. The Holocaust, being the most horrific of all Jewish tragedies (the Jewish people lost one-third of its brethren; out of eighteen million worldwide, only twelve million remained, while in Europe, almost 90 percent of all Jews were killed), convinced the survivors that unless we will fight for our own, independent homeland, the persecution and murder will never end.

Perhaps the anti-Semites should take notice: adversity works in strange miraculous ways, for all these centuries of persecution and forcible conversion have only made the Jewish people stronger.

The Land of Israel thrives since our return; even the desert blooms. Despite the arid conditions, Israeli farmers and horticulturists grow every imaginable fruit and flower. It must be the mutual love between the people and its Land.

But Israelis excel in other fields as well; whether it is science or medicine or cultural endeavors, Israel can be proud of its people.

I feel as though I myself have been wandering for these two thousand years. It's good to be home at last!

Chapter XI

The Ingathering of the Exiles and Arab Propaganda

Jewish history is unique in the annals of human existence. The Jewish people survived horrible persecution during the time of their forced dispersion, culminating in the horrors of the Holocaust. No other people in recorded history have survived as a people during their absence from their homeland for nearly nineteen centuries.

After the destruction of the Temple and the destruction of Jerusalem during the forced exile, our people took with them into exile not only their religion and devotion to One Almighty G-d, but also their love and longing for their Land — *Eretz Yisrael*, and *Yerushalayim* (Jerusalem). Their faith never faltered, even as they were burned at the stake by the fanatical Roman Catholics.

The Jewish people finally returned to their homeland after the Holocaust, although in greatly diminished numbers. As stated earlier, there always was a Jewish presence in the Land of Israel, even after the dispersion; some Jewish people managed to hide and lived in Safed and elsewhere, some eventually returning to Jerusalem.

As for those who were exiled, their longing for their Land and their holy city *Yerushalayim* never abated through two thousand years of wandering. The prayer books are permeated with that longing, and it is no wonder that it was passed on through the generations.

The Law of Return of the exiles was enshrined in the legislation of the reborn state as one of the most important rights — a right which could never be changed or abrogated, even by government decree.

It is interesting how the Arabs have borrowed the language of the Jewish people for the purpose of their own agenda and for their own nefarious propaganda. Thus the word "Diaspora" is used to describe Arabs who emigrated out of choice to better themselves in other countries of the West. Even the phrase "Right of Return" is utilized by the Arabs to further their propaganda machinations with regard to Arabs who emigrated for their own reasons or those Arabs who left of their own accord and who have deliberately been kept in "refugee camps" since the 1948 War.

It is important to note that the Jewish people in 1948 had no problem living side by side with the existing population, whether Christian or Muslim. But it was the Arabs who — together with their brethren from five other states (Egypt, Syria, Lebanon, Jordan and Iraq) — attacked the Jewish people on the eve of independence. In fact, they had been attacking the Jewish people living in *Eretz Yisrael* for at least a century prior to the Declaration of Independence; even before the 1929 massacre in Hebron and the 1936–39 attacks in Jerusalem, there were both isolated and organized terrorist attacks against Jews living in the Land.

The Arabs and the world should be reminded that aggression is not rewarded in international law; aggressor nations forfeit land from which they launch wars. This law has many precedents in Europe, particularly where borders were moved as a result of German aggression in WWII. But in Israel's case, it is the intended victim who is pressed to pay the price.

As for the Arabs' "right of return," the question is: "where to?" If they wish to return to their countries or origin, that very well may be their right, but that is something the Arabs have to work out for themselves.

It is a historic fact that *Eretz Yisrael* is not the Arabs' country of origin. In total, the Arab states have a land mass twice the size of the US, larger than Canada, and about two and a half times larger than the continent of Europe.[1] What rights do the Arabs have to Judea? And since when is Jerusalem important to the Arabs? This relationship gained mysterious currency only after the Jewish people re-established their state, rebuilding the land and its cities.

Before Jewish people started returning in large numbers in the eighteenth century, the land was neglected and sparsely populated. There were no millions of Arabs in *Eretz Yisrael* — Palestine — prior to the beginning of the twentieth century, nor indeed prior to 1948. In the mid eighteenth century, there were only fifty thousand Arabs in the Land of Israel.

The fact is that the re-established Jewish state is not merely an inconvenience to the Arabs, but an opportunity to have an external enemy. It is an

---

1. See Appendix 8.

inconvenience because Arab rulers have always been unable, even with their oil riches, to provide a decent way of life and standard of living to their people, similar to that of Israel's Western standards. And so, an external enemy is most desirable in order to mobilize their people against an external "threat" rather than turning the mobs against themselves.

As for the "brouhaha" of creating yet another Arab state on this tiny, tiny piece of land, there are several things to keep in mind. First, there has never — in all recorded history — been an Arab state in Judea and Samaria. Second, if there is such a desperate need for yet another Arab state, why was it not created when Judea and Samaria were illegally occupied by Jordan following the 1948 War and prior to 1967? Third, when Israel was willing to cede some land in the Oslo Accords, in a sort of "land for peace" deal,[1] the only requirement for the Arab "Palestinians" was for violence to cease. Israel had no desire to rule over a foreign, hostile people, and so the Oslo Accords were born. But Oslo provided for limited autonomy only. There very simply is not enough land to provide for two viable states, as anyone who knows the land will readily attest.

Judea, it must be stressed again, is not Arab land. As the name itself implies, Judea is Jewish land; indeed, that is where the Jewish people derive their name from. Further, Judea and Samaria lie literally in the heart of the Jewish state. If anyone had a design to attack Israel, certainly Judea and Samaria would be an ideal strategic location.

The history of Arab aggression against the State of Israel is long, bloody and treacherous. There is no reason to believe that the Arabs, or their terrorist proxy the PLO, will suddenly reform themselves because Israel "took risks for peace" and made itself vulnerable to attack!

But for the moment, at least, Arab propaganda is holding sway, still propagating the old, long discredited libel that Jewish people are using Arab children's blood to make pastries for Purim and matzah for *Pesach*. Such propaganda was still being printed in the Saudi press as late as March 2002. This, from the "moderate" Saudi Arabia which proposed a new "peace plan" provided Israel goes back to its indefensible pre-1967 borders, minus Judea and Samaria!

The ongoing terrorist attacks on Israeli civilians, in restaurants, shopping

---

1. Note that this term rings differently in Arab ears than in Western ones; see Bat Ye'or, *Eurabia*, and Robert Spencer, *Onward Muslim Soldiers*.

malls, on buses and at bus stops, finally prompted the Israeli army to retaliate to curb the never-ending violence.

Israel — forced in April 2002 to re-enter Jenin, an area known for its terrorist enclaves and bomb factories — was later accused by the Arabs of perpetrating a "massacre." The dupes and do-gooders of the Western world, ready to believe anything the Arabs can concoct, called for a UN investigation. On the ground, the investigation confirmed no more than fifty-two bodies, mainly those of terrorists who set booby-traps against Israeli soldiers. Israel lost twenty-three soldiers, dead as a result of the same booby-traps. Still, there is no end to Arab propaganda.[1]

It was reported that an anti-Semitic riot broke out at San Francisco State University following an Arab-instigated student propaganda campaign featuring posters depicting a can labeled with a picture of a baby and the following inscription: "Palestinian children's meat, made in Israel, slaughtered according to Jewish rites, under American license"!

It took the university's president a week to speak out, after Jewish students were attacked and yelled at: "Hitler didn't finish the job!" "Get out or we'll kill you!" The university president finally called on the district attorney to investigate certain students after months and years of unrest caused by Arab students instigating violence and spreading anti-Semitic hate propaganda against Israel and Jewish people in general.

But the outrage at San Francisco State University is not an isolated incident. Arab students throughout North America and Europe have been involved in anti-Semitic, anti-Israel propaganda for decades. It is the outrage of the poster depicting a baby as "Palestinian meat" that finally prompted some action.

---

1. As in the Arab-produced propaganda film *Jenin, Jenin*.

Chapter XII

Anti-Semitism, Israel and the Brits

When one looks at anti-Semitism and its roots from a historical perspective, one gets perhaps a better picture of what happened before, during and after the Holocaust. The indifference so openly displayed in the Western democracies to the persecution and then mass murder of the Jews of Europe during the Holocaust perplexed many contemporary Jewish writers. How, they argued, could a civilized world have allowed this atrocity to happen? How indeed could a civilized society like Germany become the willing executioners for Hitler? But one has to first understand that anti-Semitism was not merely an aberration in Western Christendom, but a deeply entrenched dogma, inculcated openly and consistently by the Christian Church over a span of centuries.

This anti-Semitic propaganda of the Christian Church was part of Christian belief. It was so deeply entrenched that few if any Christians ever questioned its veracity or reason. Nor was this attitude any less vigorous in the twentieth century. In Britain — the Mother of Parliaments, an "enlightened" and modern society, even at the beginning of the twentieth century — the worst calumnies against the Jews were spread by, of all people, the British. Parliamentarians themselves.[1]

Jews were blamed for all the ills of British society and the world, including alleged attempts to bring about the downfall of European Christian civilization.

It now appears that the Jewish Zionist leaders of the day somehow misunderstood the motives behind the genteel anti-Semitism of that time. In hindsight, some of the major figures behind the Balfour Declaration — apparently including Lord Balfour himself — may have been motivated by their anti-Semitism more than anything else, in their bid to get rid of British and

---

1. See Harry Defries, *Conservative Party Attitudes to Jews 1900–1950*.

foreign-born Jews. Palestine was the answer for these anti-Semites, motivated by their hatred and contempt for Jews rather than support for Zionism or Jewish rights in their homeland as some Jewish leaders were led to believe. Of course the Balfour Declaration said all the right things, but the motivation behind it, it appears, may have been sinister from the start. Apparently, Dr. Weizmann and others were too naïve and not sophisticated enough to fully appreciate the sophistry and hypocrisy of the British gentry.

Again, the Jews were dumbfounded and surprised that the same British leaders who brought the Balfour Declaration into being, supporting a "Jewish Homeland" in Palestine — because of Jewish "historical roots and attachment to the Land" — could subsequently, when given the Mandate to implement the League of Nations Resolution, put all possible obstacles in the path of the Jewish community in Palestine which was ready to bring about the realization of the dream of ingathering the exiles.

But the Brits had their own agenda. By 1917–18, at the conclusion of WWI, having driven the Turks out of the Middle East, the Brits were now looking to expand their own influence in the region. And so the British influenced events, to play up to the Arabs. Arab riots and even massacres in Hebron, Jerusalem and elsewhere were not only tolerated by the Brits, but were even instigated, at least initially.[1] Extremists in Arab society — both local and "imported" — were major players in the violence against the Jewish community in *Eretz Yisrael* (Palestine) and were helped by the Brits to positions of power.

The height of British hypocrisy motivated by anti-Semitism reached its zenith when, even in 1941–42 (when the Nazi annihilation policy was already known), they blocked desperate Jews escaping Nazi hell from entry to *Eretz Yisrael*. One is hard pressed not to call this British perfidy collaboration with the Nazis in the mass murder of Europe's Jewry!

The assassination of Lord Moyne (by a Jewish underground fighter), who was responsible for the implementation of the British "White Paper" which at the most critical time restricted and later completely blocked entry to Jews trying to escape the Nazi Final Solution, gave the British the "right" to now openly declare their animosity and contempt toward the Jews, and to openly declare the support of the "Arab cause," in the words of one British leader.

But what was the "Arab cause?"

The Jewish people did not take Arab land. It was the Arabs who usurped

---

1. See Samuel Katz, *Battleground: Facts and Fantasy in Palestine.*

and despoiled the Jewish land and defiled the Jewish Temple Mount by erecting a mosque on the Holiest of Holies.

And so, the act of one man (or perhaps a group of men), the assassin of Lord Moyne, gave the British the excuse of now declaring war on Zionism. But the war was not only against Zionism; it was on Jews everywhere, and on the Jewish community in *Eretz Yisrael*. Lieutenant General Barker, the general officer commanding in Mandatory Palestine, commented that by excluding British troops from Jewish establishments, the Jews would be punished "in a way the race dislikes as any, by striking at their pockets and showing our contempt for them"!

As history can testify, this was neither the first nor the last time the Brits showed or felt contempt for the Jews (or is it "the Zionists"?). The British press apparently had no problem with any of this.

We have heard similar murmurings from the House of Lords. In the late summer or fall of 2002, the *Jerusalem Post* reported on a comment (originally published in the *Spectator* magazine) by a British Member of the House of Lords who, venting his feelings about Israel and the Jewish people, was heard to say: "Well, the Jews have been asking for it and now, thank God, we can say what we think at last." This episode happened not too long after the French Ambassador to Britain referred to Israel as "that shitty little country," in the refined atmosphere at the dinner table of Conrad Black, owner of the *Telegraph* newspaper (whose Jewish wife later wrote a column exposing the ambassador's anti-Semitism).

The British created a great deal of damage to the future Jewish state by failing to implement the Balfour Declaration and the League of Nations Mandate. Not only did they cut off some 80 percent from the original land mass of Palestine.[1] to create yet another Arab country, later called Trans-Jordan (and then Jordan), they also attempted to further divide the remaining 20 percent of the land into two states, one Arab and one Jewish.[2] The proposed boundaries of this Jewish state were totally indefensible. Perhaps that was exactly what the British had in mind.

But the British did not leave Palestine until May 1948. Between 1945 (the end of the Nazi regime) and 1948, the Brits managed to inflict even more pain on the Jews; the British even stopped the survivors of the Holocaust

---

1. See Appendices 2 & 6.
2. See Appendix 7.

from entering their land. Ship after ship was sent away from the very shores of *Eretz Yisrael* to Cyprus where the Jews were interned behind barbed wire! These people — the remnants of European Jewry — who somehow survived Nazism, had to be traumatized yet again, this time by the British. How much hatred and contempt does this kind of action require?!

Chapter XIII

Israel and the Legacy of the Brits

To this day, Israel is suffering the results of British perfidy and betrayal. The British-recommended second partition of *Eretz Yisrael* (the Peel Commission Partition) was unfortunately eventually adopted by the United Nations. This clear betrayal of the Jewish people by the British government was even denounced by David Lloyd George himself, the British prime minister during WWI, as well as by the British press. The *Manchester Guardian* lamented the failure of the British government to re-establish a Jewish National Home in Palestine.

The Jewish people and their leaders were devastated at the betrayal by most of the very same British leaders who promulgated the Balfour Declaration. They seemed to be at a loss to explain even to themselves how Palestine — which originally comprised some fifty-five thousand square miles on both sides of the river Jordan (later reduced to a mere 20 percent of the original, or 10,800 square miles) — could be further divided into two states, one Arab, one Jewish.

That would make not one, but two Arab states, comprising most of the land designated for the Jewish homeland. But the Arabs refused the two-state solution, claiming that Palestine would "remain" an Arab state (at that time, no one spoke of a "Palestinian" state, but rather an Arab state). The Balfour Declaration, however, did not refer to any Arab rights within Palestine — *Eretz Yisrael* — except the rights of residence, equal to all other residents.[1]

Clearly, the creation of this new entity (Transjordan), which had no precedence in the history of the region, was more than an act of premeditated betrayal of the Jewish people by the British. It was also an act in blatant disregard of their commitment to their own Balfour Declaration.

But the worst was yet to come. What followed was the curtailment of the

---

1. See Appendix 1.

ingathering of the exiles in 1937–38, when atrocities against the Jewish people in Germany were already known. This culminated in the greatest tragedy ever to befall the Jewish people. But even the surviving remnant of European Jewry following WWII were refused entry into their own land; turned away from the very shores *of Eretz Yisrael* by the British between 1945 and 1948.

The 1947 UN Partition of the land west of Jordan into two states and the indefensible borders assigned for the Jewish state were just the beginning of problems yet to come. It seemed that Britain was now determined and the world did not much object that the fledgling Jewish state would not long survive.[1]

Before its departure in 1948, Britain left armaments and defensive structures to Jordan, as well as the British-trained Arab Legion, under the command of Glub Pasha, a British officer. How far did the Brits travel from the promise of the Balfour Declaration?

In a strange way, it was perhaps a miracle that the Arabs refused the two-state solution. Five Arab armies attacked the fledgling state on all fronts. G-d only knows how the small local community and the few thousand Holocaust survivors managed to fend off the attackers.

There was little if any ammunition to speak of. But with a great deal of perseverance and improvisation, plus a few hardy souls (including some non-Jews who stood by us at the hour of peril), the Jewish people managed — with great loss of life — to survive and even gain some badly needed defensive lines. But despite tremendous valor on the field of battle, the heart of Jerusalem was lost.

Part of Jerusalem, Judea and Samaria were lost in the battle, and Jordan illegally occupied even those lands, as well as Jerusalem's Old City, which, of course, included the Temple Mount where both the First and the Second Temples stood, the Western Wall being their only remnant.

The Arabs not only illegally occupied these lands, they forcibly evicted the Jewish population of the Old City — east Jerusalem — and the world community did not appear to be terribly troubled by all this. In east Jerusalem, the territory they had taken, the Arabs also destroyed the synagogues and defiled graves in the ancient Jewish cemetery on the Mount of Olives. Still, the world community had no problem with any of it, only a few years after the annihilation of six million Jewish people at the hands of the Nazis.

---

1. See Appendix 4.

Very telling was how the Arabs, in their war of aggression in 1948 — only three years after the Holocaust — openly threatened to destroy the Jewish people. Yet still the world did not appear to have any problem with that, nor did it attempt to send any arms or reinforcements to the beleaguered Jewish people, who received only sporadic, unofficial shipments of arms smuggled in from a few European countries. How that bespeaks the conscience of world leaders.

The interval between the 1948 War and the 1967 War was marked by ongoing aggression and provocation on the Egyptian, Jordanian and Syrian borders. One example is the cross-border terrorist attack in Ma'alot (at the Syrian border), where schoolchildren were held hostage for many days. During the rescue attempts by the Israeli army, some were killed.

There was ongoing harassment and shootings from the Golan Heights, then held by Syria, at the farmers below on the Israeli side. The almost daily provocations and hit-and-run terrorist attacks from across the border with Egypt (See *Jerusalem Post* archives, 1950s) were ongoing, as were the terrorist attacks from across Jordan. Any one of these attacks could have been sufficient to be regarded as an act of aggression, and certainly each was a breach of the Armistice Agreement of 1949 between Israel and its neighbors, but complaints to the UN produced practically no results.

By May and early June 1967, the proverbial writing was on the wall. Egypt amassed its army across the border, and demanded that the UN Peace-Keeping Force leave the area. A clear sign, if ever there was one, of things to come.[1] Israel was not at all well prepared for war. It could not possibly match Egypt's superior armament, either quantitatively or qualitatively.

After many sleepless nights in the upper echelon of the Israeli leadership and armed forces, a critical decision was taken. The country, which had limited resources, was facing an overwhelming enemy force. The painful decision was made to launch a preemptive strike on Egypt before the country was overrun.

Israel could not afford a prolonged war; it had neither the resources nor the manpower. And so the Six Day War was launched. For some time afterwards, military magazines and the general press around the world lauded the Israeli victory as "masterful." But the world soon forgot how a beleaguered

---

1. Yet some apologists claimed many years later that it was all a "misunderstanding" and a "miscalculation."

small nation — repeatedly attacked by its much stronger neighbors — had to fight this lonely battle for survival.

Either there is greater ignorance in the Western world today than one can possibly excuse, or simple indifference, or worse. The current barrage of verbal attacks against Israel, its leaders and Jewish people in general is a worrisome manifestation to Jewish people everywhere. Many wonder how malicious Arab propaganda has managed to pervert all sense of history, simple justice and morality.

That the average person may or may not be totally conversant with the history of the Middle East (including the relatively recent history of the past 150 years or so) is not surprising, but that the news media betray such ignorance should be neither acceptable nor tolerated, whether such ignorance is feigned or real.

I suppose the more naïve among us still expect the press to be the watchdog of society, and to be sure, we are fortunate enough to have a few who still consider their job as journalists a sacred trust; but unfortunately, not nearly enough of these individuals exist. The greatest majority of today's journalists have adopted a herd mentality, and follow the line of least resistance. And so, we observe in the world today a deplorable situation in which falsehoods and outrageous propaganda can be presented to the general public in various media interviews without challenge or comment.

Interestingly enough, this does not apply to every conflict or to every party of the conflict in other parts of the world. It is troublesome to watch and listen to how prejudices are openly practiced both by the media organizations — such as the BBC, CNN and CBC — and their spokesmen, as well as reporters. Reports are no longer straightforward; they are laden with innuendos, sensationalism and distortion of the very subject matter they are supposedly reporting.

The current Arab-Israeli conflict and the Arab terrorist war against Israel has many layers and a long history behind it, yet rarely if ever are these facts taken into consideration in reports, editorials or even documentaries. Depending on the political bent of the journalist or news organization, salient facts are more often than not omitted from such documentaries, which are exactly the place where they should be more fully discussed. And so the general public, instead of being informed, is left with a distorted view of history.

In his brilliant account of the origins of the Arab-Israeli conflict, *Battleground: Fact and Fantasy in Palestine,* Samuel Katz lays bare the facts leading to the present conflict, which has persisted for the last eight decades and more.

According to Mr. Katz, the midwife in the birth of the conflict was none other than Britain. His fully documented accounts tell of Britain's duplicitous role in its quest for domination in the Middle East. He shows in myriad documented facts how Britain used Jewish leaders before and after the First World War to advance its nefarious goals in the region.

Whether this duplicity was intended from the start, going back to the Balfour Declaration, or evolved as "opportunities" presented themselves, is not entirely clear. Suffice it to say, these "opportunities" were deliberate creations of the British administration on the ground in the Middle East, and the home office did nothing to stop them.

Samuel Katz delivers for us blow-by-blow accounts of how and when the British were entrusted by the League of Nations with the Mandate for Palestine — mainly due to the Balfour Declaration. Although supported by the Jewish leadership of the time, the British perverted that trust, and in fact, actively worked against it.

The so-called "Arab Revolt" was a creation of the local British administration, which not only organized, but also incited local Arabs against the re-establishment of the Jewish Homeland in Palestine.[1] Prior to these riots, a warm relationship apparently existed between Emir Faisal and both leaders of the Jewish Diaspora, Weizmann and Frankfurter, to which their 1919 exchange of letters (see Katz's appendix) attest. In fact, Faisal voiced his appreciation to the Jewish leadership for its support of the Arab cause with the British, and expressed the hope that the Arabs would have the opportunity to reciprocate in the future.

The local British administration was opposed to the Balfour Declaration and to British support for a Jewish homeland; instead of educating the local residents regarding the goals of the British Mandate, they did everything possible to frustrate it. The British government eventually went along with the position of the local administration in Palestine. Instead of facilitating the return in large numbers of the Jewish people to their homeland as the League of Nations Mandate stipulated, British officials now, with the help of the British government, did everything they could to frustrate those efforts.

Using the Arab riots which they themselves helped to incite (these riots

---

1. See Samuel Katz pages 64–66, 124–125, re Meinertzhagen Report.

led to massacres in Hebron in 1929 and Jerusalem in 1936) as an excuse, the British claimed they could not allow larger immigration. One White Paper followed another, attempting to justify the British position, eventually culminating in the Peel Commission's recommendation for a further partition of the remaining 20 percent of the original area of Palestine.

The British also used the Jews, and the creation of a viable Jewish homeland, as a reason for obtaining the eastern part of Palestine from the French, who relinquished their control over the area in consideration of the Jewish homeland. The Brits then — without qualm — created TransJordan on the very area obtained from the French for the Jewish homeland! The perfidy of the British was seemingly endless; they further attempted in a pernicious way to gain control over Syria, also under French control at the time.

On August 11, 1937, the Jewish leaders debated the infamous Peel Commission Report, which was tantamount to the acceptance of the second partition of *Eretz Yisrael*, at the Twentieth Zionist Congress in Zurich. Menachem Ussishkin, one of the leaders who desperately attempted to prevent the adoption of the resolution, uttered these prophetic words: "The acceptance of this proposal means an end of our historic hope... It will mean that a great misfortune must befall us..."

And so it did.

It was the beginning of the situation that still plagues us to this very day, for it was the first time the local Arabs were given — by the British — an excuse to demand yet another Arab state.

Worst of all, what followed were the worst restrictions for Jewish immigration. Massive immigration, as envisaged in the Mandate, could have saved tens if not hundreds of thousands of Jewish lives. In fact, if Britain had not prevented the Jewish people from leaving Europe in great numbers, the outcome of history would have — or at least could have — been very different.

To add insult to injury, the British administration issued additional prohibitions concerning the purchase of land by the local Jewish population! It was not enough that the Jewish people were willing to purchase back their own land; now the British overlords forbade them to do even that.

While the Jewish people of Europe were being prevented by the British from escaping certain death, Arabs from neighboring Arab states kept coming to the Jewish homeland in great numbers, without restrictions. And so the Arab population in *Eretz Yisrael* grew, and grew...

Chapter XIV

Have We Learned Anything from History?

Have we come full circle?

In 2002 I was asked by a rabbi acquaintance of mine how I saw the rise of far-right parties and their accompanying anti-Semitism in recent months in Europe and elsewhere, from the perspective of a survivor, and also in view of my involvement in this issue for a very long time.

The answer is perhaps simpler than it first appears.

First, there had been no "sudden" recent rise in anti-Semitism. Anti-Semitism and fascism do not emerge overnight. These trends may lie dormant, or be less public when the conditions are not favorable, but fascism, anti-Semitism and xenophobia emerge when there appears to be a change in those conditions.

Whether economic, social or political, any change for the worse will also bring with it dissatisfaction in a segment of the population, which then seeks a convenient culprit or scapegoat on which to pin its anger and frustration. But anger and frustration can be manipulated by propaganda and ruthless regimes or individuals, or both, as we have seen many times in history, most dramatically during the Nazi era. We are witnessing this again now.

The present restlessness and even anger on which ruthless men feed is in origin partly economic and partly social, but also political and religious. Those on the fringes of society may feel affected as a result of recent changes, and can easily become the prey of either leftist or rightist political movements, which eagerly exploit such individuals.

International terrorism, in particular the September 11, 2001, suicide bombing attack on the Twin Towers in New York and the Pentagon in Washington — using domestic airlines as destructive bombs and missiles — rudely awakened the Western world. There was a sudden realization that people who were welcomed to various countries in Europe and North America as students, foreign workers or refugees, were involved in causing harm to their host country.

There was something terrifying and unprecedented in this event. Even though there had been other terrorist attacks against Western countries, by Arabs and/or Muslims, this event was particularly shocking both in its execution and planning. Years must have gone into the planning of these attacks, which included recruitment, training, fund-raising, secrecy, and the collaboration of so many willing to kill and be killed in the process.

And all this, for what reason? Surely it did not benefit the killers who themselves were killed. Who then did benefit? This question is not sufficiently explored, but we will deal with the possible beneficiaries further on.

Meanwhile, a world shocked into disbelief has still not come to grips with the reality of international terrorism. Some practice avoidance and try to live in denial; others — like Israeli citizens — do not have the luxury of living in denial. The reality of terrorism stares Israelis in the face daily and they have to deal with it as best they can, while facing daily criticism from those who seem to suffer from something akin to the "Stockholm Syndrome," identifying with the terrorist perpetrators in fear for their own lives.

Others — and here we can come back to the issue of xenophobia — will blame the influx of foreigners to their homeland and will become unwitting dupes of today's far-right fascists who see this as an opportunity to bring forward their perverted ideology and once again infect society.

Is all this inevitable? Not necessarily. Much depends on each and every one of us.

For example, even France, with the worst case of xenophobia, gave Le Pen only 17–18 percent of the vote, less than a fifth. What about the other four-fifths who rejected fascism? Perhaps it is time for the silent majority to be more proactive. We have already seen protest marches by those who thankfully reject fascism and anti-Semitism; we must hope society continues to make the fascists increasingly uncomfortable through the Internet or other mass media, thereby denying any gains to the fascists or their would-be followers.

One must hope that the world has learned something from the Holocaust, when all that was heard was deafening silence while the Jewish people were being slaughtered. When I say "the world," I really mean the silent majority. I would like to count on the decent people of the silent majority to be silent no more. Silence was regarded as acquiescence by Hitler and his cohorts!

Hitler tested the water carefully. He deprived the Jewish people of their rights by denying them the right to practice their professions, thus denying them the right to earn a living, and eventually denying them the right to live. The world was silent throughout. The infamous 1935 Nuremberg Laws further eroded any semblance of Jewish rights, and still the world was silent.

And so Hitler unleashed his goons on helpless Jewish communities throughout Germany; on the night of November 9–10, 1938, a coordinated pogrom erupted in every city, town and village. Jewish people were beaten and abused, their homes were vandalized, their synagogues set on fire and their holy books desecrated and burned. Many Jewish men were rounded up and sent to Dachau, the first concentration camp in Germany. The Nazis called this pogrom *Kristallnacht*. Still the world remained silent. Deportations of Jewish people followed, and still the world said nothing!

By September 1, 1939, the German Nazi army invaded Poland. In short order World War II began. In Europe, one country after another fell to the Nazis. Even if the silent majority had wanted to speak out at this point, they would have been quickly silenced by the Nazis!

As the famous poem attributed to Pastor Martin Niemoeller says:

> First they came for the communists, and I did not speak out — because I was not a communist… then they came for the Jews, and I did not speak out — because I was not a Jew; then they came for me — and there was no one left to speak out for me.

This kind of silent acquiescence must never again be allowed to happen, for as the popular quote goes, "All it takes for evil to triumph is for good people to do nothing." The lessons of the Holocaust are many, and the world owes it to itself to heed them if it is to survive, if it is to retain a modicum of morality…

For the Jewish people, the rise of fascism at the start of the third millennium is most disturbing, particularly in combination with the "Stockholm Syndrome" whose "victims" may not even realize that they are aiding and abetting not only anti-Semitism, but their own enemies!

All this is happening while some survivors of the Holocaust are still alive. And thus wonder whether the world has learned anything from the tragic past. Not from the tragic loss of some six million Jewish people, nor the deaths of forty-five to fifty million Allied combatants.

No, they did not die to save Jewish lives; tragically they learned too late that their own freedom was at stake if the Nazis were not removed from power in Europe. Britain and America sent their young men to defend their freedom. For the record, Jewish men enlisted in disproportionate numbers to fight Nazism, and they also died on the battlefield in disproportionate numbers.

Many lives would have been spared (both those of combatants and Jewish victims) had world leaders understood early on that this was not "merely" about "the Jews." Today, the world is facing yet another challenge — the Islamo-Fascists — and it is not only against "the Jews"!

September 11, 2001, was not the only Islamo-Fascist attack on a Western nation, nor have they been aimed only at the US. More recently (July 2005), Britain suffered a horrendous attack on its civilian population in London. France too is experiencing a new challenge. Some call it an "intifada."

France has a very large Muslim population, estimated today at ten million, most of whom entered the country as a result of the Europe-Arab League pact;[1] a pact in which Europe, led by France, promised the Arab League "cooperation" against Israel, for various economic benefits and arrangements.

Now France is reaping what it has sown. No, it never ends with "the Jews." It just begins with "the Jews!"

Other countries of Europe, too, are beginning to feel concern over their Islamic population. There is no denying the fact that all terrorist attacks in recent decades — whether on Israel or others — have been committed by Islamo-Fascists.

Following the unrest in France — where fires were set to cars, etc., every night for more than two weeks — France issued a state of emergency and took other measures. Thousands of cars were burned and other acts of wanton destruction were committed during that time.

Germany and Belgium, too, suffered similar attacks, but on a smaller scale. Now all of Europe is bracing itself for the unforeseen.

As a result of the Europe-Arab League pact, all European countries have committed themselves to unrestricted immigration of Arab Muslims; a sort of invasion, by other means.[2]

---

1. See Bat Ye'or, *Eurabia*.
2. See Robert Spencer, Onward Muslim Soldiers.

Chapter XV

The Vatican Statement
on the Holocaust

The long awaited statement — ten years in the making — was not merely too little, too late, it simply avoided dealing with the issues it allegedly attempted to address, as well as the very real concerns regarding the role of the Vatican during WWII and thereafter.

To simply state that the Vatican "did not do enough" during the Holocaust is to miss the whole point. To say that "some" Christians harmed the Jews is to totally avoid responsibility for the centuries of persecution of the Jewish people which led to the Holocaust.

And what about the evidence that the Vatican was running what is referred to as the "Rat-Line" — the infamous "underground train" helping Nazi war criminals escape justice and flee to the safety of various South American countries sympathetic to them? This intricate effort to provide false passports, funds and visas to high-ranking Nazi leaders in the aftermath of WWII is a well established fact of history.

That fact alone — more than any other — betrays the mindset of at least some Vatican officials and shows that the Vatican was not merely "neutral" during the Nazi era, nor incapable of doing more for Jews.

The history of the relationship is also quite clear. The demonization of the Jews by the Church over the centuries — according to many Christian clergy themselves — not only contributed to the Holocaust, but actually created the atmosphere of hatred and suspicion towards Jews that facilitated Hitler's work. Hitler could tap into the preexisting hatred in Christian society and build on it. Considering those facts — first acknowledged by Pope John XXIII in the 60s during his very brief papacy — the Church could have simply opened up its archives and told the world what really happened both during and after WWII.

As it is, we are left wondering whether the "Rat-Line" was merely the work of a few unauthorized personnel at the Vatican, or the unfortunate policy of the existing hierarchy. If in fact the "Rat-Line," with its extremely complex structure involving the acquiescence of governments in several countries, was the work of unauthorized personnel in the Vatican, then why not state it openly and unequivocally?

But then there remains the other most troubling question: If Pope Pius XII was in fact predisposed to helping Jews as maintained in the document, then why not simply provide the relevant evidence? And then how does one explain the pope's silence in the initial stages, when as some maintain, the power of the Church could have stopped the Holocaust in its tracks before it developed?

Considering the power of the Church during that period, an unequivocal statement condemning racism and anti-Semitism would have had a profound influence on the masses throughout Europe that relied on the Church for guidance. But this is what could have been.

Today — when all acknowledge that the climate of hate against Jews was in fact created by the Church itself — there can no longer be any excuse for a perfunctory and meaningless statement acknowledging the suffering of the Jewish people, along with the Armenians, the Gypsies and even the Ukrainians. But the Church has never preached hatred against the Armenians, the Gypsies or the Ukrainians. In fact, the Ukraine was notorious for its pogroms and massacres of Jews, motivated largely by Christian zeal.

Chapter XVI

Understanding the Roots
of Anti-Semitism

In the immediate aftermath of the Holocaust there was the inevitable soul-searching by decent people who could not understand how a mass murder on the scale of the Holocaust could have been committed in what was believed to have been the center of Western culture and civilization, in largely Christian Europe.

The shock of the ongoing revelation of the mountains of unburied skeletons of human bodies found in many concentration and death camps by the Allies as they entered these hellish places after the defeat of Germany was more than an ordinary human being could bear.

Even though the beleaguered Jewish people tried desperately to convey, early on, the message of the unfolding tragedy to leaders in Britain and the US, the information appears to have been deliberately suppressed, with very little mention of it in the general press. And yet there was some general knowledge at least. Despite that, General Eisenhower appeared stunned and bewildered as he entered one of the camps in Germany. The photographs taken on his order at the time say a thousand words, and yet nothing on this earth could describe the enormity of the horror…

For some, it has taken time to really look at the horror of human bestiality and savagery perpetrated against innocent and helpless men, women and children, and even elderly people, all put to death for no other reason but for being Jews. What on earth could be the cause of a hatred so immense it knows no bounds?

Over time, films like *The Deputy* attempted to uncover the role of the Church and its silent pope during the Holocaust. No protest or outcry was uttered by the Church or Christian leaders in the free world, despite their early knowledge of the atrocities committed against innocent human beings in broad daylight.

Why? Was it solely because they were Jews?

Eventually, even Christian clergy began to speak out — some three decades after the Holocaust — quite openly laying the blame on the Church itself. It was not, they said, that the Church "didn't do enough," but that the Church itself laid the groundwork for the Holocaust!

Hitler found a receptive audience in many quarters, among people imbued by Church doctrine, blaming the Jews for deicide, preaching contempt and humiliation of the Jews for "failing" to embrace Christianity, and worse. Jews were blamed for every evil that existed in the world — and even some that did not exist.

Some sixteen centuries of such Church dogma cannot help but have an effect. The persecution and violence that befell the Jewish people during the Nazi regime was but a culmination of all that came before.

History is filled with hundreds if not thousands of incidents of persecutions, expulsions, violence and murder of the Jewish people, after the expulsion from our homeland by the Romans. The Crusades, the Inquisition and the forced conversions are but the better known historical events.

And yet, Christians, even to this day, use the word "Crusade" as if it implied a benevolent or noble event, rather than the brutal massacres of Jews and Muslims, as well as pillaging and merciless persecution!

In recent years a number of books have appeared by Christians, some of them clergy, questioning the role of Pope Pius XII during the Holocaust. Some reviewers closely connected to the Church, in defending the pope from charges of anti-Semitism, have given the most ironical defense imaginable: the pope was a product of his time; all his contemporaries were anti-Semitic!

Quite a defense, and quite a revelation for some who are ignorant of these simple facts! Most people — most decent people, and Jewish people in particular — do not understand anti-Semitism. Most people — including Jewish people — do not have all the facts concerning the Christian roots of anti-Semitism.

Most know the major facts of history: the Crusaders, the Inquisition, forced conversions, burning at the stake, persecution, pogroms and more persecutions. But very few have read Christian sources dealing with the history of the Church, including the early followers of Jesus, the Gospels and their sources, and the development of Christian dogma, particularly after the "marriage" of the Roman Empire with Christianity.

It is critical in this context to understand the issue of supersession, whereby Judaism was declared null and void, being superseded by a "more perfect" religion. This, as Christian theologian Franklin H. Littell states in his book *The Crucifixion of the Jews*,[1] basically constituted a warrant for murder.

But how did we get there? How did a small band of followers of a humble Jew — Jesus — become the Holy Roman Catholic Empire?

Clearly, there is very little known about early Christians, and even less about Jesus himself except that he was a practicing Jew, and that he was preaching to the Jews, not gentiles.

We also know that early "Christians" (i.e., Jews) — before they were called Christians — were persecuted by the Romans, as were Jews in general. Crucifying Jews was a known Roman practice, which Josephus describes as being used against rebels and others by the tens of thousands, although he does not mention Jesus by name.

The fact that Jesus was declared a deity at the Council of Nicaea in 325 CE, with Emperor Constantine presiding over the proceedings, is interesting in itself for a number of reasons. First and foremost, because he was a Jew, crucified by the Romans (all the subsequent whitewashing of Pontius Pilate notwithstanding). Also, most importantly, Jesus — as a Jew, believing in the One Almighty G-d — would himself call it blasphemy to be regarded as a deity.

We need a better understanding of the transformation that took place over time in the development of early Christianity, but unfortunately there is not a great deal to go by. We know that Saul-Paul preached to the gentiles; according to some Jewish sources, this was simply because he was eager to make it easier for new converts to Judaism, not Christianity. We do not even know at what point the Christians began to call themselves Christians, although we do know the religion was well established as a form of worship by the second century. (Very recently, November 2005, the *Jerusalem Post* reported that archaelogists had identified the remains of a floor of a church which is said to be the earliest church in Israel, dating approximately to the second century.) Perhaps the name of the religion came after acknowledging Jesus

---

1. New York: Harper and Row, 1975.

as the Messiah — Christos in Greek. But still this does not explain the deity issue.

Even the Gospels are not much help. They were written, we are told today, some 150 years after the fact by persons unknown, and somehow attributed to the apostles.[1]

I must state at this point that my intention is not to be disrespectful of other people's religion. My desire throughout my research of different sources — both Christian and Jewish — is simply to understand the roots of hatred against our people, many of whom to this day are still groping for answers.

While I do not wish to injure or besmirch another religion, I do believe that the time has come for the Western world in general, and the Church in particular, to look — really look — at the roots of anti-Semitism, and to put an end to anti-Semitism based on Christian prejudice.

Pope John XXIII, of blessed memory, started to put forward the proposition that the Jews cannot be blamed for deicide, or words to that effect, in the Second Vatican Council — *Nostra Aetate*.

Pope John Paul II claimed to have many Jewish friends — which is good as far as it goes — but his so-called apology before his visit to the Holy Land (Israel) at the beginning of the new millennium was anything but fulsome.

The pope acknowledged that the Jewish people suffered at the hands of "some Christians," etc. But it was not merely "some" Christians who caused Jewish suffering for many centuries during the Jewish Diaspora. The Church has to make it abundantly clear that it was in fact Church doctrine that caused that horrible suffering for such a long time. If the Church really follows the teaching of Jesus to "love thy neighbor" — a precept taken from Judaism — then it should be faithful to his teaching and stop persecuting Jews and the Jewish state, which appears to have recently yet again become the scapegoat for anti-Semitic hate.

Propaganda and distortion based on revisionist history are easily believed when there already exists a predisposition to hatred and prejudice.

---

1. See *Encyclopedia Americana*, vol.13.

Chapter XVII

The Sources of Hatred of the Jews

In preparing this material I have attempted to read as many historical sources as possible, including Edward Gibbon's *The Decline and Fall of the Roman Empire*. Having found his references to the Jews most offensive, and unceremoniously so (particularly as he is still regarded as a respected historian), I turned to others. I will admit I particularly sought out those who at least appeared to be sympathetic, works whose title or foreword implied an "objective" or philo-Semitic view.

My survey of the literature shows that modern, post-Holocaust writers — be they historians or theologians — have had a more sensitive ear and pen towards the Jewish people. They are also more likely to point to the origins of anti-Semitism (regardless of when that term was first used formally).

In the last decades of the twentieth century, several young Christian historians and clergy made the "astounding" admission that it was the Christian Church which had laid the groundwork for the Holocaust. Previous works, such as *The Anguish of the Jews* by Edward Flannery (1965), although seemingly concerned with the suffering of the Jewish people during dispersion, nonetheless found it possible to blame the victim!

James Parkes, in *The Conflict of the Church and the Synagogue*, a study of the origins of anti-Semitism first published in May 1934, despite his reputed philo-Semitism, somehow misses the whole point. The title of his book seems to imply a two-way conflict. But what "conflict" was there when the Church saw itself as triumphant while oppressing the Jewish people throughout Europe from its inception?

It is difficult to establish a precise date, but one can safely assume that it was approximately when Rome imposed the Christian religion on its citizens, or possibly even somewhat earlier, that there occurred a change in the followers of Christianity. The simple faith practiced by the early followers of Jesus appears to have changed when membership became predominantly gentile.

Even before the Nicaean Council of 325 CE, the new followers of Christianity were already beginning to clamor against the Jewish religion, which, up to that point, enjoyed equal status with Christianity in Rome.

Parkes admits that no written document of the Jewish leadership of that time indicates a struggle or a conflict with the Church. Even the earliest references provide no information on any kind of conflict, but rather refer to the persecution against the Jewish people by the Church. Documents on Christian attacks against the Jews are suffocating by their intensity and sheer numbers. Parkes tells of how Jewish people were persecuted and of the various "disabilities" imposed on them, but somehow — being a man of faith, a Christian, informed by the Christian doctrine — he cannot help but see this as a "conflict" which he aims to prove as a Christian.

Christian theologian Franklin H. Littell, on the other hand, in his book *The Crucifixion of the Jews*,[1] opens with an attack on the Christian Church and the failure of Christians to understand the Jewish experience. He makes the obvious case that the Jews should be allowed to choose their own faith.

It is interesting that it took a tragedy of the magnitude of the Holocaust for some decent Christians to finally realize that simple truth. Parkes wrote in 1934, a time ripe with anti-Semitism and the early stages of intensified persecution. Despite this, he is somehow still unable to see the obvious. It would seem that years and centuries of Christian indoctrination are not easy even for decent people to shake off.

For Jews, the painful and deadly time spent in foreign lands during the dispersion — persecuted, humiliated and massacred at will simply because they chose to remain faithful to the One Almighty G-d — is still difficult to understand, why were they hated? It is baffling for the Jewish people that Christians should care one way or another what they, the Jews, believe in.

The reason Parkes could find no documented response from the synagogue to the constant attacks by the Church on the Jews after the dispersion is that the Jewish people, dispersed and in disarray, had enough difficulty simply dealing with day-to-day survival as foreigners in foreign lands. The struggle was not with the Church, but to provide leadership to a nation in exile.

The leaders who survived in *Eretz Yisrael* after the destruction of the Second Temple and Yerushalayim, and the murder and enslavement of so many of their people, had the greatest challenge before them. How, after the

---

1. New York: Harper and Row, 1975.

abolition of statehood, could the Jewish communities in the Diaspora be sustained? Clearly the challenge before them was of immense and unprecedented proportions. Without current methods of communication, it's hard to even imagine how this was accomplished.

It was the Jewish people themselves, with their strong and abiding faith in the Almighty, who were largely responsible in the Diaspora for their cohesion, to the degree permitted by the local authorities. With every change in the emperors of Rome and the governors of Judea, new and often conflicting decrees made the lives of the Jewish people either somewhat easier, or more miserable.

The "conflict" between the Church and the Synagogue existed only in the minds of the Church Fathers who were in competition with the Synagogue for new converts from among the pagans.

What motivated the early Christians' intense hatred, which appeared to grow exponentially with every venomous sermon, such as the anti-Judaic teachings of Christian luminary Chrysostom at Antioch in 378 CE? The campaign of vilification of the Jewish people by Church Fathers — even before Rome adopted Christianity as its official religion — is hard to explain as no sources exist on when exactly it began, and why.

Some sources claim it was due to the intense hatred pagans harbored towards the Jews; but there were also many pagans who converted to or sympathized with Judaism. On the other hand, many pagans obviously converted to Christianity. Still, these are only speculations, and nothing concrete with regard to the origins of the intense and horrible hatred that survived almost two millennia, causing untold suffering and the massacre and torture of countless innocent people, for no other reason than that they continued to believe in One Almighty G-d, the Creator of the Universe.

Just prior to the Nicaean Council of 325 CE, Jews and Christians were treated equally under the Roman Empire. It was only after Constantine I apparently gave direction to the Roman Catholic Church — despite the fact that he himself had yet to become a Christian — that certain issues took shape in Christian religion. The Nicaean Council under Constantine, though deeply divided on the question of Jesus' deity, was nonetheless forced through. The issue continued to simmer for several hundred years thereafter. Unitarians to this day do not believe in the deity of Jesus.

One is more than a little puzzled by the concept of a small band of Jews — merely an offshoot of Judaism — becoming a powerful religion, and then attacking and attempting to destroy its own, all the while claiming to be a merciful religion that teaches its adherents to "turn the other cheek" and "love thy neighbor as thyself."

One also has to wonder how and why the early "Christians" (Jews really), persecuted by Rome and fed to the lions at the Coliseum for the amusement of the Roman aristocracy, had their religion adopted by Rome.

It would appear, however, that by the time Rome adopted Christianity, there were no Jews left in the movement. Who then were the Christians at the time of the Nicaean Council in 325 CE?

They were certainly not the followers of Jesus, who remained a Jew to the very end. In his lifetime, he preached to the Jews and not to "Christians" — although that is rarely remembered today.

(Saul-St. Paul was also a practicing Jew until his death at the hands of the Romans, although he encountered problems with Jewish religious leaders when he attempted mass conversion of pagans who were attracted to Judaism and wished to become Jews. Saul, eager to convert the pagans, attempted to forego the accepted practices of Judaism such as circumcision and the prescribed commandments.)

Jesus was a kind man who preached love and understanding, a man who was seen as a Messiah by some, when Jews suffered under the Roman occupation and longed for the promised Messiah. He was a Jew who was likely seen as a threat to the Romans, at a time when many other Jews rebelled, and were sought out and killed by their oppressors. Jesus, as a Jew, was flogged by the Romans as he proceeded to his crucifixion, a punishment regularly used by the Romans.

How was it, then, that Pontius Pilate, who ordered the crucifixion and the flogging of Jesus, could later be portrayed in Christian tradition as a benevolent man who "washed his hands" of the whole affair, when many if not all Christian theologians today refer to him as a ruthless and brutal tyrant?

Christian theologians today admit or acknowledge that the "whitewashing" of Pontius Pilate was done to appease Rome. But again, the nagging questions remain: When and how and by whom was the history of Jesus and Christianity rewritten to suit the Romans, when it became the Roman Catholic religion? And who benefited from scapegoating the Jews for centuries to come? When and why did the followers of Jesus' teaching turn to brutal persecution of the Jews and embrace the persecutors of Jesus?

Was it mere coincidence that the Roman Empire, the very regime that destroyed the Second Temple in Jerusalem, sacked the city, banished and murdered many of its inhabitants, and renamed the Jewish State "Palestine" and Jerusalem "Aelia Capitolina" in order to erase "for all time" the Jewish history from the Land of Israel, later claimed that the Roman Catholic religion superseded Judaism as the "true" religion?

Chapter XVIII

The Church, the Jews and the Rest of the World

As already stated, the sort of apology the pope offered to the Jewish people at the turn of the third millennium was no apology at all. An apology suggests a desire to change as a result of recognizing a terrible wrong committed against a people over a period of centuries. Such a wrong, if it is to be corrected, must first and foremost be sincerely acknowledged, and it must involve a change of attitude on the part of the Church. There must be a new policy that is visible to the followers of the Church, as well as to the rest of the non-Catholic world, including the Jewish people to whom the apology was directed.

So far, more than two years into the third millennium at the time of this writing, no outward sign in the changing of the Church's policy has been noted. Quite the contrary; the commission set up by the Vatican to look into the reign of Pius XII was refused access to original documents, and in particular, documents covering the Nazi period of 1939–1945 in the Vatican's possession.

If the Vatican has been made uncomfortable over the public resignation of the Jewish members of the commission in view of the Vatican's refusal to provide the important documents, it has itself to blame.

There are many — far too many — troubling and unanswered questions about the Vatican's role during the Nazi period, including the immediate post-WWII period. It is alleged that the Vatican, or some of its functionaries, facilitated the escape of major Nazi war criminals to South America (Argentina in particular).

The question of whether Pope Pius XII "did enough" is a red herring. If the pope was anti-Semitic, as claimed by both his critics and even his defenders (the "defense" that he was merely a product of his time is outrageous), then to the question whether he did enough, the answer is likely that he did far too much!

The moral and humane Christians who did save Jews were very simply committing acts of great personal courage, very often at risk to their own lives. There was a very real concern of being exposed by their own Christian neighbors, who would have no qualms over denouncing them to the Nazis, knowing full well the tragic consequences not only to the Jews they were hiding, but also to those who harbored them.

The Church bears total responsibility for the hatred of the Jewish people that was so deeply imbedded in the psyche of the Christians. Until the Church not only properly acknowledges that fact, but takes remedial action, the apology of Pope John Paul II is quite meaningless.

For it wasn't, as the pope implied, that "some" Christians did wrong to the Jewish people. No, it was the Christian Church itself that initiated these wrongs, including the forced conversions, the Crusades and the Inquisition. All the suffering and terrible massacres and the death at the stake in flames, not to mention the centuries of ongoing persecution, all of these were the direct result of the Church's policies and directives.

The Church's continued accusation of Jewish guilt in Jesus' death at the cross fuelled the flames of hatred, which only seemed to grow with time. That Jesus was crucified by the Romans, as were countless other "rebellious" Jews, was apparently never acknowledged. That Jesus was flogged by the Romans, on the way to his crucifixion, is rarely if ever acknowledged.

I, as a Jewish person who somehow survived the Nazi hell on earth that we now call the Holocaust, find it ironic in the extreme that a Jew, Jesus, was "deified" by the Roman Catholic Church.

Surely, it must be the ultimate irony that the Romans, having pillaged and defiled and burned down the Jewish Holy Temple, having crucified and otherwise murdered many thousands of the Jewish people in *Eretz Yisrael*, having exiled most of the remainder, then decided to deify one of those they crucified.

Jesus, of course, did not leave any written record of his life or works. But what is known — at least as far as we can assume — is that he was a practicing Jew, and as such, he believed, like all believing Jews, in One Almighty G-d ("Thou shalt have no other gods but me," said the Almighty).

As a practicing and pious Jew, Jesus would be the first to refute his deification; he would have rejected it as blasphemy. The irony becomes even greater as the Romans, having adopted Christianity, claimed to have "replaced" Judaism, and superseded it!

The real question is, has the Roman Catholic Church really followed Jesus' teachings? Can the Roman Catholic Church really claim to have followed in Jesus' footsteps, even as they murdered and persecuted Jewish people? Was that the perfect religion that the Roman Catholic Church gave to the world, to supersede the "imperfect" Jewish religion?

As we witness the re-emergence of anti-Semitism in the world today, can the Church still remain silent as it sees its followers reverting to their old ways? The Vatican still claims that Pope Pius XII remained silent during the Holocaust because he did not want to make things even worse for the Jews. (How much worse could it possibly have been?) But why is the Church silent now? What is the Church afraid of now?

Thankfully, now, as during WWII, there are some, perhaps even many Christians who oppose anti-Semitism and support the Jewish state and its people; whether the Vatican is among them is still an open question. We are waiting for an answer...

Just as I finished these lines, I read with disbelief in the morning paper, June 14, 2002, that Spain's Roman Catholic bishops want Queen Isabelle, the queen of the Inquisition, beatified! Is there no end to hypocrisy?

Apparently not. In the same paper, on the same day, more news on the soon to be opened (July 1) International Court of Justice. Or should we call it by its proper name? In an Orwellian twist, the I.C.J. has already lined up a number of cases against — guess who?

Not Nazi war criminals guilty of mass murder — they are "too old now"! Not the terrorists who dispatch suicide bombers who almost daily kill and maim innocent human beings, and seem to target particularly babies and children... No. They are in effect the "aggrieved" party!

Has the world gone completely mad?

According to the news report, the Geneva Convention of 1948–1949, which came into being in the aftermath of the Holocaust and was set up to protect non-combatants in time of war, has now been twisted to accommodate an Egyptian resolution which apparently considers it a crime if an "occupying power" transfers its own population to "occupied territory." This is an interesting twist, with perhaps unforeseen results for the Egyptians, since it could fly straight in the face of what they are attempting. Note that Yasser Arafat was a native Egyptian whose ragtag band of terrorists came from all over the region.

(Jordan also has had to import Arab residents — now around five million — from the entire area to populate its nearly empty land).

The Geneva Convention of 1948–1949 applied to transferring populations *from* (not *to*) occupied territories, which referred of course to the Jewish people during the Nazi era being transferred from their homes to ghettos, to slave labor camps and finally to their deaths. Redressing this was the purpose of the Fourth Geneva Convention.

Egypt's president, clever and cagey, thought up the additional resolution to imply that Israel transferred its population to Judea and Samaria, and therefore is guilty of a war crime! But Judea and Samaria are historically part of the Land of Israel!

This land was always seen, at least by those who are interested in history, as the Jewish homeland. It was so recognized after WWI by the international body the League of Nations. And furthermore, there was always a Jewish presence in the Land of Israel — *Eretz Yisrael* — even after the savage expulsion of the majority of the population by the Romans, during the countless occupations by various foreign forces, and throughout the exile. Those occupying forces included Egypt itself; the reason we now have the so-called "Palestinians" is because some of them stayed behind after their occupying forces retreated. Who then are the illegal occupiers of Judea and Samaria?

Following Egypt's logic, it is the Arabs in Judea and Samaria who live there illegally and should be tried for war crimes!

Israel's tremendous blunder was to be willing to cede even part of Judea and Samaria, where there are heavily populated Arab areas. But that was in the vain hope that giving up part of its own land would lead to peace.

But this is not about peace. This is about conquest. The Arab States have tried to destroy Israel in several wars of aggression; through economic boycotts; through the Arab "oil weapon"; through maneuvering at the UN and by attempting to isolate Israel by exerting all sorts of diplomatic and economic pressure on countries formerly friendly to Israel. In short, the Arab League, a sworn enemy of Israel which openly declared its genocidal intentions against the state of Israel and its people, in several wars of aggression (a recognized war crime in international law), is now accusing Israel of war crimes! This Orwellian concoction says that Jewish people living in their ancestral home are war criminals! And they, the Egyptians, who promised to annihilate the Jewish people only a few years after the Holocaust and eradicate the state of Israel, are the brazen accusers.

In a similar spirit, Queen Isabella I — the queen of the Inquisition — is to be nominated for sainthood! Spain, with its black history of persecution that lasted some 340 years and was not abolished until 1834, shows us through this nomination that we still live in the Dark Ages!

Pope John Paul II has a historic responsibility to reject Spain's request out of hand if indeed he meant even partly what he said when he sort of apologized to the Jewish people on the eve of the third millennium. (Written in 2002; Pope John Paul II died April 2, 2005, with Queen Isabella's canonization still uncertain.)

The Vatican made a terrible mistake in wanting to bestow sainthood on Pope Pius XII. Having relented after an outcry against this beatification, its choice to bestow sainthood instead on Pope Pius IX was an even greater mistake. Pope Pius IX is best remembered for forcibly removing a Jewish child from his parents and raising him a Roman Catholic!

The Vatican, if it is even to retain a shred of moral integrity, dare not follow the wishes of the Spanish Roman Catholic Bishop.

Chapter XIX

From Nicaea to Auschwitz

There appears to be a direct line from Nicaea to Auschwitz.

No doubt, to some, it will appear far-fetched to make such a statement. The Council of Nicaea took place in 325 CE; the Nazi regime took hold in 1933, some 1,600 years later. But if you look back at history and what has transpired in those sixteen centuries, history speaks for itself.

Hatred and contempt feeds on itself, particularly if an agenda to vilify "the other" exists.

The agenda of the Roman Catholic Church was to proclaim itself the "new Jerusalem" which claimed to supersede the "hateful Jews." To this day, the Vatican proclaims itself the only "true" religion.

Of course the fact that Israel was reborn created some problems for the Roman Catholic Church. If the Jews were "condemned to wander and suffer humiliation forever" as a result of refusing to accept a different religion, then that concept became invalid the moment the Jewish state was reborn.

But the Jews, being a minority always deferring to others, never challenged the Church and its concepts. The New Israelis simply went about rebuilding their homeland, and were quite ready to defend it, even against overwhelming odds.

In spite of everything the Jewish people have suffered throughout their exile, they are on the whole a generous and peaceful people. But even peaceful people have a right to defend themselves.

Auschwitz had a profound impact on the Jewish psyche. Immediately in the aftermath, the motto *"Never again"* was repeated frequently. The Jewish people realize the world had stood silently by, while every day our people were being gassed and massacred by the tens of thousands.

Neither the Americans, nor the Canadians, nor the British showed any mercy to help or accommodate those Jews able to escape the Nazi horrors and murders, or even offer them temporary asylum.

The British perfidy was particularly vile. Having been given the League of Nations Mandate to help the Jewish people rebuild their ancient homeland, the British turned the Mandate on its head, and worst of all, prevented a large number of Jews from returning to their homeland.[1] Not even at the worst time — 1933–45, when the terrible persecution was well known to the British, the Vatican and all Western nations — not even then did the world extend a helping hand.

In 1941–42, when mass killing of the Jews became the order of the day throughout Nazi-occupied Europe, Britain still refused entry to *Eretz Yisrael* to many Jewish people whose lives could have been saved. They initially insisted on a quota and later blocked entry completely — reneging on all their obligations to the Jewish people, as well as the League of Nations, choosing instead to curry favor with the Arabs.

Even after 1945 when WWII ended, the British still barred Jewish survivors of the Holocaust from coming to their homeland, turning away ship after ship from the very shores of their homeland. The would-be immigrants — survivors of the Holocaust — did not merit the return to their own homeland, even after the most gruesome mass murder ever committed against any people!

What motivated the British policies?

Various excuses were offered, one of which was that it would be difficult to absorb too many new arrivals (which was not true). The existing Jewish communities were growing and desperately needed more working hands, quite apart from their concern of rescuing their brethren. Many appeals were made to the British asking for an additional workforce, all to no avail.

Why were the British so indifferent to Jewish suffering? Why were they so indifferent to the survivors of the Holocaust after the indescribable ordeal the Jews had suffered?

Why indeed were the Americans indifferent, and the Canadians?

Why? Why?

Could the centuries of vilification of a people so predispose the adherents of the Church as to make the lives of the Jewish people meaningless, their suffering meaningless?

Was this the same Church that purported to be following the teachings of Jesus? The same Church that described itself as kind, decent and fair?

Clearly those Christians who were, in fact, kind, decent and fair, who

---

1. See Appendix 1.

cared about human life, and who saved some Jews, were few and far between. They were motivated by their personal decency, rather than the teachings of their Church. They did, in fact, risk their own lives to rescue fellow human beings, in secrecy, lest their own neighbors denounce them for hiding Jews.

They will never be forgotten; they in fact deserve our eternal gratitude for their sense of humanity, decency, and kindness.

But then there were the other kind, who, during the Nazi tyranny, upon spotting a Jewish person would almost instinctively denounce him to the Nazis, knowing full well that it meant certain and cruel death to the Jew. There were also those who themselves killed Jews escaping from concentration camps.

In Poland, even those Jews who had the opportunity and courage to escape from ghettos and concentration camps, if they were not killed by the Nazis in the process of escape, were more often than not killed by Polish people themselves.

In this case, in Nazi-occupied Poland, "the enemy of my enemy is my friend" did not hold true.

Even after the war, in 1945, some Polish people were involved in a massacre of the Jewish people who had survived the Nazis! Jews were dragged off trains and massacred by the mob. My father's cousin — one of the only three surviving relatives — and his fiancée were beheaded by a mob while sitting on a park bench, during the pogrom in Kielce almost immediately after the war.

Even the Polish underground (one of the two official ones) — the nationalist *Armia Krajowa* — was just as interested in killing Jews as they were in resisting Nazis.

What drives people to such unspeakable acts?

At Nicaea, the policy of humiliating Jews began. The hatred and contempt against the Jews grew stronger over the years; the Jews were persecuted and accused of horrible crimes they knew nothing about.

Jews who took refuge in various European countries following the expulsion from their land suffered all manner of humiliation: head taxes, wearing a yellow star, being forced into ghettos, forced conversions or death at the stake, to say nothing of periodic expulsions from the host nations, and massacres both during the Crusades and after. The Jewish people were persecuted almost constantly; even if occasionally some bishop offered them asylum to prevent massacres, the reason for the asylum was that, in the reasoning of the

Church, "Jews should not be killed, only humiliated to bear witness to the Church 'triumphant'"!

Can this be the religion, the Church that Jesus had in mind?

Between the two Jewish revolts in 70 CE and 132 CE, Jewish religious practice was restricted, and eventually forbidden by the Romans, and the Jews were forbidden from setting foot in Jerusalem. As explained in *Carta's Historical Atlas of Israel: Survey of the Past and Review of the Present*,[1] "Hadrian then rebuilt Jerusalem as a Roman city and renamed it 'Aelia Capitolina.'" Jews were forbidden to set foot in the city, and were also severely restricted in Judea, which was renamed "Syria Palestina" and settled with gentiles.

Carta's Historical Atlas of Israel continues (p.16), it was not until the "Roman Empire officially adopted Christianity in 313 A.D.," that "Palestine" "suddenly gained prominence as a focus of Christian pilgrimage." The new developments "brought some prosperity [to the area], but the Jews were forced into a state of subjection that was to continue under the Byzantine emperors."

Exactly when and how the followers of Jesus became Christians is not clear. We do understand that the early Christians (or were they still Jews?) were fed to the lions at various Roman spectacles. So it is hard to comprehend why and how exactly the New Christians embraced Rome or vice versa.

Despite the loss of political independence, the Jewish people continued to live in "Palestine" under a self-imposed regime of Nesi'im, or Patriarchs, and later enjoyed a larger degree of cultural and religious autonomy up to approximately the fifth century.[2] During that time, the *Mishna* (Oral Law) and the Talmud were compiled.

The Jewish people did not disappear from their land or history, although they suffered severe persecution from various waves of invaders over the centuries. To many Jews, the issue of "supersession" is still a puzzling question. Why did the Catholic Church not simply call it a new religion? And why did the Church have to go to all this trouble to convert Jewish people to Christianity?!

The Jews, on the other hand, did not force their religion on Christians. That being the case, what "conflict" was there on the part of the Jewish people towards the Church, except wanting to remain faithful to their own religion?

---

1. Jerusalem: Carta, 1983, p.16.
2. See again *Carta's Historical Atlas*, p.17.

What would motivate the Church to persecute, torture, and burn at the stake a people who were steadfast in their own religious beliefs, and who did not require conversions?

One almost wishes that one could leave well enough alone, but one runs into such quotes as: "the Council of Nicea met pursuant to an imperial summons in the Year 325 A.D." Bishop Eusebius of Caesarea, playing (likely) a very important role "being seated (likely) to the right of the Emperor Constantine".

Despite the fact that at the Council of Nicaea in 325 CE the issue of the deity of Jesus was sort of resolved, the controversy with the Arians continued for some time. Also, at the same time, the Christian Church formulated its policy towards the Jews: "The Jews must continue to exist for the sake of Christianity in seclusion and humiliation" (*Encyclopedia Judaica*, vol. 8: Chronological Chart of Jewish History, following p. 766).

And, of course, these precepts were instituted all over the Christian world from then on. The following is a partial litany showing some of the tragic results of the Roman Catholic Church's policy adopted in 325 CE, an almost uninterrupted string of violence, repression, oppression and murder, to say nothing of humiliation.

Jews were expelled from the Frankish kingdom in 628; from Mainz in 1012; Crusaders massacred the Jews of Rhineland in 1096.

Blood libel in Norwich, England in 1144; France expels its Jews in 1182 and recalls them in 1198; anti-Jewish riots at York, England, 1190; Council of Oxford introduces discriminatory measures 1222; Domus Conversorum established in London 1232.

In Italy: Fourth Lateran Council introduces the "Jewish Badge" in 1215 (although in 1249 Pope Innocent IV issues bull against blood libel).

Again persecution in France 1236; disputation of Paris 1240; burning of Talmud in Paris 1242; blood libel in Lincoln, England 1255.

Disputation of Barcelona 1263; Jews of London sacked 1263–64; *Statutum de Judaismo* 1275; expulsion 1290; Jews burned at Troyes, France, 1288; expulsion 1303.

In France, Jews recalled by Louis X in 1315 only to be expelled again in 1322; in 1328 anti-Jewish riots at Navarre, Spain.

More blood libels in Germany and Austria and destruction of communities. In Poland, Boleslav V the Pious (Hrobry), issues a charter which is extended in 1334 by Casimir III.

But by 1348, "Black Death" is blamed on the Jews, and massacres of Jews follow in Spain and France.

Again, 1391 massacres and conversions in Spain, followed by oppressive legislation in 1411–12; Disputation of Tortosa 1413–14, followed by more massacres and conversions of the Jews of Majorca in 1435.

Yet more massacres in Spain, this time of converted Jews — Marranos of Valladolid and Cordoba in 1473, followed by massacres of Marranos of Segovia in 1474. Then, the Inquisition is established in 1480, and yet another blood libel in 1490–91; the expulsion from Castille and Aragon in 1492; expulsion from Portugal and mass forced conversion in 1496–97; massacre of Marranos in Lisbon in 1506.[1]

All this after Pope Martin V expressed himself "against forced conversions" in 1419. Still, in 1427 papal edict prohibits transportation of Jews to *Eretz Yisrael* in ships of Venice and Ancona.

Again, in Italy, 1475–94 Jews are expelled from several towns; in 1475 another blood libel in Trent. And yet more expulsion from Sicily in 1492–93.

The Jews were being expelled from town after town in Italy, and yet not allowed to go to *Eretz Yisrael*. Where did the Christian leaders expect them to go? Why prevent the Jewish people from going back to their Land?!

After Casimir III extends the Charter of 1334 in 1364–67, and Witold of Lithuania grants the Charter in 1388, there is yet again a blood libel in 1399, this time in Poznan, Poland. In 1454 privileges are revoked in Cracow, Poland, followed by riots, and the expulsion from Warsaw in 1483. There is yet another expulsion in 1495, this time from Lithuania.

Germany and Austro-Hungary: a massacre of a Prague community is recorded in 1389; expulsion from Austria in 1421; from Cologne in 1424; from Augsburg in 1439; 1452–53 John of Capistrano incites persecutions and expulsions; 1473 expulsion from Mainz; and 1499 expulsion from Nuremberg.

In 1510, expulsion from Brandenburg; 1519 from Regensburg; 1541, expulsion from Prague and crown cities; 1544 Luther attacks Jews and 1551 expulsion from Bavaria.

In Italy: 1516 Venice initiates the ghetto; 1541, Jews are expelled from Naples and in 1550 from Genoa. In 1553 the Talmud is burned; in 1554, there is censorship of Hebrew books. In 1555, Paul IV orders that Jews be confined

---

1. See *The Last Kabbalist of Lisbon* by Richard Zimler (London: Arcadia, 1998), based on eyewitness accounts of the massacre of 1506.

to ghettos. In 1556 Marranos are burned at the stake in Ancona; 1567, expulsion ordered from the Republic of Genoa; and in 1569 expulsion from Papal States. In 1584, Gregory XIII orders compulsory sermons to Jews.

In Italy, Jews are still expelled in 1593 from the Papal States, and in 1597 from Milan; 1624 ghetto is established in Ferrara.

In Germany, the Jews of Frankfurt are attacked in 1614, and in 1615 the Jews are expelled from Worms; in 1616 Jews are readmitted to Frankfurt and Worms, but in 1649 they are expelled from Hamburg. In 1671 they are permitted to settle in the Mark of Brandenburg, but Vienna expels its Jews in 1670. The same year there is again a blood libel in Metz, France.

In Poland: in 1648–49 the Chmielnicki massacres; more massacres in 1655–56 during wars of Poland against Sweden and Russia. In 1680 are the riots against Jews in Brest-Litovsk, and in 1682 more riots erupt in Cracow. In 1687 the Jews of Poznan are attacked; and in 1712 Jews of Sandomierz are expelled after a blood libel.

In 1761 Cardinal Ganganelli issues a memorandum against blood libel, only to be followed by an anti-Jewish edict of Pius VI in 1775. In 1793 an attack on the ghetto of Rome is recorded.

In 1738 in Germany, Joseph Suess Oppenheimer — "*Der Jud Suess*" — is executed on trumped-up charges; he refuses to convert and is hanged. In 1750 severe legislation against the Jews in Prussia is enacted; in 1781 there is actually a Christian plea for Jewish emancipation.

Austria-Hungary: in 1745, Jews are expelled from Prague; and in 1748 they are allowed to return.

In Poland-Lithuania: in 1734–36 Jews are attacked by the Haidamacks; 1757 disputation with the Frankists at Kamenets-Podolski; 1759 disputation with the Frankists at Lvov; 1768 Haidamack massacres.

In Germany: in 1808 emancipation in Westphalia, 1811 emancipation in Hamburg and Frankfurt, 1812 emancipation in Prussia; but in 1815 the Congress of Vienna permits the abolition of the emancipation laws in the German states; in 1819 riots; in 1833 emancipation in Hesse-Kassel, but in 1847 anti-Jewish riots erupt in Prussia before emancipation in 1848.

Despite the emancipation in several European states, anti-Jewish riots continued in Austria-Hungary in 1848, as did oppressive laws. In Russia, in 1826–1835 Velizh blood libel, and in 1853, another blood libel in Saratov.

Not until 1860 were Jews allowed to own real estate in Austria, but Rome did not abolish the ghetto and end Jewish disabilities until 1870.

In 1871, Germany abolished Jewish disabilities; in 1876 Orthodox Jews are permitted to found an independent congregation in Prussia, but in 1878, an anti-Semitic movement starts in Berlin (headed by A. Stoecker); 1879–80 anti-Semitic articles by H. von Treitschke are published; 1881 sees the anti-Semitic petition; and in 1885, Russian refugees are expelled; 1891 again blood libel, this time in Xanten; and in 1893 fifteen anti-Semites are elected to the Reichstag (German parliament).

In France: in 1886 E. A. Drumont publishes his anti-Semitic tractate *La France juive*; and in 1894, the infamous Dreyfus trial is held.

In 1867, Austrio-Hungarian constitution abolishes Jewish disabilities; but in 1871 A. Rohling publishes his anti-Semitic *Der Talmudjude*; in 1882, another blood libel in Tiszaeszlar; and in 1891 thirteen anti-Semitic members enter the Austrian Reichsrat (parliament).

In Rumania, in 1871–72 there are attacks on Jews. In Russia, in 1871 there is a pogrom in Odessa, after some relaxation of disabilities; in 1879 a blood libel in Kutais; in 1881–1882 pogroms sweep southern Russia and mass emigration follows; in 1891 Jews are expelled from Moscow. The year 1881 sees the beginning of mass immigration from Eastern Europe to the US.

In France: in 1898 Emile Zola publishes *"J'accuse,"* his indictment of institutionalized anti-Semitism in the Dreyfus Affair; in 1899 Dreyfus is re-tried and pardoned; in 1906 Dreyfus is rehabilitated.

In Germany, H. S. Chamberlain's anti-Semitic *Die Grundlagen des neunzehnten jahrhunderts* is published in 1899. In 1890 there is another blood libel in Konitz. In Rumania, in 1895 the anti-Semitic League is organized.

In Russia and Poland: in 1903 a pogrom in Kishinev is recorded; 1905–1906 more pogroms, followed by mass emigration; 1909–10 Polish boycott against Jews; and in 1910 expulsion from Kiev. In 1917 anti-Jewish laws are abrogated; and in 1919, again, pogroms in Ukraine and Poland, and community organizations and Jewish institutions in Russia are abolished.

In 1919, there are pogroms in Hungary. In 1922, the advent of Fascism in Italy.

In Poland: in 1924 economic restrictions on Jews in Poland, and an attempt to "settle" Jews in Crimea. Today we would call that ethnic cleansing, but then, Jewish people were "ethnically cleansed" from virtually every country in Europe as we are about to see.

In Germany, in 1925–27 Hitler's *Mein Kampf* is published.

In Russia, in 1928, Jewish people were being "settled" in Birobidzhan, part of it becoming an autonomous Jewish region (or was it a large ghetto?!).

In 1933, Hitler is elected German chancellor. In the same year, anti-Jewish boycott is instituted in Germany and the first concentration camp is established.

In 1934, Poland annuls Minorities Treaties; and in 1936, there is a pogrom in Przytyk; in 1937 there is discrimination in Polish universities; and in 1939, pogroms follow the Nazi invasion.

In *Eretz Yisrael* ("Palestine"), in the meantime, Jewish people desperate to leave Europe are now restricted from coming to their own land, due to various British "White Papers." In 1934, they resort to "illegal" *aliyah* — immigration to "Palestine."

In 1935, the Nuremberg Laws come into being, depriving Jewish people of all their rights; in 1936 Hitler begins his expansion and invades and occupies Rhineland; and in 1938, after the Munich fiasco of Chamberlain, Czechoslovakia falls victim to Hitler's aggression.

In 1938 Austria is annexed, and in 1938 there are pogroms in Vienna, and anti-Jewish legislation, followed by deportations from Austria.

In Italy too, racial legislation is established in 1938.

In Germany, on the night of November 10–11, 1938, a pogrom erupts in every city, town and village; they call it *Kristallnacht*, the night of broken glass, a dress rehearsal for things to come.

In 1938 there are pogroms in Vienna; in 1939, anti-Jewish laws in the Protectorate of Czechoslovakia; and in Slovakia in 1941.

In 1937, there is more anti-Jewish legislation in Rumania; and in 1938 anti-Jewish economic legislation in Hungary; in 1939 many Hungarian Jews lose their citizenship — all this even before Nazi-Germany entered their states!

In 1939 Poland is overrun, and WWII begins. By 1940, Western Europe is overrun by the Germans, and in 1940, the French Vichy government — collaborating with Nazi Germany — institutes discrimination laws against Jewish people, followed by the opening of a concentration camp in Drancy in 1941. Between 1941 and 1944, eighty-three thousand French Jews are deported and murdered.

In 1941, there is a pogrom in Rumania, this time in Jassy, and anti-Jewish laws are passed in Slovakia.

In Germany, Jewish emigration is prohibited in 1941; and in 1942, at the Wannsee Conference a decision is taken on "The Final Solution." But as we have seen, anti-Jewish pogroms and laws predate Hitler's Final Solution in Christian-dominated countries including Russia.

Between 1942 and 1944, there are mass transports to Auschwitz from Belgium, Holland.

In Poland, now under the Nazis, ghettos are established in 1940; and in 1941, there is a pogrom in Kaunas and Lvov, as well as massacres by *Einsatzgruppen* — Nazi "Special Units" — in occupied western Russia and eastern Poland. In 1941, too, there are continuing expulsions from the Reich to Poland; the first death camp is established in Chelmno, Poland.

In 1942, massacres continue in occupied Russia; and in 1942 death camps of Auschwitz, Maidanek and Treblinka begin to function at full capacity; transports from the ghettos to death camps continue.

In 1944, Hungary helps the Nazis "remove" its Jewish population to Auschwitz and slave labor camps; but not before the local gendarmes humiliate the Jewish people by keeping them in pigsties and open fields during rain for weeks, awaiting deportation.

The only country that stands out in all this horror is Denmark, whose people organize a rescue by sea, using all available fishing boats and other vessels to smuggle the Jewish people to Sweden.

This heroic deed will forever be remembered by the Jewish people, as will other heroic deeds of those who rescued Jewish individuals, and often families, at the risk of their own lives. There were a number of such heroic figures, but not nearly enough; before Hitler's Nazis were done, some 90 percent of European Jews were murdered.

The above record states only major historic events and their dates. It says nothing at all about the human suffering; nor does it mention the families worried about their children during expulsions, pogroms, riots and massacres; nor indeed anything about the deliberate humiliation inflicted. These crimes cry out to heaven!

Only those who have witnessed such horrors can understand the human suffering and despair imposed on the Jewish people throughout our exile.

I, unfortunately, lived through such horrors. I saw with my own eyes the persecution, the selections in which families were torn asunder, and the suffering. Most of the families separated during these "selections" never saw each other again.

But, even before all that started, I witnessed with my own eyes how Jewish Orthodox men were humiliated in the middle of the street in Lodz, Poland, where I was born. Their beards were torn until the flesh bled! They were made to kneel in the street to clean the gutters with toothbrushes!

As I go over this horrific litany of persecution and murder of our people throughout the centuries, I feel as if I personally experienced each and every indignity visited deliberately on our people; all this horror nearly uninterrupted until the Holocaust!

To say let well enough alone is easier said than done. I have personally suffered persecution due to anti-Jewish hate propaganda, culminating in the Holocaust. We are experiencing, yet again, a fierce revival of anti-Jewish hate propaganda, often repeating the old libels and canards used to demonize our people. This time it comes mainly, though not exclusively, from Arab-Muslims. But there are not a few Christians in high places, such as the French ambassador to England, or the member of the House of Lords who recently said, "We can finally say what we think of them," or words to that effect. What does this tell us? The British Lord apparently always had animosity towards our people — but he senses that this is yet again an opportune time to "finally" say it!

The hostility, hate, and murderous attacks by the Arabs on our people seem boundless. The mixture of Christian and Arab-Muslim hate is a dangerous brew.

If Pope John Paul II really meant to apologize to the Jewish people for past misdeeds, prior to his visit to Israel, he certainly had an opportunity to speak out, and to stop the revival of Christian anti-Semitism in its tracks before it gets out of hand. He had the power and authority to do it.

I hope that from now on the Vatican will not miss the opportunity, and will not remain silent in the face of very real and present danger.

Chapter XX

The Church's Relationship with Israel

The fairly recent realization by many Christian scholars and clergy that the Church must recognize the Jewish people's right to practice their religion without interference from the Church is still at best a work in progress.

The fact that Israel exists — despite all difficulties — in its own homeland puts an end to the Christian theory of the "Wandering Jew."

The fact that the reborn nation flourishes is no small miracle.

Of course it is difficult for survivors to talk of miracles. But the fact that this nation survived almost two thousand years of exile — scattered to the four corners of the globe, preserving its religion and fidelity to G-d, Jerusalem and *Eretz Yisrael* — is nothing short of amazing and totally unprecedented.

The love of Jerusalem and the land of Israel was repeated in the daily prayers of the Jewish people in exile, and preserved in their hearts in spite of all the adversity, in spite of the persecution. The way Israelis rebuilt their land shows that love and devotion.

The unprecedented change that took place in the young state, in a mere half a century, has not been seen in any other country that has gained independence from colonial powers at approximately the same time. Israel excels in the fields of medicine, science, technology, agriculture, horticulture, etc., on a par with many developed countries.

All this, despite the many wars of aggression by its Arab neighbors who still have not given up the idea of eliminating the reborn state.

One has to wonder, when will the Arab-Muslims give up their murderous intent? When will they realize that this is the only piece of land — small as it is — that we Jews can call our own? Two thousand years in exile have proven that the Jewish nation can only exist in its own land, and we are not about to relinquish our cherished Land and freedom!

We have lost so many of our people during dispersion; before, during and after the Crusades. Despite the Church's claim that we should not be killed but "merely" live in humiliation forever, the Church's vile propaganda against the Jewish people amounted to a prescription for murder.[1]

In fact, that is exactly what happened during the Inquisition and continued after, finally culminating in the Holocaust.

Following the Holocaust, voices of conscience were heard (here and there), even among some Christian clergy, to the effect that the teaching of contempt towards the Jewish people led to the Holocaust. Recently, these voices have become even more pronounced. But the Church's ambivalence towards Israel as a state still remains.

It took almost two decades after the Holocaust for Pope John XXIII — in his all too short reign — to pronounce that Jews today are not guilty of the death of Jesus!

Jews today refer to John XXIII as a saintly person, and rightly so, for it was he who may have started the new way of looking at the Jewish-Christian relationship.

In more recent history, John Paul II, despite his strange apology to the Jewish people, still did not see fit to recognize Jerusalem as the capital of the state of Israel, which it physically is; it was never a capital of any other state.

The state of Israel was recognized by the Church only after several decades of existence. (One wonders how all of that affected the Arab attitude towards Israel, or was it the other way around?)

Arab countries, meanwhile, use economic relationships with the Christian world and coerce them into putting even more pressure on Israel to relinquish even more land to the mythical "Palestinian" people.

---

1. See Franklin Littell, *The Crucifixion of the Jews*, on the implications of supersession.

Chapter XXI

The Arab War against Israel

Jewish people everywhere are rightly concerned about the re-emerging anti-Semitism in many areas around the world. We know only too well that anti-Semitic hate propaganda and incitement inevitably lead to violence. Our long history — particularly in exile — provides ample proof for those still in doubt.

Here in the Middle East, the almost daily violence and terrorism against Israel are a direct result of anti-Jewish, anti-Israel hate propaganda emanating from the leadership of the Palestinian Arabs, including clergy, the mosque, schools and universities, the news media, as well as education in the home.

This propaganda unfortunately is not limited to the Palestinian Arabs. It is equally — if not more virulently — in major Arab states, including what in years past were referred to as "moderate" Arab states such as Saudi Arabia. Egypt and Jordan still indulge in this hostile practice regardless of official treaties with Israel; hostility has gone on unabated and uninterrupted for many decades despite the "peace" treaties.

It turns out that the very same schoolbooks that teach even small children in "Palestinian"-controlled territories to hate and kill Jews are also used in the erstwhile "moderate" countries of Jordan and Egypt!

Of course these books give the young students a reason to hate and kill by inculcating the nasty lie that Israel "stole" Arab land, and therefore it is a holy duty of every Arab and Muslim to do whatever it takes to punish the "usurpers," "those sons of dogs and monkeys — the Jews." And, of course, since this is taught as a "holy duty" ordained by Allah, young, impressionable children — preschoolers, and even young toddlers barely standing straight on their feet — are often portrayed in the Arab media as would-be fighters, "martyrs" for the cause!

It is probably no wonder, then, that children who are instilled with this kind of indoctrination from such an early and impressionable age become willing tools at the hands of their unscrupulous leaders. And so we see young children as young as seven or eight years old, together with older ones of sixteen, seventeen and older, confronting Israeli soldiers and even vehicles and tanks with stones and fire bombs.

Of course this makes for terrific pictures for the foreign press, particularly if any of the boys get injured or occasionally killed in the crossfire, and ignoring the fact that behind them are the older combatants with guns! Israel is then blamed for "killing children" when in fact they may have been killed by "friendly fire"!

I would not put it past the terrorists to deliberately engage in such dastardly acts since they are, after all, training these children to become future suicide bombers. Such acts would gain them world sympathy and condemnation of the Jews. And is this not after all a battle for the hearts and minds of the world community?!

The world media laps it up; world leaders can feed on this propaganda, and can be "excused" of any hostile feelings towards the Jewish state, including their not so well disguised anti-Semitism. This also helps them in no small measure to follow their own agenda whether economic or political, without any major guilt feelings.

And so, the world leaders can continue to import Arab oil in exchange for war materiel; the Arabs are relatively satisfied, as long as those leaders continue to be pliant, as long as they "deliver" Israel in this seemingly never-ending Arab-Israeli conflict. Or perhaps we should stop using euphemisms and call it what it is — a war.

But those leaders — who are no strangers to appeasement, so long as it is "only" "the Jews" the Arabs are after — are committing the same mistake as their forebearers did in the 1930s; they continued trading with Herr Hitler no matter how far he oppressed the Jews. But eventually, they themselves paid the price of appeasement.

The Arab-Muslims today have greater plans than "merely" to harass and murder Israeli civilians and children. There are many signs of those designs already. The Western leaders will, to use Lenin's famous phrase, "sell the rope which will eventually be used to hang them."

Meanwhile, the "helpful" media, too, is helping in the process by being respectful and pliant with the Arabs, and hostile and nasty with the Jews. The Arab propaganda line is helped along by most of the Western press, including news media that report Arab lies whole without question or challenge.

It has indeed been so long since anyone openly challenged Arab lies and assertions, that today they are accepted by many in the general public as if they were true.

To quote Goebbels, Hitler's propaganda minister: "People will believe a big lie sooner than a little one; and if you repeat it frequently enough people will sooner or later believe it."

And so it is!

Judea and Samaria — the heartland of the ancient Jewish land of *Eretz Yisrael*, and recognized in history as such — is presented to the public by the world media as "occupied" Arab land, or even "occupied Palestinian land"! And Jerusalem, the ancient capital of *Eretz Yisrael*, is referred to as part of "occupied East Jerusalem," the future capital of a "Palestinian" state!

Never mind that Arab land is in Arabia and that *Eretz Yisrael* is historic Jewish land; and never mind the fiction of a "Palestinian people." And never mind that the Temple Mount, including the Western Wall (Judaism's holiest site), is located in east Jerusalem.

It is interesting that Jordan never rushed to create a Palestinian state for the "Palestinians" following its illegal annexation of Judea and Samaria — the "West Bank" — nor did they ever demand such a state be created for them during the nearly two decades they lived under Jordanian rule.

Interestingly too, when the "Palestine Liberation Organization" (PLO) was created by the Arab League in 1964 in Cairo, wasn't it very clear to all, which territory the PLO terrorist organization was created to "liberate"? The PLO Covenant is certainly very clear about that, but how many people would bother to find and/or read the PLO Covenant?[1]

The Arabs in their war against Israel in 1948 promised local Arabs that they would push the Jews into the sea — read: commit genocide against the Jewish people (some of whom barely survived the Holocaust). The Arabs never stopped the war against the Jews. During the time between the wars — 1948–1967 — terrorist attacks never ceased on the Egyptian, Jordanian as well as the Syrian borders. Economic measures by all Arabs continued unabated, with blockades of international waterways, including the Suez Canal. All these harassments, and the terrorist attacks on all of Israel's borders, can each separately be considered acts of war.

After months of blockaded shipment to and from Israel, and appeals to

---

1. See Appendix 10.

the UN with no recourse whatever, Israel finally, in 1956, joined the French and British in the fiasco of the Suez Campaign, which was abandoned without result under pressure from the government of US President General Eisenhower.

The Arabs' determination to fight and obstruct Israel "by any means necessary" — military, economic and terrorist — continues. What a legal state could not do officially, the PLO terrorists could and did, causing countless victims in its terror campaigns, doing damage not only to Israel but also to international aviation. But even in the host countries of Jordan (and later Lebanon), the PLO, the monster, created a state within a state and was eventually unceremoniously driven out of Jordan in September 1968. The Jordanians killed many of the terrorists in the process. No one officially complained about Jordanian "draconian" measures. Not about driving out the terrorists nor about the massacre.

It appears it was perfectly "legitimate" for the Arab League to create the PLO monster, as long as the victims were Israeli schoolchildren and civilians. When, however, the PLO threatened the local authority of the Jordanian government, that could not be and was not tolerated.

Again, the PLO was created by the Arab League with one goal, to do the job for the Arabs that five Arab armies did not succeed in doing in 1948! Let us remember that the PLO was created in 1964, some three years before Israel took Judea and Samaria in 1967 in a defensive war — after being attacked by Jordan.

Again, which territory did the Arab League want the PLO to "liberate" in 1964?

And for the record, for those who may still be lost in the thick fog of Arab propaganda: according to international law, you do not reward the aggressor by restoring to him the land he used during the aggression. There is a great deal of precedence in the rules of war, where borders were moved and land taken from the aggressor. As for instance after WWII, when the borders of Germany were changed considerably, and German population was removed from lands occupied through aggression.

Even if Israel did not have historical rights to Judea and Samaria (and it does), those lands — taken illegally by Jordan in the first place — would not have to be given to Jordan. The question of whether the Arab population of parts of Judea and Samaria have any rights in those lands, other than simple residence, is equally clear. The illegal and unjust partition the British concocted in their Peel Commission Report does not bestow any rights on the Arab residents of Judea and Samaria, except to live in peace and respect the laws of the land.

The Arabs of Judea and Samaria did not accept the UN Partition in 1947, even though it created indefensible borders for the state of Israel and was totally unjust historically. The supposed right of the "Palestinians" to a state of their own was simply a ploy, used to this day by the Arabs to make Israel indefensible once again. The clear evidence that it was in fact a ploy by the Arabs is the reality that the so-called "Palestinians" did not create a state during the nearly two decades when Judea, Samaria and Gaza were in Arab hands as referred to above.

The Arabs are very strong on pride. "Humiliation," as they see it, at the hands of the "infidels" — the Jews in this instance, who defeated them in several wars — must be avenged!

What they do not seem to appreciate is that the Jews did not intend to humiliate them. It was not the Jews who went out of their way to attack their much stronger neighbors on all their borders; clearly that would be folly.

But seeing how the Arabs swore before each aggressive war to annihilate the Jews and remove the state of Israel from the map, they do not leave the Jews much choice. In the post-Auschwitz age, there are two options: fight back or be annihilated.

The Arab propaganda war against the Jewish state and Jewish people in general has perverted not only the UN and its lofty goals, but influenced many in Western societies through their various institutions, including universities.

Having lost several wars against Israel, the Arab states are now conducting the war through other means.

Over the past few decades, many Arabs have migrated to Western countries; they are now said to be numbering in the hundreds of thousands in several countries. As of 2004 the figures were as follows: In the US, they claim their numbers exceed well over two million; Canada is said to have some seven hundred thousand Arabs; Britain 1.3 million; France has 7.6 million (this is an estimated number not counting the "illegals"; some sources estimate the number to be ten million plus) and Germany three million plus. Even Belgium is said to have as many as over six hundred thousand "Palestinians"! "Palestinians"?! Where are they all coming from? We have become accustomed to Arab exaggerations, but these numbers are preposterous.

There were only some four hundred thousand Arabs living in the former "Palestine" in 1948. In the mid-eighteenth century there were only fifty thousand Arabs in all of "Palestine," the overwhelming majority — poor fellahin — working the unproductive soil for foreign masters.

Various travelers of that period — pilgrims, archaeologists, writers[1] — describe an empty landscape with hardly any population. The British, during their unfortunate Mandate for Palestine, helped to bring in Arabs from adjacent Arab states, while curtailing and eventually preventing Jews from coming back to their homeland. In those days the Arabs, of course, did not call themselves "Palestinians."

The reason I bring up the issue of large numbers of Arabs living in Western countries is because their numbers appear to wield considerable political power. Their children, too — at Western universities, together with other Arab foreign students — cause a great deal of noise using Arab propaganda against Israel, and lately also against Jewish people in general, leading to anti-Semitic attacks on individuals as well as Jewish institutions such as schools and synagogues.

Long discredited canards against the Jewish people are gaining a whole new life in the hands of these "students," who flood university campuses with anti-Israel, anti-Semitic propaganda, allegedly in their "fight for inalienable Palestinian rights!"

Many Western students have little or no knowledge of the roots of the contemporary Arab-Israeli conflict, now almost a century old (to say nothing of the older conflict, during the Islamic conquest in the seventh century).

Western students' ignorance of history becomes a fertile ground for Arab anti-Israel, anti-Semitic propaganda. And we have seen already recently anti-Israel, anti-Semitic riots at various universities, both in the US and in Canada.

Freedom of speech and thought in Western universities and societies are being perverted to preaching hate and bigotry. Incitement to violence, and language such as "Hitler didn't finish the job" and "get out or I'll kill you," has been heard at the San Francisco State University in recent riots. Concordia University in Canada has recently experienced anti-Semitic rioting when former Israeli Prime Minister Binyamin Netanyahu was invited to address the students. As a result of the riots, Netanyahu's address was canceled. So

---

1. See Mark Twain's *Innocents Abroad*.

much for freedom of speech on Western university campuses, thanks to Arab influence and propaganda.

All this while the American president, George Bush, is hoping to help establish democracy in Arab states, in particular, among the "Palestinians."

I suppose it is difficult, if not impossible, for the Western mind to comprehend the mindset that exists in the Arab world. But a sampling of Arab students' behavior in Western universities should give us some idea how these people think.

If Arabs living in Western countries cannot adapt to Western-style democracy, how can anyone expect democracy to take hold in Arab states? They are rooted in a different tradition, closely aligned to their religion. Progress, if it exists at all, is very, very slow. Even Arab leaders educated in Western countries disparage Western culture. The populace of Arab countries appears to despise Western democracy and culture, having been indoctrinated by Arab anti-Western propaganda.

What is most galling is that Western leaders for the most part turn a blind eye to these Arab attitudes.

Shouldn't Western opinion-shapers wonder why the Arab leaders, even those who have signed peace treaties with Israel — Egypt and Jordan — are never heard condemning the ongoing terrorist attacks on Israeli civilians, and most especially children?

During the period of September 2000 to December 2004, dozens of suicide bombers attacked civilian buses in Israel, deliberately targeting buses with schoolchildren and restaurants frequented by families. Markets are attacked by terrorist bombers when there is a good chance that many people will be shopping for the Sabbath. In one hotel, in Netanya, there was a particularly gruesome attack on families during the holiday of Passover; elsewhere attacks have been perpetrated on those celebrating bar and bat mitzvahs!

And still, we have not heard a word of condemnation from Arab leaders. On the contrary, constant demands are made on Western leaders to put more pressure on Israel, and/or to stop supporting the Jewish state!

Arab propaganda and coercion are so widespread that only two countries supported Israel at the UN during the annual Israel-bashing "fest." Those two countries are the US and Micronesia.

The US, however, despite its alleged support of Israel, over time "merely" abstained from voting on critical issues at the UN. American support was not always there, depending on the makeup of the US administration. Recently, despite the so-called support of the current US administration, US President Bush has come up with a "new" idea. If the "Palestinians" make democratic reforms and stop terrorism, Israel should agree to a "Palestinian" state in Judea, Samaria and Gaza. This is the first time an American president actually *demanded* the creation of an Arab state on historically Jewish land.

The US president then added that this should be "a viable state living side by side with Israel in peace." Apparently the president forgot that mollifying the Arabs has been tried before. Adding the word "democratic" to the equation is not going to change how the Arabs will or will not act.

Meanwhile, the Arab states — latching on to this "new idea" — are pushing and prodding and getting support from the Europeans as well as the Russians and the Brits. It appears that it was the Saudis with whom this "new idea" originated. The Saudis proclaimed through a "third party" that if Israel returns to its 1967 borders, the Arabs will make peace with Israel. In other words, if Israel will commit national suicide, that is!

Very clever, isn't it?

The Europeans and the Arabs are busy constructing the "Road Map" to the Arabs' liking, which they hope to force on Israel, even if the Arabs just pay lip service to peace and democracy.

More than five decades after the re-establishment of the Jewish state, and several wars of aggression by the Arab states, the Arabs still cannot or will not accommodate themselves to the fact that the Jewish people returned to their homeland, that this is our historical right, and that we are here to stay.

In the early days of negotiating boundaries of *Eretz Yisrael* (Palestine) following the Balfour Declaration, then Emir Faisal welcomed the return of the Jewish people to their homeland. He saw benefits to both peoples, the Jews and the Arabs, in mutual cooperation. But this was, of course, at a time before the British administration in Palestine had artificially created the so-called Arab "revolt," inspired by none other than the local British officers themselves. This was also a long time before local Arabs took to calling themselves "Palestinians."

The tragedy is that after all the wars of aggression by the Arabs — including the "War of Attrition," which involved continuous terrorist attacks against the state of Israel and its civilian population; and the "Arab Boycott" as well as other economic measures such as blockading international waterways to Israel, and all the wars that promised to annihilate the Jewish people and eradicate the Jewish state — the Arabs still persist. And the so-called "refugees" still linger in "refugee camps" which have now grown to small towns or satellite towns, with ever growing unemployment and terrible sanitary conditions.

The Arab propaganda blames it all on Israel and strangely enough, the international press — for the most part — buys into this horrific canard.

The Arabs, especially the very young, believe the propaganda, which has become part of their daily diet. They believe they were the original inhabitants of the land of Israel, and that they were "dispossessed" by the Jews and/or Zionists. The unfortunate result is that many young Arabs are willing to commit suicide in order to help "liberate their country."

Perhaps the unemployment, the raw sewage and the misery are all part of the same plan: keep people miserable and ignorant and they will fight for "a better tomorrow."

But this so-called "better tomorrow" is nowhere in sight. The Jewish people are not going to commit suicide to please the Arabs.

Despite the attempt by Western nations to whitewash Islam and the Arab culture of violence, the facts on the ground belie these attempts. And yet, the Western nations turn a blind eye to what is really going on.

Europe, particularly, continues to fund the PLO-PA despite the fact that those funds do not help the local Arabs, but simply pay wages of the various factions of the PLO, some of whom openly claim "credit" for suicide attacks and drive-by shootings at civilian motorists on Israeli roads!

The US ultimately refused to deal with Arafat, putting the blame where it belongs. It is a bit surprising though that it took as long as it did for the US to recognize Arafat as the mastermind behind all the terrorist attacks on Israel.

Considering his past as a mastermind hijacker of civilian aircraft, and various kidnappings of diplomats, including Americans, why would anyone be surprised? His entire behavior after the Oslo Peace Accords which were supposed to bring "Peace in our Time" (echoes of Munich) witnessed constant doubletalk from Arafat; he broke every agreement he signed, and in Arabic spoke openly of the "temporary" agreement. (As the prophet Mohammed likewise did with a certain tribe, in his time. Mohammed signed the Hudaybiya Treaty with various pagan tribes, as well as Jews of Mecca, only to violate it several years later when his forces overran the Jewish and other non-Muslim clans.)

In the 1930s the world turned a blind eye, as it turns a blind eye now, on the farce and hoax that the Oslo Peace Accords turned out to be. What is even more disturbing is that Western diplomats still speak of "the peace process"! Terrorism continues unabated, hundreds of people are being killed and many more thousands maimed for life, but still the Western world insists there is a peace process!

And the Arab states, including the "moderate" Saudi Arabia and Egypt, as well as Jordan, are still prodding and lobbying the US to create a "Palestinian" state!

Everyone seems to have forgotten that the PLO — the terrorist group created by the Arab League in Cairo in 1964 — was in fact a proxy for those very Arab states! No one seems to be saying it, but the PLO is still a proxy for the Arab League.

There were no "Palestinians" before 1964 when the PLO was created. They were, and they are, only Arabs. There is nothing to distinguish the Arabs living in Judea and Samaria or indeed in Haifa and elsewhere from their Arab brothers living throughout the Middle East. They are *not* a separate nation — they are part of the Arab nation. They speak the same language, practice the same religion and there is nothing that distinguishes them from other Arabs. (Our thanks to Joseph Farrah, an Arab-American journalist and editor of the *World Net Daily* Web site, who said as much.)

Yet the Arabs have always had a genius for using propaganda to manipulate world opinion. Imagine if the Arab League, during their meeting in Cairo in 1964, had decided to call their terrorist organ not the Palestine Liberation Organization, but rather "The Arab League Liberation Organization."

This — calling the terrorist PLO the "Palestine Liberation Organization" — was a stroke of genius as far as Arab propaganda was concerned. The name "Palestine Liberation Organization" had future implications that the Arabs themselves could not possibly fully imagine. It played on the ignorance of the general public, as well as the Arab masses themselves. In one stroke, this name gave the Arab masses a cause to fight for, as well as a unifying force against a common enemy that had to be defeated at all costs. It also portrayed the Arabs as the "injured party" in the conflict, gaining them world sympathy.

Suddenly the tables were turned. Despite numerous Arab wars of aggression against Israel and their collective pledge to push the Jews into the sea and annihilate them, in what could only be referred to as an Arab call to commit genocide against Israel and its people, the "Palestinian" Arabs are now portrayed as "victims," and the Jewish people as "usurpers" in our own land!

But what happened to history?

Why is the world at large swallowing whole this big lie?

By creating the PLO — "Palestine Liberation Organization" — the Arabs must have been hoping to establish several fictions. One, that it was the Arabs of Palestine, and not the Jews, who were dispossessed. Two, that it was the Arabs, not the Jews, who were defending their land. And three, that the Arabs were the underdog in this struggle, something the Arabs could not claim when several Arab armies attacked Israel on the very day of its rebirth!

The PLO as a terrorist organization was thus able to hijack civilian aircraft and commit other outrages, and claim "credit" for it, while the Arab states could stay in the background and remain "innocent" and silent.

Now we had a new category of "victimhood." Terrorists attacking children in Ma'alot in northern Israel became "freedom fighters"!

Terrorists could kidnap diplomats, even shoot them, shoot innocent civilians on the beaches of Tel-Aviv, and be seen as the "victims" by the world!

The Arab nation already comprises some twenty states in an area of 5.3 million square miles. Israel has this sliver of land (10,800 square miles) and does not covet other people's land.[1]

If the PLO is still a proxy for the Arab League, and there is every indication that it is, then a PLO state in the very heart of Israel would become the proverbial Trojan horse. And the Arabs will yet again try to annihilate the Jewish people and their state!

Such a scenario is unthinkable and must not be allowed to happen.

The Arab propaganda against the Jewish people and the state of Israel is ever increasing. The vilification of the Jewish people and its state continues, and Israel is continually under attack in every international forum, especially at the United Nations. Is it because the Arabs feel "humiliated" that they lost every war they started since 1948, promising to annihilate the Jewish people?

Israel and the Jewish people will not allow themselves to be annihilated, just so that Arab "humiliation" will disappear.

The violence that Arafat unleashed following the Camp David negotiations in July 2000 caught Israelis by surprise. How, they wondered, could Arafat's response be violence, when then Prime Minister Ehud Barak offered

---

1. See Appendix 8.

the "Palestinians" a state in practically all of Judea, Samaria and Gaza; wasn't that what Arafat wanted?

Most Israelis were surprised and many quite upset when Barak offered the Arabs far more than any other Israeli leader, considering the danger such concessions posed to Israel. That Arafat would reject this offer was beyond the comprehension of many. Isn't that what he wanted; what was he holding out for? The violent attack on Israel that followed left many Israelis — and especially those who strongly supported the Oslo process — dumbfounded.

The simple explanation, with some hindsight, of course, is that peace was never intended; that the "Oslo Peace Accords" were a sham, a pretext to get control over land from which to launch terrorist attacks on Israel.[1] Attacks continued unabated, from almost every town and village under Arafat's control.

That President Bush, a man who knows the land, who understands terrorism and apparently also the PLO's *modus operandi*, and who is purportedly a friend of Israel, would in his speech of June 24, 2002, advocate creating a "Palestinian" state "living side by side in peace with Israel," is nothing if not mind-boggling!

President Bush — who wages his own fight against terrorism following 9/11 half a world away — visited Israel years before he became president of the United States. He has seen Israel's borders and apparently understood the danger inherent in Israel's pre-1967 borders. Mr. Bush, knowing all that, ignores the ongoing terrorism Israel faces every day to its civilian population from an enemy bent on its destruction, and proposes, even commits himself personally to forcing Israel into what amounts to committing national suicide!

The Arabs have never relented. Most of them still openly scream for Israel's destruction; what kind of blindness or pretence does it take to ignore all these dangers to Israel?

Is America's "friendship" a meaningless gesture simply designed to use Israel and the Jewish people, yet again, as scapegoats in the never-ending charade of pleasing the Arabs?

Mr. Bush decided to disarm Saddam Hussein of weapons of mass destruction — a most desirable endeavor, considering the dangers they pose in the hands of the butcher of Baghdad. Bush obviously chose Israel as a conve-

---

1. See Appendix 11.

nient scapegoat to keep the Arabs at bay. To the Arabs, apparently, sacrificing Saddam Hussein — one of their own (though not well loved by his own brethren) — is not too big a price to pay, so long as Israel is the intended victim.

It is fair to assume that Tony Blair, British prime minister, contributed in no small measure to President Bush's decision vis-à-vis Israel. The papers were full of Blair's pronouncements calling for a "Palestinian" state in 2003.

Blair — Bush's close ally on the issue of Iraq — seems to have ignored even Bush's conditions for creating a "Palestinian" state; namely, a total change of the leadership still involved in terrorism.

Blair set out to meet with Yasser Arafat's cronies in London in preparation of the Road Map with specific dates leading to a creation of this PLO entity, in total contradiction to Bush's speech of June 24. Blair was apparently counting on Bush's support for his Road Map. Bush's isolation in the international arena on the Iraq issue allowed Blair to push his own agenda on the Middle East.

If Israel was not the proposed sacrificial lamb, one would have to feel sympathy for Mr. Bush seeing how his closest ally exploited the situation, when erstwhile members of NATO and others turned their backs on the US effort to dismantle Iraq's weapons of mass destruction, and unseat the butcher of Baghdad.

But Israel should not be asked to pay the ultimate price in this international intrigue!

Just as I was writing these words, another suicide attack took place in Haifa, causing horrible deaths and destruction. Early pictures of the tragedy show a man screaming in distress: "I saw dead bodies, I saw people burning." The terrorist suicide bombing in the center of Haifa, on bus 37 traveling from downtown Haifa to the university, killed at least fifteen people, many more seriously wounded, some critically; some died of their wounds on the operating table. Among the killed and wounded were many young students, some high school students as young as thirteen or fourteen.

My first reaction watching these horrific scenes of emergency workers picking up body parts of blown up people, and this young man screaming in agony of what he witnessed, was: these people must be thrown out of our country! Why are we fighting with our hands tied behind our backs an enemy that is committed to our total destruction?

Chapter XXII

The Road Map

In his June 24, 2002, speech, the US president called for a "two-state" solution to the Arab-Israeli conflict. This alleged friend of Israel is the first US president to call for a Palestinian state, rather than autonomy. Two states — one Arab, one Israel — "living side by side in peace." He envisaged the Arab-Palestinian state to be democratic and free of terrorist influence. He also envisaged that such an Arab State be "viable." I suppose to most Western ears, this must sound eminently reasonable.

In short order, a "Road Map" was created by a "Quartet" comprising the UN, Europe, Russia and the US. Many non-Jewish friends of Israel have been warning Israel against this "Road Map."

To begin with, its origins must be scrupulously scrutinized. The Saudis first floated the idea of Israel going back to pre-1967 borders. The composition of the Quartet — our detractors at the UN and our not-so-great friends the Europeans (who remained enamored with Yasser Arafat to the end), together with the Russians and the US — should give us pause.

But the content of the document itself should have raised alarms, since the Road Map provides that not Israel, but the UN, the EU, the Russians and the US (collectively the Quartet) will determine what Israel must do and when.

To offer the Palestinian Arabs a state up front within a few short months of the introduction of the Road Map is completely ignoring the past, and the violence unleashed when Yasser Arafat and his thugs turned to terrorism once again after rejecting an offer for a state by then Prime Minister Barak three years before the introduction of the Road Map. This was an offer many Israelis considered more than generous; indeed, most opposed PLO statehood altogether. Barak, however, misjudged Arafat and apparently believed in his peaceful intentions, as did many Israelis on the Left. Despite all indications to the contrary, they believed that once the Arabs were granted a state, peace and normalization would follow.

The Left in Israel totally ignored the role the Arab states played in this clever charade. Now Israel is expected to ignore these realities once again; according to the provisions in the Road Map, Israel is expected to forfeit its sovereignty!

Even UN Resolutions 242 and 338 provide for negotiations between the parties to the conflict, which really are the Arab states and Israel, not the "Palestinians," nor indeed the "Quartet."

But in this diabolic document there is no room for negotiations. Just demands and dictates by countries that in the main were not parties to the Arab Israeli conflict, countries which have no rights under international law to impose a solution to a conflict not of Israel's making.

The Quartet's Road Map attempts to start where the (failed) Oslo process left off; in effect, rewarding terrorism.

Despite all the evidence to the contrary, the Quartet implies that terrorism will cease once "dignity" is restored to the "Palestinians," ignoring the fact that terrorism feeds on the hatred and propaganda spewed not only by the Palestinian Arabs, but by all Arab states.

The US — now apparently under the influence of the other members of the "Quartet," and Britain's Tony Blair in particular — appears to have forgotten that the suicide bombers who attacked New York's Twin Towers and Washington's Pentagon buildings on September 11, 2001, were all students from wealthy Arab families, who were influenced by Islamic propaganda of hate towards Western powers.

Instead of seeing through Arab-Islamic subterfuge, they buy into the propaganda that if only Israel would agree to the pre-1967 borders and create a "Palestinian" state, all the ills of the world would be cured.

But what happened from 1948 to 1967 when all Arab states neighboring Israel sent infiltrators to commit terrorist attacks on Israeli civilians, including deliberate targeting of schools? The world's leaders appear to be suffering from willful blindness and total loss of memory.

The Israeli government, and especially the cabinet, accepted the provisions of the Road Map only after then Israeli Prime Minister Sharon had received assurances from Bush that Israel's concerns would be addressed.

Israel's fourteen reservations to the provisions stipulate certain requirements, which attempt to reverse the offensive provisions that would otherwise allow the Quartet to basically undermine Israel's very sovereignty. Instead of direct negotiations between the parties, it was to be the Quartet that was to decide whether or not the Palestinian Arabs had lived up to their obligation to eradicate terrorism and its infrastructure, as well as creating "democratic" institutions.

In spite of a very flowery speech by "Palestinian" Prime Minister Mahmoud Abbas at Aqaba, promising a new beginning and an end to violence and terrorism, nothing of the kind has happened.

Yasser Arafat was originally supposed to be sidestepped, as he was declared an obstacle to peace and a supporter of terrorism by President Bush in his June 24, 2002, speech on which the Road Map was supposed to be based. In fact the Road Map departed greatly, in very important ways, from what was articulated in that speech. Most importantly, the new "Palestinian" leader was supposed not to be tainted by terrorism. Abbas, however, is just as much of a terrorist as Arafat was (he is said, for example, to have been responsible for the murder of eleven Israeli athletes at the 1972 Olympic Games in Munich).

In any event, Arafat remained until the end courted by almost all European leaders. Mahmoud Abbas, the new, "improved" Prime Minister, reported to him dutifully and pre-cleared all decisions with Arafat.

Despite the fact that the Road Map — as flawed as it is — provides for immediate and unconditional cessation of all violence and terrorism and incitement to terrorism, confiscation of weapons as well as dismantling the terrorist infrastructure, terrorism still continues. None of the provisions of the Road Map are taken seriously by the PLO-PA.

Although there has been a bit of a letup in terrorism, there are still several attacks reported every day, and almost daily the Israeli army reports apprehending would-be terrorist suicide bombers. July 23, 2003, for example, there were two such incidents.

Special commissions charged with monitoring incitement in the PA media and schools reported that even the new eighth grade textbooks include almost the same type of incitement and propaganda, and practically no general change.

Due to the new "prime minister's" efforts, a *hudna* was proclaimed between the various terrorist factions and the PA. The *hudna* is a temporary ceasefire, but not with Israel; rather it is between the terrorists themselves! They even had the temerity to proclaim that the *hudna* was only to last for a mere three months. The terrorists are now making demands to have terrorists released from Israeli prisons!

And so the Road Map is being gradually perverted and stood on its head;

instead of having an immediate and unconditional ceasefire, and an end to terrorism including the confiscation of weapons and arrest of the terrorists, the terrorists have declared a "temporary" ceasefire and demanded the release of terrorists!

The new "prime minister," Mr. Abbas, repeatedly told us after signing the agreement that he will not confront the terrorists and that he will continue to dialogue with them. He also invited Hamas and the other terrorists to join his government, as well as the police force.

As preposterous as all this sounds, Israel was urged by the US and others to release terrorists to placate the "Arab street," and to improve Abbas' standing and credibility!

If this is how the new PA "prime minister" achieves credibility, then, of course, the whole exercise is nothing but a sham.

Abbas, in the meantime, was also criticized by the PA Council for being a "novice" and "not knowing how to deal with the Israelis."

Now we suppose he knows, as he was briefed by the Egyptian president, Hosni Mubarak, prior to his first visit to Washington for a meeting with President Bush; the Egyptians of course are past masters at this sort of game!

After Abbas's Washington visit, we were told that President Bush was very sympathetic to Abbas's demands that Israel: (1) release large numbers of prisoners; (2) freeze further settlement activity and roll back recently established outposts as well as transfer additional cities to "Palestinian" control; and (3) halt construction of a security fence wall.

What is striking is that we did not hear Bush demand that "Prime Minister" Abbas immediately dismantle the terrorist infrastructure and arrest the terrorists, and do a better job of stopping all violence (which still continues) in accordance with the provisions of the Road Map, as well as stop incitement in all its institutions.

There are no provisions in the Road Map to release terrorists; that would be shocking indeed. Nor is there any reference to stopping the construction of the security wall that was designed to prevent shooting incidents at Israeli citizens from Arab villages, as well as infiltration of terrorist suicide bombers. In fact, the security fence was the product of the previous defense minister, Mr. Benjamin Ben Eliezer, who was a member of the previous coalition government of the dovish Labor faction. Many Israelis support the security fence as one of the ways of preventing much of the bloodshed caused by suicide bombers.

One can see a repetition of the Oslo process; not only do the Arabs have no intention of fulfilling their only obligation under the agreements, but furthermore they put the onus on Israel on issues that are not even part of the agreement. They somehow managed to put Israel on the defensive when Israel should be on the offensive.

According to Bush's vision of a "two-state solution" (as if the conflict were merely between Israel and the Palestinian Arabs), the new leadership was supposed to be untainted by terrorism. Abbas himself, of course, is not exactly "untainted." He has been a terrorist for as long as Arafat was, and some of his interviews and activities vis-à-vis Israel and the Jewish people in general do not really make him a convincing leader for peace and democracy. His early assertion that he would neither confront nor use force against the terrorists belies his promise at Aqaba. He instead stated that he will dialogue with them, saying that the only alternative to dialogue is dialogue! During the *hudna* "negotiations" Abbas invited all the terrorist groups to join his government.

When Bush spoke of a democratic "Palestinian" state living side by side in peace with Israel, a state untainted by terrorism, did he have in mind a government including all terrorist groups? Clearly not. Then why didn't Bush raise this disturbing issue with Mr. Abbas? Or did Abbas keep Bush busy with demands on what Israel must do to placate the Arab street?

Also, the temporary *hudna* between the terrorists is clearly not what the Road Map calls for (according to Arabic language experts, the *hudna* is merely a temporary truce, borne out of convenience for the weaker party in order to rebuild or regroup), particularly in view of the still ongoing violence, including two kidnappings. One of the victims, a young soldier, was found dead on July 28, 2003, buried in a shallow grave.

During his visit to Washington, July 28–30, 2003, Israeli Prime Minister Ariel Sharon was to express his concern over the terrorists building up their strength during the three-month ceasefire and urge the US president to pressure the PA to crack down on Hamas and Islamic Jihad (*Jerusalem Post*, July 28, 2003).

Before his departure, the Israeli prime minister managed to convince his cabinet to agree to release additional prisoners, as a gesture of goodwill to bolster PA "Primer Minister" Abbas! It should be noted that Israel holds only criminals who were convicted of serious crimes and who belong to various terrorist organizations. Many important members of the cabinet voted against this decision, obviously concerned that these criminals would only continue doing what they did before their incarceration. (With good reason; there were in fact many instances of terrorists committing the same crimes immediately upon being released from prison.)

Altogether, Israel was to release some one thousand prisoners out of about six thousand it was holding in prisons.

Still, the Palestinian Arabs said this was not enough. And so we witnessed again the same scenario where Israel, trying to be forthcoming, gives in — even against its better judgment. But the more it gives, the more the Arabs demand!

The PA, although calling the prisoner release a "positive move," still called for the release of all the prisoners. "Israel must release all the prisoners," said Hamas leader Abdel Aziz Rantisi (later killed in an Israeli airstrike on April 17, 2004). "Israel's refusal to release all the prisoners is a grave violation of the *hudna*" (*Jerusalem Post*, July 28, 2003).

Oh? But perhaps Rantisi forgot that the *hudna* was only among the terrorists and the PA. Israel was neither consulted nor indeed included in the temporary truce. All this is however part and parcel of their deceitful propaganda.

Rantisi went on ranting and raving: "What Israel announced today is a deception and fraud!" In a similar vein, Islamic Jihad leader al Hindi — another archterrorist — accused Israel of "deceiving world public opinion."

Israel is not obliged to release convicted criminals, most of whom are involved in terrorist acts of one kind or another. Nor is this a requirement under any international law.

Also on July 28, 2003, victims of terrorism organized as Victims of Arab Terror petitioned the High Court of Justice for an immediate injunction on the release of prisoners pending a hearing on the case (*Jerusalem Post*, July 28, 2003).

Despite all the smiles exchanged at Aqaba between Sharon and Abbas (aka Abu Mazen) during their acceptance of the Road Map, Abbas did not mind attacking Sharon in public for not doing enough to conform with the requirements of the Road Map! This, despite Sharon going out of his way to help Abbas placate the Arab street.

Abbas's conversion to non-violence, one must remember, occurred only after he and others realized they were losing the terrorist war. Even the *hudna* was only announced after Israel seriously targeted the kingpins of the terrorist organizations.

The "Road Map to peace" between the Palestinian Arabs and Israel is not only a sham, but also a sorry commentary on Western leadership.

The Oslo Peace process which preceded the Road Map promised peaceful co-existence between Arabs and Jews in *Eretz Yisrael*. Israel promised the Arabs autonomy, while the Arabs, under their chieftain Arafat, promised to renounce violence and terrorism.

The terrorism and violence never stopped during the seven years of the "Oslo process" while Israel continued to make irreversible concessions of handing over territory in Judea and Samaria (and Gaza), historically and biblically Jewish land.

The "process" which started under the left-wing Labor government continued under the centrist Likud government. Then Prime Minister Netanyahu, feeling duty-bound by the previous administration's commitment toward a peaceful solution to the Arab-Israeli conflict, forged on even though the violence and terrorism continued. Despite Netanyahu's insistence that Oslo would not continue in the absence of reciprocity, it did — under US pressure.

The Labor government's duo, Prime Minister Rabin and Defense Minister Peres, referred to the sporadic acts of terrorism against Israeli civilians as the "price of peace" during the initial stages of the Oslo process. They paid no attention to Arafat's duplicity; while speaking of the Oslo peace process in English for the benefit of the Western leadership or Western media, he cavorted openly with violent terrorists Hamas and Islamic Jihad, calling suicide bombers "martyrs," and paying homage to their "proud parents." All this was screened live on "Palestinian" TV, paid for by none other than the Americans.

Then opposition M.K. Benjamin Begin provided tapes of Arafat's duplicity to members of the Israeli government, but to no avail. Even though all this was going on fairly early in the process, the Israeli Labor government turned a blind eye, perhaps hoping that all this was only for local Arab consumption. The reality, however, was that Arafat had developed an elaborate fiction of a peace process, and while negotiating autonomy, continued with terrorism and vile propaganda against Israel and the Jewish people in general in its media and school system. All this while every effort was made at accommodation on the Israeli side.

Arafat even developed a "defense force," which, according to the Oslo

Accords, was supposed to be a police force of some eighteen thousand men. The "defense force" grew to some forty to fifty thousand soldiers, marines and even air force, all with appropriate insignia, etc!

The Israeli Labor government still ignored this reality — the US, now under President Clinton, kept twisting Israeli arms for the sake of "peace." Following elections and the defeat of Netanyahu, Israel had a new prime minister, Barak, again of the left-wing Labor Party, who was ready to bend over backwards to conclude a peace agreement with Arafat, eventually offering the Arabs almost all of Judea and Samaria — 97 percent, plus 3 percent of the Negev.

An outrageous concession by any account, and wonder of wonders, Arafat refused, claiming that the Israeli concessions were not good enough since they did not include some "three million" alleged "Arab refugees" from the 1948 Arab war on Israel. (Note that according to various accounts, the number of so-called "refugees" who left voluntarily, despite Israel's urging to stay in 1948, was two hundred thousand, to four hundred thousand. I recall reading in 1948–49 of three hundred thousand.)

Arafat thought that he now had an excuse to openly start violence all over again. But what happened to foreswearing terrorism and bloodshed? The terrorism Arafat unleashed in September-October 2000 — following seven years of the Oslo farce — was worse than anything Israeli civilians have ever experienced.

The three million figure is clearly a fiction. The so-called refugees still lingering at UN refugee camps — again at the urging of Arab leaders — have no claim on Israeli citizenship either, since they left voluntarily at the urging of the leaders of five Arab countries.

It is these Arab countries and their leaders who bear responsibility for the displacement of these people who left at their urging and were promised the spoils of war, when these five Arab armies would finish off the Israelis! At best, these "poor refugees," or their forefathers, are guilty of collaborating in attempted genocide against the Jewish people. Now that they have not succeeded in their vile and criminal design which they are still pursuing in their overwhelming majority, the Jewish people are expected to accept them and their offspring, and all those thousands of others and their offspring to form a fifth column?

The "refugee camps" have become towns supported for all their needs including health and education, paid for by UN member states for the last fifty-five years! These towns — refugee camps — are hotbeds of terrorists who have been brainwashed since childhood by vile Arab propaganda, both in schools and local media. This outrage is allowed to continue to meet the demands of the very same Arabs who are still at war with the state of Israel. These Arab states have conducted a war against Israel at every possible level — using all possible means, including blackmail. These so-called refugees were to be used as leverage against the Jewish state.

No other state except Israel appears to be protesting this hoax, or the other almost totally forgotten Arab outrage — the seven or eight hundred thousand Jewish people expelled from Arab countries where many of them had lived since before the Muslim period. These people — true refugees — were unceremoniously driven out from their homes, having to leave all their belongings behind.

We do not hear anyone speaking of these refugees, most of whom were forced out of (ethnically cleansed from?) the various Arab countries in 1948–1950. These refugees have long since been absorbed into Israeli society as well as other countries.

What will it take for the world to recognize that the current crisis is not of Israel's making, that it is not an "Israeli-Palestinian" conflict, but an Arab-Israeli conflict which started with Arab aggression against the reborn Israeli state in 1948? This state of war still exists — despite Egypt and Jordan signing peace treaties with Israel — only now the war is conducted by other means.

The so-called "Road Map to Peace," concocted by the Quartet at the suggestion of Saudi Arabia, would push Israel to the indefensible borders of 1967. The suggestion that the Arabs would conclude "peace" with Israel is nothing but a hoax and such a peace would not be worth having, nor does it appear to be forthcoming any time soon (note that the Saudis threatened to boycott any meeting if Israel were to attend; so much for the Saudi "peace"!).

Meanwhile, Israel is asked — nay, forced — to promise to create a "Palestinian state" up front as a confidence-building measure, while terrorism and violence continue unabated. Is this what Bush had in mind when he declared all-out war on terrorism? Or is there still a different standard to be applied where Jewish people are concerned?

Why should Israel be obliged to create an enemy state based on terrorism? A state that has never before existed; a state on Israel's own soil, of which there already is precious little?

The Arab war by "other means," which aims at Israel's destruction, continues. The idea of an Arab state called "Palestine" is yet another ploy towards that goal.

The new, "improved" Arab leader, Mahmoud Abbas, has, the *Jerusalem Post* reports, written an essay addressing the issue of whether peace or war is more likely to split Israeli society. What does that tell us about this new "prime minister"?

Whatever happened to Bush's demand that there be a change in "Palestinian" leadership? That those like Arafat and his cohorts who are "tainted with terrorism" must be replaced by a "democratic leadership"? Just where is this democratic leadership supposed to emerge from? Among people who do not know or even understand the meaning of democracy? A people who reject democracy as a "Western plot"? A people whose overwhelming majority — 70 to 80 percent — support terrorism and suicide bombing against Israeli civilians? A people so radicalized and brainwashed that they would sacrifice their own children to become suicide bombers and even be proud of sacrificing them? A people that overwhelmingly supports Hamas and Islamic Jihad? A people who vilified Abu Mazen, whom they have branded a traitor and a Western puppet, for even mouthing the words "peace" and "ending terrorism"?

Is that what Bush had in mind? Is that what he intended?

Even as Bush twisted Israeli arms to agree to give away part of its land, its very heartland to this sworn enemy, Hamas's outspoken chief, Abdel Aziz Rantisi, swore never to conclude peace with "the Zionist entity," calling Abu Mazen a traitor because he called for an end to terrorism.

According to Rantisi, attacks on civilians are not terrorism as long as it is "within Palestine"!

Land for Peace

Someone once said that peace is its own reward…

Various impositions forced on Israel from time to time by various "friendly" governments, particularly after the 1967 Six Day War (when Israel was openly to be annihilated by its surrounding Arab neighbors), have nothing to do with "peace" or indeed international law. Even though under international law aggression must not be rewarded, Israel is incessantly pushed and prodded about "returning land," its own land, to the enemy, to the very aggressors who would use the land to attack Israel yet again.

Clearly, neither Syria nor Jordan should be rewarded since they were the aggressors not only in 1967, but both before and after. It is true that Israel launched a preemptive strike against the most potent of its enemies, Egypt, in the 1967 War, thus preventing the annihilation of its people, but under international law, given the circumstances at the time and the fact that Egypt was poised for the attack and asked the peace-keeping force to leave, there was very little left for Israel to do.

Today, some revisionist historians would have us believe that it was all a mistake, a "miscalculation." I do not know if other nations, given the same set of circumstances, would have acted differently and waited for the fulfillment of the Egyptian threat.

Israel gave the Sinai Desert back to Egypt for an incomplete promise of peace.[1] A last-minute amendment to the peace agreement was added by then Foreign Minister of Egypt Boutros Boutros-Ghali. The amendment, an outrageous add-on to an all but completed document, stipulated that if any Arab country was to be engaged in a war with Israel, Egypt for all intents and purposes would be released from the peace treaty! Then US President Jimmy Carter, no friend of Israel, as an "honest" broker, shepherded the agreement through with another twist of the arm of then Prime Minister of Israel Menachem Begin. His closest friends and advisers, among them Samuel Katz (whose book *Battleground* is much cited here), were perplexed that Begin had allowed himself to be cajoled into such a devious treaty.

I have many doubts whether Sadat was as well-meaning as some people in Israel and elsewhere believed and still believe. Sadat wanted the Sinai back and was prepared to play the part expected of him. But surely it was not Boutros-Ghali's idea to add the amendment to the peace treaty; he was simply chosen to play the bad cop.

Sadat was assassinated not so much because he managed to get the Sinai back through peace with the hated Israel, but because he even negotiated with the Israelis at all! He was a pragmatist and a clever manipulator who gave to Israel almost nothing in exchange for getting back the Sinai. The assassins of Sadat could not forgive him for the "humiliation" of going to Jerusalem to negotiate, even if that was an empty gesture.

The normalization of relations between Egypt and Israel which the peace treaty provided for never materialized, even before Sadat's assassination. The

---

1. See Katz, *Battleground: Fact and Fantasy in Palestine.*

Israeli ambassadors in Egypt felt isolated. There were no exchanges, cultural or economic. In fact, it was what has come to be known as a "cold peace." The anti-Israel, anti-Jewish propaganda that existed prior to the peace agreement continued unabated, and continues to this very day.

Old and new propaganda of the most outrageous kind, such as the long discredited *Protocols of the Elders of Zion*, as well as new bloodcurdling stuff produced by prominent Muslim clerics and "scholars," is circulated freely by the Egyptian government-controlled press.

Today's ruler of Egypt, President Hosni Mubarak, has only set foot in Israel once, at the funeral of Prime Minister Yitzhak Rabin, one of the leaders of the Oslo process. Clearly the Oslo peace process was more process than peace. In fact, there were more terrorist attacks at the beginning and during the peace process than at any time before.

Arafat was seen again and again on "Palestinian" TV glorifying terrorists and calling them "martyrs," and promising his audiences, again and again, that sooner or later the PLO flag would fly over Jerusalem!

That Israel gave Sinai to Egypt was one thing. The Sinai's strategic significance pales in comparison to that of Judea, Samaria and Jerusalem.

The Oslo Peace Accords were about limited autonomy, but before long, it was turned on its head as the Arabs began a process of "land for peace"!

The pressure on Israel exercised by the various US administrations, and particularly the US State Department, had no historic reason, nor indeed international law to justify it.

Israel agreed to a truncated land in 1947 out of desperation, but never agreed to the boundary imposed on it after UN Partition in November 1947. Abba Eban — one of the first Israeli foreign ministers, and himself a "dove" — called the 1948 boundaries of Israel Auschwitz borders!

The League of Nations did not authorize the creation of yet another Arab state out of thin air, nor was there any partition envisaged.

What, if anything, could compel Israel to give up its own land — Judea and Samaria — land essential to its defense and its very survival, to its sworn enemies?

Jordan, after a time, gave up any claim to Judea and Samaria, the "West Bank," following the Six Day War. This was likely in order to step aside to allow the "Palestinian" Arabs to claim the land. But *even if* this land was not part of *Eretz Yisrael* (and, as I have repeatedly shown, it in fact *is*), Jordan forfeited the right to Judea and Samaria when it attacked Israel in June 1967 from that very land.

And what right does the PLO have to Judea and Samaria?

Arafat was born and educated in Egypt. We do not know how many of the current residents of Judea and Samaria, and Gaza, have illegally entered the territory. Most of the PLO chieftains and terrorists were imported. Furthermore we do know that in 1948 the original number of so-called "refugees" was about three hundred thousand. Out of the original "refugees" most have likely died, but there is now a third generation still living in those slums.

But many of the "refugees" were not originally from "Palestine" at all; they came from Syria and other areas. Impoverished people came to the camps where everything was provided to them free. What's more, no one asked any questions, since the camps, even though run by the UNRWA, were administered by local Arabs. In 1948, the only qualification required to become a "bona fide refugee" was a two-year residence in "Palestine." But even those who came from other countries were allowed in on humanitarian grounds.

Everyone seems to know — but no one seems to be doing anything about it — that the Arabs exaggerate the numbers of the so-called "refugees," that they never report any deaths to reduce the existing numbers of "refugees," and that their overlords refuse to resettle them into normal housing and proper living conditions. The so-called Arab "refugees" remain a drain on the public purse of the international community and a threat to Israel as they breed terrorism.

By contrast, some eight hundred thousand Jewish refugees who for the most part were forced out of Arab lands between 1948 and 1952 — even though they had lived there for centuries — were long ago, in fact within a year or so, resettled mostly in Israel.

Similar to India and Pakistan in 1947, there should have been an exchange of population. I remember clearly how refugees from India went to Pakistan and vice versa; in fact, front-page newspaper articles showed how the two streams of refugees traversed the same road in opposite directions.

It was clear that the Hindus in Pakistan no more wished to remain under foreign Pakistani control than the Muslims in India wished to live under Indian rule. However, there are still millions of Muslims living in India; either they feel satisfied to live there and do not feel hostile, or perhaps there are other reasons for their remaining.

The so-called Arab "refugees" — contrary to legend but based on reports of the day — left for the most part at the urging of Arab leaders to make it easier for them to "massacre" the Jews. They were promised to come back within days to inherit the spoils of war and take over the homes of the slain "infidel" Jews!

That is part of the record, part of history.[1] Should we Jews feel sorry for them because they did not succeed in their evil design?

Should Israel now reward them with a state for which there is neither historic reason nor any precedence in international law, to say nothing of the danger such a terrorist state and its sponsors would pose?

Is there a humanitarian problem in the PLO-controlled territory? Absolutely, but it is a problem of their own creation which they make no effort to remedy. And they must be convinced by the international community to resolve it, but not at Israel's expense.

They almost succeeded in having a state, when Barak offered them nearly all of Judea and Samaria in July 2000, but they refused the most generous offer they are ever likely to see.

There is higher unemployment in those territories than ever before; previously more than a hundred thousand Arabs worked in Israel daily. The PLO chieftains were neither willing nor able, apparently, to create an industry in the territory under their control to benefit their people. Instead, the PLO was busy building an army of some forty thousand with the help of foreign support — at first perhaps unknowingly helping the PLO terrorist infrastructure.

As far as Europe is concerned, they continued to support the PA (read: the terrorist PLO), in spite of documents provided to them by Israel and other independent sources.

The "Palestinian" Arabs, radicalized through vicious propaganda, openly support suicide bombing and other methods of terrorism. Various surveys, including Arab surveys, show 70–80 percent of the Arabs in Judea, Samaria and Gaza supporting terrorism against Israel.

It would take supernatural kindness, or more to the point a death wish, for any Jewish person in Israel, or elsewhere, to support the creation of a state for such a hostile population.

The Oslo Peace Accords were predicated on an end to hostility and violence and terrorism. This unfortunately did not happen, and it is not likely to happen under current circumstances. A complete re-education of the entire

---

1. See Katz, *Battleground*.

population, and especially the very young, would have to take place before these people can be entrusted with even limited self-rule. But I am afraid I do not hold out such hopes, although that would be the desirable thing to happen.

Oslo did not provide for an armed state, but rather limited autonomy — a demilitarized entity, without control of outside borders — and for good reason. UN Resolution 242, passed following the Six Day War of 1967, also did not call for such a state.[1]

An Arab state with borders to Egypt in Gaza, and with Jordan in the east, was designed as a Trojan horse in the heart of Israel. Only a nation wishing to self-destruct could allow such a state to come into being.

The Pragmatist

Abbas, the PA "prime minister," discovered "peace" as a means of achieving his goal, since violence and terrorism did not seem to work as well as he had expected.

In one of his written essays, he was delving into the theories of whether peace or terrorism would split Israeli society. He apparently believes in the theory of divide and conquer. He is perfectly aware that in Israel, there is a difference in perception of Arab intentions between the Left and the Right.

The "doves" of the left-wing persuasion believe that if only the Arabs achieved a state of their own, peace would reign supreme. The fact that they refused several opportunities for just such a solution in the '30s, '40s and ever since, does not seem to get in the way of their wishful thinking. The centrist Likud, and other parties to the right of center, argue that all that has been tried already, and one needs only to listen to Arab propaganda to realize that nothing short of Israel's destruction would satisfy our Arab neighbors.

And so Abbas knows that he can play on Israel's desire for peace in order to achieve the ultimate Arab goal!

The only thing separating the Palestinian Arabs from achieving a state — if that were their goal — is to stop. Stop terrorism, violence and incitement to terrorism and violence, in their official institutions, in schools, mosques and official press and TV. But Abbas told us in his first official interview after Aqaba, the summit where the "Road Map to Peace" agreement was signed (in

---

1. See Appendix 9.

the presence of US President Bush and at his strong urging), that cracking down on Hamas and other terrorist groups is "not an option."

How then is a process supposed to move forward, seeing that this is their only obligation, and must be addressed immediately? That was supposed to have happened in May 2003, when the Road Map was accepted unconditionally by the PA, or at the latest, the beginning of July after Aqaba. But by the end of July, not only was there no crackdown on terrorist groups and their leaders, but Abbas had actually negotiated with them to join his government!

Furthermore, in July the IDF reported that Hamas was building kassam rockets and smuggling arms, ammunition and rocket components across the border with Egypt to Gaza ("Hamas Building 1,000 Kassams," *Jerusalem Post*, July 22, 2003, front page). Cross-border tunnels, many of which had been sealed or destroyed, were being rebuilt, with approximately eight to ten functioning at that time.

But the PA did nothing to stop the smuggling of huge amounts of weapons, nor indeed interfered in the production of rockets. And, as far as can be ascertained, Egypt was not troubled by all this either.

When Israel handed over security to the PA in Gaza and Bethlehem following the Aqaba agreement, it was on the understanding that the PA would act to stop the smuggling, the production of weapons and rearmament. But just the opposite appeared to be taking place. The terrorists used the ceasefire to their own advantage to rearm and rebuild, without any interference from the PA.

The IDF was obviously concerned that when the *hudna* ended, the next phase of hostilities would be even more violent. But the *hudna* was not likely to end until at least December, when, according to the Road Map, the state could be declared and immediately recognized by the supporters of Arafat and co., i.e., Europe, the UN and, of course, all assorted Arab and Islamic states. In fact, however, the terrorists could not even wait until December. August 19, 2003, a terrorist attack on a double bus killed twenty-two Israelis and injured over 130, including children and two babies!

But what happened to monitoring the progress, if any, of the Arab PA undertakings? The Quartet appeared to be ignoring the PA's failure to deal with terrorism and to build democratic institutions (as was its obligation), free of terrorist influence.

A *Jerusalem Post* writer, Evelyn Gordon ("Plain-speaking Abbas," *Jerusalem Post*, July 29, 2003), warned that "if there is one thing that the Oslo process proved, it is that words are often no less important than deeds" — referring to comments in an interview with *The New York Times* Abbas made July 20:

> Asked about Israel´s refusal to release prisoners with "blood on their hands," Abbas replied that this was unacceptable. "We were in a war," he explained, "and in war, all prisoners are freed once hostilities end."

Obviously the fact that such provisions do not exist in international law with reference to terrorists, or indeed in the Road Map itself, did not appear to faze Mr. Abbas. Nor indeed that the hostilities never appeared to end!

The writer continued:

> Abbas' statement is tremendously important because it means that even he, the man who publicly denounced terrorism in Aqaba due to Bush's arm-twisting, continues to believe that deliberately blowing up schoolbuses full of children, or elderly people attending a Passover Seder, is a legitimate form of warfare that entitles its practitioners to return home in triumph. Furthermore, he has no qualms about saying so, in English, to America's newspaper of record — making him even more brazen than Yasser Arafat, who usually confined his defenses of terrorism to Arabic.

The writer went on to assert that Israelis learned from Oslo that when the Palestinian leaders declare they have no intention of honoring a signed agreement, they mean it.

> [W]hen Arafat lauded terrorists as legitimate freedom fighters this was not mere idle talk; it played a major role in creating the climate that made the intifada possible — one in which, according to repeated polls, an overwhelming majority of Palestinians not only support suicide bombings but view them as a legitimate accompaniment to peace talks. [!!!]

The writer reminds us that during a press conference in Cairo on July 22, Abbas openly admitted his refusal to hold up his side of theagreement:

> "[A]sked by reporters whether he ever intends to fulfill his Road Map obligation of dismantling the terrorist organizations,

> he replied bluntly: "Cracking down on Hamas, Jihad and the Palestinian organizations is not an option at all." [!]

From this statement, taken together with some of Abbas's earlier interviews, one may get a clearer picture of Abbas, the "moderate pragmatist."

As late as March 3, 2003, in an interview with Al-Sharq al Awsat, Abbas said:

> On the basis of the talks held in Cairo (with several terrorist groups and the P.A.) we agreed upon freezing of military operations for one year... We did not say however, that we are giving up the armed struggle... The intifada must continue. [!]

Abbas's so-called pragmatism and "moderation" are valid only insofar as they will ensure a state of "Palestine" with "provisional" borders. After that, all bets are off.

Chapter XXIII

When Diplomacy
Becomes Obscene

In August of 1997, following a particularly horrific attack on Israeli citizens by Arab terrorists in a marketplace in Jerusalem, Charles Krauthammer wrote a damning essay with the above title: "When Diplomacy Becomes Obscene" (*Time*, August 11, 1997):

> The body parts had not all been collected from the victims of the latest massacre of innocents in Jerusalem when the words of condolence came filtering in from the outside world. They were not just words of condolence, however. They were mixed with admonition…

Foreign government leaders from Europe as well as Kofi Annan, the UN secretary-general, attempted to give gratuitous advice to Israelis after "perfunctory words of sympathy":

> …telling Israelis that no matter how many of their women and children are lying in pieces on the street, they must continue to negotiate with the very people who harbor and abet these murderers…

This, only about three years into the Oslo Accords!

Today, this obscenity is magnified manyfold, as the Road Map does not merely urge Israelis to negotiate with the terrorists, but imposes a "solution" on the Israeli government which not only rewards terrorism, but forces Israel to provide a "viable state" for the perpetrators, in the very heart of *Eretz Yisrael*. This is totally unprecedented in history!

After the Oslo Accords were declared officially a failure in September 2000, rejected by Arafat and his terrorist gangs following an offer which is not likely to be repeated in any future negotiations, after nearly three years of violence and suicide attacks, Israel is now being forced to forego independent decision by its government, and simply abide and submit to the will of foreign governments!

What we are witnessing is nothing less than collusion of Europe's anti-Semites with Arab-Muslim irredentism.[1]

---

1. See Bat Ye'or, *Eurabia*.

Chapter XXIV

More Propaganda and Incitement and Terrorism

I do not sleep very well these days. Once, late at night, I turned on the TV: CNN — Israel's "best friend" — is showing an exhibition of paintings. The images, sort of primitive, depict on one painting several cameo faces with head coverings — all look pretty much the same. Someone in the background explains to several adults and children that these people are "refugees." The voice explains that they want to sensitize small children to the plight of refugees who had to, or were forced (I no longer recall) to leave their homes with only what they had on their backs and what they could carry.

I look again. Are they speaking of European Jews during the Holocaust? It doesn't look like it. Are they describing Jews from Arab lands when several Arab countries forced eight hundred thousand Jewish people from their homes where they had lived for many centuries — with indeed nothing but the clothes on their backs and a suitcase? Apparently not.

They are referring to the Arabs — the poor "Palestinians" still languishing in "refugee" camps, for several decades now!

In disgust I shut off the TV, not because those Arabs, still in "refugee" camps, should not be pitied. Indeed they should… but the shameless Arab propaganda presented to the world, courtesy of CNN, implies that the Zionists (Nazis?) threw them out of their homes!

Are they sensitizing children and their parents or shamelessly indoctrinating them with this horrible calumny against the Jews?

Don't these people have any shame? Don't they read historical accounts of what really happened then?

Or are they also the product of indoctrination by Arab professors who teach "Middle East Studies"? These professors came to Western countries to do their utmost to convert Western students to their way of thinking, bringing with them their own propaganda and radicalism.

Are these journalists at CNN and other media the "useful idiots" decent journalists refer to? Are they also the product of the Left that paraded in support of Saddam Hussein in several European cities in February 2003?

Considering the radicalizing influence of Arab-Muslim students and professors over the past several decades on Western students, I suppose we should not be surprised that the hundreds of thousands of mainly young people — some with their children — came from far and wide to demonstrate in London, Rome and several other European capitols to protest the disarmament of the butcher of Baghdad! But what about the recent arrests of several Arabs, including two professors, on charges of terrorism and incitement to kill? How do these useful idiots understand that?

Do they believe — as one of the professors, Sami Al-Arian at the University of South Florida, claimed — that "it's all politics," despite the fact that the professor openly said during an interview that Israelis should be killed?

Do they believe, as some Arab-Muslim leaders claim, that innocent Arabs are being targeted because of 9/11, and that their "inalienable" right of freedom of speech is interfered with?

Do they really believe that inciting to hatred and murder qualifies as legitimate freedom of speech?

Don't they read news that many Muslim and/or Arab organizations in North America support — financially and otherwise — various terrorist groups involved in jihad?

Don't they hear that many Muslim clerics, both in the US and Britain, use their mosques to preach and incite hatred against infidels like themselves and recruit terrorists?

Should we generalize about all Muslims and/or Arabs? Certainly not. But isn't it interesting that those who complain the loudest about discrimination are the very ones who have been found involved in those criminal activities? And we are still waiting to hear from those Arab-Muslims who condemn the killing of civilians by jihadist terrorists!

According to a *Jerusalem Post* column by Caroline Glick (February 28, 2003), Professor Al-Arian, referred to above, was charged with:

> ...conspiracy to murder and maim people outside the US, conspiracy to provide material support and resources to Islamic

Jihad, extortion, obstruction of justice and immigration fraud
— charges that carry a sentence of life in prison…

But what is even more disturbing is the fact that Prof. Arian's "activities" were
known in the US since 1994:

> [J]ournalist and terrorism expert Steven Emerson produced [a
> PBS] documentary […showing] that the Islamic Jihad's head-
> quarters in the US has the same address as the World and Islam
> Studies Enterprise (WISE), a USF think-tank run by Arian.
>
> […] In the same 1994 documentary, Emerson showed Arian
> in action, making speeches in praise of jihad against Israel and
> suicide bombers.
>
> And yet the result of the documentary was that the liberal
> establishment of the US branded Emerson as a bigoted, Islam-
> bashing racist while Arian was feted as a civil rights trailblazer
> for Muslims in America.
>
> Emerson was banned from National Public Radio and Arian
> was invited to the White House on four separate occasions
> — three times by President Bill Clinton and once by President
> George W. Bush.
>
> […] Middle East studies professors, influential journalists
> and political organizers spanning the ideological spectrum
> attacked Arian's accusers as racist up until the week before his
> arrest.

Arian was suspended from the University of South Florida after an interview
with Fox TV news commentator Bill O'Reilly, "who questioned Arian about
past statements he made in favor of Jihad and suicide bombings in Israel."
O'Reilly "concluded the interview by commenting that if he were in the CIA
he would trail Arian '24 hours a day.'" The suspension of Arian was met with
protests from:

> …the political Left and in academia. The powerful and respected
> Middle East Studies Association wrote a letter to USF President
> Judy Genshaft in February 2002, decrying the suspension as an
> attack on academic freedom […and…] the basic first amend-
> ment right to freedom of speech.
>
> Here then, the most respected Middle East academic orga-

nization in the US went on record defending a suspected terrorist and decrying those who would view the issue as one of
law enforcement rather than of civil rights.

But Arian was also protected by highly placed political hacks. Arian was
reportedly the president of "an organization called the National Coalition to
Protect Political Freedoms [...among whose] members are front organizations for Islamic Jihad, Hizbullah, Hamas, the IRA, the Peruvian Shining Path
and the Basque separatists."

The *Jerusalem Post* article went on at some length about how political
advisors in the White House were influenced by political fund-raisers, etc.,
in supporting Islamic extremists and even some who had relatives involved
with an al-Qaeda leader. The article also decried the fact that those who shape
public opinion, such as Columbia University professor Joseph Massad, who
had recently (February 3, 2003) "published an article in Al-Ahram calling for
progressive circles to force the Palestinian leadership to again overtly embrace
the destruction of Israel and terrorism as official policy, are allowed to act
with impunity."

This, as if the Al-Arian case were not enough to prove that we live in an
upside-down world.

Professor Arian continues to be supported by all sorts of academics,
including the American Association of University Professors.

An editorial in the *Washington Post* on February 24, 2003, comments on
the affair that "the faculty union filed a grievance, alleging discrimination,
among other things"; others accused the university of "violating academic
freedom." The *Washington Post* reports that "Georgetown University Islam
scholar John L. Esposito canceled a scheduled speech at USF, saying it was
impossible for him to appear 'at a university that so clearly violates academic
freedom of one of its professors.'"

All in all, are we being persuaded by many "respected" academics that
academic freedom includes the open advocacy of murder and genocide?!

Meanwhile, a federal grand jury indicted Al-Arian and several others. The
editorial continues:

> But the government is alleging far more than that Al-Arian
> was a terrorist fundraiser [...] with considerable supporting
> detail that he was a top official of Islamic Jihad. [...H]e man-
> aged its money, held the wills of would-be suicide bombers,

disseminated statements claiming responsibility for attacks, helped formulate policy on behalf of the organization, and was in regular covert contact with its general secretary, spiritual leaders and other operatives.

The editorial further suggests that "people were too reflexive in their disbelief that an urbane, politically active professor — one who had been to the White House and who regularly talked to journalists — could be a genuine terrorist" and therefore misguidedly felt "that he must be a victim of university railroading and FBI abuses."

Arian and three other men are indicted by the grand jury on the following charges:

operating a criminal racketeering enterprise since 1984 [the year Al-Arian came to the US!] that supported Palestinian Islamic Jihad and with conspiracy to kill and maim people abroad, conspiracy to provide material support to the group, extortion, perjury and other charges.

The murder of one hundred innocent people, among them two Americans, is blamed on the organization Al-Arian allegedly participated in from 1984, the year he came to the US, an organization whose goal, according to a manifesto that was presented as evidence in the indictment, is "to destroy Israel and to end all Western influence in the region" (CNN, February 21, 2003).

There were many arrests reported in this time period, among them a student in Hamburg, Germany, convicted of aiding and abetting the 9/11 suicide bombers. He was convicted on 3,045 counts as accessory to murder and was sentenced to fifteen years in prison (apparently the maximum). The convicted man, Mournir el Mutassadeq, denied the charges and his lawyer demanded an acquittal, but he admitted training in one of Osama bin Laden's camps in Afghanistan. He also acknowledged knowing six key members of the suicide attack of 9/11, including the three pilots. He also signed the will of Mohamed Atta (the key terrorist of the 9/11 suicide attack), as well as approving the key elements of the attack.

Another interesting slew of arrests in Newark, NY, involved some sixty-two Middle Eastern students who were paying impostors to take exams for them in the months before September 11, 2001, among them, twenty-five Saudi students. From an AP report in the *Jerusalem Post*, March 3, 2003:

A spokesman for the US Attorney's Office in Newark said the cases were correctly listed as international terrorism. He said the high number really shouldn't be surprising. [...] "We can look right across the river and see what was the home of the World Trade Center [...] There were just a lot of cases developed here, given the proximity."

Some of the students found to have cheated on tests were pilots, among them Muhammed Al-Masari, who pleaded guilty to wire fraud. The employee of the Saudi-based Aramco oil company was learning to fly helicopters at the University of North Dakota last year. The AP report continues:

Of the two other New Jersey cases, one was the March 2, 2002 indictment of Ahmed Omar Saeed Sheikh for kidnapping *Wall Street Journal* reporter Daniel Pearl. Pearl's employer, Dow Jones Co., is based in New Jersey.

Saeed was sentenced to death by a Pakistani court, and probably will not be tried in the US.

The article also reported that "a Middle Eastern man" who pleaded guilty to using a false visa was sentenced to time already served and could be deported. Government and law enforcement officials do not seem to lay sufficient weight on false visas, a necessary tool of terrorists.

There were those who saw these arrests as "merely" cheating on exams, among them, Neil al-Juberi, a spokesman for the Saudi Arabian Embassy in Washington.

On March 3, 2003, the Israeli paper *Ha'aretz* reported an AP story out of Islamabad headlined "Alleged mastermind of 9/11 terror attack arrested in Pakistan." Khalid Sheikh Mohammed was thought to be very high-ranking in al-Qaeda. Obviously the US was extremely pleased with this arrest, apparently conducted by Pakistanis with the cooperation of the FBI (or vice versa). The US praised Pakistani President General Pervez Musharraf for his cooperation. Pakistan has handed over some 420 al-Qaeda and Taliban suspects to US custody, at this writing.

And so we see how perverted beliefs lead to false assumptions in academia and in the press, but meanwhile, there were all these cases of what can only be described as sleeper cells for al-Qaeda or other terrorist groups!

Chapter XXV

The Road Map to "Peace"

Early 2003. The US is getting ready for war with Iraq; it is issuing a final ultimatum to Saddam Hussein to go into exile in order to avoid unnecessary war and bloodshed.

It has become increasingly clear for some months that Saddam Hussein has no intention of disarming and declaring what, if anything, happened to the massive quantities of both chemical and biological weapons whose surrender the last UN resolution required.

UN Resolution 1441 called for immediate and complete disarmament of weapons of mass destruction, and giving a full and complete accounting of these weapons.

Saddam Hussein has hedged and used all manner of subterfuge, managing so far to avoid the "serious consequences" the UN resolution called for in case of noncompliance. (In all, fourteen UN resolutions were ignored by Saddam Hussein.) The "serious consequences" were clearly understood by most — if not all — as war.

But what if anything has the Road Map, referred to in the heading of this chapter, to do with Iraq and Saddam's failure to disarm? Very good question.

In the perverted logic of some leaders of the West, in order to initiate action against Saddam, the Arab leaders — who are not participating in this action against Saddam, and are in fact against it — must be mollified by sacrificing Israel!

The Road Map as currently constructed by the so-called "Quartet" does not reflect Bush's original commitment — that in order to make progress between Arabs and Jews, old hatreds would have to give way to reason and better understanding and cooperation, which in turn would lead to freedom and a better way of life for all Arabs and Jews. In Bush's vision, the first step was for the Arabs to abandon terrorism and blind hatred. He called openly for Arafat and his gang of terrorists to be replaced by leaders who are not tainted with terrorism.

What Mr. Bush fails to see is that such leaders, even if they exist, would not long survive, even if they ever got elected.

The Arabs of Judea and Samaria and Gaza, indoctrinated for decades with Arab hate propaganda and falsehoods, are still calling for Israel's destruction! As recently as this writing, tens of thousands of Arabs marched through the streets of Ramallah, Hebron and several parts of Gaza, chanting "Oh, beloved Saddam, bomb, bomb Tel Aviv!"

According to the *Jerusalem Post*, March 16, 2003, the protests were orga-nized by professional unions and took place Saturday, March 15. Many of the marchers expressed their readiness to join Iraq in their war against the US. American, Israeli and British flags were burned and the leaders of the three countries were denounced as enemies of Islam. The demonstrators urged Saddam Hussein to use chemical and biological weapons against the US and Israel!

So much for the peaceful intentions of the Arabs in Judea, Samaria and Gaza, and their readiness to live in peace and security in a state of their own, alongside Israel!

The Road Map, which calls for a "viable and credible state" for the "Palestinians," to be called "Palestine," chooses to ignore several critical realities:

1. There is no room on the tiny piece of land that is Israel — reduced from an intended fifty-five thousand square miles to less than eleven thousand square miles in its current reality — for two viable states.[1]
2. If a full-fledged Arab-PLO state were to be created in the heartland of Judea and Samaria, Israel would put itself in mortal danger and would become itself indefensible, let alone "viable."
3. The hoax of a "Palestinian people" (discussed elsewhere in this book) is nothing but an attempt to delegitimize the state of Israel; calling such a state "Palestine" is another way of saying that Israel is "illegitimate."

Israel replaced what the Romans decided to call "Palestine" (after they occu-pied the Jewish state), when the Jewish state was re-established in 1948, ending the cruel British Mandate for "Palestine." "Palestine" ceased to exist for all

---

1. See Appendices 2, 4 & 6.

intents and purposes. We must stop nurturing Arab propaganda by mind-lessly repeating it!

Creating a limited autonomy for local Arabs in areas containing an Arab majority appeared to be the only logical solution since Israel does not wish to rule over these people. This was tried and failed miserably, when Arafat and his gang of terrorists restarted a terrorist assault on Israeli civilians with renewed and increased violence. This terrorist war never let up from September 2000 to the present day!

Nearly every week, sometimes every day, there are countless victims of this endless blind hatred and violence.

How dare the Western world keep pressing Israel to make impossible concessions to the Arabs?

The Arabs already have vast areas of land given to them, following the end of WWI. An area of land approximating 5.3 million square miles is inhabited by the Arab nation. How much more land do they need? Is Israel's 10,800 square miles the only obstacle to peace?!

It should be made clear to all concerned that the most the Arabs of Judea and Samaria and Gaza can expect is a very limited autonomy comprising only the cities with an Arab majority. Again, a mere 10,800 square miles cannot hold two viable states, even if the Arabs had peaceful intentions, which clearly they do not!

As for the so-called "settlements," it must also be made perfectly clear to all concerned that these settlements are on Jewish land and they were designed to form an improved line of defense to what were previously indefensible borders. Israelis are fully entitled to settle the land everywhere, Judea and Samaria included.

Those who call for the closing of settlements either display their total ignorance of the reality on the ground, or willful blindness. Mr. Bush, as a friend of Israel and the Jewish people who knows the reality, should not ask Israel to commit suicide, even if he wants to help out his friend and ally, Mr. Blair.

It was Mr. Blair's country's — Britain's — initiative to push the Jewish state into these horrible and unacceptable borders. Israel must not now be pushed by Mr. Blair at the behest of the Arabs. The British have already done quite enough damage to Israel and its people!

UN Resolution 242 and "The Road Map to Peace"

Most Israelis consider the Oslo Peace Accords between Israel and the PA a dead letter — null and void — having witnessed how a peace accord based on the PLO foreswearing violence and terrorism in exchange for local autonomy and self government gave Israel nothing but bloodletting. Particularly after Arafat decided Israel had not sacrificed enough, and officially restarted terrorism in October 2000.

Nor was Oslo the first time that Israel offered the local Arabs of Judea, Samaria and Gaza a peaceful resolution. So far, to no avail.

One would think that Western leaders, and especially President Bush, would finally understand that the Arab-Israeli conflict is not about reasonable agreements with reasonable people. It is not even about the "refugees," nor even about compromise on land. If it were, there have been dozens of opportunities for the Arabs to address all their so-called grievances.

But what grievances, you might well ask?

It is the Arabs who committed aggression against Israel, not the other way around. And not once, but many times, through several wars of aggression, numerous violations of accords and countless acts of terrorism, since long before the Six Day Way of 1967.

To many people, it is abundantly clear that the Arabs do not want a peace accord with Israel, but rather to dismantle Israel piece by piece.

In every war of aggression against Israel by the Arabs since 1948, the Arabs promised to destroy the Jewish state, to drive the Jews into the sea. This language is about genocide, not about peace. And while two Arab countries finally signed peace accords with Israel — Egypt and Jordan — the hostility is ongoing both in the press and other media in those countries; a variety of spokesmen still advocate that nothing short of total destruction of the Jewish people will satisfy these, our "peaceful" neighbors.

The PLO, Hamas, Islamic Jihad and other assorted terrorist groups are by no means alone in their aim.

Most Arab states are still officially in a state of war with Israel. Most Arab states still support terrorism against Israel, and have for a very long time. It's only since the September 11, 2001, terrorist attack on the US that the Americans started investigating these various terrorist groups, and began to put pressure on their Arab benefactors (Saudi Arabia chief among them).

But whether the Americans fully appreciate (or care) to what extent the

Arab states are involved in keeping the misnamed "Palestinian"-Israeli conflict alive is still a somewhat open question.

On the one hand, we see the United States' unconditional and total war declared against al-Qaeda terrorists and its leaders since September 11, and on the other, the US attempt to hamper every necessary policy of Israel towards terrorist groups within its own territory; this appears at the very least a double standard. But many Israelis still wonder if there is more to this strange and incomprehensible phenomenon than meets the eye.

Do American leaders really believe that they can convert the Middle East's tyrannical rulers to democrats (or Islam to a peaceful religion) by appeasement, or is this just a game?

Do the American leaders really not understand the Arab policies toward Israel, or are they willing to sacrifice Israel on the altar of expediency and realpolitik as they play for time?

Israel is a friend and ally of the United States, but the Americans, during their various administrations since 1948, have treated Israel shabbily to say the least. Israel may be an ally, but it is not a subjugated vassal state, nor should it be treated as such.

Admittedly, there have been some good things the US government did for Israel, but more often than not, begrudgingly, and mostly at a very high price.

Supporting Israeli statehood at the UN vote in 1948 came only at the last moment.[1] In 1973, just before the Arab war against Israel, the US counseled Israel to ignore the Egyptian troops gathering at the border as if in preparation for war. In June of that year, Israel did call up the reserve force, and the Egyptians held their fire; but in October of that year, Israel, in deference to the US government, did not call up the reserves. On the holiest day of the Jewish people, Yom Kippur, the Egyptians and the Syrians attacked, and Israel suffered severe casualties on the Egyptian front particularly. The country was in dire danger, and yet the Americans withheld to the last moment military equipment which was, in fact, a matter of life and death.

There were other instances when the Americans withheld loan guarantees

---

1. The entire US administration was reportedly against it. Truman himself, who made the decision at the last moment, according to his diaries, was not exactly a friend of the Jewish people. He was moved to act based on some basic decency perhaps but, according to some, he was a man of his time — an anti-Semite.

and the like, as when Israel refused, under Yitzhak Shamir, to succumb to US dictates concerning Judea and Samaria. In 1991, too, following their first war against Iraq, the US, feeling obliged to repay the Arabs for being part of their so-called "coalition" against Iraq's invasion of Kuwait, tried to repay them by endangering Israel.

So the Road Map is really not a new invention. Only the name is new. This time, too, the US president feels obliged — not only to the Arabs who agreed to sit out the invasion of Iraq, but also to his friend, the British PM Blair, for being one of very few leaders who joined his coalition against Iraq — to repay them, not by ceding US territory, but Israel's territory!

We are often told that states have no friends, only interests. Israel is still a young state, and it's still suffering from the outmoded notion that allies could and should be friends. But Israel is learning the hard way. Israel too has interests. Its primary interest, its primary function is to protect its citizens and its borders!

This brings us to UN Resolution 242, accepted by all parties to the conflict in the aftermath of the 1967 war of aggression by several Arab states against Israel.

According to international law, the aggressor does not dictate the terms of cease-fire, armistice or indeed peace. Even if Israel did not have a historical right to Jerusalem, Judea and Samaria, international law dealing with aggression would confer on Israel superior rights over the territory.

UN Resolution 242 did not change any of these rights, but provided that Israel could, in exchange for a complete and comprehensive peace agreement with all its Arab neighbors, make some concession to its former enemies provided that such bilateral negotiations would be held in a spirit of reconciliation — without threats or coercion — and would lead to secure and recognized borders for Israel and its neighbors.

Such negotiation of course never took place. On the contrary, the Khartoum Conference of the Arab States, August 29-September 1, 1967, issued the three infamous "no's": (1) no negotiations (2) no recognition, and (3) no peace with the state of Israel!

Even during the Egyptian-Israeli negotiations (in 1977–79), Egyptian President Anwar Sadat attempted to dictate the terms of a peace treaty. The US, under President Jimmy Carter, twisted Israeli arms. Israeli Prime Minister Menachem Begin resisted as best he could — he had international law on his side, but not the US president.

Israel was quite prepared to give the Egyptians the Sinai Peninsula, under certain conditions and guarantees. But Jerusalem, Judea and Samaria are quite a different matter. In the end, Israel got nothing, just a piece of paper, and a very cold peace. Sadat was assassinated by an Islamic faction soon thereafter. His successor, Hosni Mubarak, no less sly, coached Arafat how best to extract concessions from the Israelis during the Oslo process while Arafat's terrorists smuggled illegal arms over the Egyptian border, in clear violation not only of Oslo, but of the Israel-Egypt Peace Treaty!

As for Judea and Samaria, these were not even discussed in UN Resolution 242. The Jordanian aggressor had no historical or legal rights to Judea and Samaria in the first place, and the PLO was not even part of the equation.

The Arab population in the areas grew through illegal infiltration, marriage with outside partners, etc., not merely by natural growth.

Israel, not wishing to lord over this Arab population of Judea and Samaria and Gaza, offered various compromises to the Arabs since 1967, always getting the belligerent answer "no negotiations, no recognition, and no peace" from the Arab League.

There has not been much change in Arab-Muslim attitudes toward Israel even despite the peace treaty with Egypt, which got something very tangible for nothing. The peace treaty with Jordan followed the Oslo process where again the Arabs stood to win by weakening Israel. The hostile propaganda against Israel continues in both Egypt and Jordan, and not "merely" by the local Arab population in Judea and Samaria. The PA says it is using Jordanian schoolbooks when confronted about the hate propaganda in those books instilling hatred and violence against Israel in impressionable young Arab minds!

Considering the Arab "education system," is it any wonder that 70 to 80 percent of the population of Judea, Samaria and Gaza, most of whom were subjected to anti-Israel indoctrination during the half-century they were forced by the Arabs to remain in the "refugee" camps, support terrorism and suicide bombers against Israel?

But Israel should not have tolerated such a hostile population dedicated to its destruction. Israel does not owe these people anything. It certainly does not owe them land historically Israel's, and it does not owe them a state.

What other country would be asked to do such a preposterous thing?

History — notwithstanding vile Arab propaganda regarding Judea and Samaria — is clear, and so is international law.

Let the countries that asked these people to leave their homes take them back. Those Arab states bear full responsibility for the welfare of these people — now scandalously allowed to remain "refugees" for three generations — and their resettlement.

Many Arab countries also bear the responsibility for the expulsion of Jewish families from their homes in their countries, families who lived there from time immemorial, long before the creation of Islam. These refugees, who were forced to leave all of their belongings and much of their way of life behind, were long forgotten in the shuffle.

Arab propaganda made a case for "Palestinian refugees," bogus refugees who left Israel in 1948 of their own accord, despite Israel's leaders' urging them to stay. Israel attempted several times to resettle these "refugees" in proper housing — to no avail — they preferred to listen to Arab leaders who told them to stay in miserable refugee camps, which by now have turned into towns (though slum towns, to be sure).

Israel built five universities for the local Arabs, only to see them turned into hotbeds for terrorist activity, no different than the "refugee camps." Any other country would deport such hostile people, or force those who wish to stay to swear an oath of allegiance and to obey the laws of the state.

The Americans fight terrorism halfway across the world in Afghanistan, following September 11. Israel is living daily with terrorist attacks — on its civilian population — people indoctrinated from early childhood to become killers, not unlike the Hitler Youth of the Nazi era in Germany. Israel has every right to defend its citizens against this menace, which presents a clear and present danger!

Neither the US president Mr. Bush nor anyone else has the right to impose on Israel a solution not of its own making, and not in its best national interest.

Mr. Bush should be reminded that Israel is a sovereign state, with all the rights that implies. Israel is not the aggressor in the Arab-Israeli conflict, and the US has no right to force its surrender.

Bush at Auschwitz and the Road Map to National Catastrophe

We tend to think that principled men possess a moral compass that motivates their actions. George W. Bush, the US president, is seen by many as a man motivated by strong moral principles, and yet…

During his visit to Auschwitz with his wife (while on his way to several summit meetings dealing with his newly adopted "peace initiative," the Road Map), Mr. Bush was described as visibly shaken. He was seen wiping away tears. In pictures of him and his wife in front of a crematorium, he appeared to be stunned. Their guided tour included a walk to a gas chamber. Indeed, no decent human being could see the remnants of these horrors and not be shaken.

At the end of the tour Bush exclaimed that evil must be fought, and in the guest book he wrote these words: "Never again," and signed his name to it. Strangely, the rest of the message written beforehand in the guest book referred to the suffering of the "Polish people."

Yes, the Polish people have suffered during the Nazi occupation, and yes, there were even some Polish political prisoners in Auschwitz. But the tall piles of baby shoes that Mr. Bush saw during the tour of Auschwitz once belonged to Jewish babies and children, not Polish children! The mounds of hair that Mr. Bush saw once belonged to Jewish women, who, together with their babies and children, were murdered in cold blood in those very gas chambers!

Anything of material value to the Germans, even the hair of their victims, was taken from them while they were still alive. Gold teeth were extracted after death! Nothing was wasted by these barbarians, except human life!

Did I miss something in Bush's speech at Auschwitz as it was reported? Did he in fact make some reference to the fact that all the victims of the Nazi "Final Solution" in Auschwitz, in Birkenau, in Treblinka, in Maidanek, in Sobibor, in Babi Yar, in Chelmno and other less well known places, were Jewish people deliberately and mercilessly murdered?

Perhaps I am nitpicking here. He was moved, he reacted as any decent human being would. But I am perturbed that whoever wrote in the guest book at Auschwitz for Mr. Bush about the "suffering of the Polish people" somehow, whether deliberately or not, distorted history yet again.

I don't subscribe to the idea that victimhood is something to be proud of — although we Jews are often wrongfully accused of that. But whom does it serve to misrepresent reality — as tragic and horrible as it was?

I am always concerned when reality and truth are misrepresented, whether in deliberate malicious propaganda such as that of the Nazis, which led the way to Hitler's "Final Solution to the Jewish Question," or the more recent

Arab propaganda which claims that the Jewish people have no claim and no rights to Jerusalem, to the Jewish Temple Mount or *Eretz Yisrael*, the Land of Israel.

These claims contradicting history, as preposterous as they are, have again tragic consequences for our people.

Bush, who said at Auschwitz, "Never again," is in fact, once again, endangering the Jewish people by demanding the creation of yet another Arab state on this tiny remnant of *Eretz Yisrael*, falsely proposing to call itself "Palestine."

"Palestine" — *Eretz Yisrael* — was already wrongly divided by our British "protectors" who promised to restore the Jewish people to their Land after being given the confidence to carry out the Mandate by the Jewish people and the League of Nations.

The Land of Israel is now all of 20 percent of Palestine, thanks to the betrayal of the British whose agenda after the Balfour Declaration may have been simply to dominate the region, while playing the power broker between Arabs and Jews.

The 80 percent of the Land which was given to create yet another Arab state even less populated than the part west of the Jordan River. This action taken by the British defies logic.

The population of that area thereafter increased by leaps and bounds, the majority claiming to be "Palestinians." Where did they all come from?

Had the British lived up to the Balfour Declaration and their own solemn undertaking to bring the Jewish people back to their own Land, millions of Jewish people could have come to *Eretz Yisrael* between 1919 and 1939. The existing community in *Eretz Yisrael* pleaded with the British Mandatory that more hands were necessary for work, as the League of Nations provided that the land should be settled closely. The British claimed falsely that only a trickle of new people could be absorbed.

And so, twenty crucial years were wasted while the British played up to the Arabs. Even after the 1939 outbreak of World War II, there were still many possibilities to save the Jews of Europe. But even those ships with refugees from Europe were mercilessly turned away practically from the very shores of the Land! British perfidy knew no bounds!

I believe that most Jews from Europe could have been saved had the British lived up to their solemn undertaking to restore the Jewish people to their Land. The League of Nations Mandate provided for just that. There were no provisions to create another Arab state in Palestine — *Eretz Yisrael* — not even on the East Bank of Jordan, let alone yet another one on the remaining 20 percent of the Land of Israel.

And now, Mr. Bush is participating in the British perfidy. This, after his solemn declaration at Auschwitz among the ashes of millions of Jewish men, women and children — Never again!

What could possibly motivate Mr. Bush, a seemingly upright human being with a heart, to sacrifice Jewish security in our own Land?

It cannot be overemphasized: there is no room for "two viable states" in this already once divided *Eretz Yisrael*!

Mr. Bush fights terrorism half a world away, in the aftermath of the September 11 terrorist attack on the US — yet Israel is not "allowed" to fight terrorism in its own land! Does Israel, a sovereign nation, require permission to defend itself?

Clearly in a sane world it would not. No sovereign country requires permission for self-defense, for defense of its own population. Why is Israel treated differently?

Because we are Jews?

Because we live in a perverted world, where the United Nations created after the defeat of Nazism — after the genocide perpetrated against our people — which promised to strive for a different future, was itself perverted by Arab manipulation. Over several decades, after several aggressive wars against Israel, after decades of Arab-sponsored terrorism, all of which was designed to weaken and eradicate the Jewish state and its people in its own land, the Arabs discovered the "oil weapon."

Using the halls of the UN, the Arabs cajoled, blackmailed and otherwise "convinced" nations dependent on Arab oil to toe the line — or else.

And so, the automatic majority at the UN was born! Truth and reality no longer matter, and anti-Israel, anti-Semitic propaganda is now openly proclaimed from the very forum that sought to prevent it. To grasp the extent to which this evil has permeated the United Nations one has only to look at some if its many resolutions over the years as well as recent events.

Syria — itself in noncompliance for harboring and supporting terrorist organizations that regularly attack Israel — has recently been elected to preside over the Security Council while it debated Iraq's noncompliance with UN resolutions! (These were Security Council resolutions dating back a dozen years to the Gulf War, when Iraq was defeated after invading Kuwait. The outcome of that war obliged Iraq to submit to inspections for weapons of mass destruction.)

History records that all of those UN resolutions were defiantly disobeyed by Iraq, making a mockery not only of the inspections, but of the UN itself. The strange bedfellows that now occupy the Security Council could not decide how to exact compliance from Iraq, and eventually the US, exasperated, went to war to unseat the Iraqi regime and prevent Iraq from using its weapons of mass destruction.

During Iraq's war with Iran, such weapons were in fact used against Iran's soldiers. These weapons were used as well on Iraqi Kurds — men, women and children! And during the Gulf War (1991) Iraq threatened that it would use such weapons on Israel, despite the fact that Israel was not involved in the so-called coalition that included several Arab countries. Israel was attacked with scud missiles in several cities. Despite the threats, the scuds were not armed with chemical weapons. Nonetheless, the Israeli population was forced to prepare for chemical warfare. This, while the US government forced the Israeli government to refrain from self-defense!

During the second US-led war against Iraq, Iraq threatened again to attack Israel, despite Israel's non-involvement in this war as well. The Israeli population was again obliged to prepare for the worst. Masks were again distributed as in the Gulf War of 1991, sealed rooms were prepared as before although their efficacy was less than certain. The good sports and the stoics that the Jewish people have become in the course of various challenges, even now in their own land, played their part. The condition of uncertainty lasted months while the US prepared for war.

It is believed that the US asked Israel again, even if attacked, not to respond!

One is beginning to understand, following the same line of logic, why the US can fight its enemies, including terrorists, halfway across the globe, but Israel — Israel cannot be allowed to defend itself against terrorism even in its own land. Now, according to the wisdom not only of the Europeans, the Brits and the Russians, but even the Americans, Israel is obliged not only to negotiate with the terrorists, but reward them by dividing the land yet again to create a terrorist state in its very heartland — in Judea and Samaria!

When the Jewish people returned to our land and re-established the State of Israel, we had every reason to expect to be treated as any other sovereign

nation. But no, apparently we are treated still as "the Jew" whose very existence poses a problem!

Even our best friends, the US (in fact our only friend except for Micronesia),
make demands of our leaders that can only lead to a catastrophe. Mr. Bush
knows the lay of the land; he has seen it with his own eyes. Years before Mr.
Bush became the president of the US, while visiting Israel, he was taken on a
helicopter ride over the territory of Judea and Samaria by Mr. Sharon, then
the minister of defense. Mr. Sharon, no doubt, pointed out to Mr. Bush how
vulnerable Israel's borders were prior to 1967. Anyone, even with a modicum
of knowledge of geography and topography of the land of Israel, even without
a bird's-eye view, can appreciate Israel's position.

What in heaven's name, then, prompted Mr. Bush to make it his "personal
commitment" to divide our Land and "pledge" to create a "Palestinian" state
"living side by side with Israel in peace and security"?!

What right does Mr. Bush or the US government have to pledge our land
to a terrorist entity? Or any entity, for that matter?

Israel tried under pressure to create an autonomous area for the Arabs in
towns where there is an Arab majority… but a state with all the dangers that
entails?

In spite of all the hype of "millions" of Palestinian Arabs living in Judea
and Samaria, flying over the area I have seen vast areas of state-owned empty
land. Vast only to the extent that in this relatively small area, there can be
"vast" empty land. Standing on high ground at the river Jordan, one can
clearly see Tel-Aviv!

The Judean hills, the Judean desert, all historically Jewish land, why would
we be asked to give up to anybody uninhabited state-owned Jewish land? I
don't recall in recent or ancient history anyone volunteering to give up their
land to a hostile people.

Would America? Would Canada? Would the British? (Even though at least
the Irish have some legitimate claim to Ireland.) The so-called "Palestinians"
are simply Arabs. A hostile terrorist entity, who, together with their Arab
brothers from at least five Arab states, collaborated in attacking Israel again
and again in several wars of Arab aggression.

Since when is aggression to be rewarded with land not their own?!

The Arabs apparently believe that by inflating their numbers, the claims of
the so-called "Palestinian" will be more legitimate. And wonder of wonders,

somehow the world, for the most part, bought this propaganda hook, line and sinker.

But Mr. Bush, who stands for Justice and Democracy and against Evil, should he not be able — together with his many advisors — to see through this hoax and the subterfuge?

The Arab war against Israel has never ended; we see it at the UN, we see it in their official media. The "Palestinians" are just another way of waging war against Israel — a Trojan horse.

The Road Map to peace and the creation of a "Palestinian" state on Israel's historical land is not only a clever trap against Israel, but also a means to delegitimize the Jewish state. If "the Palestinians" create a state called "Palestine," then who or what is Israel?

"Palestine" ceased to exist when the Jewish people came back to their Land and re-established their state — the State of Israel. But reality never got in the way of propagandists and Israel's detractors.

Tony Blair, the British prime minister, decided to extract a price from Mr. Bush for being his only major ally in the war against Iraq. In a style reminiscent of Britain in the days of the Mandate, Tony Blair didn't ask for American land, but for Jewish land.

Someone should have told Mr. Bush it was not his land to give.

But what can one expect in an upside-down world, where Syria not only sat as the president of the Security Council and became the chair of the Disarmament Commission, but Libya was appointed to chair the UN Human Rights Commission!

Does all that mean that even decent men can be made to do evil, even if not intended? And does it mean that Israel, a sovereign state, has to agree to its own destruction?

Even Decent Men...

What is one to make of the US president's actions regarding the Road Map in view of his behavior at Auschwitz?

The president, viewing some of the evidence at Auschwitz, is said to have been seen wiping away tears. The remnant of evidence of the horror perpetrated at Auschwitz, where at least three million Jewish men, women and children were systematically put to death, murdered in cold blood by a regime that justified this horrific crime by vilifying and demonizing the entire Jewish people, is seen, witnessed, by mounds of children's shoes and women's hair, and suitcases that once belonged to living, breathing human beings.

These people were brought to Auschwitz from the four corners of Nazi-occupied Europe not knowing what this diabolical place was, not knowing what to expect nor what their tormentors intended for them. I myself never suspected what would greet me in Auscwhitz when I was brought there. The Nazis were very clever at keeping their true intentions secret.

Any decent person can easily imagine the agony and humiliation, the brutality these people were put through, even before their horrific agonizing death in the gas chambers of Auschwitz.

What was going through Mr. Bush's mind, when he wrote the words "Never again" in the Auschwitz guest book?

How does one square his words at Auschwitz with his deeds immediately afterwards regarding the Road Map, and the two summit meetings in the Middle East that dealt with it?

The first meeting at Sharm el-Sheikh with leaders of several Arab countries, where Bush is said to have expected some gesture of coexistence towards Israel, yielded nothing at all. Quite the contrary; Saudi Arabia threatened to boycott the meeting if Israel were to be invited.

So much for goodwill gestures, coexistence and confidence-building.

Mr. Bush said nothing following this failed attempt at Sharm el-Sheikh on "the Road Map to peace."

The next step was Aqaba, the southernmost tip of Jordan on the sea. The irony that Israel, in Jordan of all places — part of the original Mandate, which was to *restore* the Jewish Homeland — was forced to agree to give away to the Arabs Judea and Samaria — still *more* of the land originally mandated for the Jewish homeland — to build yet another Arab state, could not escape anyone...

Some writers, in the *Jerusalem Post* particularly, referred to this "Road Map" as the Arab war of "stages," pointing out yet again that during Jordan's illegal annexation of Judea and Samaria following the Arab war of aggression against Israel in 1948, no one spoke of creating a "Palestinian" state on that territory.

Why would the US government force Israel to endanger the security of its citizens in making this demand to create an enemy state in the very heart of Israel? Bush and his many sophisticated advisers know full well the danger this Road Map to disaster poses to Israel; why then the sophistry and the claim that the US government and its president are dedicated to creating peace between Israel and its Arab neighbors?

Many, if not most Israelis, were angry and disappointed at their prime minister (Mr. Sharon) for caving in to American pressure. There was no justification for American pressure on Israel to create an Arab state, openly dedicated to its destruction.

The ongoing propaganda and terrorism isn't just the work of a few terrorist gangs. Seventy percent — some surveys say eighty percent — of the Arab population in Judea, Samaria and Gaza fully support terrorist attacks on Israel, including suicide terrorist bombers!

Considering the vile ongoing propaganda and vilification of Jews and Israel in the schools and local media, these people are not ready for peace any time soon, and might not be ready for many generations even if propaganda were to stop today.

What then is Mr. Bush thinking? What makes him say that a democratic, peaceful "Palestine" can exist side by side with Israel? A limited autonomy would have been quite sufficient, but not a state.

Admittedly, there is a problem what to do with a large, hostile population — whatever its real number. The Arab states that expelled some seven to eight hundred thousand Jewish people, who had lived there from time immemorial as a peaceful minority, didn't have any such qualms in 1948–53, after confiscating their property!

No one at the UN ever raised an eyebrow, let alone helped these genuine refugees to resettle, whereas the bogus Arab "refugees" are still permitted to live off the public purse which the UN exacts from its member states. Why are we Jewish people treated differently even now when we have finally returned to our own homeland, even after the horrors of the Holocaust?

Why would the US president force Israel into indefensible borders, ceding Israel's own land to what is now a terrorist entity sworn to Israel's destruction?

Never again?

Just as the Nazi regime used vile propaganda against the Jewish people in order to pave the way to mass murder, so do the Arab states — all the Arab states, not just the "Palestinians" — vilify and demonize the Jewish people, calling for our destruction.

Arab propagandists tried to persuade the world that even 9/11 happened because of the Arab-Israeli conflict (or better yet, that it was actually the work of the Jews); in other words, if the Americans were to abandon Israel, or, better yet, deliver Israel on a silver platter to its enemies, then they, the Americans, would be safe from Arab-Muslim terrorism.

Well, think again. When Hitler started his campaign against the Jewish people, the world did nothing, thinking it was "only the Jews." Before long, all of Europe was under Nazi occupation, and Hitler showed that he had even greater designs.

"All it takes for evil to triumph is for good people to do nothing," as it has been said after the devastation of WWII and the Holocaust.

Chapter XXVI

More Arab Propaganda and Incitement!

Read this item from the *Jerusalem Post*, August 3, 2003, under the headline: "Palestinian preachers accuse Israel of destroying Aksa Mosque":

> A Palestinian preacher on Friday told Muslim worshipers in Gaza City that the Israelis have begun "destroying the Aksa Mosque," and urged them to move quickly to save the holy sites in Jerusalem. The sermon was broadcast live on Palestine TV's satellite station.

The preacher, Sheikh Ibrahim Idris, said that a special committee set up by the Wakf:

> ...has decided to highlight the "dangers and threats" facing the Aksa Mosque by instructing preachers to raise the issue in Friday sermons.
> "This is the most dangerous phase of the Arab nation and the Palestinian cause," Idris declared.

The propaganda and incitement in the sermon has no factual basis, needless to say, but the choice of words is interesting: "most dangerous phase" ... "the Arab nation" ... "the Palestinian cause."

The preacher went on at length in the same vein: "the Aqsa Mosque is suffering" and "crying out from under the yoke of occupation." He continued:

> "We appeal to all the honorable people in the Arab and Muslim world to devote their sermons this month to the blessed Aksa Mosque — to participate in defending the mosque and the holy

sites, together with the Palestinians and the rest of the Arab and Muslim world."

He stressed "the significance of the Aksa" to "the Arab and Muslim world" and the "duty to defend Islam's holy sites." "This," he declared:

> "…is the duty not only of the people of Palestine, but also anyone who believes that there is no God but Allah… [T]he Aksa Mosque is being assaulted every day…the mosque is now being subjected to demolition — a programmed and organized demolition. The occupation is destroying the blessed Aksa Mosque!"
>
> The preacher concluded his sermon by making an emotional plea to the Muslims to rescue the Aksa Mosque. "O, Muslims! They (Israelis) are working towards destroying the mosque under the pretext of searching for the purported Temple."

A call to a holy war if there ever was one. And not "merely" to the "Palestinians," but all of the Muslim world.

The preacher went on at some length calling on Muslims to save the mosque from "desecration" claiming again falsely that "they are depriving the people of Palestine from entering through its gates…"

> "The Aksa Mosque is crying out to you, O, Muslims, O, believers, save it …Isn't there a (Muslim Caliph) Omar (Ibn al Khatab) amongst you? Isn't there a (Muslim warrior) Salah Eddin amongst you? […] Doesn't the Aksa Mosque deserve that we sacrifice — all what is dear and precious to us in order to liberate it and defend its dignity?"

The *Jerusalem Post* also reported that:

> At the same time, a similar sermon was delivered in Jerusalem by Sheikh Jusef Abu Sneineh. He claimed that while Islam was under attack from the entire world, Israel has been trying to divide the Temple Mount.
>
> According to the sermon, which was broadcast live on the Palestinian Authority's "Voice of Palestine," excavation work carried out by Israel beneath the Temple Mount is aimed at destroying the Aksa Mosque.

"The Arab and Muslim world are sleeping while the Palestinians are left alone to defend the mosque as if it was their property alone," he told thousands of Muslims attending Friday prayers at the Aksa Mosque.

Here again, we can glean from the phrase "as if it was their property alone" the truth that this isn't about "the rights of the 'Palestinian'" in Jerusalem and elsewhere in *Eretz Yisrael*, but renewal of conquest of long ago. Again, shameless lies do not get in the way of Arab-Muslim incitement to violence.

The preacher in Gaza City is telling the world — via satellite, no less — that not only is the Aksa Mosque in immediate dire danger of destruction, but that the gates of the Aksa are closed to the *people of Palestine*. At the same time, thousands are attending the Aksa Mosque, listening to another preacher appealing to the Arab-Muslim world which is "sleeping" while the "Palestinians are left alone to defend the mosque"!

Interesting usage of words, *as if it was their property alone*!

In case anyone was thinking that the Road Map might finally lead to peace, that the Arabs too might be tired of bloodshed, no; here is a new bloodcurdling call to holy war — jihad — veiled in the guise of a mosque in imminent danger of being destroyed by the "infidel enemy."

The fact remains that since the so-called "Aksa Intifada" started in September-October 2000, there have not been any excavations conducted either under or near the Temple Mount. Due to the violence, the Israeli government simply halted all archaeological digs in the area.

But on the contrary, it was the Arabs who undertook wholesale excavations under the Mosque and built a whole new mosque under the Temple Mount. An area called Solomon's Stables is now a full-fledged mosque!

In fact, Israeli and other archaeologists complained that while the Arabs were excavating underground, precious artifacts from the site may have been lost forever as the debris from the excavation was simply dumped onto garbage sites!

Prior to the September-October 2000 suspension of all excavation at the Temple Mount area, archaeologists were, in fact, looking for remnants of the First and Second Temple era, always being careful not to disturb other religious holy sites.

Visits to the Temple Mount were also suspended by the government following the outbreak of violence in 2000, and only in the summer of 2003 were small groups of tourists, as well as some local Christians and Jews, allowed to visit the Temple Mount.

The terrorist chieftain Arafat soon after proclaimed it a "crime" to allow non-Muslims to visit the Temple Mount. And then only a few days after Arafat's "crime" proclamation came this claim that it is Israel that is "endangering" the Aksa Mosque.

It is interesting to note the language used in the sermon I referred to above: "*This is the most dangerous phase of the Arab nation and the Palestinian cause.*" This is all one sentence, but I find the language interesting inasmuch as it refers to "the Arab nation," rather than the "Palestinian nation," and "the Palestinian cause." Clearly, the "Palestinian cause" is the Arab nations' cause, as it becomes clear even in this propaganda piece.

The appeal to all Arabs and Muslims makes it further clear that this is a holy war — jihad against Israel, not because the Arabs need a "special" state for the "Palestinians." The "cause" of "Palestinians" is not simply a state but a religious "obligation," which according to the sermon in Gaza, affects every Arab and every Muslim the world over. The sermon at the Aksa Mosque makes it clear that the Aksa Mosque is not the "Palestinians'" "alone" and thus the "Palestinians" should not be fighting that "cause" alone.

All in all, this is most revealing and interesting; if only it were not wrought with danger.

The world is led to believe that the Arab world will be at peace with Israel if only the "Palestinians" have a state of their own. Clearly that is not the case, nor was it ever.

Even if the Arab and Muslim world do not immediately pick up the tools of war and rush to the "defense" of the "crying" and the "about to be destroyed" Aksa Mosque, there will surely be a new cadre of suicide bombers responding to this "desperate" and "urgent" call, which thanks to modern technology, will be broadcast around the world on TV and the Internet.

And this, when we were told that incitement to violence and terrorism, at least on PA TV, has been slightly toned down!

Meanwhile, we saw on Israeli TV Channel 10, Israeli Arab children in summer camps with their elders, using the same type of propaganda as their "Palestinian" Arab cousins.

The camp in the Galilee was shut down by police on July 31, 2003, following allegations that the camp organizers were inciting youngsters against the state and promulgating extremism (the *Jerusalem Post* reported August 1, 2003).

The action was taken following an investigative report on Channel 10 Israel News about activities of the summer camp "The Return," which, according to the *Jerusalem Post* is run by the radical "Sons of the Village" movement. The *Jerusalem Post* further reported that the police confirmed the raid took place due to the report on Channel 10.

Tents in the camp were named after refugee camps, and the children were taught about heads of terrorist organizations. The elementary school children reportedly started the morning singing with the "Palestinian" anthem and later sang other songs with words made up to fit popular tunes. One chorus, according to the report, went: "We don't want flour or sardines — we want bombs."

This, from Israeli Arab children who do not live in "refugee" camps, nor experience any hardship; their family's quality of life is on a par with other Israelis.

Apparently the camp counselors' literature included the following quote: "It is best to die as a martyr for your homeland, for your nation, for your land from whence you came and where you will go."

The question that one has to ask is which homeland, which nation, which land did they come from, and where do they wish to go now?

The Arab children of the village live in their own homes, where they have lived at least for some time. They were not displaced. Where their ancestors came from prior to the reestablishment of the state of Israel is still an open question.

To plant the seeds of hatred and violence and "martyrdom" in the minds of these young and impressionable children is in itself a crime.

Apparently, according to the same *Jerusalem Post* report, local residents of the village of Kabul identified the camp's organizers as outsiders. The local council head Ali Rian told the *Jerusalem Post* (July 31, 2003): "We don't want this sort of thing in Kabul."

He said they don't want these outsiders in their village.

> "We don't want them here and we don't want their activities, which besmirch the good name of the village and our residents.
>
> "We are all citizens of the State and we have to live alongside one another in peace and harmony. I won't tolerate any incite-

> ment (against the state) or anything that disrupts the good ties
> we have developed with our (Jewish) neighbors."

Would that this were so. But still, the children who are sent to the summer camp must have been sent by their parents, one has to assume. Is coercion, reward or blackmail being used against those parents?

The children — I happened to see the report on Channel 10 — looked quite happy and even relaxed; one girl was proudly showing off a pendant she was wearing around her neck depicting the "state of Palestine" encompassing all of Israel and Judea, Samaria and Gaza!

The girl could not have been more than nine or ten years old. Where are the parents — if they claim to be citizens of the state of Israel — who are against incitement and want to live in peace and harmony with other Israelis? Surely it could not possibly escape their attention what their children are saying, especially when wearing symbols of Israel's destruction, which is still the goal of their Arab cousins!

We can only hope that this is not a "Fifth Column" in the making.

◆ ◆ ◆

The hypocrisy of the proponents of the Road Map is gradually coming into focus, as more and more of the support of even the most hardy "true believers" in the "peace" and "coexistence" with the Arabs begins to crumble in the dust.

People are beginning to see that since the declared *hudna*, not a day has passed without violence of one kind or another. Of course we have to keep reminding ourselves that the *hudna* (temporary ceasefire) was not between the Arabs and Israel, but simply between the various factions of the terrorists.

This *hudna* includes — or was supposed to — all factions of the PLO (PA), but some factions claimed even early on that they were not told to be part of the *hudna*!

During the six-week period prior to the two suicide bombings on August 12, 2003, which took two Israeli lives and left some fourteen wounded — some gravely — there were at least two hundred incidents of violence, including three kidnappings, many roadside shootings, and one attack on an Israeli home where a suicide terrorist bomber blew himself up killing an elderly woman and injuring her two grandchildren. In Israel this is considered as "low level violence."

Some of the attacks were "allegedly" carried out by so-called "splinter" groups, which did not adhere to the *hudna*.

But even following the two suicide bombings on August 12 — one of which Hamas claimed as their own — the Hamas terrorists announced that they "remain committed" to the *hudna*, through to its September 29 "expiration" date! (*Jerusalem Post*, August 13, 2003, front page: "Attacks claimed by Hamas, Fatah shatter six-week-old *hudna*").

Expiration date? And then what?

What a preposterous thought, that terrorists can order or decide to call temporary ceasefires with a predetermined date of expiry, and continue what some call "low level violence" at will as part of a peace process. While claiming "credit" for the suicide bombing, they "remain committed" to the *hudna*!

The other terrorist suicide bombing was claimed by the terrorist Fatah's "al-Aqsa Martyrs' Brigades" — Arafat's own — which denounced both the Road Map and the *hudna*.

US Secretary of State Colin Powell said on August 13, 2003, only one day after the two terrorist attacks, that the "Road Map is still on track."

What will it take to convince the US State Department, and Mr. Powell, that one cannot expect "democracy" and peace from people who support terrorism against civilians, and do not know the meaning of the word "law"? Democracy is not part of their lexicon, nor is peace. The overwhelming hatred that permeates Arab society is fed by decades of propaganda nurtured throughout Arab societies, not merely "Palestinians."

People — including leaders of the Western world — appear to once again practice amnesia. Everyone appears not to remember that all the wars between Arabs and Israel were of Arab aggression.

When "Palestinians" claim that Israel "stole their land," along with other concoctions, the Western leaders remain mum and appear to have conveniently forgotten not only the history and geography of the Middle East, but also the fact that the "Palestinians" were not even officially part of the Arab-Israeli conflict!

Then what in heaven's name justifies the creation of yet another Arab state on this tiny, tiny land already once divided?

Unless the leaders of the Western world want the world to believe the Arab propaganda that "Israel stole Arab land," not vice versa, then there cannot possibly be any justification for creating an Arab State called of all things "Palestine" on the territory of the historical land of Israel.

Why Israelis go along with this charade is beyond comprehension.

Israelis must have a terribly short memory. They even seem dismayed that the Arabs of Judea, Samaria and Gaza, instead of being grateful that Israel released a considerable number of prisoners as a gesture of goodwill — not even required under the Road Map — are, instead, protesting that all terrorists must be released! And here we naïve folks thought that all the remaining terrorists should be arrested instead!

Some Israelis still do not seem to understand that this is not about goodwill, or accommodation, or even giving away your own land in order to make peace. People who have for decades been fed propaganda that "Israel stole their land" are not going to be satisfied, show gratitude, or live in peace.

Whatever Israel is willing to give, they want more; they are infused with anger and even righteous indignation, that we do not do their bidding! And no wonder; they appear to believe their own falsehood and propaganda. This propaganda is still fed, and passions still more inflamed, when some of their leaders, not satisfied with a new state of their own, demand the "right of return."

Nabil Sha'ath, PA "foreign minister" said August 16, 2003, that the "right of return" of Palestinian "refugees" to their former homes inside Israel is no longer an "illusion": "We see no solution for our people in Lebanon other than the right of return to their homeland. [...] There is no other political solution and the right of return to the homeland is guaranteed," he said (*Jerusalem Post*, August 17, 2003).

Subsequently, spin doctors tried to soften the language, saying that Sha'ath did not know that his statements would be quoted by international news agencies (*Jerusalem Post,* August 19, 2003, p. 11). At another gathering of Arabs in Ramallah, the same *Jerusalem Post article* quoted some Arab leaders, emboldened by Sha'ath, as saying in a statement "that there would never be a just and comprehensive peace in the Middle East unless all refugees are permitted to return to their original homes inside Israel."

A PLO spokesman said the gathering "came to reaffirm the Palestinian people's determination to hold on to the right of return" and that the "Palestinians are united in their refusal to make any concessions on the right of return." Other Arab leaders also condemned attempts by some "Palestinians" to "compromise" on the issue. Elsewhere, the press reported (*Jerusalem Post*,

August 17, 2003, p.3) that a poll shows that only "10 percent expect the right of return."

All this is creating a great deal of frustration among Israelis, even among such "doves" as Yossi Beilin, the original engineer of the Oslo "peace process," saying that "Sha'ath's comments were damaging and hurt the chances of seeing the Road Map carried out" (*Jerusalem Post*, August 19, 2003, p. 11).

But isn't that exactly what derailed Oslo? The "refugee" issue was deferred to the last, just as it is in the Road Map.

Would it not make more sense — having learned from the Oslo fiasco — to simply draw some red lines making clear once and for all what will not and cannot be negotiable? Such as the Jerusalem issue, which was proclaimed by the state as the undivided capital of Israel. Such as the issue of borders — Israel cannot, will not, and should not ever sacrifice the security of its borders.

All of these critical issues are left for the last segment of negotiations.

It should also be made perfectly clear that Arab propaganda notwithstanding, the Arabs of Judea, Samaria and Gaza are not native to the land of Israel; Israel's largesse will only go so far and not permit a full-fledged state, but only a limited autonomy with no borders to Israel's neighbors. Such a state is to have no army, no air force and Israel is to control both the airspace as well as the borders.

It is extremely doubtful that this is doable. We know what happened during the Oslo process and what still continues today. But this is what Israel's prime ministers believed and still believe all parties of Israel could live with.

Clearly, that is not what the Arabs expect, and as long as the Arabs continue with their falsehoods, vicious propaganda and false expectations, the Road Map will go the way of Oslo.

As far as the "refugees" are concerned, there are historical records of the fact that they left Israel in 1948 of their own accord, after having been promised a share in the spoils of war by the five Arab aggressor nations. Does Israel owe them something for their failed attempt in collaboration with the enemy in what was clearly attempted genocide?

This, only a few years after the Nazi Holocaust.

Today, Arab terrorists, whether they call themselves "Palestinians" or not, are still attempting to do what their brethren failed to do in 1948 and 1967.

Chapter XXVII

Arabs and Jews

In the fall of 2003 Mahmoud Abbas (Abu Mazen) quit as the "PM" of the PA-PLO, some PLO members claiming that "he was humiliated and deeply insulted because he was neither supported by Arafat nor given the chance to do anything" (*Jerusalem Post*, Sept. 8, 2003: "Arafat taps Abu Ala for prime minister").

A day after delivering his one-hundred-day "progress" report to the PLO Council, sensing that he had no support there and facing a possible forced resignation, he announced that his resignation was final.

Arafat did not waste much time in announcing his real choice for "prime minister," the ever-faithful Ahmed Qurei (Abu Ala), the former "speaker" of the "Palestinian Legislative Council." The trappings of statehood are to all appearances there, except that instead of real statesmen, we are still looking at the same old terrorist hoodlums in suits and ties.

Over the weekend, US administration officials "expressed doubts that any progress could be achieved in the peace process unless a new Palestinian Authority prime minister is chosen who is empowered and given the resources to fight terrorists" (*Jerusalem Post*, Sept. 8, 2003, front page: "Powell opposes expelling Arafat").

It appears that those spokesmen for the US administration still do not get it. They are, in fact, asking the terrorists to fight terrorists.

The same Sept. 8 article reported that Secretary of State Colin Powell (since replaced by Condoleeza Rice) told one of the American talk shows on Sunday following Abbas's resignation and in reference to a new "PM": "'If that person does not make a solid commitment to follow the road map, go after terrorism, and stop these terrorist attacks, then it's not clear that we'll be able to move forward.' [...] Powell blamed Hamas and Islamic Jihad for the breakdown" of talks and Abbas's resignation, and "he also faulted PA (PLO) leaders for not giving Abbas the 'support he needed...so he could go after the terrorists.'"

Apparently Powell is not reading newspapers or paying attention to what Abbas himself was saying only days after signing the Road Map in Aqaba. Abbas's way to deal with terrorists was to invite them to join the PA "government" and work together as one big happy family of terrorists.

On the issue of expelling Arafat, Powell did not believe this would accomplish much, and indicated that he would not support it. On the issue of targeting Hamas leaders, he said: "We don't support that policy. It's never been our policy to support that kind of action…"

One assumes that Powell is only against "that kind of action" where Israel is concerned. Clearly we did not hear Powell complain when the US Air Force dropped "daisies" (several-ton bombs) on the possible hideouts of Osama bin Laden, often causing numerous civilian deaths in Afghanistan, as well as repeating the same performance in pursuit of Saddam Hussein, with similar results.

In its editorial (*"Don't stay the course,"* September 8, 2003), the *Jerusalem Post* bemoaned the US-imposed restrictions on Israel and that the consequences of "inaction" are not an option Israel could afford, although it was hoped that the US would somehow come to understand:

> What is needed is for Bush to return to the moral clarity of his June 24 speech. This means, at least, pulling the plug on the road map until a Palestinian leadership truly committed to combating terrorism emerges. At a minimum, that means a leadership that does not include Yasser Arafat. It would be greatly preferable if the US and Israel were to come to this conclusion together. But even if the US refuses to join us or lead the way, Israel should lead the way in the hope that the US will follow.

It is interesting to note the two op-ed pieces on the same day. One, on "Being a Jew" by Israel's President Moshe Katsav, consisted of reflections on the last words of Daniel Pearl, telling the terrorist "I am a Jew" before being murdered. Pearl was an idealistic young man who wanted to bring to the public both sides of the story behind the Afghanistan war. His good intentions of trying to be even-handed did not impress the terrorists; what mattered to them was that he was an "infidel" — a Jew!

But President Katsav wanted to tell the world, or whoever would listen, what being a Jew really means, and briefly described the history of the Jewish people and its "belief in one G-d and universal values, which have accompanied humankind since the founding of the nation 3,313 years ago at Mount Sinai, when we sanctified our faith and received the Ten Commandments."

He referred to the numerous challenges and tribulations that the Jewish people have withstood with steadfastness and determination for thousands of years. The destruction of our First Temple and the exile to Babylon, the attempted annihilation of our people by the Persians and the Purim miracle which saved the Jews. He referred to the Greek invasion and the attempt to Hellenize the Jewish people, which also did not succeed, and the revolt under the Maccabees against the Greeks, which prevented the loss of independence.

He then referred to the "loss of independence a second time…to the Roman Empire, resulting in the exile of the Jewish People from its country," and all the resulting suffering which the Jewish people were forced to endure for close to two thousand years:

> …expulsion, forced conversions, exiles and inquisitions and, worst of all, the terrible Holocaust by the Nazis and their collaborators. The Jewish people rose up from the ashes and succeeded in reviving and obtaining sovereignty and independence in its homeland.

The Israeli president went on to refer to the modern democratic state of Israel, its liberal policies and its advanced scientific and technological achievements as well as its moral values based on the Prophets of Israel, the values which are shared by much of the civilized world. He referred to the laws of the Bible, dealing with social justice, and concern for the weak, the orphan, the widow, the poor and all those who cannot fend for themselves. He stressed:

> The prayerbook and the Bible, on which our national and religious life are based, bound thousands of Jewish communities, cut off from each other for thousands of years and scattered throughout the world. In this way Judaism and the Jewish people were preserved.

In this essay the president reemphasized Judaism's universal and humane values and laws concerning man's conduct towards his fellow men and towards G-d:

> To be a Jew means to belong to a nation whose people are spiri-
> tually and emotionally connected to each other, to belong to a
> group which shares a common magnificent past, one tradition
> and a common destiny and fate. The Jewish people are the sons
> of one father. We are one big family.

There was much else of great value in what the president wrote, which unfortunately I had to leave out. Thank you, Mr. President, and thank you, *Jerusalem
Post*.

The other op-ed piece in the *Jerusalem Post* titled "Reject the Or
Commission," by Josef Goell, a journalist and a lecturer in political science,
referred to the Or Commission, established to deal with the riots of Israeli
Arabs in September-October 2000, which coincided with the so-called second
intifada.

The "second intifada" — the outbreak of violence instigated by Arafat
and his cohorts following Arafat's rejection of the Oslo Peace Accords — was
apparently coordinated by and with Israeli Arabs.

"The report of the Or Judicial Commission of Inquiry into the Israeli Arab
riots of September-October 2000, released September 1, 2003, was already
being roundly criticized," stated the *Jerusalem Post* editorial the following
day.

The Israeli Arabs were already critical days before the commission's report,
demanding the commission go far beyond its mandate and address "all their
grievances."

The commission — in its attempt to be "even-handed" — and sensitive
to the Israeli Arabs, did, in fact, appear to go beyond its mandate in an effort
to appease the Arab population, but what it failed to address at all was the
issue of sedition, which Goell referred to in his op-ed piece (Sept. 8, 2003).
As reported in the *Jerusalem Post* editorial on September 2:

> Thirteen Arabs died in those riots at the hands of the police,
> and one Jewish Israeli died when his car was stoned by the
> rioters. The report satisfied neither the families of the victims,
> Jews and Arabs, nor the police and their defenders.
>
> [...] The report tended to confirm two common sense con-
> clusions that many Israelis have already come to: The riots were
> inexcusable, but it should not have been necessary to kill 13 of
> the rioters to restore order.

The *Jerusalem Post* editorial went on at some length about the pros and cons of the Or Commission report, among others, the fact that "the Or Commission touched upon, but did not really study, the reason for the radicalization of Israeli Arabs."

The editorial further pointed out that "Israeli Arab leaders, such as MK Azmi Bashara and Islamic Movement leader Raed Salah, were blamed for encouraging the rioters and promoting the idea that Israel has no right to exist"!

I find it difficult to go on with the rest of the report blaming the police for not being sufficiently well prepared, for using improper rubber bullets, and in some cases live fire when the police found themselves outnumbered by the rioting mob. Equally, the issue dealing with improving the lot of the Arabs and improving relations with them had nothing to do with the Or Commission's mandate.

When one deals with sedition and a rampaging mob for several days running, it is difficult to worry about how to improve the rights of the rioters!

When I hear the words "Israel doesn't have a right to exist," I wonder why those who say these horrible things expect to receive rights from the very state they are attempting to destroy.

The rioters were primarily from small communities in the Galilee, and it is more than likely that some of the things they feel need to be improved are probably correct, especially as compared with their counterparts in cities. But to say that Israel has no right to exist is sedition pure and simple; add to this the violent riots, and there isn't very much one can say in their defense.

Still, the Or Commission tried to be "even-handed." Even the Israelis writing about the Or Commission report tried hard to support some of the legitimate grievances of the Israeli Arabs. But take almost any small Israeli community, and you will find that they too have complaints regarding municipal services and the like.

People tend to forget that communities, large and small, are supported by local taxes. That tax base determines what services the community will receive, or can afford. And yet, if the Israeli Arab population compares its living standard to any Arab country such as Egypt, Syria or Iraq, their standard of living is significantly higher.

Goell in his September 8 op-ed piece also makes that point, even though he feels very sympathetic to some of the Arab grievances. But he seems to be categorical regarding the fact that there is not the slightest connection between Arab grievances and what happened in late September and early October 2000:

> The timing, the locales and the identity of the participants of those violent riots were the giveaways: They broke out in different parts of the Arab populated areas in the north within a day and in apparent coordination with the launching of the intifada in the territories by the Fatah Tanzim; they broke out nearly simultaneously in Umm el-Fahm, Sakhnin, and Nazareth, areas especially noted for the vitriolic anti-Israel hatred spewed out for years by local leaders; and the participants were all teenage boys and young men in their 20s, who have been the main imbibers of that vitriol.

Goell comes to the conclusion that "what occurred three years ago had all the markings of a seditious uprising by rebellious local Arab supporters of the anti-Israel Palestinian terrorists who were simultaneously attacking Israeli forces in many parts of the territories." He goes on to say, "As such, that seditious rebellion should have been put down with full force." He further asserts that it was "perfectly legitimate" for the police "to resort to even more lethal live fire," if they were attacked and outnumbered by the mob.

He further asserts that despite the simmering hostility between Arabs and Jews since those tragic events, there was no breakdown into further violence, which must be attributed to the "realization that Israel would not blanch at using deadly force to put down seditious uprisings."

He then gives us the benefit of what he wrote a few days after the end of those riots (in October 2000):

> Vastly outnumbered police first tried normal riot-control methods, then tear gas and rubber bullets, and only then, in life-threatening situations, resorted to live fire… That police restraint is why there were "only" 10 (the figure known at the time) Arab rioters killed.

The Or Commission failed miserably in that it dealt very harshly with the police and some of their supporters as well as the minister of internal security, but the seditious rioters as well as those who incited them, among them MK Azmi Bashara, got off practically scot-free.

Perhaps the time has come for the Israeli government to institute harsher laws dealing with sedition, incitement to sedition, and related offenses. Whether or not MKs have immunity, they must not be allowed to act with impunity and become the leaders of the fifth column in Israel.

Sedition is one of the most serious crimes in most countries, democracy and freedom of expression not withstanding.

What Is the Alternative to the Road Map?

No one has ever accused the Arabs of ethnic cleansing or racism even though most Arab states, in fact, became *Judenrein* after expulsions of their Jewish citizens during the period of 1948–52. Also, Saudi Arabia, once called "moderate," has racist restrictions on Jewish visitors.

Somehow the Western countries do not seem to object to these racist attitudes where Arab Muslims are concerned. Worse, they seem to go along with them.

One of the provisions of the Road Map to peace is the dismantling of "unauthorized" Jewish settlements in Judea and Samaria. It is quietly understood that Jewish residents who established their homes there legally for decades will be uprooted and forced to leave if and when the Road Map comes to fruition (something that largely depends on the Arabs' willingness to stop terrorism).

Is that not ethnic cleansing? And this in Israel's own land, government-owned land, on empty stretches of Judea and Samaria.

How is it that Arabs can ethnically cleanse not only their own states of Jewish people, but also Jewish land without any protest from the UN or Western countries? (If the state of Israel ever contemplated such a move, there would be hell to pay.)

How is it that a new state to be established on historically Jewish land has to be ethnically cleansed of its Jewish population?

And how is it that Israeli Arabs — despite the fact that they have comfortable lives in Israel — are more and more acting like a fifth column within Israel. How can they support the "Palestinians" in all their outrageous demands and yet have a right to live in Israel?

These, the Israeli Arabs, who did not leave during the 1948 Arab-Israeli war, enjoy all the same rights and privileges accorded Jewish citizens. They make full use of all Israeli institutions, attend universities, practice medicine in hospitals and privately. They own businesses of every kind; they are involved in construction of every kind, including private home building. In cities particularly, they very much enjoy the good life. Their standard of living is on par with their Israeli counterparts and is certainly far superior to the average Arabs elsewhere in any Arab state.

But now that the Palestinian Arabs are about to have a state of their own, these Israeli Arabs — at least some of them — are becoming quite restive and support the "Palestinian" actions no matter how lawless or hideously violent!

The Arab Members of Knesset (the Israeli parliament) openly support and visit countries such as Syria which in turn supports Hizbullah and Hamas, Islamic Jihad and assorted other anti-Israel terrorists clearly in breach of Israeli law.

Is this not treason?!

If this were Jewish activity in an Arab state, they would very likely pay with their lives, or if they were "lucky," they could be expelled.

This behavior of some Israeli Arabs is extremely dangerous, and Israel is ignoring it at its peril, particularly now, with all the terrorism going on. Some Israeli Arabs have, in fact, in recent months, been found guilty and are serving prison terms for aiding and abetting "Palestinian" terrorists, such as providing them with transportation and other support while on their way to commit terrorism. These Israeli Arabs who can move freely through Israel make possible many suicide terrorist attacks that could not have happened were it not for their help.

Israel should be very clear to its Arab population that if they have any problems with Israel's sovereignty, they are free to leave. If, however, they wish to remain, they have both privileges and also obligations to abide by the law of the land, and demonstrate allegiance to the state. That is the minimum requirement in every democracy, and Israel should not be timid about enforcing these basic principles.

The same principles should apply in Judea, Samaria and Gaza. (This was written before the Gaza pullout-more on this later.) Israel cannot part with its historically Jewish land if it is to survive in this dangerous region.

Limited autonomy, akin to municipal autonomy, is all that Israel should offer. In such an environment, the Arabs could rule themselves municipally, continue being Jordanian citizens and not be subject to Israeli intervention so long as they abide by the law of Israel and do not turn to criminal behavior, treachery and terrorism.

Those Arabs who find it anathema to live under Israeli sovereignty are free to leave, and to return to their ancestral countries.

Whether or not that is doable — considering the decades of Arab hate propaganda and indoctrination for an Arab populace that has practically no other source of information — cannot play on Israel's goodwill. To continue to tolerate this cancer, this Trojan horse in our midst, is not an option.

Israel's first obligation is to protect its citizens. Israel is not obliged to facilitate its own destruction.

◆ ◆ ◆

The Road Map is an "innocent" or euphemistic garb for something far more sinister. The Road Map appears to imply how to get from here to there… But there really is not any "here" in place, to get to "there." The Arab-Israeli conflict remains unresolved. The Road Map does not address this very serious conflict at all.

As far as the Arab "refugee" problem is concerned, this has been tried before in many different ways during the now dead Oslo peace process, and long before. Any attempt by the Israeli government to resettle the "refugees" into proper housing was met by refusal from both the Arab states and the "refugees," who preferred to stay where they are getting all their needs looked after by the UNRWA. The Arab states — as is becoming increasingly clear to everyone by now — are committed to holding the "refugees" where they are, to further their propaganda campaign against Israel.

Unless one believes the Arab propaganda, there is absolutely no justification, moral or legal, for creating yet another Arab state.

We still do not understand how Bush in his wisdom decreed that there should be "two viable states" on this very small area, given the fact that there is no justification, legal or moral, to create such a state at all.

The Arab "refugee" problem is the creation of several Arab states, as is the perpetuation of the problem of these "refugees," and therefore must be resolved by them on their own land. The Arab states, with their vast areas of land, can easily absorb these people since originally they all came from these very states.

The myth of "Palestinian" peoplehood must be exposed once and for all, as must be the inflated numbers they allegedly comprise. A proper census might be a good way to start to determine the real number of the Arab population and its national origins.

Every so often we hear of illegal "Palestinian" Arabs found living in Jerusalem.

We must not forget that the original inflow of Arabs started somewhere at the beginning of the twentieth century and continued throughout the British Mandate, even as the Brits blocked — illegally and unilaterally — Jewish immigration from Nazi Germany and Europe. (Again, it is useful to remind ourselves that the entire population of "Palestine" numbered some one hundred thousand in the mid eighteenth century, of which the Arabs comprised some fifty thousnd. Most of the Arabs — poor fellahin — were tilling the poor soil for foreign overlords. Of course, back then, nobody referred to the Arabs as anything other than Arabs.)

The fact that the Arabs inflate their numbers does not entitle them to a state of their own. Clearly, their numbers — inflated or otherwise — do not by themselves give them the right to a separate state; neither do UN Resolutions 242 and 338. Those resolutions speak about the need to resolve the Arab-Israeli conflict, and yes, they do speak about refugees (both Arab and Jewish refugees, one has to assume).

But neither Resolutions 242 nor 338 speak of creating a state for a mythical people — the "Palestinians."

Clearly one has to believe that world leaders are fully aware of all those facts; therefore, it makes it difficult to understand what motivates them. A dose of old-fashioned anti-Semitism is clearly still discernable here and there of late (and has only became more evident as the twenty-first century progresses).

The Arab hatred toward the Jewish people and the Jewish state is now common knowledge, but what about the Western leaders? By what moral or legal right are they attempting to make Israel more vulnerable to further future Arab aggressions by forcing Israel to create this terrorist state?

Clearly neither Europe nor the UN nor Russia possesses the moral underpinning to give them credibility as honest brokers. The US, too, by becoming part of the unholy Quartet, can no longer claim to be an honest broker interested simply in furthering democracy in the Middle East and Arab-Israeli peace.

The US is fully aware of the hostility towards Israel and Jews in general prevailing in the Arab states. And nowhere does the Road Map address the issue of the wider Arab-Israeli conflict. To simply follow the Arab propaganda line and to force Israel to allow the creation of a state for a mythical "Palestinian people" is not only sinister, but also poses an existential danger to the very survival of the state of Israel and the Jewish people.

There is no criticism of the PA-PLO — as should be expected — by the other members of the Quartet, and the provisions in the Road Map for an immediate and unconditional end to violence and terrorism and incitement are totally ignored. Violence and terrorism and incitement still continue, although at "a lower level." Still, no level of violence or terrorism should be considered acceptable. Incitement is probably the easiest thing to stop if the PA really wanted to, and yet, that continues as well, not only in schools and media, but also by its very leaders.

Abbas, for example, a la Arafat, keeps saying that "Israelis are not complying with the provisions of the Road Map." Such talk only exacerbates existing propaganda. The claim by the Arab leader that all terrorist prisoners must be released fuels the incitement even further and leads to false expectations, as the general populace clearly has no idea that prisoner release is not part of the Road Map provisions, nor indeed is there any such requirement under international law.

Kidnapping Israelis is a new phenomenon not widely seen before the institution of the Road Map. In fact, after the *hudna* Hizbullah-type tactics have generally been seen more frequently.

The Arabs — far from being grateful that the Road Map provides for a state of their own if only they could bring themselves to stop violence and terrorism — are now even more emboldened in their demands. Obviously that boldness is a result of their belief that their propaganda campaign has finally succeeded.

Hizbullah, too, is now apparently helping and collaborating with the Arabs of Judea and Samaria and Gaza to extend the range of their Kassam rockets, which, up until recently, have nearly always caused little or no damage or loss of life. And so the *hudna* is being used to great advantage by the Arabs as they produce more and more "improved" Kassam rockets that will now enable the terrorists to reach Israeli cities. The Israeli security fence will then be of little use.

Hizbullah has also called for more kidnappings of Israelis. And here, too, we have seen the results: three young Israelis have been kidnapped, among them, a young soldier barely nineteen years old, a young girl of seventeen and a young Orthodox youth.

The spokesman for Hizbullah, Hassan Nusrallah, recently "offered" an exchange for several kidnapped Israeli soldiers — now believed to be dead — and Israeli businessman Elhanan Tannenbaum. The Israeli soldiers were kidnapped on the Israeli side of the Israel-Lebanon border in the year 2000. Tannenbaum was kidnapped by Hizbullah operatives shortly thereafter while on a business trip abroad, in October 2000.

On August 19, 2003, the *Jerusalem Post* (p.3) reported Germany's attempt to facilitate a prisoner exchange between Israel and Hizbullah. Nusrallah, in an interview with the Saudi newspaper Al-Wattan, expressed the "hope" that negotiation "would produce a happy outcome"! But, "he warned that if Israel refuses Hizbullah's terms, the organization would kidnap more Israelis to increase its bargaining power"!

Whatever happened to international law?

That appears to be the way of life if you happen to live in the Middle East! The same Middle East US President Bush is committed to convert to a democratic, law-abiding way of life.

The demand of the Hizbullah in this prisoner exchange is "the release of Palestinians [whatever that means], Jordanians, and Syrians, as well as over a dozen Lebanese, mainly members of Hizbullah, in return for the release and return of Tannenbaum and three dead IDF soldiers."

And so, the Hizbullah is rapidly becoming the "Godfather" for all the terrorists.

Chapter XXVIII

Savage Barbarity

A horrible bomb blast, unprecedented in its ferocity, tragically ended twenty lives (and two more who died following the blast, succumbing to their wounds), including several young children and two babies. There were over 130 wounded, many critically, and among the critically wounded were several small children.

The double accordion bus which carried families returning home from prayer at the Western Wall was apparently boarded by a suicide bomber, who, according to reports, may have been dressed as a *haredi* (Orthodox) Jew. He was carrying a backpack loaded with explosives and nails and bolts, in an effort to cause maximum casualties.

This horrific barbarity that occurred on August 19, 2003, destroyed the lives of many families; in some cases, several members of the same family were killed. One woman and her baby died in the blast; a father and his nine-year-old son died; a young pregnant woman also was killed. G-d only knows how many of the 130 wounded were maimed for life, and of the tragedy engulfing the families of those who lost children, wives, husbands, grandmothers, grandfathers!

It is not possible to describe the depth of the tragedy or the depth of depravity of the terrorists and those who send them on these missions of mass murder.

The early scene of the blast was shown following the evening TV news, as the blast occurred shortly after 9:00 p.m. It was impossible to look at the horror: the wounded, the dead, and parts of human remains all over the pavement. I do not cry easily — but I cried and cried that evening and the following morning.

How does one deal with this kind of savage barbarity? How will the families deal with their terrible loss, and above all, the loss of little children and babies?

The same night Israeli TV rebroadcast from an Arab TV station the suicide bomber as he was depicted prior to the attack, with a weapon at his side, recording his last message to the world. I could not make out what he was saying, but apparently, the tape was provided by the Hizbullah.

This was followed by other scenes where an older woman was pushed out of the way crying, while the suicide bomber's wife was seen praising Allah — "*ham dililah, ham dililah*" — quite serenely! His wife, according to reports, is five months pregnant and they also have two other children… In this kind of family, will their offspring also grow up to be killers?

The bomber, Raed Abdel-Hamid Mesk from Hebron, was a member of Hamas, according to reports. Hamas claimed responsibility for the suicide bombing (as did Islamic Jihad initially, claiming revenge for one of their leaders; one has to ask what were the motives for all the other murders?).

Mesk, who was 29, "was a faithful Muslim" — according to his first cousin Nabil Mesk — "who taught the Koran and knew it by heart; he knew what a sin was and what was not."

In an interview with the *Jerusalem Post*'s Matthew Gutman, "asked whether they [the family] were shocked by the monstrosity of such a bloody attack on civilians, Nabil casually denied that those killed were civilians. 'In Israel, people are soldiers from the age of one to 100.'"

The suicide bomber, a graduate of the "Palestine" Polytechnic University, "was an imam who had studied theology and was also completing a master's degree at A-Najah University in Nablus" (*Jerusalem Post*, August 21, 2003, page 2: "In Hebron while a 'martyr' is lauded, no sympathy is found for the victims").

The *Jerusalem Post* writer conducted several other interviews in the Arab village in the neighborhood, finding nothing but hatred and utter hostility, and absolutely no remorse or concern for the victims of this vicious killer.

This vicious murderer was not "destitute," as some apologists for these murders want to claim. He was an educated man, a theologian, an imam! According to his cousin, he knew right from wrong, and as his cousin put it, "what is sin and what it is not." Is his cousin — who claimed that all Israelis "are soldiers from the age of one to 100" — the next ticking bomb?

To all appearances this entire society appears to be infected by this fanatical, vicious behavior. If there are any who think or feel differently, we have not heard from them yet. Not in Judea, Samaria or Gaza — not even in any Arab country did we hear any unequivocal condemnation of the murderers or their bosses. The only phrase Mahmoud Abbas could bring himself to utter was that this action did not help the Arab cause!

Chapter XXIX

Jews, Arabs and the Western Countries

In Israel (and even in the Diaspora), people are blaming themselves and their government for failing to make their case to the world. They believe that the foreign ministry failed in its *hasbara* (providing information or explanation) on the realities Israel lives under, as well as the history of the Jewish people in *Eretz Yisrael*. They continue to believe that if only the outside world understood and knew the facts on the ground, if only they were informed about Israel's rights to its own homeland, all this negative propaganda and biased news reporting would change.

That sadly reminds me of how, during the Nazi period, Jewish people — myself included — in ghettos and concentration camps (and later in death camps) truly believed that if only the world knew what was happening to our people, surely they would not permit this to continue.

Of course (thankfully), today's situation is completely different. We are no longer a people without a state, with nowhere to go, at the mercy of others.

Jews today still believe in the basic decency of humanity. One recalls Anne Frank's words in her diary while still in hiding before she was sent to her death (betrayed by one of her neighbors!): "I still believe that people are basically good…" But history, and the sad and tragic truth, proved us wrong.

The world knew of the persecution of the Jewish people at the hands of the Nazis, and it knew about the death factories of the Nazis almost as soon as they were established, but did absolutely nothing.

Couriers from the Warsaw Ghetto and Polish underground were dispatched to Britain and elsewhere, only to be met with stony silence and indifference to the horrible truth. Western leaders did their best — with the obvious help of the press — to suppress the information of the mass murder of European Jews.

Is there any similarity to our present predicament?

Our immediate neighbors — the Arabs — are still bent on our destruction; they still cannot bring themselves to declare an end to war or belligerence. Their hate propaganda against Israel — using Nazi-style caricatures and old canards, including Dark-Ages blood libel — is circulated in the press and general media without shame or apology. This includes Egypt and Jordan, both of whom have signed peace treaties with Israel. (Their hate propaganda against Israel and Jewish people in general, in fact, contravenes the provisions of those treaties.)

Needless to say, none of these countries have condemned terrorism and suicide bombings against Israel. Nor do we hear the "vigilant" press or news media condemning the hate propaganda of the Arabs against our people; nor is there ever any recognition that the Arab states, in fact, nurture terrorism against Israel through their hate propaganda campaign.

It has yet to be fully recognized how Nazi hate propaganda against the Jewish people was instrumental in facilitating the mass murder. The Arabs have learned well from the Nazis, but we, the Jewish people, should also have learned. We have not!

We are very good at commemorating *Yom Hashoah* (the day of remembrance of the victims of the Nazi Holocaust). We commemorate the destruction of our Holy Temples, both the First and Second, on the mourning day of the Ninth of Av in the Jewish calendar. We remember well the many tragedies that befell our people following the expulsion from our Land, and we remember well some of the good people who occasionally, during those terrible times, changed our lives for the better — even if for short periods of time. And we still believe in the basic decency of humanity.

Some of us have trouble understanding why anti-Semitism still flourishes in Europe even after the Holocaust — an anti-Semitism that in fact appears to be growing, according to reports.

Much of the anti-Semitism in Europe and elsewhere can be attributed directly to Arab influence, both in international relations between Arab and Western countries, and because of the influx of Arab-Muslim population in those countries. The universities in most — if not all — Western countries have come under this influence, both through faculty and students.

It is quite amazing and almost beyond belief how much effort and energy the Arab Muslims spend instilling hatred against the Jewish people and Israel. It would seem that if they spent half as much effort in developing their economies and improving the lives of their own citizens in their own countries, the lives of ordinary people in those countries would have — could have — improved manyfold. But, as it is, we Jews are the targets of their hatred and all their efforts, and their own people in the meantime suffer from deprivation and neglect in many areas of human endeavor, including culture, health and the economy.

Seldom, if ever, do we hear or read in the general media any criticism of these deliberate, poisonous and maligning efforts of the Arab-Muslim people against us. Thankfully, there are still a number of decent people, both academics and journalists, who attempt as much as possible to be a counterweight to this poisonous onslaught. They provide those who are open-minded with information, so badly needed, against this horrific anti-Israel, anti-Semitic, anti-Western Arab-Muslim propaganda.

I always believed — based on my own observations over many, many years — that anti-Semitism never really dies. It seems to recede into the woodwork, as it were, from time to time — as was the case immediately after the Holocaust — only to emerge again, if the world will tolerate it. And apparently now the world tolerates it again!

The residue of the old, Christian-based anti-Semitism is supplanted now by the Arab-Muslim variety, which proves to be quite a deadly weapon. We have observed the phenomenon for some time now of various derogatory utterances against Israel in England and in France; we ignore them at our peril.

The UN and its various agencies have long been perverted into an anti-Israel, anti-Semitic forum. The fact that no Western country has ever attempted to speak out against this poisonous atmosphere permeating the UN should speak volumes to us.

Many Israelis get very upset when these goings-on receive more than the usual publicity in the Israeli press, but they don't really see it as a potent danger; rather, they see the UN as an irrelevance. Unfortunately, they are wrong. Belittling the UN, referring to it as "UM-SHMUM" (as Ben-Gurion did, with contempt), does not quite change the fact that it is, and has been for some time, the "dangerous place" referred to in the title of Daniel Patrick Moynihan's book of the same name (which describes his time as US ambassador to the UN).

When one contemplates what the UN has become and the support all this gets from the European Union, there is every reason for serious concern. Most

European counties are doing the Arabs' bidding not only at the UN, but in most other situations.

The Road Map was concocted by the Arabs in collaboration with Europe. One of Israel's elder statesman, Samuel Katz, historian and writer, says the road map was "made in secret, hostile in purpose, prepared in collusion, with some of Israel's worst enemies…" (*Jerusalem Post*, August 8, 2003, page B11, "Ariel Sharon trips on the road map"). That pretty much says it all!

Many Israelis still believe — in spite of all the evidence to the contrary — that it is possible to forge some sort of peaceful coexistence with the Arabs. Bush's speech of June 24, 2002, calling on the Palestinian Arabs to democratize their institutions, abandon support for terrorism and choose new leaders untainted by terrorism, gave some of those still indulging in wishful thinking an unexpected boost.

Many Israelis who initially saw a win-win situation in the Oslo Peace Accords leading to limited autonomy for the Palestinian Arabs were shocked to discover that the entire "process" was, from the Arab point of view, a way to attain as much land from Israel as possible, and then use it as a base of operations from which to attack Israel. In fact, this was precisely what the Arab process of stages has called for, and that is exactly what happened following the collapse of Oslo.[1]

Bush, the US president, is still widely regarded as a friend of Israel, and his June 24 speech helped to raise new hopes for some. But what was new, unexpected and dangerous in that speech is that for the first time an American president called for establishing a "Palestinian state" on historically Jewish land — Judea and Samaria. Not merely an autonomy for the Arab residents of those areas, but a "viable state" with contiguous land!

It is not as though Bush is not familiar with the territory or the history of Judea and Samaria. As a fervent Christian, he knows whose land Judea is. He also saw with his own eyes how dangerous such a "solution" would be for Israel. As previously discussed, there simply is not enough space nor strategic depth for two viable states.

The Road Map in its wording proved to be even more worrisome than Bush's speech. It dictates to Israel what it must do, as if Israel were the aggressor and not the Arabs in this long and protracted conflict. Whatever Bush's intentions were, the results could only spell disaster for Israel.

---

1. See Appendix 11.

We are reminded what former Prime Minister Begin said to Carter, the US president during the Israeli-Egyptian negotiations, about Judea and Samaria: "Whosoever sits in these mountains…holds the jugular vein of Israel in his hands." He also stated categorically, referring to the 1967 borders: "Gentlemen, there is no going back to those lines. No nation in our merciless and unforgiving neighborhood can be rendered so vulnerable and survive."

Bush knows it as do his advisors, as well as the US State Department, and yet, the pressure on Israel continues. Even as the first hundred days of the Road Map proved disastrous, without letup in violence and terrorism, the Americans kept up the pressure on Israel.

The August 19, 2003 attack on the double-accordion bus filled with families and children returning home from prayer caused an outrage everywhere in Israel. Still, the US kept insisting the Road Map was not dead!

The musical chairs charade in the PA-PLO saw one "prime minister" resign, only to be replaced immediately by another, of Arafat's choice.

According to Bush's vision, Arafat was to be sidestepped in favor of a prime minister untainted by terrorism. Perhaps many ordinary people in the West are not aware that the first "Palestinian prime minister," as we have discussed, was a terrorist for as long as Yasser Arafat. Mahmoud Abbas-Abu Mazen accompanied Arafat through the Oslo process and the violence that followed, reporting directly to Arafat throughout this period of his involvement as "prime minister." He repeatedly stated in public forums that "the struggle must go on." All this is apparently not enough to convince our American friends.

The Road Map's first political "achievement," of a supposedly untainted "Palestinian" leadership, only put us back to square one. Arafat reminded everyone — if there was any doubt — that he still ran the show. His newly selected "prime minister" made acceptance of the post conditional on US, European and Israeli approval. But in the end he decided to take the post regardless.

US Secretary of State Colin Powell still hoped that Arafat would give the new "prime minister" the power to run "all the forces" (then under Arafat's command) so he could go after the terrorists! Powell also "assured" us of Bush's continued commitment to the Road Map. The Americans' dogged insistence that the Road Map was still valid — in spite of everything — should have put in question their friendship to Israel.

Given that the PA-PLO did not even put on any pretense of following

Bush's vision of "two States living side by side in peace and security," it must be astounding even to the most cynical how the Americans are mollycoddling the terrorists and their sponsors. Israel is meanwhile being pulled and pushed, and told what it can and cannot do!

Israel was put on warning not to harm or even expel Arafat, even if the US agreed that he instigated the violence during and before the so-called intifada, to say nothing of his terrorist past. According to our Western "allies," Israel must not build a security fence even if its government believes it will prevent the infiltration of suicide bombers and the killing and maiming of countless civilians. Israel must not support in any way the existing settlement in Judea and Samaria (and at the time Gaza), lest the US deduct such support from loan guarantees it promised as a result of the ever-worsening economic situation caused by terrorist violence, as well as the "preparation" connected with the US war against Iraq (the gas masks distributed to Israeli citizens fully expecting an attack by Iraq with biological or chemical weapons). In 2003 an amount calculated to be the cost of building the security fence, which the US opposes, was also deducted from loan guarantees!

Meanwhile, despite the PA-PLO's failure to reform in any way whatsoever, the US government expressed no concern, but promised economic assistance to the unreconstructed terrorist PA-PLO! It is useful to remember that the Arab population of Judea and Samaria (not to mention the newly "disengaged" Gaza) still supports terrorist attacks on Israel, as well as suicide bombers. Polls in 2003 indicated that some 70–80 percent of Palestinian Arabs support these attacks! When Israel's government declared that Arafat must be be removed or deported if peace was ever to reign in the area, the "Palestinian" population openly declared their support for Arafat's continued leadership.

It should also be pointed out that while Israel has suffered economically due to terrorist violence, so have the Arabs of the area, yet they rejoiced at Israel's hardship despite their own economic problems, which, of course, are of their own making!

They also celebrated openly in the streets at the news of the staggering casualties caused to Israeli civilians — including children — by each new suicide attack!

Surely Bush, the US president, was fully aware of these tragic facts. But he still opposed expelling or removing Arafat. Meanwhile an Arab resolution was introduced at the UN Security Council to condemn Israel for attempting to remove or expel Arafat. They can still count on an overwhelming majority at the UN General Assembly to support them.

Judea and Samaria

Considering that Israeli leaders such as Abba Eban, the former minister of foreign affairs (of the Labor Party), and Menachem Begin, the former prime minister (of the Likud Party), as well as former prime minister Rabin (also of the Labor Party), among others, have clearly and unequivocally made their case that Israel could not ever go back to the pre-1967 lines, it is absolutely maddening that Western leaders at the behest of the Arabs are pushing Israel to do just that.[1]

Not only Israeli leaders, but even American experts commissioned by their governments declared that Israel must have greater strategic depth to be able to defend itself surrounded by mortal enemies. We are not surprised that the Arabs would like to render Israel indefensible; but why are our American friends so dedicated in helping them to achieve their nefarious goals?

Judea and Samaria are not only historically *Eretz Yisrael*, but also belong to Israel according to international law. The fact that Israel was attacked many times from that land, by the Arabs, culminating in the 1967 War, is enough to grant Israel legal possession of the land.

There is also the issue that Jordan illegally occupied and annexed Judea and Samaria in 1948. Jordan itself is an entity having no history on this land (and I am referring not only to Judea and Samaria, but also the land east of Jordan, the "east bank"). Jordan, as already discussed elsewhere, emerged as a result of British perfidy. The Mandate for "Palestine" given to the Brits by the League of Nations with the approval of Jewish leaders did not give Britain the right to divide the land, which was a betrayal of trust.

It was the 1917 Balfour Declaration that recommended and supported the Jews' return to their homeland from exile. It further supported and recommended immediate and massive return of the Jewish exiles to their ancient land, "to settle the land closely" and bring it back to life.

Even then, 1917–20, it was envisaged that to make the country viable, a future Jewish state would require all of the land of former "Palestine" on both sides of the Jordan River. Now, should the country already once divided and

---

1. See Bat Ye'or, *Eurabia*.

reduced to a miniscule 10,800 square miles be divided yet again to make it fall prey to its Arab enemies, using a PLO state as a staging ground?

Arab propaganda notwithstanding, before large-scale Jewish return, the land was despoiled and nearly empty of people, as many travelers in the eighteenth and nineteenth centuries testified. Again, it bears repeating that in the eighteenth century the entire population of *Eretz Yisrael* — "Palestine" — consisted of some one hundred thousand people, about half of them Arab, mainly fellahin.

Despite the fact that the statistics in the following years were not terribly reliable, we know that during the British Mandate, Arabs from neighboring areas were allowed free access into the land, while Jewish immigration was ever more restricted by the Brits in total contravention of their undertaking when they were granted the Mandate.

We also know that the British subsequently manipulated how the various Arab states were to be established in the Middle East. The so-called Arab revolts were nothing but British-manipulated riots, as Samuel Katz shows in his *Battleground: Facts and Fantasy in Palestine.*

We also know from historical records that not only were many Jews killed by Arabs during those riots, but the local Arabs who refused to join the so-called "revolt" carried out mainly by outsiders were also killed.

Perhaps the Jewish people could have had a peaceful coexistence with the existing Arab residents of the area had there been no Arab outsiders involved. I maintain that the large numbers of Arabs who came from neighboring Arab states not only caused violence and death to the local population, both Jewish and Arab, but also caused the so-called "demographic" problem.

Every so often we hear of Arabs who are illegally residing in Israel being apprehended by the authorities. These are not insignificant numbers; a recent (2003) estimate is two hundred thousand. I would venture a guess that if we went back several decades, that there were hundreds of thousands more who came in the early twenties, and many thousands more when UNRWA opened its shop of freebies. These inflated numbers of Arab residents from various sources all helped the Arab "cause" in claiming that the "Palestinians" are now 3.5 million strong in Judea, Samaria and Gaza (statistical surveys carried out in 2003–04 in fact revealed only some 2.25 million in Judea, Samaria and Gaza) The Arabs also claim that "millions" more "Palestinians" are living in the "Diaspora."

It is absolutely amazing how the Arabs use their propaganda to our detriment while appropriating to themselves expressions usually used to refer to the Jewish people — such as "Diaspora" and the "Right of Return," among others.

It is also very important to point out how Arabs used forged documents not only for identification, but also to claim property that belonged to Jews, in the Jerusalem area in particular, including the Old City and elsewhere. It is likely that such properties may still be in possession of Arabs, as the forged documents were not always detected. But there were obvious cases where property was known to be Jewish-owned, and upon closer examination, the forgeries were confirmed.

So much for Arab propaganda that we stole "their" land!

The Issue of Settlements

Arab propaganda has so thoroughly influenced the news media and therefore much of world public opinion, that the big lie is now treated as fact. The infamous quote (usually attributed to Goebbels, Hitler's propaganda minister) bears repeating: "People will believe a big lie sooner than a little one; and if you repeat it frequently enough people will sooner or later believe it."

Settlement — connoting the settling of the land of Israel by Jewish people — is the noble endeavor of returning to the land, and returning the despoiled land back to useful purpose and to the people. Israelis have done great things in the last fifty years particularly, but even long before then, Jews in Israel transformed the desert to bloom and to produce again. In the early 1900s, Jewish people began re-claiming land from swamps and building roads and the like.

The barren and previously unpopulated hills of Judea and Samaria have been turned into productive communities, little garden towns and cities. These formerly barren hills are not Arab land, as I have already shown, but government land. But, if you believe Arab propaganda, Arabs were "removed" from those barren hills! If you believe Arab propaganda, Israel "stole" Arab land; not just Judea and Samaria, but all of Israel.

And so the news media obediently quotes Arab propagandists that the "settlements" are an "obstacle to peace" and somehow "illegal," as if they were a criminal endeavor! Not the terrorism perpetrated daily by these "peace-loving" terrorists, but the settlements are "obstacles to peace"!

Even the Road Map incorporated that lie into its text by demanding that settlement activity must be "frozen." Unfortunately, however, that is not the only lie that appears in that document.

In order to be "evenhanded" the drafters of the Road Map included two horrific lies: (1) Not only do the Arabs have to stop incitement to violence, but also Israelis (never mind that Israelis do not practice such vile propaganda or incitement) and (2) Not only do the Arabs have to stop violence, but also Israelis!

One can well imagine that it is our "friends" the Europeans who saw to it that these shameful equations were included in the text of the Road Map. But what about our friends, the Americans, who do know better; how could they allow this? And what about Dr. Condoleezza Rice, who declared to Israeli officials that the text of the Road Map "is not negotiable"?!

No wonder the Arabs accepted the "Road Map" without amendments. But for the Arabs, accepting something is not the same as carrying it out.

As already referred to above, the violence and terrorism, which were to stop "immediately" according to the Road Map, continued uninterrupted in spite of the solemn commitment by their new and improved "prime minister" Mahmoud Abbas, and in spite of the *hudna*, the so-called "ceasefire." He had the tenacity to declare that he would not dismantle the terrorist organizations and "risk civil war"! He proved — if one needed such proof — how hollow his declaration at Aqaba was, and how fruitless and pointless are any attempts at peace-making at this time in our history.

Now, the ceasefire that never was lies in tatters as does the "Road Map," and in their wake is ever-increasing violence such as the August 19, 2003, bus bombing which killed twenty-one people (and two more who succumbed to their wounds afterwards) and injured over 130. Many of those killed and severely injured were babies and children. The injuries — besides severe burns — included lung problems caused by the bomb blast. Many of the injured, apart from sustaining lung problems, will be maimed for life.

But officials of the US insist that the Road Map is not dead. What on earth will it take to open their eyes?!

The people on that Arab-terrorist-targeted bus were families and children returning home from evening prayers at the Western Wall. The terrorists are clearly saying — for any who will listen — that all Israelis are targets, including children. To them, there is no distinction between military and civilian. In fact, their preferred and deliberate targets are civilians and children!

How does one negotiate — let alone make peace — with these terrorists bent on our destruction? How does one make peace with brutal, savage cannibals?

And how does one reconcile the fact that according to such news media as the BBC and CNN, these vicious terrorists are merely "militants"? And what are the terrible atrocities perpetrated by these terrorists, and Israel's inevitable reaction to them? A "cycle of violence." Here again, thanks to the ever-present Arab propaganda, Israel's self-defense is equated with the terrorist atrocities!

The settlements of Judea and Samaria, far from being "obstacles to peace," are Israel's line of defense. They were put there by successive Israeli governments, both Labor and Likud. And they were put there for a very important reason.

As already quoted earlier, Abba Eban — former Israeli representative to the UN and later foreign minister — put it this way: the pre-1967 borders — that is, the armistice lines of 1949, were Auschwitz borders, and Israel could never go back to them.

Prime Minister Begin told US president Jimmy Carter that "whosoever sits on these mountains [Judea and Samaria] holds Israel's jugular vein in their hands." He too stressed that Israel could never relinquish its line of defense.

Rabin too, using similar language, insisted in 1977 that Israel's survival depended on its strategic depth and that those hills were essential to its security. Those hilltops, where settlements were built (on empty land), must never be relinquished. They are Israel's lifeline and yes, they are historically our land!

The British White Paper notwithstanding, the proposal to yet again partition the land of Israel was nothing if not a betrayal of the Jewish nation.[1] The British knew full well what such a partition would mean to Jewish survival. The subsequent UN partition in 1947 — more or less along the same lines — could not possibly have meant that these Western leaders responsible for that partition truly expected Israel to survive.

Mahathir and His Minions

The world has been exposed for decades to vile anti-Jewish, anti-Israel Arab propaganda, but Malaysia's prime minister Mahathir Mohamad clearly crossed

---

1. See Appendix 7.

the red line in his speech at the opening ceremonies of the summit conference of the Organization of Islamic Countries (OIC) in Putrajaya, Malaysia,
on October 16, 2003. He did not merely say that "the Jews control the world
by proxy" (this is an old and vile Nazi canard). He said Muslims must defeat
the Jews:

> We are actually very strong. 1.3 billion people cannot be simply
> wiped out. The Europeans killed six million Jews out of twelve
> million. But today the Jews rule this world by proxy. They get
> others to fight and die for them.

He also said that Muslims should not send their children to kill and be
killed:

> Is there no other way than to ask our young people to blow
> themselves up and kill people and invite the massacre of more
> of our own people? It cannot be that there is no other way. 1.3
> billion Muslims cannot be defeated by a few million Jews. There
> must be a way.[1]

All this he said to wild applause from approving heads of state and kings in
the appreciative audience!

This is an open call for jihad — with a difference — genocide! (This time
not only by our Arab neighbors, but now by all Muslims.)

We Jews cannot ignore Mahathir's words — where they were said, and
how they were received by Arab-Muslim leaders. Any Jew, in Israel or the
Diaspora, who still believes that "the dispute" is merely between Israel and
the "Palestinians" better adjust his vision.

The "conflict" was always between Jews and Arabs, who, simply put, covet
our land. Now, the conflict has "officially" widened. It appears that all of Islam
considers our return to our land an "offense" against their religion. Should
Islam be called a tolerant religion? Does anyone still believe that settling the
Israeli-"Palestinian" issue will bring peace?

The outgoing Malaysian leader Mahathir Mohamad, after ruling for
twenty-two years, was attempting to make good use of the bully pulpit while

---

1. Viewable at http://66.249.93.104/search?q=cache:98OUuU-qKL4J:www.oicsum-
   mit2003.org.my/speech_03.php+OIC+Summit+2003+Mahathir&hl=en&ct=clnk&c
   d=1 as cached on 24 Jan 2005 02:52:30 GMT.

he held it for the last time. As Caroline B. Glick wrote in her Column One, "Malaysian Road Map" (*Jerusalem Post*, October 24, 2003):

> Given the standing ovation that Mahathir received at the con-
> ference, as well as the daily diet of anti-Semitism broadcast
> and published throughout the Islamic world, it seems safe to
> say that the views he enunciated are more or less mainstream
> in the Islamic world today. Because of this, it is important to
> understand the "road map" set out by Mahathir in his address
> and assess its ramifications for Israel's future.

Still, there are apparently some in the West who regard Mahathir as a "moder-ate." For a long time, the Saudis too were regarded as moderates, but not so after September 11 and subsequent revelations. Some still regard Egypt as a moderate Arab state, despite the full knowledge of its official, vile propaganda against Israel and Jews in general.

In 1938, when Hitler's persecution of the Jewish people was well known (but before the "Final Solution"), Western countries, including Britain, still believed they could do business with Herr Hitler. The rhetoric of Mahathir is the uncompromising rhetoric of absolute racism and bigotry comparable only to Hitler's rhetoric.

Arab-Muslim propaganda is still not properly understood by many in the Western world as well as in Israel. Some Western analysts interpret Arab-Muslim propaganda as a feeling of weakness, inadequacy and jealousy, when they claim that "the Jews control the world by proxy," or that President Bush is not really serious about creating a Palestinian state.

Both of these statements in Arab-Muslim propaganda have nothing to do with reality, nor the beliefs of the propagandists themselves. They are simply a means of promoting a goal in their overall scheme, which is to weaken Israel, and spur Bush, as he is put on the defensive, to even greater efforts to bring about a PLO terrorist state, as well as prove to the Arab Muslims that he really is their — and not Israel's — friend.

Hitler used similar tactics. He accused the Jews of waging war against Germany and threatened to wage war and eliminate the Jews. Both statements seemed preposterous at the time. Jews were trapped in Europe, powerless and unable to escape the anti-Semitic onslaught and persecution. As for "eliminat-ing" the Jews, no one could even imagine such a thing possible.

Germans under Hitler, of course, knew all that, but such knowledge had no influence on their propaganda.

The problem with the post-Holocaust generations is that they do not understand the power of hate propaganda, nor indeed the fact that the propagandists themselves do not have to believe the lies they are spouting.

But propaganda has a purpose, and the propagandists have a goal. In the case of Nazi Germany, the vilification and demonization of the Jewish people led some to believe the horrific lies about the Jews, while inuring others to their terrible plight, all the while getting ready for a wider conquest.

This is precisely the purpose and goal of the Arab-Muslim propagandists who have managed over the last two to three decades to isolate Israel in every international forum. Now, they are trying to complete the job by depriving Israel of its remaining few friends. But like Hitler, the Muslims too have a larger goal, which goes beyond the Jews!

All one has to do is look at what has happened and is happening at the United Nations, where Israel, over the past three decades, is almost completely isolated, and where every vile resolution can be passed in the General Assembly, with only three or four countries voting with Israel out of some 192 member states.

With some fifty-seven Arab-Muslim states and various other adherents to the Arab-Muslim brand of anti-Semitism (and racism), they regularly muster overwhelming majorities of 130–140 votes at the UN General Assembly, regardless how vile and false their accusations.

The "Zionism is racism" resolution passed by the UN General Assembly in 1975 proved more than anything the perversion of the UN, and that Orwell's fantasies have been realized.

According to the automatic majority of the UN, neither the bigoted Saudi Arabia where Jews cannot set foot on its holy soil, nor all the Arab aggressors who waged several unprovoked wars against the Jewish state with genocidal intent, are racist. Rather, it is the Jewish state, which dared to defend itself and defeat the Arabs each time (thank G-d) that is racist.

In truly Orwellian fashion, those who deliberately target civilians (women and children) in their homes or in restaurants and buses are not terrorists but merely militants, but Israel attempting to defend itself is the "aggressor."

Jews who visit the Temple Mount where both the First and the Second Temple stood are committing "a crime," according to "Palestinian" leaders and

Muslim clergy. But having deliberately desecrated the holiest Jewish site on the Temple Mount by building a mosque is simply a Muslim religious duty!

It is interesting that the official Egyptian press reported recently that the Temple Mount, or the al-Aqsa Mosque, was not the site of Mohamed's "night journey." Well, how could it have been since the al-Aqsa did not even exist during Mohamed's life? We have not heard yet, however, a refutation of the Arab lie that there "never was a Jewish Temple on the Temple Mount." Clearly, the issue of the Temple Mount is part and parcel of the Arab-Muslim propaganda war against the State of Israel and Jewish people in general, as well as the larger goal of conquest through jihad.

History tells of the neglect that was rampant throughout *Eretz Yisrael* as well as the Temple Mount during the centuries of foreign occupation, including the Arab-Muslim period. The fact that the return of Israel's independence brought back to life the Land as well as flourishing cities is bound to be a thorn in the sides of the despotic leaders of the Arab-Muslim world, pointing out their own inadequacy and inability to provide a decent life for their citizens.

The fact that despotic leaders need an enemy to divert the attention of their citizens from their real problem also plays a role, but to the Arab-Muslim psyche, jihad and conquest in the name of Allah is their primary religious obligation. To conquer the "infidel" and make him subservient, or put him to the sword, is Allah's will. But the West still does not get it!

They continue pouring in millions, nay, billions of dollars to "moderate" Arab countries, including the "moderate" terrorist group the PA-PLO; but nothing ever changes. The Arab population continues to live in squalid conditions — with few exceptions — but the Western funds are being used for more and more armaments and to pay the wages of the terrorists!

The Arabs of Judea, Samaria and Gaza who used to work in Israel (since the Arabs never managed to create an economic base of their own), now unemployed, rejoiced at the news that Israel's economy is suffering as a result of years of unrelenting violence and terrorism. Obviously, doing harm to Israel is far more important to these fanatics than their own well-being.

Bush, undeterred by any of this, still pursues the misguided Road Map, still hoping to establish a "democratic Palestinian state" (on historically Jewish land) "living in peace side by side with Israel."

Condoleezza Rice, the president's National Security Advisor (before she became Secretary of State), following Mahathir's tirade, declared of his comments: "I don't think they are emblematic of the Muslim world."

But what about the standing ovation Mahathir received from fifty-seven heads of Arab-Muslim states?

Perhaps Bush should be more careful about choosing his next National Security Advisor.

Egypt's foreign minister, Ahmed Maher, said of Mahathir's speech: "I think it was a shrewd and very deep assessment of the situation… I hope the Islamic countries will be able to follow this very important road map."

Mahathir's "road map" to victory includes modernization, not for its own sake, not for the sake of improving the lot of the Arab-Muslim masses, but for the sake of victory over the "infidels." Caroline B. Glick in the same October 24 column quoted above described Mahathir's quest for "the defeat of the West by the Islamic world":

> And the shortest path of eventual victory is the destruction of Israel. Victory goes through Israel in Mahathir's view, because although the US and Europe are the true targets, they will only accept Islam as their master after their current master, the Jews, are destroyed.
>
> Aside from intra-Islamic cooperation, Mahathir pointed out that not everyone in the hated West hates the Muslims back. Mahathir counseled the Islamic leaders to use those Westerners who support them and who "see our enemies as their enemies" to advance their goal of world domination.

Glick also gives existing examples of cooperation between Muslim countries, such as the Saudis' attempt to buy nuclear weapons from Pakistan to destroy the Jewish "enemy." She also discusses their use of European useful idiots who appear to be cooperating with Arab Muslims not only against Israel but also on the matter of giving Iran more time before the International Atomic Agency turns the matter over to the UN Security Council, on the vague promise to "temporarily stop enriching uranium":

Now Iran has at least another month to enrich uranium without needing to worry about the International Atomic Energy Agency turning the matter over to the UN Security Council.

And so the Europeans, and to a large extent also the Americans, are prepared to do the dirty work of the Arab-Muslim states, even though they themselves are the prime targets!

The motives of the Americans may not be as vile as the French and Brits.

For the US, it may be more a question of playing for time. But regardless of the motives, the issue for Israel is the same.

Israel must stop playing along with this dangerous charade and tell its friends, the Americans, that it will not commit national suicide in order to nurture that friendship.

The Building Blocks of Propaganda and Its Inevitable Results

When the outgoing leader of Malaysia, Mahathir Mohamad, claimed that "Jews rule the world by proxy," and that something must be done about that, he received a standing ovation from the leaders of the Muslim nations.

Just weeks later, on Sunday, November 2, 2003, the *Jerusalem Post* reported on its front page ("EU poll: Israel biggest threat to peace"):

> A majority of Europeans says that Israel is the greatest threat to world peace, according to a European Commission survey of approximately 7,500 Europeans… Given a list of 15 countries, including Iran, North Korea, and Afghanistan, 59 percent listed Israel as the top threat to world peace.

It should be even more obvious now that Arab-Muslim propaganda is bearing concrete fruit. Of course, as far as Europe is concerned, anti-Semitism never quite died on that blood-soaked continent. There is enough confirmation of that fact, from time to time, in the expressions of various parliamentarians and diplomats throughout Europe, including Britain, France and Germany.

On November 3, 2003, the *Jerusalem Post* reported again on its front page that "Palestinians seek apology for Balfour Declaration"! And so we see how the building blocks of anti-Jewish propaganda build upon themselves, with ever more outrageous claims.

It is truly amazing how Arab propaganda has managed to take hold in the Western world, regardless of its open and repeated calls for genocide against Jews. The Arabs, having lost every war of aggression, eventually turned to propaganda and duplicitous diplomacy. Both of these tactics appear to bear far greater fruit than all their wars, including terrorist incursions and economic boycotts.

Israel eventually refused to meet European envoys and ministers who insisted on supporting and meeting with Yasser Arafat. Even the Americans acknowledged that Yasser Arafat not only facilitated but actively directed terrorism. Israel tried to make its case against Arafat by providing proof to the EU of Arafat's direct involvement in terrorism. The EU was not impressed by proof or reason, but rather threatened Israel with sanctions if it continued to "boycott" its ministers who were openly cavorting with Arafat, the archterrorist.

Apparently, logic and reason have ceased to reside in the EU. To help underline this point, we were informed by the press that the new Swedish foreign minister Laila Freivalds said that Israel is in breach of international law for building the security fence on "occupied Palestinian territory"!

And so the propaganda, originally based on a single lie — that the Arab residents of Judea and Samaria are indigenous people, "the Palestinians," descendants of "the Canaanites" and/or "Philistines" (never mind that they officially call themselves descendants of Abraham — Ibrahim — through Ishmael) — has now grown out of all proportion, as Israel is accused of illegally occupying its own land.

One cannot dismiss the role of the media in all of this. The pro-Arab bias, and the herd mentality of the media, has played a central role in the promulgation of Arab lies. There is a great deal of evidence that in order to "earn" the right to report from Arab states as well as from terrorist lairs, the reporters had to play by their rules or else.

And so the building blocks of Arab-Muslim propaganda have reached such heights that they have managed to subvert all semblance of logic, reason or reality. I suppose the next thing we can expect will be the Arab demand of the renunciation of democracy, since Mohamad Mahathir "accused" the Jewish people of bringing democracy to the world in order to avoid the persecution they suffered for centuries.

Apart from the obvious, what Mahathir was trying to tell the world was that Arab Muslims consider it their G-d-given right to persecute the Jews.

The Europeans, ever willing to facilitate Arab-Muslim goals, tried at least in their dealings with Israel to downplay the results of the survey that showed 59 percent of Europeans consider Israel "the greatest threat to world peace," but how can they explain that it was the EU Commission that commissioned the survey, which placed both the US and Israel alongside thirteen rogue states?

Europe is not only playing up to Arab-Muslim states, it is also very aware since 9/11 of its own large Arab-Muslim population and the fact that the 9/11 plot was hatched in Europe, where al-Qaeda found "a vast pool of Muslim zealots," according to some reports.

Now instead of searching for and fighting terrorists in its own territory, the Europeans are trying to appease and mollify the terrorists and their supporters.

Many so-called experts and former diplomats with experience in Europe have tried to understand the phenomenon of the transformation in Europe with regard to the unsavory survey as well as to the rise of anti-Semitism and anti-Israel sentiment. Some think Israel is itself to blame for its poor *hasbara* — explaining Israel's cause — but they also have to admit the inroads and impact on European society that Arab Muslims have made on universities, both as students and faculty, by employing professional propagandists and agitators.

European governments and their long relationships with various Arab-Muslim states have also impacted the local media, which in turn impacts society at large. Now that the EU is enlarging its membership, its imposed uniformity with regard to foreign policy will no doubt play an even greater role in its pro-Arab, anti-Israel bias.

But apparently there also exists an appalling ignorance among students themselves (*Jerusalem Post*, November 10, 2003, "Don't give up on 'Hasbara'"):

> A recent survey of European campuses found that a sizable majority of young people believe there once was an independent Palestinian state on Palestinian land that was conquered by European immigrants and Holocaust survivors — who expelled hundreds of thousands of unfortunate Palestinians.
>
> An understanding of the connection between the Jewish people and its land is nonexistent in some student circles.

Clearly, to instill this propaganda, these terrible lies, there had to be fertile ground to begin with. Why did the universities allow themselves to be transformed into propaganda organs of the Arab-Muslim big lie? Why did they knowingly expose their students to this?

Surely, the European faculty members cannot claim ignorance of Middle East history and geography, or indeed who the Jews are and where they came from.

But as already stated, anti-Semitism never died in Europe. It may have been subdued following the Holocaust and the conquest by the Allies over the Nazi Third Reich. It may have receded into the woodwork, so to speak, but it did not die.

Now our "friends" the Europeans insist on injecting themselves into the Arab-Israeli conflict to better serve their Arab allies. By becoming members of the unholy alliance called the "Quartet," they will try to determine Israel's future, determining what is Israel's land and what is "Palestinian" land!

Europe's willful blindness with regard to the Arabs is pervasive. As the *Jerusalem Post* pointed out in an editorial on November 10, 2003, many European countries, if not all, as part of the Arab-Muslim automatic majority at the United Nations, have a difficult time defining terrorism.

There apparently exists in the UN a counterterrorism committee, except that those in charge cannot define what terrorism is, or what they are supposed to be fighting. As the *Jerusalem Post* editorial says:

> Every country in the world, including those that support terrorism, is willing to say it will fight terrorism with all its might. They get away with this by claiming that they support "legitimate struggle."
>
> Syria, for example, currently a member in good standing of the UN Security Council, says this openly, to the CTC itself... [S]ince the committee "lacks any clear definition of terrorism," Syria based its responses on the 1998 Arab Convention for Suppression of Terrorism, which conveniently "distinguishes between terrorism and legitimate struggle against foreign occupation."

And so since the Arab-Muslim propaganda big lie claims that Israel is occupying "Palestinian" land, all means of resistance is deemed legitimate.

The *Jerusalem Post* editorial urged the US to make a serious diplomatic effort to save the UN from becoming irrelevant and the UN Committee on Counterterrorism from embarrassment:

"Surely there is a majority among the nations of the world that is willing to state that terrorism is the intentional targeting of civilians, regardless of cause," says the editorial, and asks the question:

> [H]ow could Europe and most peaceful developing countries vote no, if the United States made a serious diplomatic effort?

> Trouncing the minority of pro-terrorist states in a UN vote would have an immediate positive impact, even before empowering the CTC to begin to take serious international action against terrorism. It would signal to terrorism-supporting nations that the automatic majorities that protect them in international bodies are no longer there. It would show that it is not the United States and Israel that are isolated in the world, but the states that claim a right to support terrorism.

If it were only that simple! But the automatic majority at the UN encompasses many "peace-loving" countries including Europe. Are they all suffering from the Stockholm Syndrome? Will they wake up before it is too late, and recognize that appeasement of terrorists and their supporters does not work and never has? Trying to sacrifice Israel and Jewish people in general is not going to save their skins!

The Arab-Muslim world and its supporters had better understand that Israel will not allow itself to be sacrificed for their ill-conceived and genocidal ideas. Israel is here to stay, no matter the pressure, no matter the sacrifice. We will never return to the state of helplessness and *dhimmitude*.[1]

I wrote these words November 10, 2003, not being able to forget for a moment the significance of the day. *Kristallnacht*, the day of horrors, a pogrom in every town and city in Germany on a scale only the Nazis could invent. A night of violence unprecedented — Jewish people beaten and killed, synagogues burned to the ground and holy books desecrated by Nazi hordes unleashed by their Führer — a dress rehearsal for what was to come: the Holocaust!

Postscript

The *Jerusalem Post* reports on its front page (November 10, 2003): "Rajoub to Arabs: Resist US in Iraq":

> Palestinian Authority National Security Advisor Jibril Rajoub on Sunday launched a scathing attack on the United States and called on Arabs to support "resistance operations" against American troops in Iraq.

---

1. Living under Islamic rule; see Bat Ye'or, *Eurabia*.

"This US administration is unreliable and unrealistic and does not deal with Arabs and their aspirations with the minimum level of respect," Rajoub said in an interview with the Saudi daily Al-Jazeera. "This requires a unified Arab position to mobilize all energies and capabilities to face the American aggression."

This from the PA "national security advisor"!

The same one to whom Israel is still urged by the US to make concessions in order to "live side by side in peace and security"!

How does the US administration feel about this call for jihad against America, a call for a "unified Arab position to mobilize all energies and capabilities…" against the US?

Or perhaps no one is listening to al-Jazeera…?

Chapter XXX

Conspiracy

Europe's Demonizing Israel Not Spontaneous!

And so, dear reader, you have read in the last few chapters the echoes of the infamous, long discredited calumny *The Protocols of the Elders of Zion*, circulated freely in Arab states, some of whom allegedly are at peace with Israel.

First we heard Mohamad Mahathir tell his Muslim brothers that "the Jews rule the world by proxy," and that "1.3 billion Muslims cannot be defeated by a few million Jews," and that a la Hitler something would have to be done about it!

Next, we heard several European members of parliament and cabinet ministers making all manner of incendiary accusations against Israel, and shortly thereafter a European community commissioned poll "informed" the world that Israel, from among fifteen nations, is the "greatest threat to world peace," with the US tying for second with North Korea and Iran, both of these democratic nations being lumped together with thirteen rogue nation states!

All this while anti-Semitism is running rampant in Europe. Jewish schools and synagogues are desecrated and sometimes even set ablaze, or attacked by suicide bombers; Jewish men are assaulted once again on the streets of Europe and elsewhere, and cemeteries are desecrated. All of this is not only reminiscent of the early days of Nazism in Europe, but far more murderous, as we saw in the almost simultaneous November 15, 2003 attacks on two synagogues in Turkey, where twenty-seven people were killed and many more wounded — both Jews and Muslims. Five days later, another two terrorist attacks in Istanbul, this time on British targets, took many lives and hundreds were wounded.

These terrorist murders tell us that even though the Jewish people are — again — the first target, almost anyone can also be a victim of these savage terrorists.

In Israel itself, of late, many terrorist attacks have been foiled but certainly not eliminated. Drive-by shootings, very difficult to control and prevent, are still going on, as are attacks on homes in certain areas of the country, as well as soldiers.

The "al Aqsa Martyrs' Brigades" — Yasser Arafat's own — now boldly and brazenly claim responsibility for these dastardly acts as though it were a badge of honor to kill and maim innocent human beings.

There was a time when Arafat claimed to be unable to control terrorism in areas ceded to him under the Oslo Peace Accords. By late 2003 all pretense was gone. All of his thugs — whether the Tanzim, al-Aqsa Brigades, or Fatah generally — were involved in terrorism in one way or another. Everyone knew that nothing went on in "Arafat-Land" without Arafat's knowledge or approval, including graft of every kind.

Still, the Europeans insisted on official contacts with Arafat, in spite of their knowledge of all the above. Many have wondered what it would take to convince the Europeans that Arafat, the archterrorist, remained to the end very much "hands-on" in all the terrorist acts.

The Europeans steadfastly refused to listen or look at proof of these allegations. This, in spite of the fact that they wanted to be the prime movers of the so-called "Road Map," and the main authors of its provisions!

The Europeans, as members of the "Quartet," are supposed to be "neutral" and "evenhanded" in their approach to both parties in this latest "peace process." But how, many wondered, can they claim neutrality and evenhandedness when they fail to notice even the most egregious acts in contravention of the provisions of the "Road Map" dealing with the dismantling of terrorism?

Well, now we know!

The *Jerusalem Post* published revelations of a study by an Islamic scholar, Bat Ye'or, pointing to the truth behind the strange goings-on in Europe, as well as the actions of their politicians and diplomats. The revelations in the *Jerusalem Post*, November 27, 2003 (page 6), under the headline "Europe's demonizing Israel not spontaneous," we learn in the first paragraph:[1]

> The anti-Semitism sweeping much of Europe is a concentrated
> effort led by the political and intellectual elites of Europe,

---

1. See also Bat Ye'or, *Eurabia*.

driven by a pact between the European Community and the
Arab League.

We are further informed that this pact goes back nearly three decades:

> Following the 1973 Yom Kippur War and the ensuing oil crisis
> launched by Arab countries, the French led the EC [European
> Community] into the Euro-Arab Dialogue (EAD). In return for
> granting Europe the right to develop the economic possibilities
> of Arab lands and its oil, the EC (later the EU) agreed to align
> itself with the Arab stance vis-à-vis Israel.

The results of this pact have been both obvious and alarming for many years
now, but no one dared to call them by their proper name. Many suspected
— due to the unmistakable EU pro-Arab, anti-Israel bias — that there is more
there than meets the eye, and yet, no one dared to call it by its name.

What is even more disturbing now is that people do not seem shocked by
these revelations. People no longer appear to be capable of a sense of outrage.
But even allowing that we shouldn't be surprised, why do we in Israel allow
Europe to be involved in the so-called "peace talks"?

Knowing what we know, how do we, as a sovereign state, allow Europe to
dictate to us what land we must cede to the Arabs and their proxy the PLO?
Knowing what we know, how do we permit Europe — under Arab urging
— to denude us of the ability of self-defense? Knowing what we know, and in
the face of ever-increasing Arab-inspired anti-Semitism in Europe, we must
confront these dangers head-on, before they get out of hand.

The old European-Christian-inspired anti-Semitism, dormant for a few
decades following the Holocaust, now appears to be fusing with Arab-Muslim
Jew-hatred. A dangerous mix, to say the least.

The Israeli government, though it must avoid being alarmist, must nevertheless take concrete action.

First, the so-called "Road Map" must be put aside, if not scrapped altogether in the face of Arab intransigence. The Road Map is only the latest phase
of Arab subterfuge — offering Israel a "peace plan" but no peace, preparing
instead to destroy Israel in stages.[1]

Israel must not uproot Israeli towns and villages in Judea and Samaria

---

1. See Appendix 11.

(Gaza residents have since been uprooted by the Israeli government under former Prime Minister Sharon) in the face of this reality, long suspected, but now finally confirmed. If anything, it has to be made clear to all and sundry that Israel is not going to abandon its land, which is vital to its existence and survival.

The Jewish people have not returned to its historical Land to abandon it to impostors and propagandists, whose nefarious goal — and no longer even a secret one — is Israel's destruction! The Jewish people have suffered far too long in exile to now allow themselves to be deluded by this subterfuge.

Admittedly, there are some among us who still delude themselves as to the true intentions of the Arab states and their willing European partners, but they are not speaking in the name of the people, and are a small minority. They are the "useful" idiots that the Arabs and their European friends exploit for their own nefarious goals.

I have written in a previous chapter about Arab-Muslim influence on university students by their Arab professors, both in North America and Europe; I also noted that such undue influence could not have been exercised, let alone achieved, without considerable help and cooperation from the university hierarchies. And indeed the revelations referred to by Bat Ye'or point also to the incredible influence allowed the Arab League and its agents. The November 27 *Jerusalem Post* article referenced above continues:

> The EAD structure is led by a joint presidency of the head of the EU and the Arab League, whose decisions are implemented by scholars and technocrats…
>
> Over the years it has ushered in a complex set of agreements that included mass immigration of Arabs to Europe, school textbooks written under Islamic supervision, the teaching of the Arab language and Islamic culture throughout Europe, and European recognition of the greatness of Arab civilization.

Bat Ye'or is an expert and world authority on *dhimma*, a status of inferiority imposed by Islamic civilization for centuries on Jews, Christians and others living under Arab-Muslim rule. She wrote, among other groundbreaking works, *The Decline of Eastern Christianity under Islam: From Jihad to Dhimmitude*. Bat Ye'or — who is Jewish and was born in Egypt, experienced firsthand the life of a *dhimmi*. Her Egyptian nationality was revoked in 1955, and along with hundreds of thousands of Jewish people who lived under

Arab-Muslim rule, became a stateless person and refugee. Ye'or, who lives in Europe (in Switzerland), is now also experiencing firsthand the Euro-Arab alliance, and refers to this transformation of Europe as "Eurabia."

Ye'or also refers to the constant European media bombardment the average European is exposed to about "Palestine":

> From the moment the average European gets up in the morning and turns on the radio he is bombarded by the message that the world revolves around Palestine — not on the Muslim-perpetuated genocide in the Sudan with its 2 million Christian and Animist victims, or any other ongoing atrocity of a similar scale.
>
> [...] On the theological front, Christianity is being detached from its Jewish roots as the Jewish Jesus is replaced by an Arab Palestinian one, emphasizing the traditional Muslim view that Jesus was a Muslim prophet. Yet the dialogue of this Christian-Muslim symbiosis carefully hides the Islamic belief that Jesus will come back to destroy the Christian faith.

It is interesting in a tragic sort of way that this "dialogue" between Christians and Muslims does not appear to trouble the Christian clerics. Hypocrisy and mendacity, it appears, are alive and well.

Arab-Muslim Propaganda and Jihad

I should point out again that the so-called "conflict" between Arabs and Israel is pretty much one-sided. Israel has no problem with the Arabs per se. It is the Arabs who have a problem with Israel: in fact, with the very existence of the Jewish state! But to understand that, one has to understand the teaching of Islam. The idea of conquest of "the other," the "infidel," is deeply imbedded in the Arab-Muslim psyche, as are jihad (holy war) and *dhimmitude*.[1]

To the Arab Muslims, their conquest in the seventh century and their subsequent defeat in the fourteenth century are as alive today as they were then, and their idea of conquest and forced conversion or death by the sword is what still motivates and animates Muslim society.

To that end Arab Muslims have employed all the weapons at their disposal.

1. See Robert Spencer, *Onward Muslim Soldiers*.

Naked aggression with the aim of killing the Jews and eradicating Israel from the face of the earth was openly proclaimed in all their wars in 1948, 1967 and 1973. During all the years in between the wars, they have used terrorism and cross-border incursions into Israel to attack and hold hostage schoolchildren, and other forms of attacks on the Israeli civilian population. The Arab Muslims apparently consider terrorism to this day a "legitimate" form of warfare. But they did not stop there. If they have not succeeded in annihilating Israel it is certainly not for lack of trying!

Where they have succeeded beyond their wildest dreams is in their propaganda campaign against the Jewish state.

The "Zionism is racism" resolution was particularly galling. The UN passed it with a majority vote! Israelis and Jewish people everywhere were stunned. They could not believe that such a thing was possible, of all places, at the UN. But the UN is only as good as its member states, of whom Arab and Muslim states comprise nearly one-third; add to this all the "non-aligned" nations (which were both oil dependent and also aligned with the former Soviet Union) plus Western nations, Europe and Japan, and presto — you have an automatic majority.

The Arab Muslims could now introduce any anti-Israel resolution they wished at the UN, and it would pass, which they did, and still do. More than one-third of all UN resolutions deal with Arab-Israeli issues (and are all anti-Israel!).

For all intents and purposes, the Arab Muslims could now introduce a "flat Earth" resolution at the UN and that too would pass! If it weren't so serious, it would be funny indeed.

The UN, created after WWII — which cost some fifty million lives — was created to prevent wars, promote conciliation, and prevent hate propaganda, discrimination and genocide. This very same UN has now been stood on its head and is used as a forum for hate propaganda and discrimination against Israel by the most bigoted and racist of nations. These are the very same nations who attacked Israel in several unprovoked aggressive wars launched with the declared purpose of genocide against our people. They are the very same nations who practice jihad and discrimination and persecution against peoples of different religions, and had no problem expelling hundreds of thousands of Jewish people who had lived in those countries since long before the Muslim religion came into being.

Now, the Arab hate propaganda that found its way into the UN has also found its way into Western society at large, using universities, of all places, to spread its venom.

All of this is old news. But unfortunately, insufficient attention has been paid to all of this, even by Israel and Jewish people generally. Now the Jews are once again reaping the fruits of neglect — unbridled anti-Semitism.

The venom the Arabs have been planting worldwide since the creation of the "Palestinian" myth some three decades ago is beginning to bear fruit. What would have been unthinkable some thirty years ago is acceptable once again. Jews are being targeted once again for "special treatment" at universities and elsewhere. What purportedly started as "anti-Zionism" has now blossomed into full-blown anti-Semitism.

Israel is being constantly demonized while Jewish people are being attacked. Synagogues and Jewish cemeteries are being vandalized; in Turkey on November 15, 2003, two synagogues in one day were bombed, killing many and injuring many more, including passersby. More and more prominent people say such things as "the Jewish state has no right to survive"!

In late 2003 one of the most senior Anglican bishops in Britain, the Bishop of Durham, the Right Rev. Tom Wright, said in an interview published in the *Independent* daily (as reported in the *Jerusalem Post*, December 30, 2003):

> I'm not anti-Israel, but when I see what's been done to the Palestinians over the past 50 years, I say, "Well I'm sorry, but if you put people behind barbed wire, keep them caged, take their land despite international resolutions, and bulldoze their homes, you are asking for trouble."

His comments followed another suicide bombing near Tel Aviv, which killed four Israelis.

Now let's take apart this quote and see what the good bishop really means. Since this was said following another suicide bombing, the bishop clearly implied that the suicide bombing was justified considering what the bishop believes Israel is doing to the poor Arabs. And this for the past fifty years! Which land exactly did Israel take from the Arabs fifty years ago? When exactly were any Arabs put behind barbed wire? And which Arabs are being kept in cages?

Let us take each part of his statement one by one. The last part of his statement was about bulldozing their homes. Bulldozing homes of terrorists — and those are the only homes being bulldozed by Israel — was something his own countrymen introduced during the British Mandate of "Palestine." "Palestine" is and always has been Jewish Land, the land of Israel — *Eretz Yisrael.* It never was an Arab state, nor was there ever an Arab state called "Palestine."

The barbed wire the bishop is probably referring to is the fence (which is not barbed wire) which separates Gaza — a hotbed of terrorism — from other parts of the Land to prevent terrorists from attacking Israeli civilians. There is also another security fence, part of which is a wall, to prevent Arab snipers from killing Jewish people both in their homes and in drive-by shootings, which have cost many Israeli lives.

And as for cages, Israel of course does not keep terrorist prisoners in cages. Duly convicted terrorist perpetrators are held in prison cells in Israel, as is the right of any sovereign government. The bishop's remarks only help to spread Arab propaganda and justify their horrendous crimes!

But this is only one small example of how horrific Arab propaganda is, and how it perverts reality to the point where a prominent religious leader can say to the world that Israel is asking for trouble because of its treatment of "Palestinians." Doesn't the Bishop know whose land it is?

Israel didn't ask for trouble in 1948, nor indeed before 1948 when Arabs, incited by their leaders, attacked and massacred Jews in Hebron, in Jerusalem and elsewhere in 1929–1939.[1]

There was no problem for the Israeli Arabs who remained in their homes in 1948 despite their leaders' urging them to leave; those Arabs who remained continued to prosper.

The Israeli government didn't ask for trouble in 1967, either, when several Arab armies stood poised to kill Jews. I do not recall there being an outcry against these Arab states anywhere in the "civilized" world. Nor was there any outcry against Arab states, particularly Egypt and Syria, when they attacked Israel in a surprise attack on Yom Kippur in 1973, on Israel's holiest day!

Miraculously Israel survived all these attacks by far superior Arab armies. In the Six Day War Israel took Judea and Samaria as well as the Old City of Jerusalem, all of which are historically — not just biblically — Jewish land.

How the Arabs managed to pervert history and reality with their vile propaganda is nothing short of astounding. If the Arabs had put their minds to better use in order to improve the lot of their long-suffering people instead

---

1. See S. Katz Arab Revolt p. 45, 72–76.

of pursuing this single-minded effort to destroy the Jewish state and its people, they probably would have succeeded beyond their expectations.

But this is not about improving the lives of their people, this is about jihad, as Allah ordained, and the world at large still doesn't seem to get it; although of late there have been some signs that some leaders, including the Vatican, are beginning to grasp what this is all about.

It's interesting, isn't it, how the confluence of events is capable of changing the tide of history. Just as the assault on Israel and Jewish people everywhere seemed to reach alarming proportions not seen since the Holocaust era, so too new revelations about the true nature of Islam have finally come to the fore.

It's not so much that these revelations are "new," but that till recently no one dared to speak of them. Knowing full well that there are many scholars of Islam, including in Israel, I often wondered what it would take for these scholars to finally let the light of day reveal, for the common good, what motivates Muslim parents to indoctrinate their young children to become human bombs.

Particularly confounding is watching these young children (girls in particular) on TV, their faces shining with a not-of-this-world glow, declaring proudly how wonderful it is to die for Allah. Asked what is better, peace or martyrdom, they declare without hesitation, smiling: martyrdom!

One has to ask, where does this kind of fanaticism come from? Yes, we know about the fanatic propaganda these youngsters are fed continually in their schools, their mosques, on TV — certainly all this can amount to brainwashing. But there must be a fundamental source of all this, which permeates Arab-Muslim culture or religion, since as we know, most — if not all — Arab states in the Middle East provide the same indoctrination.

The two Arab-Muslim states with whom Israel has peace treaties, the erstwhile "moderates," provide the same indoctrination the PA-PLO uses to great effect on its schoolchildren and general media. Egypt of course infamously broadcast on TV a long series of propaganda based on various calumnies including *The Protocols of the Elders of Zion*. As we know the Saudis have sponsored *madrasas* (Islamic schools or learning centers) which were educating for jihad in Afghanistan and Pakistan, among other places, prior to 9/11. Apparently, they also sponsor *madrasas* in Europe to this day.

The brouhaha over headscarves in France is also very telling. Belatedly, France came to "recognize" that the *hijab* represents more than "mere modesty," and that the *hijab* is in fact a symbol of "Islamism." The attempt by

France to curb the influence of "extreme Islam" starting in its public schools has provoked an outcry by Muslims not only in France but well beyond its borders. Thousands of Muslim girls and women in headscarves were seen marching through the streets of France in protest of the proposed law to do away with religious symbols in public schools. But apparently this "religious" symbol dates back only some two hundred years.

We have been treated recently to a number of revelations about the "peaceful and tolerant" Muslim religion by scholars of Islam, as well as some former Muslims.

Bat Ye'or — Jewish, born in Egypt, and exiled from that country — who became a scholar of Islam, has also the added knowledge of personal experience. She describes how Islam treats "the other" — the "infidel" — and informs us of the basic tenets of jihad and conquest deeply rooted in Islam. *Dhimmitude*, the subjugation of the population of conquered land, gives us a frightening glimpse into the culture of Arab Muslims, and what makes them act the way they do.

Similarly, a recently published book by Robert Spencer under the title *Onward Muslim Soldiers: How Jihad Still Threatens America and the West*[1] gives us a deep insight into the central political tenets of Islam. Hugh Fitzgerald — a lecturer on the manipulation of language for political ends — reviewed the book in the form of an essay published in the January 2004 edition of *Outpost* (a monthly publication of AFSI — Americans for a Safe Israel). According to Fitzgerald's essay:

> In a rightly ordered world [Spencer's] book would be translated into all major languages; it would be on the shelves and, more importantly, in the minds, of all those whose duty it is to instruct us. For *Onward Muslim Soldiers* explains, clearly, scrupulously, meticulously, the central political tenets of Islam (not the tenets of "political Islam"), that make so many of its adherents such a threat to the entire non-Muslim world — the world of Christians, Jews, Hindus, Buddhists, Sikhs, Confucians, agnostics, atheists and others. Though few non-Muslims seem to realize it, they face not a "war on terror" ("terror" is merely

---

1. Washington, DC: Regnery Gateway, 2003.

a tactic, and by no means the most effective one) but a world-wide *Jihad*…

He goes on to explain that this jihad is "deeply rooted" and is "central to Islam," and part of *shari'a*, the law of Islam. Jihad, Fitzgerald explains, will use many different instruments, "until all non-Muslims, ultimately, are subjugated to the rule of Islam."

Fitzgerald allows:

> It sounds fantastic, but it is deeply rooted in an ideology that is not tangential but central to Islam. And all non-Muslims are the targets of this military, economic, propagandistic, and demographic campaign.

Fitzgerald tell us: "Spencer links the latest pronouncements of Bin Laden, al-Zawahiri, Sheikh Rantisi of Hamas, and others," not only to twentieth-century Islamic extremists, but "to the central texts of Islam: Qur'an and *hadith* (the sayings and acts of Muhammad)":

> [T]hese texts, and the tenets they give rise to, cannot be changed or interpreted away. "Moderate" Muslims…who suggest otherwise, are often wilfully misleading… [I]t is the so-called "extremists" who articulate what is mainstream and orthodox Islam, and who would have been so regarded by any Muslim writer of significance in the past, from al-Ghazzali to Ibn Khaldun.
>
> Spencer shows us just where in the Qur'an and *hadith*…hostility and aggression toward non-Muslims have been expressed, and forever fixed. Whatever else it may be, the Qur'an is also a manual of war, and it gives a great deal of attention to the Unbeliever, his perfidy, his hostility, and what must be done with him. When the founder of the Muslim brotherhood, Hassan al-Banna, wrote that "Islam is to dominate and not to be dominated," he was merely echoing words of Muhammad. When *mujahideen* invoke deception as a religiously sanctioned weapon to protect the faith and fight the Infidels…, they are following Muhammad's declaration that "war is deception."

The entire essay, and certainly the book by Robert Spencer, should be required

reading for everyone and especially our Western leaders who still mouth plati-
tudes about Islam being a religion of "peace and tolerance."

Spencer gives us an insight into the mindset of Arab-Islamic leaders, who
are not at all fazed when they pronounce the most outrageous lies. All in the
service of Allah!

Conquest, genocide or subjugation by any means possible are the goals
of Islam. This seems fantastic as Fitzgerald admits, considering the odds they
are up against, but in the Islamic mind, they were conquerors once and they
believe they will conquer again. They will use terrorism, the oil weapon, or
any other economic weapon including boycotts, blackmail or bribery. They
believe nothing will stop them.

They will use demography as a weapon, deception, propaganda — no
matter how transparent — and they use outright lies without compunction.
As in the case of the Temple Mount in Jerusalem, they claim that "there never
was a Temple on the Temple Mount" or that "the Jews stole" their land, or
that "Jews have no connection" to *Eretz Yisrael*. All this in the face of known
history!

They have managed to populate our Land both illegally and otherwise,
and managed to convince Western leaders that they are entitled to a state (yet
another Arab-Muslim state, of which there already are some twenty, comprising huge areas of land).

The idea of course as we all well know is to weaken Israel, to the point
where conquest over the "infidel" will become more plausible.

"Islam," to recall the words of the founder of the Muslim brotherhood,
Hassan al-Banna, "is to dominate and not to be dominated."

Again, Fitzgerald discusses Spencer's explanation of Muslim theology:

> [C]entral to the belief-system of Islam is the doctrine of Jihad,
> the "struggle" to enlarge the borders of the *dar al-Islam* (the
> House, or Abode, or Domain of Islam, where Muslim popu-
> lations predominate and Muslim rule is established) until it
> completely swallows up the *dar al-Harb* (the House, or Abode,
> or Domain of War, where non-Muslims still remain unsubju-
> gated to Muslim rule).

He reiterates again that:

> *Jihad* is a solemn religious duty, and the surest way to Muslim

> Paradise is not to have a lifetime of good works, of charity and mercy, but to die in the service of *Jihad*, fighting Infidels.

That would certainly explain why young girls of eight or ten are so intent on "martyrdom"!

He goes on to explain how "*shari'a*, the Holy Law of Islam, ...enshrines Muslim attitudes towards non-Muslim peoples whom early Muslims conquered."

He expresses his regret that "some Western statesmen, such as Tony Blair," are not conversant enough (if at all) with the Qur'an and its related traditions. Fitzgerald asserts that misinformation of that sort is dangerous, and insists that if those at the top do not have time to study Islam, then they should have their aides do it, to "put an end to the notion [that Islam is] a 'religion of peace and tolerance.'"

> Spencer explains the best-known excerpts routinely invoked by Muslim apologists, and brings to bear both the classical commentators, and what Muslim history reveals about the application of these excerpts to dealings with non-Muslims.

He gives ample examples of what type of quotes Muslim apologists generally use: "appeals to an utterly false solidarity among the three monotheistic faiths: 'we are all monotheists'; 'we are all People of the Book.'" Then he makes the following startling assertion, which all Westerners would do well to heed:

> If they are truly believing Muslims, they represent a permanent threat to the well-being, beliefs, and entire way of life of non-Muslims.

Again, he cautions that:

> *Jihad* is not an invention of a "handful of extremists"; it does not date from the twentieth but from the seventh or eighth centuries.
>
> [...] Spencer shows that *Jihad* and *dhimmitude* work together, first to conquer, then to consolidate the hold of the Muslim conquerors over initially far larger populations of conquered non-Muslims. Islamic doctrine is used to explain and justify the oppression of the conquerors, even to make it palatable to those conquered by offering them an ideology

(a religion) which contains bits and pieces of the pre-existing religions of those conquered — both of Western religions, Christianity and Judaism, and those of Persia, Zoroastrianism and Manichaeism.

The status of *dhimmi* is linked to *Jihad*, for it follows immediately upon the initial successful conquest. It imposes a status of permanent humiliation, degradation, and insecurity (witness the massacres and forcible mass conversions of "protected peoples" throughout Muslim history, despite their supposed "protected" status). The host of financial, legal, economic, political, religious, and social disabilities inevitably led to the slow asphyxiation of non-Muslim communities, which became "Islamised" [and then] "arabized" as well.

Finally, there is the latest and most potent weapon of *Jihad* — that of demography. It is discussed openly in the Muslim world as a weapon of *Jihad*... The mass movement of Muslims to the dar al-Harb [the western world], where their presence, under Infidel rule, is ordinarily forbidden under Islam, is now justified by Muslim theologians, who see it as promoting Islam.

Both conversion of Infidel peoples and the much higher Muslim birthrate lead inexorably to gradual takeover of non-Muslim lands from within, where outright military conquest would be impossible. It is a strategy that is succeeding.

He bemoans again how the failure to understand the Muslim world undermines Western society. He says that the war on terrorism is "imperfectly understood and imperfectly articulated by those whose duty it is to instruct and to defend us against the *Jihad.*"

There is certainly much more that can be gleaned from this vast study, including an understanding of local jihads, from China (1930), to India (the Moplah Insurrection) to Israel (one long jihad against the "Infidel" state).

He gives a number of other examples: East Timor, Pakistan, Bangladesh, Nigeria, Sudan and others. He tells us that an accident of geology endowed Muslims with the wherewithal for a worldwide jihad using a full range of instruments. The five to six trillion dollars that OPEC states have received in the last thirty years has helped to buy hundreds of billions of dollars in arms, to corrupt diplomats and journalists, to build mosques throughout the *dar al-Harb* and *madrasas* throughout the *dar al-Islam*.

Certainly in the case of Israel, we have unfortunately a perfect example of how Arab propaganda — outright barefaced lies — has perverted how the world views Israel and Jewish people in general.

As Spencer points out, "demography" is created by transferring populations into "infidel" territory, etc. Birthrate alone did not produce millions of Arab Muslims in Judea, Samaria and Gaza, as well as allegedly more millions in their so-called "Diaspora." Deception as a weapon has helped to convince many — through propaganda — of the fantastic claims of the Arabs.

We know for a fact that the British invited many Arabs to work on infrastructure in what was then the League of Nations Mandate for "Palestine." These workers did not necessarily come here with their families. We also know that following 1948, UNRWA "decreed" that a mere two-year residency qualified Arabs for "refugee status." We also know, even by UNRWA's own admission, that the numbers of the so-called "refugees" were grossly exaggerated, and deaths were never reported, only births. There was also the additional issue of poor Arabs from neighboring countries who were allowed into the "refugee camps" simply because they were needy, which again helped to swell the number of Arabs in the so-called "refugee camps."

I have no objection to helping the needy, but that alone does not make them "refugees." Since the Arabs were employed by UNRWA and were running the camps practically all by themselves, their numbers were not questioned, lest of course they would feel offended or worse.

There appeared to be a deliberate effort to manipulate numbers and falsify documents. The intermarriage of Arabs from neighboring states with local Arabs helped again to swell the numbers, which is also a documented fact.

As described above, the Arabs have skillfully exploited demography, subterfuge and propaganda surrounding the whole issue of population. Worse, the world leaders helped, and were instrumental in the Arab endeavor to delegitimize Israel's rights to its own Land.

The British, and old Europe in general, still believe that playing along with the Arabs against Israel will save their skins. Just as they offered up Czechoslovakia to Hitler in the 1930s "for peace in our time," they are now offering up Israel to the Arabs as a sacrifice for the "greater good."

They are, of course, playing a dangerous game, and one day soon, one must hope they will wake up from their delusion.

Europe Playing a Dangerous Game

One of the most important reasons why I have written this book is that as a survivor of the Holocaust — the greatest crime ever perpetrated against any people — I indeed understand the roots of anti-Semitism. I have been forced to confront the kind of boundless hatred that is capable of such horrific crimes, and also what motivated the free world to be so indifferent to what was happening to our people. How could it be, I puzzled, that an entire world, with precious few exceptions, a world that believes itself moral, could stand aside and allow the mass murder of the innocent to happen, with full knowledge?

The free press reported these atrocities somewhere on the back pages; the horrors were more often suppressed than not. There was no one to protest! World leaders themselves did their best to suppress the news of the mass killings, but people knew. They kept quiet for a variety of reasons.

The Jews in the "free" world, with few exceptions, kept quiet because of fear for their own safety, as anti-Semitism was still deeply imbedded in society at every level. In certain societies, open Jew-hatred was more pronounced than in others, but on the whole, various governments and their officials did nothing to prevent open hostility to Jewish people. Quite the contrary. In Canada, for instance, it was official government policy to discriminate against Jews, even to the point of preventing the entry to Canada of any Jewish person who could have escaped the Holocaust! The British — who did their utmost to prevent Jews from coming to their own land — allowed some transport of young children into Britain. In the US, in response to entreaties to save Europe's Jews by allowing larger numbers to immigrate, President Roosevelt was said to be preparing "relief" for those who would survive!

For all practical purposes, the doors were closed shut to any escaping Jew, let alone families. Some Jewish people of means, certainly few in number, were able to find refuge in the East, in Hong Kong, then under the governance of China. Some young people were persuaded by their parents to simply cross the border to the former USSR, many with no success; others found themselves continuously on the run as the Soviets were not very hospitable either.

What was that hatred that knew no bounds? What motivated ordinary people to become killers? What indeed motivated German society, a "civilized" society, to become savage, cold-blooded killers of children and defenseless human beings?

There were few answers that could explain such a total breakdown of morality in what seemed educated, enlightened and civilized people. And yet, we see a similar phenomenon, as shocking and disturbing as it is, even today.

Recent revelations that 59 percent of Europeans consider Israel "the greatest threat to world peace," according to a poll commissioned by an official body of the European Union (EU), sent shock-waves across the globe, and of course, in Israel.

Of course, these sorts of things don't happen by accident. The recent revelation that the former European Economic Commission had a pact with Arab states since 1973 to collaborate against Israel in exchange for unimpeded oil supply[1] is nothing short of shocking.

That the Europeans played along with the Arabs to advance their "cause" vis-à-vis Israel was obvious for a long time, but an actual pact? And this at the time when the Europeans — the creators of the unholy "Road Map" — claimed to be "honest brokers" in search of "peace" in the Arab-Israeli conflict!

The "Road Map to Peace," which is supposed to divide further this tiny land in order to create yet another Arab state, a hostile terrorist state at that, is nothing short of a disaster for Israel. But now it's clear! If anyone was wondering why Europe — claiming to be an honest broker — would wish Israel to become indefensible, we now finally have an answer: the European-Arab pact!

But the story is even more sinister. While no one was paying much attention, the Arabs have, for the past three decades, been given wide scope to influence the news media and the universities in Europe, and thereby influence European society in general. In fact, even more immoral, the leaders of Europe have actually helped to reinforce Arab hate propaganda against Israel both in their own countries and at the UN by voting with the Arabs and supporting the most outrageous UN resolutions against the State of Israel. As well, Europe's constant criticism and reprimand of Israel's defensive actions against terrorists and would-be terrorists further reinforces Arab propaganda.

How is it possible, one might ask, that European leaders and their states were giving unanimous support to the Arabs? Very simple. The European Union dominated by France, Germany and also Britain, as members of the EU "club," must support the common EU foreign policy. And now, with the acceptance of some additional member countries to the EU (including the

---

1. See Bat Ye'or, *Eurabia*.

Czech Republic, Poland, Latvia, Estonia and Lithuania, among others), some voices previously more favorable to Israel will find themselves stifled.

That anti-Semitism is now so widespread in Europe and much of the world may be surprising to decent and moral human beings who know the truth about the Arab-Israeli conflict and who are knowledgeable about the history of the region, as well as Israel's history and its current predicament. How can Israel be seen as "the greatest threat to world peace" when it faces almost daily terrorist attacks on its civilian population, surrounded by intractable enemies sworn to its destruction?

All this is true. But hate propaganda repeated daily has a way of eventually being believed, as seen in Hitler's infamous propaganda strategy. Blaming the intended victim has always been a useful and often lethal tool of dictators, despots and bigots.

Hate propaganda combined with violence can often even disorient an intended target, particularly when interspersed with periods of relative calm or quiet. This was the tactic the Nazis used on the Jewish people. Their intended victims were kept busy trying to understand what it all meant, never suspecting what the Nazis really intended, often to the last minute before death!

I do not wish to draw any close parallels here to the present situation of the Jewish people, but one cannot help but notice the method.

The Jewish people, thank G-d, are in their own Land finally. During the Nazi period we were totally at the mercy of our oppressors, unwanted and hated in our "host" countries of Europe. But Europe, it now appears, has not changed very much since the early '30s and '40s, to say nothing of its long history of anti-Semitism. It appears that the seeds of centuries of indoctrination of Jew-hatred and contempt are still alive and well.

Europe, it is now clear, has no problem vilifying Israel in order to play along and do the bidding of its Arab enemies. Allowing Arab anti-Israel propaganda to go unchallenged in the universities has now produced two generations of young and middle-aged people fed on poisonous Arab hate propaganda against Israel. Maybe those polls showing Israel as "the greatest threat to world peace" could have been predicted if people had paid more attention to what is happening on university campuses as well as in the official Arab and European press.

People still don't understand the power of hate propaganda and incitement based on falsehoods, intended to isolate Israel with the aim of destroying the Jewish state.

The role of the news media in all of this cannot be overstated as the media repeat — parrotlike — the Arab propaganda, painting Israel as the "villain" in this seemingly never-ending Arab-Israeli conflict, which seems to have become an obsession of the Arabs.

It is clear, when one listens to Western journalists, that with very, very few exceptions, they are reporting according to Arab dictates. It seems that they have learned that in order to report from terrorist-held territory, they better do the bidding of the terrorists or else.

The Lynching!

It is instructive to remind people at this point of the lynching of two Israelis who strayed into PLO territory and were attacked by an Arab mob at a PA-PLO police station! The mob appeared to go wild with fanatical blood lust! All of this was filmed by an Italian TV crew, and was broadcast in Israel and elsewhere. Arafat then "punished" the Italian crew for daring to show the Arabs in a negative light. The following was reported in *Outpost* (a monthly publication of AFSI, Americans for a Safe Israel), November 2000:

> Richard Cristiano, the representative of Italian state television…wrote a letter of apology to the Palestinian Authority (his letter was published on October 16 in *Al Hayat al Jedida*). He said he worked under the PA's rules for journalists, blames his competitors in the Italian media for broadcasting the pictures and promises never again to film events liable to cast a negative light on the PA. To underscore the point, Italian TV put large ads in all the West Bank papers apologizing for inadvertently putting the PA in a bad light.
>
> […] [A]ll the foreign press works under the same PA rules (ever wonder why CNN and BBC coverage is so ludicrously one sided?)…

Has anyone heard any protests or cries of outrage in the hallowed halls of the UN, the EU, or what were still in those days described as the "moderate Arab states," namely, Saudi Arabia, Egypt and Jordan, at the atrocity of the blood-curdling, bloodthirsty blood lust of the Arab mob? Indeed has any concern been expressed at the collaboration of the Western media with terrorism?!

For any society to function properly, the news media must be a diligent watchdog. Europe has lost its way once again, and there is no one to tell the people that the emperor has no clothes.

Israel is a young democracy, and yes, Israel too has its useful idiots. But, Israel will somehow muddle through.

The Jewish people have lived through many calamities. It's true, we have lost many of our people during our long exile, but Israel will endure; the Jewish people will endure, with G-d's help.

But whether Europe — or as some refer to it now, *Eurabia* — will endure, with its *madrasas* preaching hate against not only Israel but all Western countries — collectively "the infidels" — is another question.

Europe is playing a dangerous game — dangerous not only to Israel and others, but dangerous to itself and the Western world in general. After the fall of Afghanistan, Europe now serves as an incubator of Arab-Islamic extremism and terrorism, playing along with the terrorists, hoping to be spared.

Europe is sick! But whether it is suffering from the "Stockholm Syndrome" or some other pathology that is affecting a high percentage of its people, it is clear that this epidemic, before it's over, will cost Europe dearly.

As far as Israel is concerned, we Israelis (and Jewish people in general) should make it clear to the leaders of Europe, Tony Blair included: Now that your pact with the Arabs is out in the open, stay out of our domestic affairs!

Bush, too, should be told clearly — if need be — that the "Road Map" to disaster is a non-starter, and that on this particular issue he won't be able to help out his friend, Mr. Blair.

Israeli leaders must learn to assert themselves, and be less accommodating to all concerned. Compromise and willingness to appease the Arabs have led absolutely nowhere, except to ever-greater demands based on their falsehoods. Their big lie must be exposed once and for all. Compromise has been interpreted by the Arabs as a sign of weakness, and the weak will not exist long in this dangerous neighborhood and increasingly more dangerous world.

Chapter XXXI

Vatican Releases New Data on Inquisition

The Vatican, in its "new revelations" on the centuries-old Inquisition released June 15, 2004, claimed that the Inquisition torture, burning at the stake and other punishments by Church tribunals were "not as widespread as commonly believed" (*Jerusalem Post*, June 16, 2004):

> The research, presented at a news conference, grew out of a conference of historians and other scholars in 1998 at the Vatican as John Paul sought to objectively assess the Inquisition, which stretched from the 13th to the 19th centuries.
>
> The experts involved in the research included historians and other scholars, with specialties ranging from the medieval period to more modern times, and included non-Catholics from various countries of Europe including countries involved in the Inquisition such as Spain, Portugal and Italy, as well as the United States and Canada.
>
> "Before seeking pardon, it is necessary to have a precise knowledge of the facts," John Paul wrote in a letter Tuesday in which he expressed his "strong appreciation" for the research, which is contained in a 783-page book.
>
> At the news conference, Church officials and others involved in the project said statistics and other data demolished long-held beliefs about the Inquisition, including that torture and executions were commonly used.
>
> [...] [W]hile there were some 125,000 trials of suspected heretics in Spain, research found that about 1 percent of the defendants were executed, far fewer than commonly believed.

Many of the burnings at the stake which took place during the centuries of the Inquisition actually were carried out by non-church tribunals, experts told reporters.

Cardinal Georges Cottier, a Vatican theologian, stressed the need to have the facts before making judgments about a period of history. "You can't ask pardon for deeds which aren't there," he said.

Indeed…

I referred to the pope's "non-apology" earlier, also renouncing all responsibility for acts committed by "some Christians" in the name of their religion.

Curious, isn't it? Here we have a study which reports that the Church in Spain, for instance, was responsible for "only" one percent of the executions of some 125,000 trials of "suspected heretics." We are also told that many burnings at the stake were not officially perpetrated by the Church.

Aren't we all relieved by these revelations?!

I am sure this made all the difference to the innocent victims of these Church-supported horrific atrocities!

Even if the Church was "responsible" for only one percent of these atrocities, the Church was certainly responsible for the dogma which led to the infamous Inquisition, lasting well into the nineteenth century. The Church's teachings were most certainly responsible for violence and hatred towards the Jewish people and even the newly converted, as well as other "heretics"!

And what about the non-official mass slaughter and torture carried out by incited mobs in Portugal and other places, all due to the teaching of hatred and contempt towards the "G-d killing" Jews?!

Pope John XXIII declared some four decades ago that Jews were not responsible for the killing of Jesus. Why was his legacy not carried to the logical conclusion that the Church should condemn, once and for all, all manifestations of anti-Semitism, which at least among Christians were still based on the previous teachings of the Church?

The Church — if it is at all serious about soul-searching — should once and for all renounce its former teaching of hatred and contempt towards Jews which led to so much suffering, so many deaths and massacres!

Today, more than ever, when anti-Semitism is once again accepted even among the elites, the Church has the opportunity — and the responsibility — to denounce anti-Semitism for what it is in the strongest possible terms.

The Vatican protested Pious XII's anti-Semitism in various ways, claiming that he could not do "any more" during the Nazi era; what is the excuse for the Vatican's silence now, when anti-Semitism is once again openly displayed?

There are many Christian denominations that support Israel and the Jewish people, and to those we are most grateful, but the Vatican itself must finally speak openly and unambiguously. The Church has a powerful influence among many and it could certainly be a force for good. We are still waiting…

Chapter XXXII

The Battle Ahead

While one can easily agree that Western leaders have difficulty reading and comprehending the Arab Muslim psyche — which cannot be separated from the teaching of the Qur'an and the *hadith* — one cannot accept the notion of their total ignorance of these teachings. The issue is rather that they do not see themselves threatened by those teachings, since the conquest of the world by Islam — at least at present — appears to be a fantastic notion at best.

The fact that the Bush administration declared war on Iraq — which may well have been justified in the face of available intelligence and due to Saddam Hussein's continuous failure to comply with UN Security Council Resolutions over a period of a decade — did not appear to move the EU to support that effort.

The near certainty that Saddam had both chemical and biological weapons ready for use as he threatened numerous times — as well as nuclear weapons allegedly in their final stages according to available intelligence which Saddam himself did little or nothing to dispel — may well have been sufficient grounds for war, but not for the EU!

The real miscalculation on the part of the US was that they were not prepared to find such strong opposition from their erstwhile friends the Europeans — with the exception of Britain — and therefore no support from the UN Security Council. One must suppose that the Americans miscalculated to what extent France and Russia were beholden to Saddam, and to what extent Europe in general was doing the bidding of the Arabs. The other miscalculation was, of course, Saddam's deception, as he very cleverly postured as if indeed all those weapons of mass destruction were ready to go at his command. But perhaps the Western world pays little attention to what extent the Arab Muslims use deception as a tool of war.

Saddam himself miscalculated when he hoped that his posturing and deception would prevent rather than cause war, occupation, and ultimately, his own capture and humiliation.

There is no doubt that Saddam did possess chemical and other deadly weapons, which he has used against his own citizens, the Kurds. He also used these weapons against Iran in their war, and threatened twice within a decade (1990–91 and 2000) to use them against Israel. What is not yet clear is what happened to those weapons; are they hidden, or were they transported to a friendly Arab country, or elsewhere?

The most glaring miscalculation of all by the US administration was, of course, the totally unexpected reception they received from the Iraqi population, and that does show an unpardonable ignorance of the Arab-Muslim psyche. According to the Qur'an and *hadith*, it is they, the Arabs, who must be conquerors, not conquered! They, who "must dominate, not be dominated." It is they who will humiliate the Infidel, not be humiliated. That is why they vociferously demonstrated against the occupation by the US; that is why they demand an end to the occupation, and that is why almost every Arab country reacted with alarm to Saddam's "humiliation" and capture.

Even if they disagreed amongst themselves, or disliked Saddam, they viewed an attack on a Muslim country as an attack on all of Islam, and the humiliation of Saddam was by extension a humiliation for all of Islam, and therefore all Muslims.

The "cooperation" of some Arab states during the first Gulf War (1990–91) was an aberration; the excuse may have been that Saddam invaded another Arab-Muslim country, Kuwait. But, of course, that cooperation was very limited — the Arabs merely promised not to oppose or interfere. In exchange, however, they were very handsomely rewarded; the Americans promised to "deliver" Israel! Israel was also infamously prevented by the US (in 1991) from responding to the Iraqi missile attack, which Saddam promised would carry chemical or biological weapons!

In the eyes of the Arabs, Israel was severely humiliated, which in itself must have been a most satisfying reward.

Israel's government and defense forces were forced by the US to sit on their hands, while the Israeli public, expecting the worst, was obliged to prepare sealed rooms and carry gas masks with them wherever they went, for several months. Again, that too was a war of deception, and one that cost Israel dearly. The thirty-nine scuds that fell on Israeli cities in 1990–91 thankfully caused no casualties or major property damage. The damage this war caused, at least in the Arab mind, was that Israel became vulnerable to pressure; and so the Arabs have used pressure ever since on Western leaders, who in turn have pressured Israel into unconscionable compromises!

But, the Western world itself is becoming more and more subjected to that pressure, which is beginning to have an effect on them directly.

The pact that Europe forged with the Arabs[1] following the oil embargo in 1973 has affected in no small way the lives of their own population. Even though many Europeans may enjoy the *Schadenfreude* (enjoyment of other people's troubles) derived from the pain they together with the Arabs inflict on Israel and Jews in general, they are only now beginning to wake up to the fact that the European-Arab pact affects their own lives. And the Arab impact on Europe is only just beginning. The huge Arab population — which was transported to Europe as a result of that pact — is growing not only in number but also in influence. France alone has now a population of five to six million Arab Muslims (latest estimates are closer to ten million, not counting illegals). In another generation, this could easily be increased at least four- or fivefold, and what then?

The Americans — who expected to be greeted as liberators by the oppressed Iraqis — are now pressured to leave Iraq, while their goal of democratizing that country is quickly becoming a nightmare. The Americans are learning very quickly that democracy is not necessarily translating into one man, one vote, at least not in this part of the world. In fact, that principle would very quickly transform Iraq into a Shiite state not unlike Iran; since the Shiite — oppressed under Saddam — are the majority in Iraq. Certainly this is another surprise the Americans were not really prepared for; another miscalculation.

The other miscalculation — which may or may not affect the US immediately, but which may have catastrophic effect on Israel and its people, and eventually the rest of the world — is the US president's dream of transforming all of the Middle East into Western-style democracies, starting with the PA-PLO.

The incentive for the Arabs is yet another Arab-Muslim state (at Israel's expense, of course). The possibility of transforming the PA-PLO into a democracy is of course a pipe dream, and even more so the remaining Arab states. Here, it is quite clear that the Americans have failed completely to understand the Arab-Muslim psyche, their behavior or their actions.

---

1. See Bat Ye'or, *Eurabia*.

Israelis, too, once harbored such dreams of coexistence in a more liberal if not democratic Middle East, but most of us have been jarred into reality by the ongoing terrorism and propaganda war.

How much longer will the US keep pressuring Israel on behalf of the Arabs and/or Europeans? But even more importantly, how much longer will the Israeli government bend under these pressures, and how much longer will it continue to compromise the security of its people?

By 2004 Israel's prime minister, Ariel Sharon — once regarded as Israel's greatest hero who was instrumental in turning the tide in the 1973 Egyptian war of aggression against Israel — seemed to have lost his nerve under the constant American pressure. Despite the fact that Bush's vision of a "two-state" solution — at Israel's expense — under the so-called "Road Map for Peace" is not working, Sharon seemed to carry on regardless.

The Road Map was not working for two main reasons, as well as major miscalculations by Bush and his administration. Bush in his "bold vision" — enunciated in June 2002 — saw a "Palestinian" and Israeli state "living side by side in peace." The bold vision, however, provided that "the Palestinians must first democratize all their institutions and renounce terrorism forever." This sounds like a noble endeavor — especially if it isn't your land being traded! And, of course, the other "minor" problem is that the Arabs, and especially the "Palestinians," don't see anything wrong in using terrorism as yet another tool of war.

Has anyone ever heard of any Arab state condemning terrorism?

One must be reminded here that practically all the Arab states still consider themselves in a state of war with Israel, not merely the "Palestinians." And, of course, practically none of them have shrunk from using terrorism against Israel in between wars!

It is very telling indeed that the only two Arab states which have peace pacts with Israel withdrew their embassies from Israel following Arafat's terrorist attacks in September-October 2000, in the aftermath of the failed Oslo Accords.

As for democracy in the PA-PLO, Arabs and Muslims in general consider democracy a Western idea that has no place in their culture or religion.

Considering that Bush's idea to end terrorism and democratize PA-PLO institutions has no chance of working in the foreseeable future, one would have hoped that the pressure on Israel to make fateful concessions would have stopped. But no!

Despite the fact that terrorism continues unabated, despite the knowledge that the Arabs of Gaza, Judea and Samaria have been radicalized beyond redemption, our friends the Americans behave as if nothing has happened to change their vision of a two-state solution.

Sharon, then the Israeli prime minister, floated a disengagement plan to separate from the "Palestinians," and even decided to leave Gaza and uproot fairly large Jewish communities in parts of Gaza. Sharon's own cabinet was opposed to these ideas; senior members demanded that no decision be taken by the government on this critical issue unless approved by both the cabinet and the Knesset (the Israeli parliament). Sharon planned to visit Bush to present to him his plan, but his ministers demanded that until he had agreement from his own government and a vote on the matter, nothing should be done.

Sharon therefore postponed his visit to the US. "Obligingly," however, the US quickly dispatched three senior officials from the State Department so Sharon could present them his plan. Whatever happened to such concepts as sovereignty, and yes, democracy?

Israel was apparently being treated as a vassal state for being a true and faithful ally. The Arabs, however — despite the fact that their long-range plans do not bode well for the West — were (and continue to be) accorded every courtesy in their relationship with Western leaders, including America.

If the Americans and the European leaders are taking into account the confrontation with Islam they will face in the not so distant future, they are certainly not letting on. In the meantime, they hope to appease the Arab Muslims by offering up Israel as a sacrifice, not unlike Chamberlain in the 1930s. The Europeans seem to be suffering from amnesia regarding the results of appeasement; Chamberlain sacrificed Czechoslovakia to Hitler for "peace in our time," but what he got instead was the invasion of all of Europe, and near invasion of England as well.

Interesting Times

To say that we live in "interesting times" is the understatement of the last two centuries. The goings-on in the world we live in are beyond comprehension.

Israel's prime minister decided — without much support from his cabinet, nor indeed his own party, the Likud — to unilaterally withdraw from Gaza, a hotbed of terrorist activity. Sharon's "logic" was that since there is no "partner" on the "Palestinian" side to conduct any sort of (meaningful) negotiations for peaceful coexistence, it would be in Israel's best interest to disengage from the Arab population in Gaza.

There were, however, several serious problems with this unilateral decision. First of all, the terrorists would consider that they were winning the war, that their terrorist tactics were working. Secondly, this move would force Jewish communities living in the area to abandon their homes, their livelihood and way of life, leaving a lot of very unhappy families who see this as an ethnic cleansing of Jews. Thirdly, and most dangerously, the Western world was to see all this as a positive development (not at all as Sharon saw it), inasmuch as it would lead to the creation of a "Palestinian" state.

No one in the Western world appeared to be concerned that such a state would be a terrorist state, and they continued mindlessly repeating their mantra, typified by the G8's official statement in June 2004 on "Gaza Withdrawal and the Road Ahead to Middle East Peace":

> The G8 hopes that this disengagement initiative will stimulate progress towards peace in the region, the realization of Palestinian national aspirations and the achievement of our common objective of two states, Israel and a viable, democratic, sovereign and contiguous Palestine, living side by side in peace and security.

Of course the G8 consists of the usual suspects: members of the Quartet (Russia, the European Union, the US and the UN), plus Canada and Japan.

All this, as if oblivious of the fact that various PA-PLO leaders have said time and again that they will not fight against jihad. They have openly stated that they will not interfere with Hamas and Islamic Jihad and "risk civil war."

The Arabs seemed to be hoping that they would be handed a state of "Palestine" on a silver platter by the Western world, without stopping their terrorist war against Israel. And the Western world was doing its best not to disappoint.

The Western leaders speak of reform; but what reform is possible when terrorism continues unabated and will remain for the foreseeable future?

In another misguided move, Israeli prime minister Sharon turned to Egypt's President Mubarak to help fill the vacuum when Israeli defense forces would depart from Gaza. Mubarak readily agreed, and why not? This would allow Egypt to bring in considerable reinforcement to the border with Israel, which it was prohibited to do according to the Israeli-Egyptian Peace Treaty.

Israel apparently was hoping against hope that the Egyptians would suddenly now prevent the arms smuggling by terrorists across the border with Israel, which had already continued for years without Egypt lifting a finger.

It is true that the Israeli Defense Forces (IDF) have destroyed over time many tunnels through which most of the arms smuggling activity was carried out, but new ones were being added all the time.

The IDF successfully eliminated many terrorist kingpins in Gaza primarily among the Hamas leadership, but Hamas was (and remains) very popular among the Arab population.

What reforms, in any event, are possible in a society so brainwashed by Arab propaganda that parents readily send their young on suicide missions? The attitude is endemic to the entire Arab world, and by no means exclusive to Gaza. A *Jerusalem Post* report on June 9, 2004 revealed that the government of Iran (a non-Arab but Islamic state) had flooded its mosques and universities with tens of thousands of applications for suicide missions. As of the date of the report, ten volunteers had already applied for "martyrdom operations…against Israel and US forces in Iraq, according to the recruitment group, the Committee for the Commemoration of Martyrs of the Global Islamic Campaign"! The spokesman for the campaign explained that "our targets are mainly the occupying American and British forces in the holy Iraqi cities (Najef, Karbala, Kufa and others), all the Zionists in Palestine, and Salman Rushdie."

The *Jerusalem Post* also carried a translated copy of the recruitment form, and noted that Iran not only is intimately involved in all the actions of Hizbullah, but also supports and sponsors Tanzim (which was Arafat's own) and Islamic Jihad cells all over the "West Bank" and Gaza:

> A senior Israeli intelligence source told the *Jerusalem Post*… that complementing Iran's imminent nuclear capability are its efforts to infiltrate terrorists, weapons, or information into the West Bank and Gaza Strip. There is no way to over-emphasize this danger.

And as if on cue, it was reported in the *Jerusalem Post* on June 13 that according to Iran's foreign minister, Kamal Kherrazi, Iran "won't accept any new internationally imposed obligation regarding its nuclear program," and that "the world must recognize Iran as a nuclear-capable nation."

Several months before, Iran had claimed that its nuclear program was for "peaceful" purposes only and the EU had urged the UN to delay the scheduled Nuclear Inspection Agency's visit to the nuclear site!

All of this is disturbing enough, but Mubarak's "help" in Gaza should give us all concern. The G8 at its summit meeting in the US widely praised Egypt for all its efforts "to resolve critical security issues relating to Gaza." UN Secretary-General Kofi Annan also praised Mubarak "for his involvement in the process"!

It is beyond credulity that Israel would ask Egypt to help control the situation in Gaza; some described it as sending the cat to watch over the milk!

One remembers how Egypt tried its best to unify all the different terrorist groups on several occasions. Egypt, whose official television station broadcast a twenty-one-episode series based on the infamous scurrilous libel against Jews, *The Protocols of the Elders of Zion*; Egypt, whose peace pact provided nothing but a very cold peace; Egypt, where Israel's ambassador is treated as a pariah; Egypt, who withdrew their ambassador following Arafat's open terrorist war with Israel.

And this man, who openly works with terrorists at war with Israel, this man, a dictator in his own impoverished, underdeveloped country, is worthy of praise among the important leaders of the West...

Meanwhile, Arafat issued a call to the al-Aqsa Martyrs' Brigades — a terrorist group which claimed "responsibility" for many suicide attacks on Israeli civilians — to join his "security forces." The al-Aqsa Martyrs' Brigades, an offshoot of Fatah, however, recently threatened to abandon Arafat's Fatah because its gunmen were not being paid.

A spokesman for the PA-PLO said that they could not abandon these men, as they have a "moral responsibility" towards them, because "they have sacrificed everything they have for the sake of the cause" (*Jerusalem Post*, June 13, 2004)!

During an emergency meeting of the central committee of Fatah in Arafat's office, the previous day (June 12, Sunday), "Palestinian" leadership discussed "how to contain the mutiny of the Fatah militia." "Prime Minister" Ahmed Qurei made it clear that "the most important mission now was to guarantee the safety of the gunmen who are wanted by Israel for carrying out terrorist attacks" (*Jerusalem Post*, June 15, 2004).

[T]he commander of the Aksa Martyrs Brigades in Tulkarm told the Jerusalem Post that the PA stopped paying his salary a few months ago [and] that was the main reason why he and his friends had halted their attacks against Israel.

"The Palestinian leadership in Ramallah told us that we must now sit quiet and that because of pressure from the international community they would not be able to continue paying us our salaries," he added.

So now we know that pressure from the international community has an effect...sort of. Temporarily.

The article confirmed the official role terrorists were playing in the PA-PLO government:

Senior PA officials in Ramallah on Monday [June 14] confirmed that Arafat had invited the Fatah gunmen to join the reformed security services.

Former PA cabinet minister Abdel Fatah Hamayel...said the idea of recruiting the gunmen to the Palestinian security forces was not a new one. Hamayel said there were at least 450 Fatah gunmen in the West Bank and Gaza Strip who had "made many sacrifices for the Palestinian cause."

He added: "After all these sacrifices, we can't tell these men that we don't need their services any more. The Aksa Martyrs Brigades have a big role to play and they are committed to the decisions of the political leadership."

So in case anyone still had any doubts about the intentions and actions of the PA-PLO, now you know. Qurei's statement is particularly galling: "the most important mission now was to guarantee the safety" of these terrorists!

As if we needed any more proof of what Qurei stands for, we were informed yet again, Sunday, June 20, 2004, by the *Jerusalem Post*, that after meeting with Egyptian president Hosni Mubarak the previous Friday, "Qurei confirmed" that an agreement was being put together between the PA-PLO and other terrorist groups for power sharing after Israel's withdrawal from Gaza! He added that the agreement would be completed after additional talks in Egypt, the very government Sharon was asking to police the border against arms smuggling.

"The Egyptians have pledged to send military advisers to help
train and reform the Palestinian security forces and are seek-
ing assurances from Israel that it will halt all military strikes
in Gaza well before the pullout, to allow the advisers to work,"
Qurei said in a telephone interview.

[...] Egypt is trying to broker an agreement between the
Palestinian Authority and rival factions — including Hamas
and Islamic Jihad — on how to run Gaza after a pullback, a PA
official said.

Of course this is not the first time Egypt was trying to "unify" all the terrorists in their common cause. How very clever of the Egyptians, too, to "seek
assurances from Israel that it will halt all military strikes in Gaza well before
the pullout."

Now that Israel has managed to contain to some degree the terrorist assault
on Israeli civilians by cutting off the heads of the multi-headed cobra, Israel
is asked — or given an ultimatum? — to stop its so-far successful operation
against the most dangerous chieftains of the terrorists.

But what else should Israel expect from Egypt, a country supposedly at
peace with Israel, which still spreads the worst calumnies against Israel and
the Jewish people in general in its official media?

All this however did not seem to dampen the enthusiasm of Shimon Peres,
the engineer of the Oslo blunder. He still believed that Ahmed Qurei was a
"peace partner." Peres could not wait for Israel to withdraw not only from
the Gaza Strip, and Judea and Samaria, but to set a "specific timetable for
withdrawals" regardless of conditions on the ground!

Peres still hoped to join the government in a "National Unity" coalition,
so he could put into effect his failed policies. At the age of eighty, Peres still
believed naively in a "New Middle East" despite a put-down by various Arab
countries in the heyday of the Oslo process; when he envisaged his grand
ideas of economic and other cooperation of all states in the "New Middle
East," he was told unceremoniously that he would first have to convert to
Islam!

During all this maneuvering we were meanwhile also treated to yet another
calumny by the Saudis. After the recent kidnapping and beheading of two US
citizens (one of whom was apparently Jewish) in Saudi Arabia by al-Qaeda,
and other recent terrorist attacks on the kingdom, Abdullah, the de facto ruler

of Saudi Arabia (who has since inherited the throne of his brother Fahd, who died in 2005), said:

> Zionism is behind it. It has become clear now. It has become clear to us. I don't say, I mean… It is not 100 percent, but 95 percent that the Zionist hands are behind what happened.

This in a tape obtained by NBC News, as reported June 20, 2004 by the *Jerusalem Post*:

> Other senior Saudi officials reaffirmed the claim that supporters of Israel — Zionists — were behind the terrorist attacks. Prince Nayef, the Saudi Interior Minister said, "Al-Qaida is backed by Israel and Zionism."

What can one possibly say? Certainly this is not the first such pronouncement by the Saudis; nor unfortunately will it be the last. After all, dictatorships need an enemy on whom to blame all the problems of their people. Some perhaps naively believe that the people of Saudi Arabia are not stupid enough to believe such stuff. Saudi Arabia after all financed, and still does, all the *madrasas* which gave birth to al-Qaeda. The monster that the Saudis created to attack Western targets is now turning on its master!

Will the West ever wake up?

On June 20, 2004, we were also treated to two other important pieces of information as related by the *Jerusalem Post*. One, that the newly appointed French foreign minister, Michael Bernier, on his first official visit to the region, would visit Egypt, Jordan and Yasser Arafat, but not Israel. While it is true that Israel as a matter of policy did not meet with foreign dignitaries who still insisted on courting Arafat, it was interesting that the French preferred the archterrorist Arafat to the state of Israel.

According to the *Jerusalem Post*, the French and the European Union wished to "reiterate the determination…to seek solutions to break the current impasse in the Israeli-Palestinian peace process," and their minister was to "reaffirm [their] commitment to the road-map"!

One can only wonder about the extent of French hypocrisy. Have the French not heard that the "Palestinian" leadership, one after another, have refused to end terrorism — practically the only requirement under the Road Map? Were they deaf, dumb and blind to the pronouncements of all assorted terrorists to join forces under the guidance of Egypt?

The other interesting but more disturbing piece on the same page of the June 20 *Jerusalem Post* (page 2) is the claim by British MPs that the IDF fired at their convoy. Three British Members of Parliament, who were apparently on a UN-sponsored visit to Rafa (or at least were riding in UN vehicles, which are at the disposal of many Arabs who run the UN missions) to inspect damage to Palestinian homes, "charged [the shooting] was meant to prevent them from conducting their tour and making first-hand assessments"!

The real question that has to be asked is, why was this allegedly UN-sponsored mission not coordinated with Israeli officials as is the custom, particularly since the area was a war zone?

It is highly unlikely that IDF soldiers would shoot at civilians, let alone UN-sponsored missions! The IDF is very scrupulous about any unauthorized fire.

Perfidy

Just when you think that things couldn't get any worse, they do!

The ruling of the International Court of Justice (ICJ) released July 9, 2004, regarding the Israeli security fence, proved even more perfidious than initially anticipated.

It was clear from the start that the court was not an independent judicial body, but a highly politicized entity and a creature of the UN General Assembly, where Israel-bashing is a regular event, sponsored by Israel's virulent enemies and their obedient lackeys; yet even so the final decision was far worse than anticipated.

While the ICJ ruling was non-binding, it nonetheless reinforced the Arab propaganda against Israel. As some experts on international law stated, the only "positive" thing about the ICJ decision was that it was so one-sided that no sane person could possibly take it seriously. My concern of course is with all the countries which supported the original UN General Assembly resolution, which took it to the ICJ in the first place. It isn't the sanity of all those countries — the automatic majority of the UN General Assembly — but the slavishness with which they support all Arab "causes," no matter how abhorrent, no matter how one-sided, no matter how outrageous, no matter if they are based on total falsehoods.

The decision of the court was based on the false premise that Israel was "occupying Palestinian land," and referred to the Hague and Geneva Conventions, both of which are falsely applied here.

Both articles of the Geneva and Hague Conventions applied by the court deal with the rights of civilian populations, during wartime, who have laid down their arms — that is key.

The issues the court took upon itself to deal with are "occupied" territories, or worse yet, "occupied Palestinian territories," which of course is a false premise. As already discussed, the territories Judea and Samaria are historically Jewish land, annexed illegally by Jordan in 1948, an entity which itself has no history on the land but was created by Britain in 1922 out of the League of Nations Mandate for Palestine, which was to become the re-constituted Jewish homeland. Even according to the League of Nations Mandate, "Palestine" was acknowledged as the historical Jewish homeland.

So the issue of "occupied territories" of Judea, Samaria and Gaza is bogus at best. Add in the fact that Jordan — which illegally occupied Judea, Samaria and half of historic Jerusalem in a war of aggression in 1948 and subsequent terrorist raids into Israel culminating in another war of aggression in 1967 — lost whatever bogus claims it may have had. Similarly consider Egypt's several wars of aggression in 1948, 1967, 1973 and all the terrorist raids against Israel, and other acts of war enumerated elsewhere regarding international waterways, etc. Egypt too has no legal claim on any part of Israel's land under international law.

As for the "Palestinians," they were not officially party to these wars, although many participated along with their Arab brothers, particularly in 1948. The original Mandate for Palestine was very specific about the rights of Arabs residing in Palestine. They were specifically addressed in that their rights as residents should be preserved; nothing more, nothing less.

But of course even residency in any country bestows certain rights on people, as well as certain obligations under the law of the land. Of course at that time there were no "millions" of Arabs in "Palestine"; they deliberately swell their numbers with many illegals as well as exaggerations.

The original Mandate for Palestine did not bestow on the Arabs of Palestine any additional rights, nor were they ever considered anything other than Arabs — full stop. The invention of calling themselves "Palestinian" didn't occur until much later, when the Arab League decided in 1964 on this propaganda ploy, and the PLO was invented as the "Palestine Liberation Organization," complete with a charter calling for the destruction of Israel.

So let us be clear, when the Arabs talk of the "legitimate rights of the Palestinian people," that these are code words for the destruction of Israel.

The Arabs — having openly proclaimed their aim of destroying Israel and "pushing the Jews into the sea" in all their wars of aggression against Israel, and having failed — created the PLO as their proxy. This plus their unrelenting propaganda against Israel and Jewish people in general, and their successful manipulation of the UN General Assembly and many of its agencies, have brought us to this point.

The ongoing terrorism, suicide bombing, killing and maiming of Israeli women and children — civilians — is supported by 70 to 80 percent of the Arab population of Judea, Samaria and Gaza; how can the International Court of Justice regard them as innocent civilian population per the Geneva Convention?

The security fence erected by the Israeli government which was the subject of the ICJ ruling — erected in order to prevent suicide bombers and their accomplices from entering major Israeli population centers — was deemed "illegal" by the court since it "interfered" with the daily activities of the "Palestinians," causing hardship.

The court did not consider at all the "hardship" suicide bombers caused every day for at least the previous four years to Jewish people, causing more than a thousand deaths, and thousands more wounded and maimed for life, to say nothing of the heartbreak of the bereaved families and orphans as a result of this monstrous terrorism.

Terrorism as a tool of war was unknown during the time of the 1905 Hague Convention, or the later Geneva Convention of 1949. Both of these conventions deal with the protection of civilians during the time of war. Civilians — not armed thugs and terrorists!

Israel, its government and its defense forces are doing their best to avoid civilian Arab casualties in this terrorist borderless war, often putting its soldiers at risk, and paying a heavy toll in human lives as a result of these efforts to save innocent civilians. But Arab propaganda against Israel is obviously succeeding in pointing at Israel and its defense forces as doing just the opposite!

Several countries, including the US, the EU, Canada and Australia, objected (initially) to giving jurisdiction to the ICJ on the matter of the Israeli security fence, deeming it outside ICJ jurisdiction, and a matter of legitimate self-defense under section 51 of the UN Charter. Many have expressed their dismay and concern regarding the ICJ ruling. We still have to wait and see where all this will lead, and whether these democratic countries, which were against the court's jurisdiction in the first place, will in fact remain steadfast.

At this time in history — when not just Israel but the whole civilized world is facing a terrible war against terrorism — moral clarity and steadfastness must become the order of the day.

The court's ruling is preposterous — basing its decision on the bogus claim that Judea and Samaria are occupied "Palestinian land." Its reference to Israel being in breach of international law is equally bogus since neither the Geneva nor Hague Conventions deal with international terrorism. Israeli spokesmen referring to the ruling said had there been no terrorism there would be no need for the security fence.

EU — Sharon Must Be Ready to "Tango" on the Fence

So reads the headline in the July 13 *Jerusalem Post*, only a few days after the July 9, 2004, ICJ ruling.

So while hope springs eternal, our European "friends" didn't wait long to let us know — again — where they stand.

While the EU along with several other countries initially voiced strong opposition to the ICJ jurisdiction over the issue of Israel's anti-terrorist security fence; the EU now appears to want to extract a price for any support Israel may get from them at the UN General Assembly: the price Israel must pay for such support is dependent on a more active role for the EU in the proposed Israeli disengagement process (the high-handed and insulting attitude of the EU is fully explained in Bat Ye'or, *Eurabia*, the EU-Arab League axis).

This from the Dutch foreign minister, Bernard Bot, whose country then held the EU rotating presidency.

The disengagement process itself was still being hotly debated within the ruling Likud Party, and was by no means a forgone conclusion. The disengagement idea came into being following the failure of the Road Map to elicit from the PA-PLO the hoped-for response of disavowing terrorism. As already referred to in previous chapters, terrorism never stopped and in fact intensified following the Road Map, with PA-PLO chieftains "refusing to fight their brothers," Hamas and Islamic Jihad. In fact, various Fatah factions, including the al-Aqsa Martyrs' Brigades among others, claimed "responsibility," often together with Hamas and others, for many terrorist bombings.

Israel's IDF had no choice but to re-enter various areas, in attempts to arrest fugitives and destroy their bomb factories. It was these preventative actions by Israel's defense forces that foiled many terrorist acts against Israeli cities and their populations.

Since the Road Map failed in its goal to stop terrorism and create a "Palestinian" state, one supposes that Prime Minister Sharon, being fed up with the Road Map and its process, decided that unilateral disengagement was the next best thing. However, many Israelis saw unilateral disengagement as a "reward" and a victory for terrorism and were adamantly opposed to it. Even Sharon's party — the Likud itself — was deeply divided on the issue, with the large majority of the Central Committee voting against it in a partywide referendum.

Now the EU, as part of the so-called Quartet — the inventors of the Road Map to nowhere — wanted to inject themselves in the unilateral disengagement. But unilateral means just that: unilateral — without interference by other parties, particularly those who still held court in Arafat's Ramallah.

All this, despite the fact that the PA-PLO did not show any sign of giving up terrorism as a tool of their war against Israel. As already discussed earlier, terrorism is only one of their tools and they consider it legitimate, as do their Arab and Islamic co-religionists. Their concerted propaganda campaign against the Jewish people and the Jewish state seems to have affected even "enlightened" nations, as one can observe in their attitudes! Or is it coercion and blackmail levied against oil-dependent states that seems to work wonders? But even states which are not oil-dependent, such as Canada, toe the Arab line, as if hypnotized into submission.

Again, the United Nations is only as good as its member states, and since the Arabs have over time managed to acquire an automatic majority at the UN on any issue they wish to pursue — particularly their obsession with the State of Israel — the UN General Assembly can be counted on to deliver, no matter how obscene the resolutions the Arabs put forward.

And so the obscene "Zionism is racism" resolution came into being in 1975 at the UN General Assembly (since rescinded thanks to the untiring efforts of US Ambassador John Bolton and US Senator Daniel Patrick Moynihan in 1993 — the Arabs still voted against!) and dozens of other resolutions directed against Israel and its sovereignty. The UN General Assembly's overwhelming majority of (thankfully non-binding) resolutions are directed against the State of Israel, while serious abuses of human rights and killings of innocents in southern Sudan and throughout Africa go unnoticed.

The problem is that the UN General Assembly's non-binding resolutions have nonetheless caused irreparable harm to Israel.

The United Nations, which was built on lofty goals, has over time become perverted into a tool of Arab manipulations. And so, even the International Court of Justice, which was supposed to function as an arbitrator between nations to resolve disputes between them in an amicable manner, has now also become a tool of the Arab automatic majority at the UN.

The ICJ never dealt with the central issue of the Arab-Israeli conflict: the wars of aggression Arab states waged against Israel. That conflict is still unresolved, and is the real problem of the Middle East, despite the peace accords signed between Israel and its immediate neighbors Egypt and Jordan.

The ICJ decision to deal with the security fence Israel is erecting in order to prevent the suicide bombers from killing Israeli citizens on buses, in cafes, in shopping malls and elsewhere, is nothing but a sham!

Several important issues need to be pointed out here:

1. The ICJ is supposed to resolve issues between states through arbitration, provided the court has the consent of both parties to a dispute.
2. Israel never gave its consent to the court to deal with the issue of the security fence; in fact, it objected officially that the court has no jurisdiction in the matter.
3. The PA-PLO is not a state; it is a terrorist organization, which exists at the behest of several Arab states. The Arab states use smoke-and-mirrors propaganda to render the Arab-Israeli conflict a "Palestinian"-Israeli conflict.
4. The real issue is not the security fence but an attempt by the Arab Muslims to push Israel to its pre-1967 indefensible borders.
5. Judea, Samaria and Gaza and the Old City of Jerusalem are historically Jewish land. And Israel has no intention of going back to the suicide borders of 1949, which invited Arab aggression against Israel in the first place.

There is no international law in existence that would give the Arabs possession of Judea, Samaria and Gaza, as well as the Old City of Jerusalem, if the Arab-Israeli conflict were brought before an independent court of justice. But, of course, the current ICJ is not a court of justice; it is a kangaroo court, which in this ruling ignored every aspect of international law. And it didn't even deal with the reason why the security fence was erected in the first place — the issue of ongoing terrorism!

It is interesting that the day after I wrote these lines, Charles Krauthammer, in an opinion piece in the *Washington Post* (reprinted in the *Jerusalem Post*, July 19, 2004), used similar language to condemn the ICJ decision. Calling the ICJ a kangaroo court, Krauthammer points to its hypocrisy, and states:

> Not since Libya was made chairman of the Commission on Human Rights has the UN system put on such a shameless display of hypocrisy.
>
> [...] Among various principles invoked by the International Court of Justice in its highly publicized decision on Israel's security fence is this one: It is a violation of international law for Jews to be living in the Jewish quarter of Jerusalem. If this sounds absurd to you — Jews have been inhabiting the Old City of Jerusalem since it became their capital 3,000 years ago — it is. And it shows the lengths to which the United Nations and its associate institutions, including this kangaroo court, will go to condemn Israel."
>
> The court's main business was to order Israel to tear down the security fence [...]. The fence is only one-quarter built, and yet it has already resulted in an astonishing reduction in suicide attacks in Israel. In the past four months, two Israelis have died in suicide attacks, compared to 166 killed in the same time frame at the height of the terrorism.
>
> But what are 164 dead Jews to this court? Israel finally finds a way to stop terrorism, and 14 eminences sitting in The Hague rule it illegal — in a 64-page opinion in which the word terrorism appears not once (except when citing Israeli claims).
>
> Yes, the fence causes some hardship to Palestinians. Some are separated from their fields [but have access to them], some schoolchildren have to walk much farther to class. This is unfortunate. On any scale of human decency, however, it is far more unfortunate that 1,000 Israelis are dead from Palestinian terrorism, and thousands more horribly maimed, including Israeli schoolchildren with nails and bolts and shrapnel lodged

in their brains and spines who will never be walking to school again.

From the safe distance of 2,000 miles the court declared itself "not convinced" that the barrier Israel is building is a security necessity. It based its ruling on the claim that the fence violates Palestinian "humanitarian" rights such as "the right to work, to health, to education and to an adequate standard of living as proclaimed in the International Covenant on Economic, Social and Cultural Rights and in the United Nations Convention on the Rights of the Child."

I'm sure that these conventions are lovely documents. They are also documents of absolutely no weight — how many countries would *not* stand condemned for failure to provide an "adequate standard of living"? — except, of course, when it comes to Israel. Then, any document at hand will do.

What makes the travesty complete is that this denial of Israel's right to defend itself because doing so might violate "humanitarian" rights was read in open court by the chief judge representing *China*, whose government massacred hundreds of its own citizens demonstrating peacefully in Tiananmen Square.

[...] Moreover, [the ICJ] had no jurisdiction to take this case. It is a court of arbitration, which requires the consent of both parties. The Israelis, knowing the deck was stacked, refused to give it. Not only did the United States declare this issue outside the boundaries of this court, so did the European Union and Russia, hardly Zionist agents.

Krauthammer went on to enumerate various further elements of the court's anti-Israeli prejudice and corruption, with reference to the security fence as a wall, and the Arab aggression during the several wars against Israel by several Arab armies openly aiming at Israel's destruction passively described as "armed conflict broke out between Israel and a number of Arab states," emphasizing particularly the May 1948 Arab aggression. "Broke out?" Krauthammer asks:

As if three years after the Holocaust and almost entirely without weapons, a tiny country of 600,000 Jews had decided to make war on five Arab states with nearly 30 million people.

Israel will rightly ignore the decision. The United States, acting honorably in a world of utter dishonor regarding Israel, will support that position. It must be noted that one of the signatories of this attempt to force Israel to tear down its most effective means of preventing the slaughter of innocent Jews was the judge from Germany. The work continues.

Thank you Charles Krauthammer — again — for your clear-minded analyses, and thank you, *Jerusalem Post*, again and again…

The letters to the editor from Jews and gentiles alike also expressed outrage at the ICJ "advisory opinion" which added fuel to the Arab propaganda war against Israel. Many thanks to those letter-writers, too, for their expression of unwavering friendship during these particularly difficult times.

The UN General Assembly Vote

We didn't have to wait long. The General Assembly of the United Nations voted like obedient dogs 150–6, with ten abstentions, on the International Court of "Justice" advisory, non-binding opinion: Israel "must" dismantle its security barrier, being built to stop terrorist incursions into major population centers, because the security barrier "inconveniences" the Arab population.

The 150 nations which voted in favor of the "Palestinian"-sponsored resolution included all twenty-five member states of the European Union, including the ten newly-joined states, which some in Israel naively hoped would perhaps influence the EU for the better. So much for vain hopes.

The six member states that voted in favor of Israel and against the UN resolution included the United States, Australia, Micronesia, the Marshal Islands and Palau. It is interesting to note that among the ten abstentions was Uganda which in 1975 was the sponsor of the infamous UN resolution that "Zionism is racism."

Even Italy — considered by Israel as a friend — voted with the EU, as a block. Britain — no surprise here — voted with the EU as well.

Israeli officials' response to the ICJ vote was: Israel is determined to build the security barrier.

The prime minister's spokesman, Ra'anan Gissin, said, "Israel will continue to build the fence in accordance with the ruling of Israel's High Court of Justice." He dismissed the UN General Assembly vote as a "tyranny of the majority, by a majority of tyrannies," according to the *Jerusalem Post*, July 22, 2004. Also according to the *Jerusalem Post*:

> The Foreign Ministry issued a statement following the resolution expressing Israeli "disappointment" that the UN's agenda was once again "hijacked" by the Palestinians to pass yet another resolution against Israel.
>
> "Not only does this position by the United Nations not help the peace process, it encourages Palestinian terrorism," the statement read.

It was apparently the Dutch, who held the EU rotating presidency, and the French who led the charge.

The EU — which had voted the previous December against sending the issue of Israel's security fence to the ICJ in the Hague, saying it was not appropriate for ICJ adjudication — didn't seem to have any problem reversing itself, now voting yet again for the "Arab cause."

The Israeli UN ambassador, Dan Gillerman, called the resolution "one-sided and totally counterproductive" (*Jerusalem Post*, July 22, 2004):

> Addressing the assembly after the vote Gillerman was…dismissive of the resolution. "Thank God that the fate of Israel and of the Jewish people is not decided in this hall," he said.
>
> Gillerman [...] said construction of the security fence will continue in compliance with the requirements of international law as decided by Israel's Supreme Court. Gillerman added that the resolution "cannot but embolden the true enemies of the Israeli and Palestinian people."
>
> "It is simply outrageous to respond with such vigor to a measure that saves lives and respond with such casual indifference and apathy to the ongoing campaign of Palestinian terrorism that takes lives. This is not justice but a perversion of justice," he said.
>
> [...] The PLO observer, Kidwa, on the other hand, praised the vote as "magnificent," calling it "perhaps the most important development in the situation since the partition plan."

Meanwhile, we are being informed that the "Palestinian" schoolbooks for the first time delineate the borders of the "West Bank" and Gaza Strip on maps, but the entire territory encompassed by Israel, the "West Bank" and Gaza is referred to as "Palestine." Nothing new here, either, in terms of calling the entire area of Israeli land "Palestine."

One would think that such barefaced provocation and propaganda would have some influence on the nations of the world and that simple decency would have prevented them from supporting the "Palestinian" resolution, but apparently there is precious little decency left in the UN.

As the Israeli Ambassador said, the UN resolution was nothing but a perversion of justice.

Coming back to the abstentions to the "Palestinian" UN resolution — among them Canada and Uganda — one has to appreciate how far Uganda has come. Admittedly it has not come far enough, but it has to be remembered that Uganda assisted the 1970s terrorist hijackers who singled out Jewish passengers on a civilian flight and abducted them to Uganda.

Some will recall how Israel managed to rescue the hapless Jewish captives from Uganda, only to be accused by Uganda of trespassing its sovereign territory. Apparently, at that time, Uganda had no problem with the terrorist hijackers "trespassing its territory."

Yes, considering all that, Uganda has come a long way…

Not so Canada, one of the other abstainers.

Canada has not only been a haven for "Palestinian" terrorists and an incubator for would-be terrorists, but also a haven for Nazi war criminals. Many hundreds of Nazi war criminals with blood on their hands have lived out their lives in Canada, many under their own names, without fear of prosecution.

This, despite existing legal means under the Hague and Geneva Conventions to bring them to justice in Canada's own courts. These conventions provide a mechanism for a country to try individuals accused of serious war crimes provided that they are resident of that country.

Despite efforts by many Jewish survivors of the Holocaust, this writer included, Canada's governments and judiciary have obstructed every effort to bring these murderers to trial.

There were few attempts at deportation, although some of these individualso obtained their citizenship under false pretences; but surely deportation of criminals, many of whom committed mass murder or were complicit in mass murder, can hardly qualify as punishment.

After stalling for decades, when individuals were taken to court in private lawsuits, several such individuals were treated with sympathy by ignorant jurors because of their advanced age — even if only in their mid-seventies.

The newly appointed UN High Commissioner for Human Rights, Louise Arbour (a Canadian), who gave up her seat on Canada's Supreme Court, did not concern herself at her first news conference with the horrible tragedy of the Sudanese Christians, persecuted and decimated for decades by their Islamic overlords and driven out of their homes, with nowhere to go. Some estimate that a million of these refugees were driven out of their homes, with very few means of survival. These unfortunate true refugees did not arouse Ms. Arbour's humanitarian concerns, but the security fence Israel is erecting was uppermost on her mind (*Jerusalem Post*, July 23, 2004): Louise Arbour said that Israel's barrier was "not conducive to the resolution of the conflict" in the Middle East. She also said that "one has to hope that the government of Israel will reconsider the wisdom of ensuring its security — which I concede is a most pressing concern — through means other than this particular one."

If Ms. Arbour had any specific advice as to what alternate means those would be, she left us guessing! "All authorities point more or less in the same direction and that is that as presently conceived and erected, this barrier should be removed," Arbour said.

She did not quote any authorities and experts in international law including the only American judge sitting on the ICJ, who totally disagreed with the majority non-binding ICJ ruling. Ms. Arbour did pledge to devote her four-year term to the rights of "the most vulnerable and disenfranchised, the targets of intolerance and hatred." We will wait with bated breath.

She continued, warning against the "rollback in human rights... In particular, legitimate and robust responses to terrorism, must be made to operate within legal constraints... Moreover, the war on terrorism should not obscure all other pressing social problems."

How easy to say all these things without referring to the real issues plaguing the world and from a safe distance...

At the Mercy of Others

It would seem that many Western powers still don't grasp the simple proposition that while they were used to the persecution and injustice they meted out against the Jews collectively for centuries during our absence from our Land, we on the other hand never got used to it.

What we are witnessing today is still the same offensive, high-handed "high-minded" disapproval of all we do, and all we are, even in our own Land!

In their minds we do not seem to deserve the same kind of justice or consideration that applies to others. Thankfully — thank G-d — we are no longer at the mercy of others, back in our own Land. But many leaders of the so-called "enlightened" nations behave as though we are, and still treat us with belligerent bellicosity and contempt.

A case in point was the recent verbal attack by New Zealand's prime minister, Helen Clark. Her belligerent outburst was only magnified by her menacing facial expression, as she delivered herself of an undiplomatic barrage of insults, in public.

Silly me, I always believed that issues between "friendly countries" are resolved diplomatically, away from public scrutiny. I guess Clark believes otherwise, especially where Israel is concerned.

The public "dressing down" of Israel was apparently a result of some Israelis attempting to obtain illegally a New Zealand passport. She publicly accused them, even before they were brought to court, of being Mossad agents, and publicly demanded an apology from Israel.

Israeli officials apparently did not apologize, publicly or otherwise; one official claimed that the Israeli government cannot be held responsible for any transgression an Israeli citizen may commit abroad. The Israeli minister of foreign affairs tried to play down the entire affair, saying Israel hopes that the friendly relations between the two countries will soon be restored.

Meanwhile, Clark — delivering another slap in Israel's face — announced again publicly that no Israeli representative will be welcomed in New Zealand, and that in the future, even Israeli representatives will have to apply for a visa!

An apology came in the July 19 *Jerusalem Post* — from a reader, a New Zealander who apologized on behalf of her country and its leadership for the false passport debacle regarding the Israeli "agents": "I am ashamed of the outcry, and I'm positive it would not happen if another country were involved," she wrote.

Here it must be stated that Clark branded the two Israelis as Israel's agents, though their conviction was not on charges of espionage.

The letter writer continued:

> It is yet another face of anti-Semitism respectably dressed up as a diplomatic row. I call upon my government which says it has been on "friendly terms" with Israel to apologize for its interference in Israel's self-defense against terrorism, its damning silence on the Israeli victims of homicide bombers, and its votes against Israel in the UN… While Israel has many friends among New Zealanders, I am ashamed of my government.
> Signed Angela Paul, Auckland

Thank you, Angela Paul, for your honesty and decency, which are rare in today's world.

It was reported, subsequent to Ms. Clark's undiplomatic outrage, that Jewish graves were destroyed in New Zealand (*Jerusalem Post*, July 18):

> Jewish graves were vandalized at a cemetery in Wellington, New Zealand, after two Israelis were sentenced by an Auckland court after admitting to trying to obtain a New Zealand passport. […] The graveyard attacks came just hours after the two were imprisoned.

I would venture to say that the graveyard was desecrated as a direct result of the prime minister of New Zealand's Israel-bashing!

Chapter XXXIII

Chaos, Mayhem and Total Anarchy

The United Nations did not call an emergency meeting of the General Assembly or otherwise in the face of total chaos and anarchy being played out in Gaza and elsewhere. There was no condemnation of the apparently random violence, abductions, etc., openly displayed on TV for the whole world to see.

No country expressed shock or dismay. Apparently nothing the Arabs can do has any shock value anymore.

The kidnapping of several PA "officials" was orchestrated by Arafat himself as reported in the *Jerusalem Post* (July 20, 2004); this according to "official sources" in Gaza and the "West Bank":

> One source said those who were behind the kidnapping were on Arafat's payroll. Another source said it was Arafat's way of removing the unpopular police chief from his post.

Ahmed Qurei, the PA "prime minister," announced yet again that he remains "steadfast" on his "resignation," but that he was "still waiting for a response from PA Chairman Arafat on his demands for 'security reforms.'" This is of course not the first time Qurei "threatened" to resign, only to change his mind soon after. As for the so-called "security reforms," they of course mean different things to different people. To the Americans, one supposes it means turning more than a dozen separate militias into one coherent force under — they hope and apparently believe — "responsible leadership." But, of course, that is mere wishful thinking.

The violence and mayhem that always existed in Gaza has now turned into total anarchy, with the various "militias" — or shall we call them what they really are: terrorist thugs — fighting for turf, often against each other, apparently with Arafat's blessing.

According to some, it was Arafat's way of staying in power. All these disparate terrorist groups were on Arafat's payroll. They were all in their own way loyal to Arafat. Nonetheless, it served Arafat's purpose to keep them at each other's throats.

So one can really appreciate how naïve and ignorant are all those who called for the "unification" of all "security" forces! Whether Europe is as naïve in this respect as the US is less clear.

One thing, however, is certain — these thugs are no "security forces"; they are terrorists with blood of the innocent on their hands, no matter how much the Europeans or the UN or the US attempt to put a positive spin on this bloody reality.

Nothing in this world can change the fact that Israel is dealing with a society that is violent by choice. A society that has been brought up on hate propaganda and total falsehoods about history, about the Jewish people, the state of Israel and its historical rights to the Land of Israel — including, of course — Judea and Samaria. These falsehoods, this hate propaganda promoting violence, terrorism and suicide bombing were for decades taught in schools to young and impressionable children, and we are now reaping the unfortunate results of these teachings. But we must also finally acknowledge that these teachings are not only reinforced by the Arab media, but have as their sources the mosque and the Qur'an itself!

On May 16, 2004, the *Jerusalem Post* quoted Arafat invoking the Qur'an, calling on the "Palestinians" to "terrorize" their enemy. On the fifty-sixth anniversary of Israel's independence — which the Arabs refer to as "the catastrophe" because they did not succeed in committing genocide against Israel and the Jewish people — Arafat quoted a phrase from the Qur'an that tells Muslims to "find what strength you have to terrorize your enemy and the enemy of God," referring to Muslims' war against pagans. According to the *Jerusalem Post*'s Khaled Abu Toameh, "Arafat, however, also signaled that he was ready for peace when he referred to another phrase reading: 'If they want peace, then let's have it.'"

The same article also carried a picture of a "map of Palestine" — depicting all of *Eretz Yisrael* from Jordan to the Mediterranean Sea — carried by protesters during a march in Gaza City, this also coinciding with the anniversary of Israel's independence.

The "peace" Arafat was referring to is further elaborated in the Qur'an to the effect that the infidel can either convert and give up his land, or die by the sword. That is Arafat's "peace of the brave."

On July 13, 2004, the *Jerusalem Post* reported on its front page an article also by Khaled Abu Toameh, including a picture of young "Palestinian" children from a Hamas "summer camp" in Gaza, taking part in a "ceremony," receiving "diplomas" as "graduating" terrorists:

> The children, aged 7–15, are taught, among other things, how to use automatic rifles and pistols, assemble and dismantle explosive charges, and jump through burning tires.

Several TV stations broadcast footage of the video depicting the Arab children at "summer camp," including the Saudi-owned Al-Arabiya news channel, as well as Sky Television and Israeli television. The children were seen wearing military fatigues and brandishing a variety of different weapons.

The report showed children being trained how to "rescue hostages" from hijacked cars, but the footage I saw looked more like how to take and subdue a hostage! The "trainers" were masked men carrying Kalashnikov rifles and rocket-propelled grenade launchers. Some of them belonged to Arafat's Fatah's al-Aqsa Martyrs' Brigades, according to the *Jerusalem Post*. Also in the same report, we are informed that the most popular camps are the "mosque camps" which offer lessons in Qur'an, computers, as well as various sports activities:

> "We hire professional captains and teachers to polish up the physical and mental skills of our children, who, God willing, will liberate Palestine," Yasser Al-Mashoukhi, the imam of Al-Farouk Mosque in Rafah, told the Islam on Line Website.

It's extremely difficult to believe that our erstwhile "friends," the Europeans, who told us they will be involved in the (nonexistent) "peace process," whether we like it or not, are not aware of all these goings-on.

On the same day, the *Jerusalem Post* reported that Terje Roed-Larsen — the UN envoy to the Middle East, best known for his close relationship with Arafat — in an uncharacteristic way criticized Arafat in his "carefully balanced" briefing to the UN Security Council ("Israeli Gaza withdrawal offers unprecedented opportunity for progress towards peace, if implemented in right way, Security Council told," UN Press Release SC/8146, July 13, 2004). Larsen merely said what he should have said but did not say for the longest time, namely, that "despite consistent promises" by the PA:

> [Its leadership] had made no progress on its core obligation

to take immediate action on the ground to end violence and combat terror, and to reform and reorganize the Palestinian Authority.

This Larsen said July 13; it must be remembered that several days before, total anarchy took place in the PA-controlled Gaza Strip.

But the faithful UN bureaucrat that Larsen is, he nonetheless "for balance" took a swipe at Israel as well:

> The Israeli Government had made no progress either on its core obligation to immediately dismantle settlement outposts erected since March 2001 and to move towards a complete freeze of settlement activities.

And so the faithful UN envoy equated terrorism (not only practiced, but also encouraged and taught) with Israel's building settlements on its own government-owned land!

Someone should tell Larsen, and through him, the UN powers-that-be, that Israel is not obliged to give up its own land to build a state for a terrorist entity totally dedicated to its destruction!

The failure of Oslo and the Road Map, due entirely to Arafat's terrorist activities, should by now be ample proof that peace is not attainable, at least not any time in the foreseeable future.

After what can only be characterized as fairly mild criticism of Arafat's PA by the UN envoy Larsen, the following day (July 14), the *Jerusalem Post* carried a banner headline: "Arafat bans UN envoy." Larsen was declared "persona non grata" and was accused, of all things, of "being biased in favor of Israel."

Larsen threw in for good measure after several "balancing" acts, that "Israel's lack of compliance on the sensitive issue of settlements is equally frustrating. Territory lies at the heart of this conflict"!

May I remind the kind reader yet again, that none of the so-called "settlements" or "outposts" were built on anything that could be remotely referred to as "Arab land," let alone "Palestinian" land. Many of today's journalists and so-called free world leaders, in fact, refer to Judea and Samaria, apparently in compliance with the Arab propaganda line — as "occupied Palestinian land"!

That is indeed most frustrating.

And yet, in spite of Larsen's so-called "evenhandedness," the PA-PLO, including its "permanent observer" at the United Nations, Nasser al-Kitwa — Arafat's nephew — lashed out at the UN envoy, accusing him of serving as Prime Minister Sharon's cheerleader.

According to the *Jerusalem Post* (July 15, 2004), Arafat's spokesman, Abu Rudeineh, termed "Larsen's remarks 'suspicious' — a term used by Palestinians to suggest collusion with Israel." Rudeineh went on:

> ... that Larsen's attack was designed to undermine last week's ruling by the International Court of Justice in The Hague against the security fence — a decision he described as a "great victory" for the Palestinians.
>
> "As of today we consider him unwelcome in the Palestinian lands because he has violated all the conventions and agreements signed between the UN and the Palestinian Authority."

Well, it would be interesting, to say the least, to see such "agreements" (if in fact they exist), wouldn't it?

Qurei, who threatened to quit earlier, once again kissed and made up with Arafat. We were told that the mayhem and anarchy, which broke out allegedly between the old guard and the younger generation over corruption, was merely a pretext. One of Arafat's strong supporters who met with US representatives "assured" them that Arafat was still running everything in spite of his confinement in Ramallah. And in spite of all the corruption (of which he is the main culprit).

According to press reports, the lawlessness and anarchy were still going strong, with the warlords fighting amongst each other. Some foreign aid workers were kidnapped in the PA-PLO controlled territories, but were released after several hours.

"Two suspected collaborators killed in Gaza," read the headline in the *Jerusalem Post* on August 13, 2004. The alleged "collaborators" were killed in their hospital beds after being previously wounded, when a PA-PLO policeman hurled a grenade into their prison cell, in the Gaza City's main prison, where other alleged "collaborators" were being held.

Where were the cries of outrage by human rights groups? The UN appeared equally silent. It seems there is no limit to the atrocities the PLO and all the other terrorists are capable of, even against their own people. In what kind of society does a "policeman" throw a hand grenade into a prison cell? Who decides who is a collaborator? In what society does an alleged "collaborator" get killed in broad daylight in a midtown square (as also happened in 2004), while the town's people look on approvingly? And killings in hospital beds!

All this while Israel is forced to fight this borderless terrorist war imposed on us by this intractable enemy, with no help from our "friends."

Every day there are several kassam rockets targeting civilian population in the nearby town of Sderot in the northern Negev. Sometimes, these primitive rockets fall in or near inhabited areas — the last one as of this writing fell on a home in Sderot causing extensive damage. Miraculously, the family, at the urging of one of their daughters, had slept in a friend's home some distance away as the young girl seemed to have a premonition and feared to sleep at home.

There is an ongoing exchange of fire. Soldiers are regularly fired upon from private homes and sometimes from abandoned structures. Nearly every day, would-be suicide bombers are apprehended as the IDF is constantly on high alert. Road bombs and rocket-propelled grenades being fired at troops are reported daily.

It is difficult if not impossible to describe the concern one feels — in fact, the concern all of Israeli society feels — over the constant terrorist war, which goes on unabated. Every day there are reports of attempted terrorist attacks, whether it is suicide bombers and their handlers being apprehended before they are able to carry out their heinous acts of murder, or powerful roadside bombs which are miraculously discovered and disarmed before they kill and maim our people.

All this while the "free world" turns a blind eye, and instead puts pressure and restraints on the Israeli government!

World leaders do not appear concerned about the ongoing terrorism, the ugly propaganda campaign nor indeed the chaos and anarchy reigning supreme in the PA-PLO-controlled cities and "refugee camps," nor their bomb-making shops amid the civilian population, nor the ammunition smuggling tunnels from Egypt.

It is pretty difficult to imagine that the arms smuggling goes on unnoticed by the Egyptians. And yet, it is the Egyptians who are supposed to help the "Palestinians" to better "arrange" their "security" forces.

With this backdrop, the archterrorist Arafat was accorded an honorary "doctorate" from al-Quds University. Truly, one is at a loss for words (*Jerusalem Post*, August 3, 2004, page 14).

Hamas "on UN Payroll"

"Members of Hamas 'on UN Payroll'," so reads the front-page headline of the Canadian *National Post*, October 4, 2004. One reads on in abhorrence and disbelief, only to discover that Peter Hansen, commissioner-general of the UN Relief and Works Agency (UNWRA) for "Palestinian refugees," does not consider it a crime to have members of this terrorist organization on the UN payroll.

"Hamas as a political organization does not mean that every member is a militant and we do not do political vetting and exclude people from one persuasion as against another," Hansen said during an interview on CBC (Canadian Broadcasting Corporation) on October 3. "We demand of our staff, whatever their political persuasion is, that they behave in accordance with UN standards and norms for neutrality."

If we ever had any doubts what UN norms were about, now we have it spelled out in black and white!

The *National Post* reported: "Canadian officials expressed concern over Mr. Hansen's remarks — according to the story — but also pointed to the long record of UNWRA's humanitarian service in the West Bank and Gaza Strip."

As far as we know, these humanitarian "relief" works include education in Judea and Samaria, as well as Gaza. This education provided to the Arab children is nothing but brainwashing of young minds, which are trained as future terrorist suicide bombers!

A spokesman for the Canadian Foreign Affairs Ministry promised to "immediately seek clarification from Mr. Hansen directly and from UN authorities… As far as Canada is concerned, Hamas is a terrorist organization."

Is this a case of willful blindness, or one hand not knowing what the other is doing?

Surely, Canadian foreign affairs officials must be well aware of the goings-on at the UN and its various agencies — even if the average Canadian may not — considering Canada's voting record (biased against Israel) at the UN in general, there can be little doubt left where Canada stands on the issues.

The Israeli government insisted Hansen be immediately stripped of his duties and fired, after releasing a pair of videotapes they said were proof "that UN ambulances have been used to ferry munitions and gunmen…"

But, Hansen's admission that Hamas members are, or may be employed by the UN Agency, and that he does not see it as a crime, should have awakened the outrage of the world. It did not!

The world has become gradually anesthetized to terrorism and its barbarity. The world still seems to think in "us and them" terms; it's okay as long as it's "them," and not us! Most people still do not understand, or at least prefer not to believe, the ultimate aim of the terrorists and those who train, finance and recruit them.

There is a tendency to turn a blind eye and hope for the best. People are getting used to the ever-mounting atrocities, barbarity and savagery, and moral outrage is evaporating from public discourse. The world is heading for disaster and doesn't seem to know it.

At the UN Security Council, as ever, Israel is condemned for its operations against terrorists, examples in late 2004 included incidents in the Gaza Strip in the wake of ongoing terrorist rocket attacks on civilians in a neighboring town, and a kibbutz where the victims were two toddlers, cousins, two and four years old.

Russia, the great "equalizer," proposed a compromise resolution in the Security Council, to balance an Arab nations draft of a UN Security Council resolution on October 4, condemning Israel, demanding "that Israel immediately halt its incursion into northern Gaza," according to the Israeli paper *Ha'aretz*.

Curiously this comes on the heels of the admission by the UN representative in the area, Mr. Hansen, that Hamas "may be" employed by the UN agency. The "Palestinians" Israel is fighting against in Gaza are the very same terrorists who have committed outrage after outrage against Israeli civilians, including many children, often deliberately targeting buses carrying students in early morning traffic.

Hamas claimed responsibility in most of these horrific massacres of the innocent, often stating that every child is a military target, too. Meanwhile, at the UN, their Arab brothers protest loudly and condemn Israel (with the support of many "democracies," including Canada) every time Israel takes action against these terrorists!

Chapter XXXIV

Anti-Semitism,
Sixty Years after Auschwitz

As the dignitaries and heads of state gathered in Auschwitz-Birkenau to commemorate sixty years after the liberation of that infamous death factory, one could not help but wonder at the terrible irony being played out there.

These very same leaders who solemnly paid tribute to the millions murdered, mainly Jewish men, women and children, these very same leaders are playing dangerous games with the lives of the Jewish people now. They ignore Arab anti-Semitic propaganda calling for the death of the Jewish people and the destruction of the Jewish State of Israel; they play into the hands of the Arabs, to mollify and appease them; and they pressure and force Israel to commit national suicide by giving up vital parts of its homeland. As already stated a number of times in this book, Israel will not survive without Judea and Samaria, Gaza and the Golan Heights, as numerous experts and even advisors to various US governments have testified.

Israel will be defenseless without the high grounds and the depth provided by the areas of the Judean Hills and Samaria and the Golan Heights.

The leaders aligned with the Arabs in their "cause" of destroying Israel are well aware of all the facts and geopolitical realities in the Arab-Israeli conflict. In fact, the tribute paid to the dead Jews is no more than a way to soften up Israel's leaders, to get even greater concessions for their Arab clients. That is the horrible irony we witnessed at Auschwitz in 2005, and the horrible reality Israel faces from both "friends" and foes.

The various peace accords that Israel attempted to forge with its neighbors after each aggressive war the Arabs launched have led to nothing. Egypt, even after the return of all the Sinai Peninsula, remains as hostile as ever. Egypt, according to Natan Sharansky, a former minister in the Israeli cabinet, is the worst purveyor of anti-Semitic hate propaganda and incitement against Israel and the Jewish people in general.

To call the Egypt-Israel peace treaty a "cold peace" is to delude ourselves as to its true intent. The hate propaganda emanating out of Egypt is no different from that in Gaza, Judea and Samaria, and is every bit as vile and dangerous.

A headline in the *Canadian Jewish News*, February 3, 2005, following the commemoration at Auschwitz, read: "Holocaust remembered but not understood." This itself fell regrettably short of understanding.

I believe that most people still do not fully understand how propaganda — incitement to hatred and violence — led to the mass murder of the Jewish people in Europe during WWII. In the same way, people don't fully comprehend that the propaganda, anti-Semitic hatred and vilification of the Jewish people and the State of Israel by Arab leaders throughout the Middle East and the Muslim world (and now throughout Europe) has led to several wars by the Arab aggressors against Israel, as well as the terrible acts of terrorism we are still experiencing.

The hate propaganda which demonizes Jewish people and dehumanizes us is no different than Nazi propaganda. But the Arabs go one better, with the claim that the Jews — the "Zionist Entity," "stole their land."

Whether people actually believe any of this propaganda or not, Israel has been ostracized at the UN by the automatic majority in the General Assembly; in the general press, with few exceptions; in universities in Europe, Canada and even in the US where Arab professors spout out their anti-Israel venom. Several writers have pointed out in recent times that students who do not follow the anti-West, anti-Israel line touted by their professors are castigated, and their grades are affected.[1]

The universities in Europe, Canada and the US now have a large contingent of such pro-Arab professors, and in Europe especially a large contingent of Arab students as well who regularly demonstrate and use pro-Arab propaganda to promote the "Palestinian" cause.

The early signs of this dangerous propaganda were ignored; often academic freedom was cited, as well as freedom of speech. By now, campus propaganda

---

1. See Barbara Kay, "Academic freedom is under attack," *National Post*, January 12, 2005.

espouses the Arab "cause" to the exclusion of all others, and academic freedom and freedom of speech in academia have become a mockery.

Hate propaganda and incitement to terrorism and genocide often take time to explode. The Jewish people must never forget what happened to our people throughout history and culminated in the *Shoah* — the mass murder of our people by what was considered a civilized nation under Hitler's Nazis.

The current trend in the world, particularly in the Middle East, and now also in Europe, should send alarm bells throughout the world to all those who still can be called humanitarian.

In a world where terrorism and incitement to genocide in Arab propaganda doesn't seem to give anyone sleepless nights — in a world where Iran can openly proclaim its aim to destroy the Jewish people and the Jewish state, and to that end is attempting to acquire atomic weapons — the Jewish people must preserve its defense capabilities and refuse any coercion or pressure tactics in order to satisfy the Arab "claims" against our land.

Even President Bush, who might have been perceived earlier as a friend of Israel, is now moving ever closer to the European agenda. Having embarked on his "charm tour" to Europe (February 21–22, 2005), in an attempt to reinvigorate the old NATO Alliance in pursuit of his own agenda in Iraq, we were frequently treated to the inevitable references to peace "opportunities" in the Middle East, the code word for Israel's concessions to the Arabs.

Does anyone care that Israel is making these concessions at its own peril? Hardly!

That is why it was so painful and so galling to watch the procession of dignitaries in Auschwitz, on a cold night, candles in hand, paying tribute to dead Jews. We could do with less tribute and more human decency from world leaders.

President Bush, even in his charm offensive, could not help himself but remark that EU opposition to US action in Iraq was motivated by cheap oil.

Need one say more?

But here is a telling story by David Frum printed in the *National Post* (February 22, 2005, front page), quoting European sources. The Europeans are prepared now to put the argument over the Iraq war behind them:

> [A]nd real cooperation is becoming possible again — if only
> George Bush can overcome his blindly ideological positions on

Iran, Israel, the UN, etc. and cooperate with his more globally minded allies.

Does this sound familiar? It certainly should: It's repeated often enough. But repetition does not save the story from being rubbish.

But this rubbish is very dangerous to Israel's very survival.

Now the question remains whether Bush, too, will accept that "rubbish" in pursuit of his own agenda, another form of rubbish: democratizing the Arab and Islamic world…

But all is not yet well with the NATO alliance. Europe is still trying to rival the US and has in the past incited its own peoples against the Americans. Frum points out that European opposition to the Iraqi war was not, as France and Germany claimed, because it contravened international law, but rather due to the fact that both Germany and France were handsomely rewarded by Saddam Hussein, as they were "recognized and rewarded with the billions of dollars of oil-for-food money that he directed to French and German corporations and individuals."

Frum goes on:

> The Bush administration has to begin by understanding that the fundamental cause of the trans-Atlantic rift is the ambition of the leaders of France and Germany to build the diverse countries of Europe into a European super-state dominated by the largest member states; that is themselves. This project is dangerously unpopular with many European voters. To overcome that unpopularity, those leaders have needed to mobilize a countervailing emotion: anti-Americanism.

One might add that they have largely succeeded.

Frum says that to fix a problem you have to understand it. How true, how true!

There was a great deal of "horse trading" going on in Europe during Bush's four-day visit to the continent. What was observed by the press is not even the tip of the proverbial iceberg. How much was actually feigned cooperation and goodwill can be glimpsed only between the lines of what they disagreed on.

The issue of Iran's nuclear ambitions and Russia's complicity in that endeavor will not soon go away. As I write these lines, Bush is meeting with

Putin in Bratislava, the Slovak capital, to discuss this issue as well as Russia's backward slide on democracy.

Putin already announced to the world days prior to the meeting of the two presidents that Russian democracy would proceed according to Russia's own need in accordance with its history and culture. As for facilitating Iran's nuclear program, Russia insisted that it was for peaceful purposes only. But then why would Iran need the heavy water and enriched uranium necessary for nuclear bombs?

Iran has in the past supported and still does support terrorism aimed at Israel, both in Lebanon with the collaboration of Syria, and in Gaza, Judea and Samaria. Iran has on numerous occasions publicly declared its goal to erase Israel and annihilate the Jewish people from the face of the earth, using every weapon at its disposal.

The tradeoffs during the NATO talks as well as the EU-US discussions on February 22, 2005 (same players, same subjects) do not in fact endanger any of the parties to the discussions. Except for some window dressing about how much involvement there will be by the Europeans in the Iraqi "democratization" process, and how to deal with the Iranian threat, it is the Middle East "peace process" that is front and center in these discussions!

In what has been billed as a "new era" in Bush's foreign policy vision, the following quotes from his speech will make for interesting reading. The *National Post*, February 22, 2005, also provides us with a helpful map of the Middle East, showing us a sliver of land surrounded by huge territories of Arab land and Iran. The Arab territories alone comprise 5,290,888 square miles. The sliver of land referred to above is of course Israel, comprising 10,891 square miles, including Judea, Samaria and (then) Gaza.

Anyone with half a brain, even with no knowledge of the realities of the Middle East, must wonder what this is all about.

Bush's quotes are superimposed on the *National Post*'s map as follows:

> US-Europe relations: "As past debates fade, and great duties become clear, let us begin a new era of transatlantic unity."

> Israel: "Israel must freeze settlement activity, help Palestinians build a thriving economy and ensure that a new Palestinian state is truly viable, with contiguous territory on the West Bank. A state of scattered territories will not work."

Palestine: "A free and peaceful Palestine can add to the momentum of reform throughout the Middle East."

Syria: "Syria must end its occupation of Lebanon."

Iraq: "Every vote cast in Iraq was an act of defiance against terror... Now is the time for established democracies to give tangible political, economic and security assistance to the world's newest democracy."

Middle East: "Our immediate goal is peace in the Middle East...and the world must not rest until there is a just and lasting resolution to this conflict."

There were also references to Saudi Arabia and Egypt, describing how Egypt, "which showed the way toward peace in the Middle East, can now show the way toward democracy in the Middle East," and encouraging Saudia Arabia to "demonstrate its leadership in the region by expanding the role of its people in determining their future."

One has to remember that Saudi Arabia was the very country that paid for and spread *madrasas*, or schools of jihad, throughout the Middle East, East Asia and even Europe. We haven't heard yet whether these *madrasas* were dismantled or are still spreading the word of jihad. Saudi Arabia, one also has to be reminded, was rewarding families of terrorists in Israel, including Gaza, Judea and Samaria!

As for Egypt, the so-called peace treaty with Israel has changed nothing, except that Israel has handed over the Sinai Desert to Egypt following several wars of aggression that Egypt launched from that territory. It would also be useful to remember that the Gaza Strip was used as an entry point in all aggressive Arab wars against Israel. Gaza was used for years in smuggling weapons from Egypt to the Arabs in Gaza, which they used against Israel, no doubt with Egypt's connivance. Egypt is still the greatest purveyor of anti-Semitic hate propaganda against Israel. Egypt was also the preferred meeting place for terrorist groups to make attempts at reconciliation with the help of its president, Hosni Mubarak. One is at a loss to understand how Egypt has contributed or is in any way contributing to peace or democracy!

The willful blindness world leaders are now displaying, regrettably including the US president, is alarming and should give pause to all thinking people of good will.

Now the US president is praising Iraqis for defying terrorism as they went to the polling stations.

Israel has been defying terrorism and Arab aggression not only since its rebirth in 1948, but for more than a hundred years when the Jewish population in the area of *Eretz Yisrael* — Palestine — was attempting to survive against ongoing violence from bands of terrorists, mostly from neighboring Arab states.

The president's speech was remarkable for its conciliatory tone towards all concerned. Yes, Iran was told that it "must end its support for terrorism and must not develop nuclear weapons."

"For the sake of peace…"

But as the *National Post* reported: "He had markedly stiff language for the Israelis."

It is galling and totally hypocritical how Bush characterized Israel's responsibility. No nation in the world — regardless of size — would agree to give any of its territory to its sworn enemies. Israel has precious little territory as it is, against an array of large Arab armies. Let us again be reminded that the Arab residents of Judea, Samaria and Gaza are not entitled to a state of their own. They are Arabs — not "Palestinians" — no matter how much they would want to promote that fiction in their propaganda war against Israel.

No country in the world was ever asked to help create a new state for its enemies or help build for them "a thriving economy"! Contiguous territory between Gaza and Judea and Samaria would be a sure recipe for disaster for Israel, as it would split the land of Israel in two.

As already stated earlier in this book, there is no room for two viable states on this tiny, tiny sliver of land. One look at the map should be convincing enough.[1]

To quote the US president again: "Our immediate goal is peace in the Middle East…and the world must not rest until there is a just and lasting resolution to this conflict."

All these words are nothing but code words for the concept that Israel must be divided to appease the Arab and Muslim worlds and their European sponsors and lackeys. The purpose of dividing Israel is nothing more nor less than to make her totally vulnerable and defenseless to her sworn enemies!

Even commercial flights in and out of Ben Gurion Airport — the major

---

1. See Appendix 8.

airport in Israel between Jerusalem and Tel Aviv — will become impossible as they will be within easy reach of hostile fire of every kind, even shoulder-held anti-aircraft missiles.

In a world where there is a modicum of justice, the US president would have addressed himself to the real issues in the world in general, and the Middle East in particular. But given the world we live in, where old European anti-Semitism fueled by Arab hate propaganda against Israel and the Jewish people in general trumps all, perhaps one should not be surprised. Since Israel is the intended sacrificial lamb in all this horse trading, Israel's leaders and its people should take notice and respond in kind.

The meeting with Putin one can imagine went as expected. Putin made it clear that Russia will pursue its own agenda, and as far as Iran was concerned, Russia chose to "believe" the Islamic mullahs' "peaceful intentions" despite all the evidence to the contrary.

Bush said at the press conference that he and Putin are still good friends and that they had a constructive and frank discussion — in diplomatic lingo: we disagreed but chose to agree to disagree.

Europe's main concern — apart from its Middle East agenda concerning Israel's land — is that Bush will attack Iran. Ironically, their concern is not that Iran may one day attack them and the US with nuclear weapons, or indeed that a nuclear Iran would, as promised, wipe Israel and its people from the face of the earth, causing — G-d forbid — the final holocaust!

Different Rules for Different Folk

Late January to early February 2005 were witness to some unprecedented events.

January 27, 2005: We saw the first ever commemoration of the Holocaust at the UN.

January 30, 2005: The first ever (democratic) election in Iraq (following a January 9 election by the Arabs in Gaza and Judea and Samaria).

February 4: The newly minted US Secretary of State, Condoleezza Rice, set out on her maiden voyage to Europe and the Middle East, to implement her president's grand vision of democratizing the Arab-Muslim world.

Ordinarily, I would wish Bush well in his grand and noble endeavor; but I really cannot under the circumstances, since all of that is supposed to be accomplished at Israel's expense.

All the euphoria and hoopla about the "Palestinian" elections in early January as a prelude to democracy, and "peaceful coexistence" between the Arabs and Israel, is nothing but wishful thinking and ignorance, or worse!

Similarly, the elections in Iraq proved not so much that Arabs are longing for democracy as that elections do not necessarily lead to democracy. In the Middle East under current conditions, the fear is that Iraq may become a theocracy, closely aligned with Iran, which, of course, would be the worst of all possible outcomes.

As I write these words, Iran is playing a game with Europe's leaders, interchangeably claiming that it has no nuclear ambitions, and/or that it has "every right to join the 'nuclear club,'" while at the same time declaring openly that its aim is to eradicate Israel and its people from the face of the earth!

In Gaza following the elections by Fatah-PLO for their new chieftain Mahmoud Abbas (after Arafat's death), in which Hamas did not participate — since they are not members of Fatah — the subsequently held municipal elections gave Hamas a resounding victory of 70–80 percent of the vote.

So much for democracy and peaceful coexistence in the Middle East.

Despite what is being bandied about as a ceasefire (or *hudna*, temporary ceasefire), neither Hamas nor indeed the PLO (Fatah) — of which Mahmoud Abbas is the new "president" — has given up terrorism. Didn't Abbas commit to abandoning terrorism at Aqaba, when he was the newly appointed "prime minister"?

One can only shake one's head in stunned disbelief at the farce and the hoax being played out right before our eyes.

Is Ms. Rice, the new US secretary of state, so naïve as to believe that a temporary *hudna* is going to lead to peace? Are the European leaders, chief among them Tony Blair — whom Ms. Rice consulted, not by accident, before embarking on the Middle East tour — naïve?

Hardly!

Why then are Israeli leaders allowing themselves to be pushed into committing national suicide?!

It's interesting, isn't it, that Ms. Rice reassured Turkey while on her Middle East tour that the US will not allow the formation of a separate Kurdistan in northern Iraq; while in Israel, during her meeting with prime minister Sharon, she insisted that Israel must "make the hard decisions that must be taken in order to promote peace…and the emergence of a democratic Palestinian state" (*National Post*, February 7, 2005).

Israel is a tiny, tiny country, less than eleven thousand square miles, including Judea and Samaria and (now no longer) Gaza. The Arabs who have formed a majority over time in several towns are not — contrary to their propaganda line — indigenous people, but rather as I have shown Arabs from surrounding countrics, including Egypt, Syria, Iraq, Yemen, etc. Israel does not owe them a state on its own tiny land. The entire enterprise of creating a "viable" "Palestinian" state on historically Jewish land has two aims: (1) to delegitimize the Jewish state and (2) to make Israel totally indefensible militarily.

There simply is no room for two viable states on this tiny territory, even if the Arabs of these arcas were capable of peaceful coexistence. The last (at least) hundred years have proven that they are not — in spite of Israel's best efforts at coexistence, going even so far as to create the possibility of self-governance for the Arabs in a municipal-type autonomy.

The Oslo Accords — which provided initially for municipal autonomy for areas with an Arab majority — eventually led to demands for creating a state, and led to the violence and terrorism which Israel is still experiencing.

Israel suffered over a thousand deaths and many thousands more were maimed for life in suicide bombings against its civilian population from September 2000 until the present. The incitement to hatred and violence in schools and mosques continues and there does not seem to be any end in sight. With this kind of society, how can anyone expect peaceful coexistence?

In Turkey and northern Iraq — where there is a large Kurdish population which indeed is indigenous in an area formerly known as Kurdistan, there is in fact both historical and legal reason for allowing these indigenous peoples to rule themselves. However, international politics, intrigues and manipulations allowed Ms. Rice to "reassure" Turkey that the US would not allow a separate state for the Kurds in Iraq, as this may also embolden Turkish Kurds to seek separation!

In the unlikely event that the Kurds in Iraq and Turkey would some day form a state of their own, both Turkey and Iraq would survive; a divided Israel however would not, given what would become indefensible borders. But, of course, that is part of the Arab plan.

Given all this, it was not surprising that the attendance at the sixtieth anniversary of the liberation of Auschwitz at the UN was minus all the Arab and Muslim states and all their lackeys. The automatic majority at the UN in all anti-Israel resolutions and in support of the "Arab cause" triumphed once again.

And so the commemoration at Auschwitz itself, which many heads of state or representatives of European countries did attend, was marked by an irony that could hardly escape anyone. Here was a place where millions of Jews died horrible deaths at the hands of what was considered a civilized society, which used "modern" methods to speed up and dispose of the evidence of mass murder!

The Americans and the British had many opportunities to save the Jewish people from this slaughter. First, they could have allowed them into their own homeland so designated by the League of Nations, which, contrary to British propaganda, could have absorbed them. They could have bombed the railway tracks leading to the death camp of Auschwitz, to prevent the slaughter of intended victims.

These things they could have done, but failed and refused to do, to their eternal shame.

Now these same countries who bow their heads in front of the memorial to the slaughtered Jews are once again ready to deliver the Jews to their current enemies — the Arabs — proclaiming once again that this will lead to peace (in our time) with the Arab world.

Strangely, as I write these words, I hear my fax machine being activated; reluctantly, but prompted by "something," I get up to retrieve the message. The title of the message reads: "Israel's Auschwitz Borders" by Joseph Farah.

Joseph Farah is an Arab who has written previously on Arab intentions towards Israel, and about the hoax of "the Palestinian people." He understands what the Arab-Israeli "conflict" is all about. Below is Farah's message in full. It deserves to be read:

> Condoleezza Rice may know a lot about the old Soviet Union, but she sure doesn't know squat about the Middle East.
>
> The secretary of state recently explained how it is necessary for Israel to give up more land to help fashion a viable, contiguous Palestinian state — from Gaza through Judea and Samaria.
>
> Perhaps if you don't understand the geography, this might seem like a perfectly reasonable demand. After all, how can we expect the new Palestinian state to function normally if its people are divided by artificial barriers?
>
> What I trust Rice does not understand — in fact, what I

hope she simply fails to comprehend — is that Israel has no more land to give. Israel has no moral obligation to give any land. Israel will be jeopardizing its own security in doing so.

Let me make this crystal clear. Look at a map of the Middle East. After glancing at it for a few minutes, can anyone honestly tell me they believe the problems of violence and terrorism there have to do with the fact that Israel has too much land?

This is apparently what we are to believe.

There's lots of land in the Middle East. Most of it is populated sparsely by Arabic-speaking people, culturally, linguistically, religiously and ethnically at one with the so-called "Palestinians," a people who have never had a country of their own in the history of the world. Why then is it Israel's obligation to carve itself up to create this Palestinian state?

The tiny sliver of land that represents the current state of Israel is, in my opinion, too small, not too big. Since Arabs living in Israel experience first-hand more freedom than any other country in the Middle East, we ought to be exploring ways to expand the Jewish state — especially if freedom and justice for Arabs is our goal.

Now, I'm not a Jew. I'm a Christian Arab-American journalist who believes in freedom first, peace second. And I've got to tell you that the demands on Israel right now are demands for the nation to commit political, military and cultural suicide.

Do you know what the new borders of Israel would be under the plans being drawn up now for a "viable, contiguous Palestine"? I call them Auschwitz borders. I don't know why the Jews don't see it.

They are willingly helping to build a national concentration camp of half the world's Jewry surrounded by hostile maniacs who want to eradicate them. Israel's new borders under a Rice plan will be indefensible. Creating a new Palestinian state with contiguous borders and relying on Israel to come up with all the necessary real estate requires cutting Israel in half from north to south.

It might create a "viable" Palestinian state, but it will destroy the viability of Israel.

If Adolf Hitler had been a little smarter, he would have helped recreate a Jewish state in the Middle East and squeezed it the way the Arabs, the Europeans and now the United States are squeezing Israel. Hitler could never have dreamed of a more expedient "final solution."

Now I am not going to suggest that Rice or the Bush administration are intentionally trying to destroy Israel or the Jews. I will give them the benefit of the doubt and assume they are ill-informed, that they are making profoundly bad decisions based on bad data and bad analysis.

But I will make no such assumptions about the leadership of the Palestinian Authority and the Arab states that back it. They are not promoting a Palestinian state because they believe in freedom and self-determination for the Arab people who live there. Instead, they are doing so to create a permanent staging ground from which they will continue their war of attrition against the Jewish infidels who have the audacity to live in what they consider to be Dar al-Islam.

It's that simple. I wish Rice and Bush and even the Israeli government could see it.

It is a national disgrace that the U.S. government is spending $350 million more to subsidize the Palestinian Authority, which holds that no Jews are permitted to live within its territory or future nation. It is a national disgrace that the U.S. government would join with the rest of the anti-Semitic world to force Israel to abandon its own security needs and its own Jewish communities on historically Jewish lands. And it is a national disgrace that the U.S. government, while supposedly fighting a global war against Islamist terrorism, is appeasing them in the Arab-Israeli conflict.

I must express my gratitude to Mr. Farah for his forthright assessment of what the world leaders call the Arab-Israeli "conflict."

Israel is being put in an untenable situation by an unscrupulous world leadership which has no qualms about offering up Israel as a sacrifice to the Arabs, merely to secure their oil supply. But for how long? Only as long as the Arabs see the Europeans as useful idiots. There will come a time in the not-too-distant future when Europe will explode from within with all the Arab-Muslim population growing by leaps and bounds.

All the appeasement in the world will not make the slightest difference. The Muslim leaders made it quite clear in Malaysia — when the outgoing leader Mahathir Mohamed was given a standing ovation by his co-religionist heads of state of Arab and Muslim nations, when he said that Islam must prevail against the infidel — that the West can be used against Israel, until its turn comes!

Another Kind of Ultimatum

Once again, Europe's notables are flocking to pay homage to dead Jews, this time in Israel. This time, the occasion is the opening of the new Yad Vashem Museum, dedicated to the victims of the Holocaust.

Poland and Switzerland are sending their presidents; Romania and Holland their prime ministers; and Germany and Spain, their foreign ministers, according to the *Jerusalem Post* (March 11, 2005). Altogether, some forty countries will be represented at the Yad Vashem dedication ceremonies, including Canadian, Australian and Dominican Republic officials, as well as UN Secretary-General Kofi Annan and Russia's National Security Council head, Igor Ivanov.

> "It's amazing," said one diplomatic official, "the willingness of so many countries to participate stemmed in large part from a desire of the world's leaders to meet with Sharon."
>
> "Two years ago no one wanted to see him; now, everyone is knocking on his door."
>
> One official said the event presented Israel with an invaluable opportunity to show the world where we came from — from darkness to light — in the hope this would lead to a better understanding of the country's present concerns.

I would be quite concerned over the misplaced hope expressed by the above official or the misreading of the intentions of world leaders by another; the fact remains that these leaders wanted nothing to do with Sharon or Israel "two years ago."

Israel faced isolation and opprobrium before Sharon took these dangerous and unprecedented steps — namely, to withdraw from Gaza and four settlements in Samaria.

It's not that these leaders are totally ignorant of Israel's situation or its current predicament. It is rather that as long as Israel will be willing to take these dangerous and totally uncalled-for steps, these leaders will feign approval.

Sharon — though misguided — knew this full well, but isolation and constant threats apparently proved too much for him.

And so, the perception here is that Israel must choose between facing isolation or committing national suicide. Quite a choice; quite an ultimatum!

So long as Israel is prepared to cave in to Arab demands put forward by their European allies, Israel will be showered with attention and promises of all sorts. But these promises and various gestures are of short duration, as the not so distant past has proven, over and over again.

Israel and the Jews cannot afford to forget that all Israeli overtures to peace with the Arabs have led nowhere.

It is not possible to forge peace with nations whose leaders and government preach the most vile propaganda of hatred and violence based on total falsehoods against Israel and Jewish people in general, and whose ultimate goal is Israel's destruction.

The "temporary" *hudna* proposed in March 2005 by the "new" ("old") Abbas, leader of the PLO, is just that: temporary! At this writing it was still being worked out in Cairo by our "friend" Hosni Mubarak, and all the terrorist factions.

But already some of the factions are openly stating that they will not abide by even a temporary ceasefire unless their demands are met. Those demands include freeing all terrorists now in Israeli prisons, as well as Israel's withdrawal from territories.

Demands? These terrorists have rights to demand? They themselves should be put behind bars pending trial!

There is no possibility for peace in the current circumstances, in the current climate of incitement and violence and vile hatred and terrorism. We really don't know if there ever will be, so long as the Arab mindset is bent on Israel's destruction. This is not about creating yet another Arab state; this is clearly an attempt to weaken Israel and make the country indefensible.

The hoax of a "Palestinian" people has not been sufficiently disclaimed for the falsity it represents. Israel's friends, if there are any, must stop ignoring the grim realities of the Middle East, and stop pushing Israel into making impossible and dangerous concessions, affecting its very survival.

All the crocodile tears shed at Auschwitz's sixtieth anniversary commemoration or at Jerusalem's Yad Vashem would be nothing but a display of shameless hypocrisy, if these countries were to continue to push Israel's population to commit national suicide. Perhaps they believe that then, they will gather again to pay homage to dead Jews!

Conspiracy Continues

It has long been apparent that there is something rotten going on in Europe. The constant mollycoddling and funding of the PA-PLO terrorists, turning a blind eye to the terrorist outrages and not responding in a realistic way to Israel's proof that terrorists are on the PA payroll, and that in fact the PA initiates all the terrorist activities, are mind boggling! The fact that the EU is again turning a blind eye to the revelations that Hamas is, or "may be" on the United Nations' payroll in Gaza, leaves one speechless.

It is Israel that is singled out in Europe for opprobrium and not the terrorists and their sponsors. Surely, the Europeans know better; so what's the problem? Why do they insist continually — in spite of the terrorist atrocities — that Israel must sacrifice its land to build a PLO terrorist state in its very heartland?

A Saudi spokesman recently bragged that they were "the inventors of the Road Map" (CNN's Late Edition, Sunday, February 5, 2006 — Wolf Blitzer interviewing the new Saudi ambassador to the US, Turki al Faisal). Their demand that Israel go back to the pre-1967 Armistice lines in order for the Arabs to make peace with Israel is nothing short of impudent arrogance.

The offensive language of the "Road Map from hell" in its moral equivalency between the terrorists and the state of Israel shows to what extent the EU, as part of the Quartet, has become a tool of the Arab League.

As already referred to earlier, the reason Israel was continually attacked by the Arab aggressors, even between the wars, was precisely because the pre-1967 borders were indefensible, and a tempting, easy target of the jihadist Arabs.

And now, finally, tragically, we can see what went on behind the scenes for the last many years!

Bat Ye'or, in her book *Eurabia*, provides a documented account of the perfidious relationship between the EU (the European Union — formerly the EC, European Commission) and the Arab League, dating back to 1973.

In 1973, OPEC[1] issued the oil embargo following the 1973 Arab war of aggression against Israel. Since the war of aggression did not produce the desired results, it wasn't beneath them to turn to blackmail and extortion. This new relationship, innocently and euphemistically called the "EU-Arab Dialogue," was, to put it simply, to enlist the EU in the "Arab cause" against Israel.

As already previously stated, the Arab cause is the destruction of the State of Israel, by all means possible, using all weapons at their disposal, including economic coercion where necessary.

It is also now far clearer why and how the UN became perverted by the Arab-Muslim influence, and why European dignitaries and foreign diplomats insisted on having "diplomatic" relations with the PLO during the Oslo Accords, even though that was clearly in violation of these accords.

It is now also clear why these meetings took place in Jerusalem, in violation of the accords, apparently creating facts on the ground, again in violation, and treating the PLO as if it were already a "state," whose capital was Jerusalem!

It was an arrogant "in your face" way for Europe to thumb its nose at Israel.

But why? And how was it coordinated? And why indeed humiliate Israel?

Well, now we know; it was coordinated. We also know now that the Arab League insisted that the PLO (the "Palestine Liberation Organization") be treated as the "legitimate" representative of the "Palestinian people." But even when the Oslo "peace talks" broke down, and Arafat declared his terrorist war in earnest, even then the European diplomats insisted on going to Ramallah — Arafat's "headquarters" — in spite of Israel's protests. All of these actions sprang from the EU-Arab League pact!

And now, since Arafat's death, they flock to see the "new improved" PLO chief, Mahmoud Abbas, while paying homage at the same time at Arafat's grave.

All this in spite of the fact that terrorism continues, every day. Not on the scale it previously did, but a sort of "low intensity" terrorism (try telling that to the victims!).

---

1. Oil Producing and Exporting Conglomerate.

The pressure continues on Israel to make concessions to the PA-PLO in order to "strengthen" Abbas, in spite of the fact that he has told the world numerous times that he won't disarm the "resistance" (*Jerusalem Post*, May 5, 2005, page 2), and, in fact, has stated on more than one occasion that "the resistance will continue"!

So now we finally know why Israel is being forced by Europe to go along with this charade, and why Europe is showing Israel the "carrot" of economic advantage. So long as Israel is prepared to give up Gaza and other territories in Judea and Samaria, and keeps releasing from its prisons Arab terrorists despite the fact that most of these terrorists commit terrorist acts as soon as they are released.

All this to "strengthen" the PA-PLO chieftain Abbas.

Of course, it is understood that if Israel refuses to go along with this charade, the economic advantage will be removed, and Israel will be isolated even more than before.

The Arab propaganda is only growing in its intensity. In April 2005 the PA-PLO was urging the Quartet to prevent construction in Ma'aleh Adumim, a town adjacent to Jerusalem (*Jerusalem Post*, April 6, 2005, page 2): "The PA urged the international community to pressure Israel to halt plans to build some 3,500 new houses in Ma'aleh Adumim, warning that the construction would damage the peace process."

What peace process?! Put pressure on Israel? That has become a constant call of the Arabs, who act as if they believed their own propaganda.

We have seen *hudnas* come and go, and now we have something unpronounceable, which is not even a *hudna*, but a ceasefire between the terrorists, as even they have their internal shootouts, reported from time to time. (Sometimes there are attacks on police stations; once there was a shooting in the direction of the convoy carrying Mahmoud Abbas himself!)

Abbas has invited Hamas to join the PA-PLO "cabinet": "The Fatah central committee, [after] three days of discussions in Amman [Jordan]…called on all Palestinian groups, including Hamas and Islamic Jihad, to join 'a national unity government'" (*Jerusalem Post*, July 3, 2005, front page: "Hamas considers PA unity call").

Is anyone listening?!

On page 2 of the same day's paper under the heading "PA condemns extortion by Gaza Strip gunmen," we are informed that "scores of Fatah gunmen raided the offices of the Palestinian Legislative Council in Rafah, demanding that the PA provide them with jobs and money."

Despite the claim by a spokesman for the PA that they will not "succumb to extortion," the armed gunmen only "evacuated the offices after receiving promises that they would be recruited to PA security forces as soon as possible"!

The story in the *Jerusalem Post* was accompanied by a picture of armed and masked gunmen occupying an office. The photographer was identified as Khalil Hamra of the AP, and the caption referred to the masked gunmen as members of al-Aqsa Martyrs' Brigades. It appears these thugs can command the attention of news media at will!

And what about the PA? Forming a "government" made up of various terrorist groups including Hamas and Islamic Jihad, and the PLO's own Fatah al-Aqsa Martyrs' Brigades, to form PA-PLO "security forces"?!

The following day it was reported (*Jerusalem Post*, July 4, 2005, page 3) that an earlier claim by the al-Aqsa Martyrs' Brigades that they kidnapped two Israeli soldiers was in fact bogus. It took however a great deal of time and effort on the part of the Israeli army to verify that each and every soldier was accounted for. What a relief to the families and the nation. Thank G-d!

The item in the *Jerusalem Post* was accompanied by an earlier picture of the al-Aqsa Martyrs' Brigades marching in the streets of Nablus fully armed, shooting in the air. On the same page, July 4, 2005, the *Jerusalem Post* reported that "Hamas bans immoral festival in Kalkilya":

> Hamas candidates won all the seats of the municipal council in local elections held last May in several Palestinian cities in the West Bank and Gaza Strip. The Kalkilya Council members then chose Wajih Nazzal, a Hamas prisoner held in an Israeli jail, as the city's mayor.

Hamas appears to be making a strong showing in elections. The *chutzpah* of the locals to choose as their mayor a convicted terrorist! The article goes on:

> "We have become like Iran and Afghanistan when it was ruled by the Taliban," one of the organizers of the festival told the *Jerusalem Post*.
> The main objection was the "mixing of sexes" and "many

other things in violation of our religious teachings and traditions." The municipality decided to turn down the request.

Meanwhile violence goes on unabated! Every day there are several shooting
incidents at Israeli soldiers and civilians. Miraculously, casualties are low.
Nearly every day the army reports intercepting would-be bombers before
they can do harm.

On the Lebanese border, too, Hizbullah attempted to infiltrate an IDF post
in order to kidnap Israeli soldiers. In the battle that ensued, one Israeli soldier
was killed and four others wounded, including an Israeli officer, a doctor
(*Jerusalem Post*, July 4, 2005, page 4).

The *Jerusalem Post* also reported that the IDF apprehended a PA-PLO
"policeman" who took part in the lynching of two Israelis in October 2000.
This is the second "policeman" accused of the lynching. (See *Jerusalem Post*,
June 29, 2005, page 2.)

Meanwhile, as if none of these events were happening, EU parliamentary
president Josep Borrell Fontelles was in Israel promoting a meeting of the
EU-Med Partnership (part of the EU-Arab Dialogue) for the "Palestinian
territories"!

Despite the oft-repeated propaganda, I still cringe each time somebody
refers to Judea, Samaria and Gaza as "Palestinian territories," particularly
when it is some EU official.

Under the heading "Europeans push for major EU event in PA territory"
(*Jerusalem Post*, June 29, 2005, page 4), we are informed that the EU "wants
to host a major diplomatic event in Ramallah or Jericho, post disengagement
in an effort to shore up the Palestinian Authority."

President of the European Parliament Josep Borrell Fontelles, who also
happens to be the head of the EU-Med Assembly now celebrating its tenth
anniversary, brings together twenty-five EU foreign ministers with their counterparts from the Arab states in the Mediterranean. In the end, the tenth anniversary of the EU-Med Assembly was held in Madrid in late November 2005,
with some Israelis participating, while the Arabs sent only minor officials.

Borrell Fontelles in response to a question said, "It was premature to hold
[the event] in Israel," for fear that "if it was held in Israel, some of the foreign
ministers from Arab countries would not come"!

The next day, June 30, 2005, the *Jerusalem Post*, on page 3, provided a picture (credited to Nasser Nasser/AP) of Borrell Fontelles paying respect at Yasser Arafat's grave prior to his meeting with Abbas in Ramallah!

In the same article; titled "Kaddumi to join Fatah central committee talks in Jordan," we are told among other things that Abbas and Kaddumi ironed out their differences when they met recently in Tunisia.

Also in the same article: "Kaddumi's supporters in the West Bank and Gaza Strip" urged Abbas "to appoint Kaddumi as his deputy in both the PA and the PLO. Such a move would automatically turn Kaddumi into Abbas's natural successor"!

(As if we didn't have enough trouble already.)

Abbas is considered a "moderate," while Kaddumi is heading "the hardliners" in Fatah's central committee "who are opposed to any form of concession to Israel"!

Elsewhere it was reported that Abbas on his recent trip to Syria and Lebanon invited various terrorist leaders residing in those countries to join him in Gaza after Israel's withdrawal. Peace, anyone?!

Anti-Semitism Now Full-Blown!

The writing has been on the wall, so to speak, for a very long time, but ignored as always. Now, it appears anti-Semites, more brazenly than ever, show their colors. Not only white supremacists and Arab-Muslim jihadists are brazenly flaunting their propaganda and hatred of Israel and the Jewish people throughout Europe, but even British academics are joining the fray.

Not so long ago, it was only individual voices that we heard with contemptible messages. To be sure, these individual voices carried weight. They included the likes of the French ambassador to Britain, an individual in the British House of Lords, a high-ranking member of the British clergy, and even a foreign minister of an EU country, not to mention London's lord mayor.

The election campaign in Britain scheduled for May 5, 2005, also denigrated Britain's Jewish population, as some individual campaigners made such unprecedented remarks as:

> *"There is no Jewish vote."*
>
> *"There are 1.3 million Muslims and only 300,000 Jews."*
>
> *"Their vote does not count."*

"We don't need the Jewish vote" …and the like.

And to top it all, there is the boycott against Israeli universities by the British Association of University Teachers Union (AUT)!

Some academics, both British and Israeli, tried to play down the significance of the union's boycott; but sadly and very tellingly, the voices of opponents to the infamous boycott were initially very, very few indeed (happily, this situation has apparently been reversed since, as more and more academics protested the boycott). The boycott includes blacklisting Jewish and Israeli academics!

Alan Dershowitz referred to this abuse as the worst since the era of McCarthyism. He accused the AUT of being "against peace." But apparently he, too, doesn't quite get it.

The professors are not merely against peace, they are active pro-Arab propagandists and their anti-Semitic undertaking is quite helpful to the Arabs and their "cause"!

The *Jerusalem Post* reported (May 2, 2005) that the chief instigator, who introduced the resolution to the AUT to boycott Israeli universities and Jewish as well as Israeli academics, a Ms. Blackwell, has links to a Nazi Web site. Stay tuned for more on this one.

Meanwhile, another Arab propagandist, this time from Dubai (*Jerusalem Post*, April 27, 2005), while claiming to advocate "dialogue with Israelis," nonetheless managed to lambaste "pro-Israeli activists" as "hate-mongering forces," among other things.

At the same time, there are two decisions pending, in two separate trials, in two countries. The revelations at the present time link terrorists from several countries. One Ahmed Ressam from Canada, accused of an international conspiracy to bomb the international airport in Los Angeles coinciding with the millennium; the other accused was part of the conspiracy of 9/11. All in all, almost every Arab country appears to have its nationals involved in both these conspiracies.

Iran has been threatening once again to resume its nuclear program. Hassan Rawhani, "the top Iranian negotiator, called the London talks 'perhaps the last opportunity' for an agreement and acknowledged Iran and the Europeans had failed to achieve a compromise." But according to a British "Foreign Office official both parties agreed to reflect on what they had discussed…and that talks would continue." (*Jerusalem Post*, May 1, 2005).

Presumably with more demands and threats from Iran!

It was also reported on the same day, in the *Jerusalem Post* (same page) that the two leading German magazines *Der Spiegel* and *Focus* reported a German company was "suspected" of "selling weapons technology to Iran," as early as 2002!

Focus reported that "intelligence agents of an ally" intercepted the deliveries in Dubai in 2004. Both magazines reported that the German technology was to be used in Iran's Shahab medium-range missile program, which is capable of reaching Israel (as well as various US military bases).

It simply leaves one speechless!

Russia's President Vladimir Putin, arrived in Israel Wednesday April 27, 2005, for a state visit. Most pundits were hard-put to figure out the timing. The first-ever visit by a Russian leader raised two questions: why — and why now?

Perhaps the most obvious reason is that the Russians, as part of the unholy Quartet, want to increase their meddling in the eternal Middle East "peace process."

Putin did not budge, despite Israel's urging, on Russia's involvement in Iran's nuclear program, nor indeed on its sale to Syria of ground to air missiles which could be converted to shoulder-held anti-aircraft missiles according to Israeli military experts. But Putin had yet another arms sale up his sleeve, this time to the PA-PLO!

Do these leaders have no shame?

All this in spite of the fact that the PA-PLO "president" Mahmoud Abbas allows terrorism to continue unabated. As if this weren't enough, Abbas appointed as overall "security chief" "'Colonel' Rashid Abu Shabak, best known as the ruthless hunter of collaborators (*Jerusalem Post*, April 27, 2005).

On April 26, 2005, the *Jerusalem Post* reported on its front page that the mastermind of the plot responsible for the killing of Israeli Minister of Tourism Rehavam Ze'evi in 2001 told his friends that he would run as a candidate in elections for the "Palestinian Legislative Council."

The mastermind, Majdi Rimawi, is serving an eight-year sentence in a PA-PLO jail in Jericho, after hiding from Israeli authorities in Arafat's *mukata* for several months prior to Arafat's death.

April 28, 2005, the *Jerusalem Post* reported that "Palestinian" "journalists refused to cover a visit by Chairman Mahmoud Abbas to the Civil Police

Headquarters in Gaza City, after some of them were beaten by security officers."

A sinister-looking Abbas "reiterated his commitment to the unofficial truce," the *Jerusalem Post* reported; Abbas added that the "Palestinians" "needed the calm more than the Israelis" and "warned that the PA would use an iron first against anyone who tried to violate the truce."

But violence and terrorist attacks and attempted suicide bombings continue every day, without letup. Apparently the truce between the different factions of the terrorists is holding; but so is the violence against Israel!

The above-mentioned police headquarters have been named "the Yasser Arafat Police Compound." It fits!

Again, Abbas is reported speaking in Gaza City, flanked by "Prime Minister" Ahmed Qurei and "Deputy Prime Minister" Nabil Shaath, under a huge portrait of a young Yasser Arafat (as reported by the *Jerusalem Post*, April 26, 2005, with AP photo). Sometimes a picture is worth more than a thousand words; I won't bother therefore to provide the text.

One only despairs what "democracy" can emerge from this anarchy.

Chapter XXXV

The London Bombing:
Part of Global Jihad

Some compare the July 7 (or 7/7) attack on London to America's 9/11, as it has become known. But Prime Minister Blair of Britain disagrees.

Soon after the bombing, he pronounced his disbelief that such a thing could happen in Britain, a country tolerant to every race, creed and religion.

I listened, astonished at how this seemingly tolerant man could, with these few words, dismiss other countries, no less "tolerant" than Britain, as if they were less worthy to be spared the scourge of terrorist savagery!

The London bombing was horrific and savage. To attack innocent human beings as they go about their daily lives is savage enough. To bomb subways where there is an additional element of suffocation and helplessness is even more barbaric. To create even more suffering to those who were not immediately killed by the bomb blast itself requires a special kind of sadism.

But here in Israel, we have witnessed every kind of barbarity, savagery and sadism, as when terrorists — or as Bat Ye'or calls them, Kamikaze-terrorists — deliberately add glass shards, nails and screws to their explosives to cause maximum pain and suffering to the surviving victims of terrorism.

Doctors and surgeons describe what terrible brain damage has been caused by this deadly material; how these screws, nails, or glass shards get imbedded in the brain or other organs or limbs, and how many people are maimed for life because of them.

The London bombing was savage and barbaric. Four nearly simultaneous explosions took place early morning July 7, 2005, killing more than fifty people and injuring some seven hundred. Three bombs were set off on three subway trains, and one on a double-decker bus.

Subsequent information revealed that all four explosions were caused by suicide bombers homegrown in Britain. Three of these bombers were of

Pakistani origin, and one Jamaican married to a Muslim. All four lived in the town of Leeds, and were all seen on cameras as they arrived together by train in London approximately half an hour before they detonated their bombs.

Detonated their bombs? Detonated themselves!

It is difficult if not impossible to comprehend how "normal" people, apparently from middle-class families, educated, one of them a father, could bring themselves to such horrific deeds, while dying such horrific deaths?

But there is nothing normal about such people — brainwashed for years by their imams, by their religion — who in their zeal try to become "martyrs" for the "holy" cause of jihad, holy war.

In their worldview, the lives of "infidels" mean nothing. "Infidels" must either be put to the sword or surrender. If they won't convert to Islam, then they are condemned to *dhimmitude*.

Such is the enemy we are facing, and claiming otherwise is willful blindness and deliberate denial. The Europeans, and Britain in particular, will have to open their eyes sooner or later; one hopes not too late.

Meanwhile, most British officials studiously avoid blaming the Muslim community, in fact, trying to get their cooperation to weed out the culprits. Good luck!

It would seem incomprehensible to believe that the parents of the bombers were totally in the dark as to the predisposition of their sons, as they claim. Surely, they also attend their mosques, where the imams openly speak of holy war — jihad — and greatly praise suicide bombers. Apparently in Britain, imams actually speak of the conquest of Britain and of the world, and preach that the queen of England would have to convert to Islam in order to avoid paying a head tax!

All this is done openly — freedom of speech, you know, and all that!

Are — or were — the imams allowed to behave this way because of the Euro-Arab pact? Or have the Brits been ignoring all the ranting as so much noise?

In spite of all the positive spin from official spokesmen, the British parliament decided on stronger legislation to deal with "terrorism and indirect incitement" that praises suicide bombers as "martyrs."

Thank G-d for small mercies!

The civil libertarians, however, are already expressing concern over the future legislation, including surveillance, as interfering with citizens' freedoms.

But what about the sleeper cells, not only in Britain, but all over Europe?

America has its own sleeper cells, as has Canada, which has been spared so far. The US had its wake-up call on 9/11. All those trying to find a root cause for terrorism — poverty, desperation, the war in Iraq, "the occupation" of the "West Bank," Judea and Samaria, Gaza — are attempting to find easy answers that their logic can accept, preferring not to believe that the entire developed Western world is facing a global jihad.

As already referred to in an earlier chapter, in his book *Onward Muslim Soldiers*, Robert Spencer shows us quite clearly the requirements of the Muslim religion. Those very requirements are often enough enunciated by a variety of Muslim clerics: every man and woman has the obligation to give his or her all to jihad, holy war. But people refuse to believe that this is what they really mean! They prefer to believe that if they will show understanding to the Muslim "grievances," they will be spared.

There apparently existed such an understanding in Britain: the British tacitly agreed to give free hand to the various terrorist groups with affiliates in Britain, provided they did not cause trouble locally. This is how many terrorist cells located in Britain were able to raise funds and plan their attacks elsewhere, including the US. The arrangement was however apparently rescinded by the jihadists following Britain's involvement in the Iraqi war.

In Britain there are 1.3 million Muslims. In London alone, there are one million. According to Spencer, demography is one of the weapons of jihad. You plant Muslim population in a foreign country, with the intent to take it over from within!

Bat Ye'or describes how the Arab League-European pact (initially originated by France in 1973 and later adopted for all of Europe) led not only to an overpowering influence of Arab-Muslim propaganda on the lives of Europeans, but to an uncontrolled influx of Arab-Muslim immigration which is reaching critical proportions. In France alone, the Arab-Muslim population represents 10 percent of the total population — that is the legal immigrants; some claim that there are an almost equal number of illegal residents.

The universities in Europe have been flooded by Arab propagandists who are clearly brainwashing the current population. As we have seen in the EU Commission-sponsored poll referred to in an earlier chapter, Israel is singled out as posing "the greatest danger to world peace" (with the US tied for second place), out of a list of fifteen countries most of which are, in fact, rogue states!

Deception, another tool of war as we have seen, is according to Spencer an extremely effective weapon. Propaganda, even despite its obvious lies and misrepresentations of history, has nonetheless provided Arab Muslims with many supporters and adherents.

It is quite amazing how both deception and demography have influenced the Arab-Israeli conflict as well; the influx of Arabs from neighboring states has tilted the balance in the Arabs' favor, as they claim that these Arabs are all "Palestinians"!

The further claim that there are "millions of Palestinians" in the "Diaspora," as well as additional "millions" of "Palestinians" in "refugee camps," should be seen for the obvious deception that it is, and yet, few seem to question these obvious lies.

Europe has sold its soul to the devil in supporting Arab propaganda and false claims against Israel. Europe doesn't seem to realize that it is being used by the Arab Muslims in their global jihad against all infidels. Mahathir Mohamad said as much in his speech to the gathering of Arab-Islamic leaders at the annual summit conference of the Organization of Islamic Countries (OIC) in Malaysia in October 2003.

Mahathir urged his appreciative audience of kings and presidents to cooperate with each other in their quest to destroy the Jews, as the first target in their quest for world domination. Mahathir pointed out that "not all non-Muslims are against us[; s]ome are well disposed towards us," and counseled the Islamic leaders to use the Westerners who support them and who "see our enemies as their enemies" to advance their goal (see Mahathir's speech in chapter 29).

Listening to Mahathir, one is likely to believe that Israel is merely a convenient scapegoat for these jihadists on their way to world domination. But Israel has proved to be more of an obstacle than the jihadists imagined.

The poor Arabs — no wonder the world has pity on them — imagine the humiliation they must feel, having been defeated by little Israel in their every effort, in every war of unprovoked, naked aggression.

In this strange and seemingly never-ending war, Israel is fighting for its very survival, with one hand tied behind its back, forced into this position by international "do-gooders" who have swallowed Arab propaganda whole.

Israel will not lie down and die. We have survived worse calamities in our long history, and with G-d's help, we will survive this one as well.

But what about Britain and the rest of Europe?

Britain should have learned a long time ago that appeasement doesn't work against an intractable enemy, and this enemy should not be underestimated. Instead of working shoulder to shoulder against this global jihad, Britain chose to enlist Bush to push Israel ever harder to give in to this enemy. After the London bombing outrage, Britain tried to play it cool; "we can take it," the British seemed to say.

But this enemy is different. This is not the Nazi blitz. With the Nazis, you knew where to find the enemy. The front lines were clear; you knew where to hit back. Now, the enemy is right in your midst, a fifth column in the very midst of your nation.

In democratic countries, it is nearly impossible to fight a fifth column. But during World War II, both the Americans and the Canadians, and to some extent also the British, incarcerated "enemy aliens," though in reality the population of Japanese origin posed no real threat in Canada or the US. Britain chose to send its enemy aliens to Canada to different camps. Ironically, even German Jews were incarcerated along with some German nationals in those camps! We will have to wait and see how Britain will rise to its present challenge.

The "Euro-Arab Dialogue" — EAD — and other such partnerships between the EU and the Arab League provided for unhindered immigration of Arab-Muslims to Europe among other things.

This curious arrangement, among the other curious arrangements between the EU and the Arab League, would normally not be permitted under Islamic law, as Muslims should not be subjects of the infidel societies. But there are exceptions in a case where Arab Muslims want to take over a nation from within.[1] The Europeans are certainly well positioned for such a scenario. They have absorbed millions of Arabs and other Muslim nationals; the time bomb is ticking.

Israel is unfortunately in this kind of situation as well, though it was not of Israel's making. In this, the British too, played a major role. As already referred to earlier, the British during their perfidious Mandate allowed countless tens of thousands of Arabs from neighboring Arab states into "Palestine" — *Eretz Yisrael* — while preventing the ingathering of the exiles from the Jewish Diaspora which they had solemnly undertaken to facilitate.

Now, Israel has its own fifth column. Not a week goes by when there are

---

1. See Spencer, *Onward Muslim Soldiers*.

no revelations of Israeli-Arab citizens helping bombers and would-be bomb-ers to get to their destinations. This, of course, is due to Israeli Arabs' ease of movement throughout the country, as they have full democratic rights as citizens of Israel.

I will cite several items from the *Jerusalem Post* in the summer of 2005.

The first item, "Three Jerusalem Arabs held for terror ties" (June 8, 2005, page 4) relates that three suspects were arrested under suspicion "of being the Jerusalem-based operators of a Palestinian terror cell from the Popular Front for the Liberation of Palestine." According to the paper:

> [They] served as a liaison between group members in the West Bank and abroad and those in the city, Jerusalem police spokes-man Shmuel Ben-Ruby said.
>
> One of the suspects, a doctor by profession, told police interrogators that he passed on messages from the imprisoned Palestinian killers of the late Tourism Minister Rechavam Ze'evi to group cell members in Jerusalem, police said.
>
> A total of 40 suspected PFLP cell members have been arrested in east Jerusalem over the last several weeks...

A second item, July 20, 2005, reveals that "Palestinians who obtained Israeli residency under family reunification laws were involved in sixteen suicide bombings since September 2000, according to data presented by Shin Bet [Israel Security Agency]...to the Knesset."

The security chief also stressed that "Palestinians" "who obtained Israeli papers had a 'dramatic weight' in bombing attacks."

The sham and deception of "family reunification" involves a "Palestinian" marrying an Israeli Arab, in most cases to facilitate terrorism. It has come to the attention of the authorities that such a "marriage" more often than not leaves the husband living where he lived previously, except that he now has an Israeli passport and therefore can move around freely. Israel is now looking at ways to prevent such terrorists from finding an easy way to commit their crimes.

The August 19, 2003, Jerusalem bus bombing which killed twenty-three people was carried out with the help of three Jerusalem Arabs with suspected ties to Hamas. The three were also planning three additional attacks; accord-ing to police the attacks were prevented when they were apprehended one month earlier. The three, all in their early to middle twenties, had Israeli ID cards and lived in the vicinity of Jerusalem. The August 19 bombing was one of the most lethal suicide-terrorist bombings ever perpetrated, carried out against civilians — families — returning from prayer at the Western Wall. All three confessed to the charges against them (*Jerusalem Post,* October 9, 2003, page 3).

Meanwhile, in the summer of 2005 anarchy continued to reign in Gaza, as the PA-PLO and Hamas battled it out between them, getting ready to "divide the spoils," as the day of the Israeli disengagement drew near.

Approximately forty thousand Israelis marched in protest towards the Jewish community of Gush Katif (in Gaza), which was to be evacuated from Gaza in accordance with Prime Minister Sharon's disengagement plan. The Gush Katif residents and other protestors demonstrated against Sharon's plan to uproot Jewish communities, which were built up from nothing on the sandy, arid soil of Gaza. These communities had become thriving little towns and villages where local farmers produced, in hot houses, the most beautiful vegetables, flowers and fruit. All this was to be given over to the assorted terrorists of Gaza, in an attempt to appease the Europeans and the US as they collectively appeased the Arabs.

Israel is supposed to appease the appeasers of terrorism.

What, we wondered in those heavy weeks before the "disengagement," will happen after Israel pulls out of Gaza? "G-d only knows" was the only answer. In one three-day period in mid-July 2005, the terrorists from Gaza lobbed a hundred kassam rockets and mortars into Jewish residential areas. In one attack, a young woman was killed while sitting with her fiancé on the porch of her house; her fiancé was wounded by the shrapnel. In other attacks there was miraculously "only" property damage. These rockets are obviously not very accurate; nonetheless, they did, over time, cause several deaths and injuries.

Needless to say, to live under a constant barrage of these terrorist attacks requires a very special kind of people, a very special kind of courage.

The Londoners, too, will have to brace themselves in view of recent realities. July 21, 2005, two weeks after the first attack, Londoners panicked as a repeat performance of July 7 appeared to be in the offing. There was an alert that three subway stations and one double-decker bus appeared to be attacked. Luckily, the four intended attacks did not produce any injuries, aside from the bomber himself.

There were various speculations as to the nature of this new attack in London; some speculated that it seemed like a copycat attack. Thankfully, the bombs did not go off this time; nonetheless, the nerves of the people of London must have been set on edge as the police and the entire population remained on high alert.

Tony Blair called for a global conference on tackling Islamic "extremism," pointing out that twenty-six countries had been attacked by al-Qaeda and associated groups, and therefore, there must be "a huge well of support and understanding for the problems that we have faced in this country just recently" (*Jerusalem Post*, July 21, 2005, page 9).

In all of his recent pronouncements, he studiously avoided naming Israel as one of the countries under attack, but he referred to "Palestine" several times.

So much for his global conference and understanding the root cause of the problem the world (yes, including Israel!) is facing.

The global jihad does not seem to spare anyone. Saturday, July 23, 2005, in the early hours of the morning, three bombs set off in the Egyptian resort town of Sharm el-Sheikh killed ninety and wounded two hundred. One bomb was set off by a suicide bomber driving a van into the reception area of the Ghazala Gardens Hotel, ripping apart the area; another explosion occurred at the same time in a crowded coffee house and a third bomb exploded in a market area.

President Mubarak of Egypt commented: "This cowardly, criminal act is aimed at undermining Egypt's security and stability and harming its people and its guests... This will only increase our determination in chasing terrorism, cornering it and uprooting it" (*Jerusalem Post*, Sunday, July 24, 2005).

It's amazing how the Egyptian president understands how to deal with terrorists when his own country is attacked and how he treats assorted terrorists who attack Israel, including Hamas and Islamic Jihad, as honored guests.

One supposes that thanks to Arab propaganda success in the world at large, he can assume that the world believes the hoax that the "Palestinians" have a legitimate "grievance"!

It was the Abdullah Azzam Brigades, a terror group apparently linked to al-Qaeda, that claimed responsibility for the Sharm el-Sheikh bombing. The *Jerusalem Post* reported that this group was also apparently responsible for the Taba bombing the previous October in which thirty-four people, mostly tourists, were killed (Margot Dudkevitch, "Who Was Sheikh Abdullah Azzam?" *Jerusalem Post*, July 23, 2005).

According to the same article, Sheikh Abdullah Azzam, after whom the

Brigades were named, "was Osama bin Laden's spiritual mentor," and "is considered to have been largely responsible for expanding the jihad into a full-blown international holy war without borders."

The article's lengthy biography of Azzam tells us that the man was highly educated, having degrees from several Middle Eastern universities, including the Sharia College in Damascus, where he received his Bachelor of Arts degree. He obtained his master's degree from Al-Azhar University in Cairo. He spent some time teaching in Jordan, and all the time in between, he appeared active in terrorist groups against Israel. He also spent some time in Saudi Arabia teaching, and eventually became "convinced that only by military force could the 'true Islam' become victorious."

In between teaching and fighting in this "holy war," he also "established the Office of Services of the Holy Warriors (Mujahideen) and advocated hatred of the West — Christians and Jews — whom he accused of conspiracy against Islam." Azzam was active in the Muslim Brotherhood and Hamas. "Attending a conference in Brooklyn in 1988, he called on participants to carry out jihad no matter where. 'Every Moslem on earth should unsheath his sword and fight to liberate Palestine,' he said."

The man was born near Jenin, in Silat a-Hartiya in 1941 (or so we are told). He attended the village school and the Khadorri College near Tulkaram. As we have seen he was not deprived; he appears to have had the means to provide him a good education.

Like many other jihadists in Saudi Arabia and elsewhere, he came from a "good family." His grievance is against the West in general, against both Christian and Jews, and was likely a product of his environment and propaganda. As we know, Bin Laden too cannot be called "deprived," as he comes from a very wealthy family.

Perhaps as we learn more and more about the perpetrators of these horrific terrorist attacks, we will also know how to defeat them.

Meanwhile the propaganda war rages unabated; the Egyptians did not hesitate to blame Israel for the Sharm el-Sheikh bombings. The Egyptian "state-run television interviewed retired army general Fuad Allam" who said that "he was almost certain that Israel was behind the attacks at Sharm e-Sheikh and Taba" (July 24, *Jerusalem Post*). Other commentators and the al-Jazeera and al-Arabiya news networks echoed the claim.

All this despite the fact that a group citing ties to al-Qaeda had already claimed responsibility!

But Israel continues to have problems of its own. As already reported, not a day goes by without shooting incidents on civilians and soldiers. On July 24, 2005, Israeli TV reported an Israeli couple was killed and a number of people wounded in a car they were driving on the way home after a visit with friends over the weekend. The same day, a number of shootings against the IDF were reported. Two days earlier (July 22) a would-be suicide bomber was apprehended on his way to Tel Aviv; "Jihad Shahada, 18, a resident of the Jabaliyah refugee camp in northern Gaza" was "a member of the Fatah Al Aksa Martyrs Brigade" (*Jerusalem Post*, July 24).

Condoleezza Rice, who arrived in Israel the previous Thursday (July 21) and visited Prime Minister Sharon at his ranch Friday, spent Saturday with the PA-PLO chieftain Mahmoud Abbas in Ramallah, and praised Abbas for his efforts at "bringing law and order in the area."

This in spite of all the above, as well as the constant barrage of kassam rockets and mortars on Israeli residents, as well as the shoot-out between the PA-PLO and Hamas. Note that the abovementioned would-be suicide bomber was a member of the PA-PLO's own Fatah al-Aqsa Brigades!

Is Dr. Rice paying attention to current events?

Facing New Realities

The world is just beginning to wake up to the fact that it is facing a global terrorist war.

The jihadist terrorist war that Israel had to face for a century, even before declaring independence, fighting the terrorists with one hand tied behind its back thanks to the constant harping and criticism of the rest of the world, is now also being faced by our critics.

It is certainly no joy to watch others suffer as we have suffered. It is with horror that we read about the carnage and the panic of ordinary civilians facing an unforeseen danger.

Global terrorism, it appears, has now reached nearly everywhere. The same weekend of the bombing in Sharm el-Sheikh, there was also a bombing in Turkey. In Iraq, the carnage goes on nearly every day, often several attacks in a day.

Some still cling to the mistaken notion that the war in Iraq provoked the terrorists. The terrorists, as recent history has shown, do not wait to be provoked. Israel did not provoke the terrorists, nor did the US. There are hundreds of examples of that for anyone who reads the news, and whose memory goes back more than the last decade. The claim that they act only in retaliation is a convenient tool of deception and propaganda that serves the terrorists' agenda.

To propagandists of every stripe blaming the intended victim is nothing new. The Jewish people have a long memory of that, while in the Diaspora. Today's terrorists and their leaders are past masters of propaganda; they unfortunately find no shortage of useful idiots who believe them.

The dangerous game that Europe has played for the last three decades is now coming home to roost. It must be clear to most that appeasement doesn't work. As Mohamad Mahathir noted in his speech at the annual summit conference of the Organization of Islamic Countries (OIC) in October 2003, those in the hated West don't always return the hatred; "some even see our enemies as their enemies" (see "Mahathir and His Minions" in chapter 29). He urged the leaders of the Islamic world to use Western leaders on their way to achieving their goals, which ultimately include the conquest of the West and the whole world!

Western leaders would do well not to ignore these bellicose statements. Nor should they ignore the mullahs in the mosques in their countries, including Europe, who say words to the same effect. As already quoted elsewhere, a mullah in London not long ago was preaching the conquest of Britain and the whole world.

Clearly, those are words of incitement meant for the jihadists, for the *mujahideen*, their foot soldiers. Britain belatedly tried and imprisoned one of the Islamist mullahs.

The July 7, 2005, attack on London is clearly a result of such incitement, as was the repeat performance on July 21, only two weeks later. Although the four bombs did not explode as planned in the second incident, the London police clearly indicated that the bombs were meant to go off. The jihadists intended to make the point that they can strike at will, even with tighter security, which was obviously present.

London's response to this threat was "shoot to kill." And so the next day, a suspicious figure wearing a "padded" coat was spotted by the police or undercover agents entering the subway, jumping over the turnstiles and running towards the train. The police called on the man to stop; when he didn't, they followed their orders to shoot to kill. Afraid the suspected man might detonate a bomb, they aimed for the head. Tragically, an innocent man was killed. But, as the police spokesman later explained — after offering regrets and sympathy for the unfortunate mistake — the situation was such that the police wanted to avert another terrorist attack, to protect the people. Clearly, the British are facing a new reality.

By contrast, in Israel on the same Friday referred to above, the IDF apprehended an eighteen-year-old would-be suicide bomber on his way to Tel Aviv, where he wanted to explode his bomb in a crowded place. The IDF managed somehow to disarm the would-be bomber, and led him away handcuffed, unharmed.

Should the Israeli army be congratulated for this? I am not sure. One thing is certain: the IDF has learned to fight with one hand tied behind its back, often at great risk to themselves.

Will Israel be criticized less in the wake of these events? I wouldn't hold my breath!

Meanwhile, some commentators referred to new slurs, insults and calumnies, which I will not repeat, issued by the "Lord" Mayor of London, Ken Livingstone. Prime Minister Sharon demanded an apology. Some letter-writers in the *Jerusalem Post* — including an Englishman — expressed concern about the extent to which Arab propaganda has poisoned Western minds. The Englishman urged Israel to promote its cause on the international stage, because people in Britain get only half the story, the Islamic version: "You Israelis owe it to yourselves to promote your cause more vigorously than ever, to reach the ordinary members of the British public," he wrote (Frank Patton, Bromborough, UK, *Jerusalem Post*, July 24, 2005, letters to the editor).

There are many letters of support from non-Jews in the *Jerusalem Post*. These clearly represent a breath of fresh air to the beleaguered Israeli public, and they are gratefully read.

One often reads with great appreciation foreign columnists, among them Amir Taheri, with his clear-minded insight into the Middle East problems: "As Britain tries to absorb the shock of 7/7, some voices are urging what would amount to the appeasement of the terrorists." (*Jerusalem Post*, July 21, 2005, page 15).

And he warned that terrorists cannot be appeased; they simply consider appeasement a victory over an adversary, which spurs them to even more outrages. He cited France and President Mitterand as an example. While France attempted to appease terrorists such as Abu Nidal and Carlos the Jackal among others, including Yasser Arafat who was still then considered the godfather of terrorism, France was attacked many times on its own soil, as were French ambassadors overseas.

Taheri concludes that "the British should know that any appeasement of terrorists could put them in even greater danger."

Blair Accepting Reality

Prime Minister Tony Blair held his monthly televised press conference July 26, 2005, five days after the second attack on London. In a wide-ranging question and answer period — which seemed unusually long — dealing with global terrorism, he took an uncompromising stand. He said there was no excuse for suicide attacks on civilians anywhere in the world. Excuses such as the Iraqi war or the situation in the Middle East are nothing more than self-serving propaganda, used to recruit would-be terrorists.

Blair urged the British people to go on as usual, even though it may be difficult at times, but he said the terrorists' aim is not only to terrorize, but also to disrupt people's lives and divide society. He gave Iraq as an example of a people who have voted for democracy, and noted that the terrorists — both foreign and local — are doing everything they can to disrupt that progress.

To a question of how today's Islamic terrorists compare to the Irish Republican Army, he responded that while he in no way condones the terrorist attacks of the IRA, there is a difference. The Islamic terrorists are aiming at the largest possible number of victims. He said that for him, 9/11 was a wake-up call that changed his thinking.

"The suicide bombers of 9/11 killed three thousand people; they would have killed thirty thousand. They kill indiscriminately." They want to divide the world, Islam against the West. He said that these terrorists must be defeated at every level: their propaganda, their recruitment, etc. To this end, he said, the government of Britain is preparing legislation to strengthen existing laws against terrorism. Indirect incitement, praising terrorists as martyrs, etc., will be considered incitement to terrorism.

There was a question from someone from al-Jazeera asking a convoluted question, which I am unable to repeat, but he took the trouble to explain again at length what he'd clearly said earlier, this time aiming at an Arab audience. Among the other questions there was one from an AP reporter — the questioner clearly had an Islamic and/or Arab name — who asked if there was genocide going on in Iraq. The prime minister again took his time, not simply dismissing the outrageous question, and patiently explained, yet again, how the people of Iraq were able to vote freely for democracy which will improve their lives and lead to a better future, and how the terrorists are doing everything they can to stop the democratization process.

Blair praised the Iraqi people as intelligent and capable, and said the coalition of the allied forces was there to help them towards a better life. He also made the point that whether people agree or disagree on the initial toppling of Saddam's government, the efforts of the allies have the backing of the international community. He also stressed the importance of the Arab states democratizing, believing that this too would help to defeat the terrorists.

It was good to finally hear Tony Blair speak unambiguously about global terrorism, and the effort the world must take to defeat them in every sphere.

I would like to add a personal observation about why the war in Iraq has brought in so many terrorists from other countries such as Syria, Saudi Arabia and others. All one has to do is look at recent wars, or other conflicts such as the Afghanistan war against the Soviets. Thousands of *mujahideen* were recruited from other Arab or Muslim countries volunteering along with the locals. Osama bin Laden was chief among them, but there were also Egyptians and even the so-called "Palestinians" among others. If the reader will recall, the same thing happened in Bosnia, which eventually led to a breakup of Yugoslavia. Kosovo too was an interesting case in point, where neighboring Albanians gradually infiltrated Kosovo, making life rather "unpleasant" for the local Serbs, eventually displacing them practically altogether, and claiming to have a right to a separate state since they, the Albanian Muslims, decided to call themselves "Kosovars."

Does that sound familiar?

The Kosovars "need" a state of their own right next to Albania.

The so-called "Kosovars" are nothing else but Albanians!

The "Palestinians" too are nothing but Arabs in every way, as already pointed out in an earlier chapter, and yet, they too believe they must have a state of their own in the very heart of the Jewish state!

Displacing Israelis proved much more difficult, even impossible. The next best thing the Arabs have attempted to do is to isolate Israel by way of deliberate lies and misleading propaganda and spread calumnies against the Jewish people and their state, the State of Israel, our historic and ancestral home.

Many Israelis unfortunately fell for the ploy of "Land for Peace," not realizing what the phrase means to Arabs. "Land for Peace" is nothing but the surest way to defeat for anyone who believes it. (And note that the land Bush and his friend Blair are willing to trade for "peace" is not their land!)

"Land for Peace," according to Muslim teaching, is taking land while subjecting the enemy to *dhimmitude*. In their history of conquest, the Arab Muslims gave the enemy a choice: convert to Islam or be put to the sword. "Land for Peace" is part of subjugation — *dhimmitude*!

Again, with regards to the Iraqi war, Arab Muslims see themselves as "natural" rulers. They see their land as holy land. According to their teaching, an attack on any Muslim state is seen as an attack on all Muslims. "Humiliation" of one Muslim leader is seen as humiliation of all Islam. Foreign troops on Arab soil are seen as a humiliation of Islam. That is why the US army had to leave Saudi Arabia, despite the fact that they were there to help the Saudis against Saddam Hussein after he invaded Kuwait and seemed to be a threat to Saudi Arabia. And that is why you have foreign terrorists — *mujahideen* — in Iraq. That is not an excuse; that is just the way these people think. This is what their religion tells them. And this is why the Americans were not greeted as liberators who liberated Iraqis from Saddam's oppression, to America's great disappointment.

Are we there yet? Do the Americans or the British now understand better the Arab-Muslim psyche? Frankly, I don't know. But I do hope they are getting closer — 9/11 didn't quite do it, but 7/7 might, eventually… Judging from Blair's demeanor, and the certitude and determination in his voice, Blair appeared to know a great deal more than he let on. If he does indeed, he will likely share his newly-acquired wisdom with his friend, Bush. I guess we will find out sooner or later when Britain will follow through on its prime minister's speech, and when both Blair and Bush stop the talk on the disastrous-for-Israel Road Map (for which there is no justification, except if you believe Arab propaganda). Then we will know — the West is finally getting it.

The Jihad Continues

Britain has introduced stiffer legislation, including security and immigration laws, following the terrorist attack on London, July 7, 2005.

Britain and other European countries have since arrested a number of suspected suicide bombers and their accomplices. Clearly Europe is on alert for acts of terrorism. There is hope that Europe will wake up, and hopefully understand that terrorism — global terrorism — is now its problem as well.

In October, Danish police arrested six suspects who were also linked to the arrest of three others in Bosnia. In the Bosnian arrest, police found explosives, firearms and other military equipment. Of the three arrested in Bosnia, one was a Turk, one a Swede and the other a Bosnian — the Bosnian was since released (*Jerusalem Post*, October 30, 2005, page 5).

Also in October, the Dutch arrested a Dutch suspect of Moroccan origin, who planned with seven others to shoot down an Israeli El Al plane! The same suspect was acquitted in April of a planned attack on a Dutch nuclear reactor! His lawyer claimed his client was innocent of the recent charges as well, despite the fact that a video was found where he made his intentions clear, and stated that he expected to die in the attack. He made vicious statements calling the Dutch "crusaders" for supporting Bush in Iraq, and threatened the Dutch people (*Jerusalem Post*, November 6, page 3):

> "You will be held responsible for this [for alleged US abuses of
> Muslim prisoners at Guantanamo Bay and Abu Ghraib prison
> in Iraq]," he was quoted as saying. "We will, by Allah, take
> revenge … you are considered soldiers because you elected this
> government … We will spill your blood here as you helped steal
> the riches of the Muslims in Israel."

Clearly, we can see the results of Arab-Muslim propaganda. It is not "merely" the "Palestinians" who have a "claim" to *Eretz Yisrael*, but even the Muslims who live thousands of miles away!

On October 29, a massive attack on the Indian capital New Delhi claimed the lives of at least fifty-eight people. There were scores of wounded in three near simultaneous (apparently coordinated) explosions on two markets and a bus. The markets were crowded with shoppers, ahead of the Hindu holiday, the Diwali Festival. About twenty children were apparently among the dead; several people died on arrival at the hospital and bodies were charred beyond recognition according to eyewitnesses.

Some believed the perpetrators may have been Kashmiri separatists who opposed the recent warming of relations between India and Pakistan, particularly in the wake of the massive earthquake in the Kashmir Himalayan region, killing some eighty thousand people on October 8, 2005. India, magnanimously, was the first to offer help to the earthquake-ravaged region, mostly on the Pakistani side of Kashmir. Pakistan strongly condemned the attack on India, calling it "barbaric" and a "criminal act of terrorism." British Foreign

Secretary Jack Straw called the terrorist attack a "cynical and callous disregard for human life," and remarked that the blasts "appear to have been targeted at heavily populated areas to produce maximum carnage" (*Jerusalem Post*, October 30, 2005, front page and page 9). That unfortunately is always the case with terrorist attacks.

Australian Prime Minister John Howard has also called for much tighter laws against terrorism. Australia has recently received warnings of terrorist threats against the country. Australia was never directly attacked by terrorists on its own soil, but its citizens and diplomatic outposts have been repeatedly targeted and attacked as in Bali, Indonesia, when dozens of its citizens were killed in 2002, and again on October 1, 2005 (*Jerusalem Post,* November 4, 2005, page 8). Also, its embassy in Jakarta was attacked in 2004 by a suicide-terrorist bomber.

Also in October, Iran's president, Mahmoud Ahmadinejad, publicly pronounced that "Israel must be wiped off the map"!

This came from a country that has been caught red-handed clandestinely producing enriched uranium for some years. This is not the first time however that Iran's leaders have called for Israel's destruction.

But this, and the fact that Iran appears now to be racing to acquire nuclear weapons and has bragged in recent months to already have a delivery system, raised some voices in the Western world, including Bush and Blair.

The UN Security Council in an "unprecedented" move "condemned the Iranian president's call to 'wipe Israel off the map' and called on Iran not to use threatening language against Israel" (*Jerusalem Post*, October 30, 2005, front page).

The Jerusalem Post article goes on to say that Iran officially declared it would "adhere to the rules of the UN," but Ahmadinejad nevertheless repeated the call to destroy Israel during "Jerusalem Day," the last Friday in the month of Ramadan, "annually used to denounce Israel."

Apparently it's not only "the Palestinians," but Iran too has a claim on Jerusalem!

Kofi Annan, the UN secretary-general, was also critical of the Iranian pronouncement, and eventually was convinced to cancel a planned trip to Iran.

Again, October 30, 2005, another "unprecedented" event took place as was reported on the front page of the *Jerusalem Post* under the headline "Israel pleased by Quartet's demand for Syria to oust Jihad."

Suspicious person that I am concerning all things European, and the Quartet in particular, I read on. Israel has of course for years demanded that Syria close the headquarters of the various terrorist organizations, including the Islamic Jihad which operated on Israeli soil causing more than a thousand civilian dead and countless wounded, always having its pleas fall on deaf ears.

What, I wondered, caused this change?

There of course was the terrorist attack in Israel's town of Hadera several days earlier claiming five lives and many more seriously wounded. A sixth person — a woman of sixty-five — died later of her wounds. The terrorist Islamic Jihad claimed responsibility for this atrocity.

The Quartet immediately issued a statement (New York, October 28, 2005): "The Quartet urges the Syrian government to take immediate action to close the offices of Palestinian Islamic Jihad and to prevent the use of its territory by armed groups engaged in terrorist acts."

The Quartet also "urge[d] all parties to exercise restraint" in order to "avoid an escalation of violence," etc. The statement concluded: "The Quartet believes it is imperative that all involved act decisively to ensure that terror and violence are not allowed to undermine further progress in accordance with the Roadmap." (It appears my suspicion was not in vain!)

And there I was, believing that the Road Map was dead as a doorknob! With all the violence and anarchy and mayhem, what is left to discuss?

Jihad has reached global proportions. All countries in the Western world are looking for ways and means to safeguard their citizens and their borders by enacting laws which will be tough on terrorists and would-be terrorists, as well as their handlers and accomplices; yet Israel is asked to do the opposite! Israel is asked to "invite" the terrorists from Gaza to set up shop in Judea and Samaria through a "special road" linking Gaza with Judea and Samaria, and give up its heartland and defensible borders to create a terrorist outpost.

Whatever happened to UN Resolution 242, and negotiations between the parties to the conflict; namely Egypt, Jordan and Syria, and possibly one or two others?

The PLO was never to be party to those discussions and negotiations, which were to be held without threats or coercion and were to lead to secure, recognized and defensible borders.

There was never talk of a PLO state, only a local autonomy for cities with a large Arab population; that was it! Again and again, there is no room for two "viable" states on this narrow piece of land, our land, historically our Land.

What right do the Arabs have to "former" "Palestine" — to our Land? What law is there in the entire world, which would bestow upon them such a right?

Yes, the British betrayed us; they went back on their solemn promise to the League of Nations and betrayed the trust placed in them. But that betrayal, that perfidy, does not bestow any legitimacy on the Arab propaganda and the myth of a "Palestinian" people.

The riots that broke out in the fall of 2005 in Clichy-sous-Bois, Paris are just the beginning. Europe has now imported twenty million Muslims into its midst, among them many "sleeper" cells, and many jihadists. Yet Europe is still intent on pacifying them, still willing to offer up Israel as a price for its own deluded perception of immunity from terrorism.

The French insurrection started in a suburb of Paris and spread to some three hundred towns across France. President Chirac imposed a state of emergency and a curfew, but at the same time, the insurrection was played down as a rebellion "of disaffected and unemployed youth" with a "legitimate grievance," since "job seekers with foreign-sounding names did not get equal consideration with those who had traditional French-sounding names when presenting CVs," French Prime Minister deVillepin said in his impassioned speech to parliament (*Jerusalem Post*, November 9, 2005, front page and page 18).

He said that the riots were both "a warning" and "an appeal." Nonetheless, he said: "The return to order is the absolute priority… The republic is at a moment of truth."

The *Jerusalem Post* reported that "the violence started October 27, as a localized riot in a northern Paris suburb angry over the accidental deaths of two teenagers, of Mauritanian and Tunisian descent, electrocuted while hiding from police in a power sub-station."

The suburb of Paris, as well as other cities in France where the riots broke out, provide subsidized housing to new immigrants, but some of these "disaffected" youth are second and third generation Arab Muslims, who rule these areas as gang fiefdoms, where police do not dare to enter. Now these gangs are attempting to spread their will elsewhere. During weeks of rioting, thousands of cars and buses were set ablaze and firefighters were attacked with stones and bats. A sixty-one-year-old man was beaten into a coma.

The *Jerusalem Post* noted that "foreign governments have warned tourists to be careful in France," and also reported that "apparent copy cat attacks have spread to Belgium and Germany, where cars were burned."

It's interesting that these riots broke out in countries that are soft on terrorism.

Are we watching now the unfolding of the pact of Eurabia, between the Arab League and Europe?

Will Europe have the courage to save itself from this grip, and will this *"intifada"* — as it is already called by some Arab countries — be stopped in its tracks?

As reported in the *Jerusalem Post* on November 8, 2005, and referred to earlier in this chapter, Australian Prime Minister John Howard warned his countrymen the previous week over a specific threat that terrorists were planning an attack on their country. In the end Australia "foiled a plot to carry out a catastrophic terror attack" (*Jerusalem Post*, November 9, 2005).

According to the *Jerusalem Post*, Australian police arrested seventeen terror suspects in Australia's two biggest cities, Melbourne and Sydney, in pre-dawn raids in which more than five hundred police took part with helicopters hovering overhead. The arrests included "a radical Muslim cleric, known to have praised Osama bin Laden." The cleric, Abu Bakr, "was charged with masterminding the plot."

A police commissioner of New South Wales, Ken Morancy, told Australian Broadcasting Corporation radio: "I'm satisfied that we have disrupted what I regard as the final stages of a large scale terrorist attack"

The accused had apparently been stockpiling chemicals similar to what was used in the London subway bombings in July. Furthermore, the would-be terrorists had undergone "military-style training at a rural camp northeast of Melbourne."

Prime Minister John Howard acknowledged: "This country has never been immune from a possible terrorist attack… That remains the situation today and it will be the situation tomorrow."

Australia — which now appears to be taking all the necessary steps to deal with terrorism, passing anti-terrorism laws that give the police greater power to intercept terrorists — has nonetheless until now allowed other extreme clerics to practice incitement and terrorism, and permitted the training of terrorists on its own territory!

Now, all of Europe is reportedly worried, while at the same time playing down their own problems and citing France as a "special case" different than their own. When did I last hear similar claims?

Desperate people always seem to practice avoidance even when the danger is starring them in the face.

People in Europe apparently still prefer to believe that the rioters are deprived in some way, and it is their poverty and possibly "discrimination" that makes them do the things they do, that makes them into anarchists or simply "rebels."

We heard the same excuses expressed for terrorist suicide bombers, who inflicted so much suffering on others, unconnected to their "misfortune" in any way! And may I remind the reader that the infamous nineteen suicide-bombers of September 11, 2001, all came from well-to-do families, were students, and could have had a good future, but their main preoccupation was to kill the "infidels." For that, they were ready to give up everything, even their own lives.

If Europe will not stop making excuses for the Arab-Muslim insurrection, then in fact Europe will be doomed.

Mark Steyn writes in an opinion piece that appeared in the *Jerusalem Post* on November 9, 2005:

> Ever since 9/11, I've been gloomily predicting the European keg's about to go up. "By 2010 we'll be watching burning buildings, street riots and assassinations on the news every night," I wrote in Canada's Western Standard in February.

In his inimitable acerbic way he says he was "wrong":

> The Eurabian civil war appears to have started some years ahead of my optimistic schedule.

The rioters see themselves primarily as Muslims:

> ...growing ever more estranged from the broader community...and wedded ever more intensely to an assertive Muslim identity more implacable than anything you're likely to find in the Middle East. After four somnolent years, it turns out finally that there really is an explosive "Arab Street," but it's in Clichy-sous-Bois.

He berates the weakness of the French and other leaders of Europe vis-à-vis their Muslim population, and says:

> Today a fearless Muslim advance has penetrated far deeper into Europe than Abd al-Rahman [during the Muslim invasion in 732 CE]. They're in Brussels, where Belgian police officers are advised not to be seen drinking coffee in public during Ramadan, and in Malmo, where Swedish ambulance drivers will not go without police escort.

Meanwhile the French cabinet is split between those like Nicolas Sarcozy, the interior minister who would take decisive action and calls the rioters "scum," and those like President Chirac "who feel the scum's grievances need to be addressed."

Steyn believes that the rioters, like their Muslim predecessors thirteen centuries ago, are:

> ...seizing their opportunities, testing their foe, probing his weak spots. If burning the 'burbs gets you more "respect" from Chirac, they'll burn 'em again, and again.

He concludes with a quote from Theodore Dalrymple in a current issue of *City Journal* on British suicide bombers and the new Europe:

> The sweet dream of universal cultural compatibility has been replaced by the nightmare of permanent conflict." Which sounds an awful lot like a new Dark Ages.

Chapter XXXVI

Tisha Be'Av

Tisha Be'Av (the ninth of the month of Av), according to the Jewish calendar, is the most wrenching day in Jewish history, commemorating the destruction of both the First and Second Jewish Temples in Jerusalem, in 586 BCE (2591 years ago), and in 70 CE, respectively. Jewish people are once again beset with traumatic realities.

One day after *Tisha Be'Av*, of all days, the Israeli prime minister, in his questionable wisdom, ordered the controversial evacuation of Jewish communities in Gaza to be carried out.

The decision, announced a year earlier, was met with a great deal of opposition in Prime Minister Sharon's own cabinet, within his party, and among his traditional supporters. After a year of deliberations and calls for a national referendum, which the prime minister rejected, the magnitude of Sharon's folly was being recognized by ever increasing numbers of Israelis.

The ongoing terrorist violence emanating from Gaza, including kassam rockets and mortar fire at neighboring civilian communities, proved over and over again that there was no good reason for this "unilateral" withdrawal from Gaza. Nearly everyone agreed that the violence would only increase once the Israeli Defense Forces left the area — there would no longer be anyone there to control the situation.

The PA-PLO told us many, many times that it had no intention of disarming the terrorists and dismantling the terrorist infrastructure; quite the contrary, PA-PLO chairman and successor to Arafat Mahmoud Abbas has stated over and over that he will not cause "a civil war" and that "the struggle must go on"!

Bush, as though deaf, dumb and blind, still calls for a "two-state solution" — "a democratic Palestinian state living side by side with Israel." Bush again praised Prime Minister Sharon's decision to withdraw from Gaza, which he says will allow for a "democratic Palestinian state" to come into being.

According to Bush's mantra, democracies don't wage war against one another. In this part of the world — the Middle East — democracy has yet to take hold. Even elections in the current context of the Middle East do not necessarily lead to democratic states. In the still convulsing Iraq, recently held elections may well lead to a Shi'a majority-led government, allied with Iran, and possible *shari'a* laws, which will have no resemblance to democratic models as the West sees them.

For Mr. Bush to imagine that the PA-PLO — which has never rescinded its charter calling for Israel's destruction — will change overnight into a democratic entity is nothing but wishful thinking. The idea that the lawless hoodlums running amok in Gaza, threatening even each other in total anarchy, are material for a lawful society is not sustained by reality. Their young, too, still indoctrinated and brainwashed from earliest childhood, can only follow in the footsteps of their elders. To demand that Israel be "courageous" in a vain and misguided hope for peaceful coexistence is, to say the least, a dangerous fallacy.

Israel wants peace; most decent people know this, only the misguided and brainwashed think otherwise.

But Israel lives in the real world of the Middle East. Here, there is no room for error, as Israeli leaders have often discovered by taking wrong advice. Israel, like all independent and sovereign nations, must decide its own destiny, and its obligation — its first and most important obligation — is to protect its people and its borders.

Contrary to the fantasies of the Arabs, Israel will not, cannot, must not, give up its land, its defensible borders. Two years into the Oslo process (and one month before his assassination), Prime Minister Yitzhak Rabin, the dovish Labor Party leader, delivered a speech before the Knesset (Israel's parliament) discussing Israel's defensible borders.

According to those borders, Israel would continue holding onto all the outside perimeters of the land, including the Jordan Valley and all the strategic high ground. With reference to the Palestinian-Arab autonomy, Oslo also called for a disarmed entity. It didn't work.

As stated earlier, the PA-PLO reneged on all its obligations throughout the many years of negotiations. When the agreement called for a police force of some eighteen thousand — already a high number — the so-called police force grew into an army estimated between forty and fifty thousand. As soon as any city or town was transferred to their autonomy, it turned into an armed camp, hostile to Israel, its "police" often deliberately challenging Israeli border police.

The PLO "police" army was divided in such a way that Arafat could play them against one another, to control them as he saw fit, and as we have seen, all of the factions including the Fatah, Tanzim, and al-Aqsa Martyrs' Brigades, among others, were in fact involved in terrorism, later openly and brazenly claiming "credit" for the most vicious terrorist attacks.

As I have said, Israel never had and still has no desire to be an overlord over this hostile population. Demilitarized autonomy, as we have seen to our chagrin, doesn't work. There is no room for "two viable states living side by side in peace." Not much hope for peaceful intentions from these brainwashed and violent people.

Israel's Defensible Borders

Israel must do what it has to do to protect its own people, first, last, and always! This is the first and most important responsibility of any government.

The whole issue of defensible borders has once again become a hot issue since Prime Minister Sharon decided on his unilateral withdrawal from Gaza.

Experts have recently written regarding Israel's defensible borders in the context of international law. Professor Paul Eidelberg, in the August 2005 Israeli edition of the *Jewish Press* (page 21) refers to:

> Israel's legal status, conferred upon it at San Remo, Italy, in 1920, when the Allied Supreme Council assembled. The decisions taken at San Remo recognized the right of the Jewish people over Eretz Yisrael, a right recognized by the 52 members of the League of Nations, thus making it part of international law.

> That right was also affirmed by the Anglo-American Convention on Palestine. The treaty was ratified by the US Senate and proclaimed by President Calvin Coolidge on December 5, 1925. This treaty remains in force to this day as the supreme law of the land. The Bush administration's support of Disengagement and of an Arab state on Eretz Yisrael therefore constitutes a clear violation of that treaty.

> After gaining control of Judea, Samaria and Gaza in June

1967, Israel decided to deal with the Arab inhabitants on the basis of the humanitarian standards of the Geneva Convention, *without having the status of an occupying force* [Eidelberg's emphasis], since the Arab countries that invaded this land in May 1948 never had any sovereign rights thereto. Hence it was consistent with international law for the Jewish people to exercise their rights over Judea, Samaria, and Gaza, including the right of settlement.

Professor Rostow, one of the drafters of UN Resolution 242, rejects the contention that Israel must withdraw from all territories it regained in the Six Day War. The Resolution merely recommends withdrawal to "secure and recognized borders" in the context of total peace. A report to President Lyndon Johnson in 1968 by the commander-in-chief of the American army said that "secure and recognized borders" mean retaining Judea, Samaria, Gaza and the Golan.

Besides, any interpretation of UN Resolution 242 that contradicts the right of the Jewish people recognized by the San Remo Resolution of 1920 — which rights are intact to the present day — is null and void.

In view of the Anglo-American Convention signed into law in 1925…it would be contrary to that law to call upon Israel to cease developing settlements in Judea, Samaria, and Gaza.

Thus, from the viewpoint of both international and American law, the right of the Jewish people over all areas of Eretz Yisrael is completely valid, including the right to settle throughout the territory.

Thank you, Professor Eidelberg!

Yes, Professor Eidelberg, with G-d's help, Jewish people will continue to settle the land. Even though our people were illegally and tragically uprooted from Gaza, I hope and pray that the trauma they have suffered will heal very, very soon; and that this terrible and cruel experience will strengthen the nation as a whole.

What we have witnessed during these terrible days will never be forgotten, but will serve to unite the people as one.

Our brothers and sisters of Gaza, of Gush Katif, are the salt of the earth.

Our soldiers, too, have proven who they really are, and we are proud of them all.

I hope and pray that our uprooted brethren will rebuild their lives soon. May the Almighty help them, and ease their pain. May they find new abodes to continue to create.

Pity Gaza

Pity Gaza, for her Children
are no more
Her cheerful, green gardens
turned to ruin, once again…!

Pity her Children,
who play no more in her sandy beaches
Who can dream no more
of rainbow days…

Their Moms' and Dads'
furrowed brows
Betray the heartbreak
of bygone days…

Pity Gaza
City of broken dreams
Pity Gaza
For her Children are no more…

Courage

The best one can say about the disengagement from Gaza is that thank G-d there was no bloodshed — no civil war. The pullout is nearly over with only a few communities remaining at this writing.

The heartbreak of the last few days will forever be etched in the psyche of the people of Israel. To watch people being torn from their homes which they built from nothing on unproductive sand dunes and turned into picturesque gardens cities was heartbreaking enough; to watch their Arab neighbors rejoicing at their misery was more than one could bear!

While one Arab group was rejoicing, another one, more menacing, was marching through Gaza — masked men carrying all sort of weapons including shoulder-held missile launchers and anti-tank grenades.

The PA-PLO "Prime Minister" Qurei promised the Arabs: "Today Gaza, tomorrow Jerusalem."

The PLO chief, Mahmoud Abbas, too, jubilantly uttered words to the same effect.

The reader will recall in a previous chapter, President of the European Parliament Josep Borrell Fontelles, visiting Israel and Ramallah a month earlier (June 29–30), was planning a major event — a celebration with many international dignitaries present, to follow Israel's withdrawal from Gaza. Fontelles claims that all this is to strengthen Abbas.

Whether Abbas needs or deserves strengthening should be the real question.

Abbas, who is supposed to reign in terrorists and destroy their infrastructure, instead allows terrorists — including his own al-Aqsa Martyrs' Brigades, to say nothing of Hamas and Islamic Jihad — to march unhindered in broad daylight, fully armed and masked.

A *Jerusalem Post* story (August 16, 2005, page 2) pictured a smiling, jubilant and apparently triumphant Abbas waving in front of his office in Gaza, as thousands celebrated "the beginning of disengagement."

"Most of the celebrations were organized by Hamas and Islamic Jihad," the article tells us, and "Abbas received phone calls from several Arab presidents and monarchs congratulating him on the beginning of the pullout."

One can well imagine who the presidents and the monarchs are. But why are they congratulating him? What precisely did he do to deserve praise?

The terrorists are still brazenly marching in broad daylight brandishing their weapons. Peace is nowhere near; what is the reason for all this jubilation and congratulating?

Apparently, these wonderful "moderate" presidents and monarchs see that their tactics are working. Not only they, but the terrorists themselves, claim that terrorism works. At least, this is how they see it: "Today Gaza, tomorrow Jerusalem," and then they, and their European partners, hope to push Israel to the armistice line of pre-1967!

Never mind that Prime Minister Sharon decided on unilateral disengagement from Gaza, seeing no end in sight in terms of a peace agreement. Never mind that Sharon declared time and time again that unless the PA deals with the problem of terrorism, there will be no more withdrawals in Judea and

Samaria, except for the four isolated settlements in northern Samaria. The terrorists are convinced that it was their doing, their "sacrifice" that led to the withdrawal.

Bush called Ariel Sharon's unilateral action a "courageous" step. Is it?

Already the PA-PLO are calling for absorption of "tens of thousands" of "Palestinian" "refugees" from Lebanon.

The same August 16 *Jerusalem Post* article quoted the committee organizing the "joint celebrations" as wanting "to show the civilized and human face of our people," and saying, "the Palestinian leadership wanted the celebrations to serve as a strong incentive for the international community to put more pressure on Israel to withdraw from the West Bank and Jerusalem."

On August 18, 2005, the *Jerusalem Post* reported (page 3) that Hamas spokesman Khaled Mashaal, normally stationed in Syria, told a press conference in Beirut (the previous day) that the Gaza pullout was "the beginning of the end for Israel."

Mr. Bush, are you listening?

An August 6, 2005 *New York Times* article, which appeared in the *Jerusalem Post*'s August 21 *New York Times* supplement, reported on a recent meeting between Saudi Arabia's new King Abdullah and US Vice President Dick Cheney, who led "a high-powered delegation" to pay respect to the new leader. The article by Jad Mouawad points to the thawing of relations between the US and the Saudis "since the strains of 9/11," and opines that the US delegation was supposed to acknowledge "a simple fact: like it or not, the United States is more dependent than ever on Saudi Arabia."

And no doubt this is the way the Saudis like it. Not only are they bleeding the world's oil-dependent nations — with sixty dollars plus per barrel of oil — but now they can also use extortion of another kind.

The writer quotes Professor Jean-François Seznec of Columbia University's Middle East Institute: "We cannot be enemies with everybody. We need their oil desperately."

Going down a list of unreliable suppliers of oil on one hand, and oil-consuming countries — mainly from Asia, including China — on the other, he refers to the Saudis' "impressive clout."

Quoting Professor Seznec again: "They can play the United States against other buyers, like China, and why wouldn't they?"

The article goes on:

American officials, furious over Saudi Arabia's handling of the investigations after 9/11, recognize this new reality. The warmer relations between Saudi Arabia and the United States were on display last April, when Crown Prince Abdullah — who succeeded his half brother, Fahd, [this month] as king — visited President Bush's ranch in Crawford, Texas. As a sign of public diplomacy, and personal bonds, they kissed on the cheek and held hands.

Anything for public relations!

The writer goes on: "Even the contentious issue of high oil prices has been smoothly swept under the rug." He goes on and on about Saudi supremacy despite the fact that the US may have hoped to be less dependent on Saudi oil, and describes in detail Saudi Arabia's dominance in worldwide oil production.

During Abdullah's visit to the Crawford ranch in April, "Mr. Bush sought relief from high gas prices and support for Middle East peace," according to the *Jerusalem Post* (April 26, 2005, page 8). Also according to the same article: "The Saudis believe the administration's strong support for Israel harms prospects for Middle East peace."

In other words, abandon Israel and you will find us more forthcoming!

But, of course, the Saudi ideas of "peace" in the Middle East are nothing new! Even towards the end of WWII when the massacre, the genocide, the mass murder of the Jewish people of Europe was well known, Saudi Arabia's King Abdul Aziz al Saud told US President Roosevelt that the Arabs and Jews could never cooperate, neither in Palestine, nor in any other country.[1]

In 1945 the Saudi monarch referred to the increasing threat to the existence of the Arabs, and the crisis which had resulted from continued Jewish immigration and the purchase of land by the Jews. His Majesty further stated that the Arabs would choose to die rather than yield their lands to the Jews. To our dismay, the president replied that he wished to assure His Majesty that he would do nothing to assist the Jews against the Arabs and would make no move hostile to the Arab people.

One could surmise from the above that hordes of Jews were let loose on Arabia, instead of the Jewish people coming back home to their own home-

---

1. See Appendix 12.

land in a trickle (rather than the large numbers the League of Nations foresaw) after the many tragedies of exile!

Mr. Bush, or his many advisers, should realize that there is nothing courageous about giving up land to an intractable enemy. It only invites more demands.

The above gives also some idea of the mendacity of the Arabs and their propaganda (the Jews were a threat to the Arabs?). You will also note there was no reference to "the Palestinians"; they had not yet been invented.

Chapter XXXVII

New Rules of the Game

As misguided as the Gaza pullout was, the deed is done. Only the future — probably the very near future — will tell.

Amazingly, the terrorists were persuaded that it was not in their best interest to continue their vile practice during the disengagement, and they did not interfere with the process, which only proves that they can be persuaded to refrain from terrorism!

At the same time, however, we read under the front-page *Jerusalem Post* heading (August 23, 2005), "Hamas and Islamic Jihad claim PA has promised not to disarm them": "The agreement was reportedly achieved during talks in Damascus between PA Prime Minister Ahmed Qurei and leaders of Hamas and Islamic Jihad."

When are we going to stop the charade of calling these terrorists "Prime Minister" and "President," and their conclaves "parliaments"?

When are we going to call their propaganda, their lies, their mendacity, by their proper names?

When are we going to tell their sponsors, the Europeans, to go play somewhere else, for we will no longer play those deceitful games; we will not "'tango' on the fence" (as the July 13, 2004, *Jerusalem Post* headline suggested) or navigate by the "Road Map" to disaster, or anything else that they and their Arab friends cook up between them.

The mask is off; the truth is out!

Eurabia — the monster they have created for the past three decades — is their problem, not ours! It takes two to tango, and we will refrain from their deceitful game!

Tony Blair announced "new rules of the game." Well, it is about time. Britain — and indeed all of Europe — becoming victims of global jihad is our loss as well. But we cannot and will not play along with the Road Map while they get their act together! As for the Arabs living on our territories of Judea and Samaria, it has to be made clear to them that Judea and Samaria is our land, not theirs, all their rotten propaganda notwithstanding.

Most of them, if not all, are citizens of other countries, including Jordan. Quite a number of them are here illegally; they should be sought out and deported to where they came from. If they continue to behave violently, they must be treated accordingly. At best, they should be considered enemy aliens, and once their nationality is ascertained, deported. For those who choose to respect the law of the land, they should be treated accordingly.

As already referred to elsewhere in this book (and explained in Robert Spencer, *Onward Muslim Soldiers*), Muslims are not permitted to live under non-Muslim rule; nobody is holding them here against their will. But we certainly should not, must not, and will not allow them to subvert our nation from within. This too is clearly one of the precepts and conditions of their religion. They are only allowed to live under non-Muslim rule in order to subvert the host country from within.

"Game over," they should be told once and for all; they will not be allowed to make outlandish demands according to their propaganda, based on vicious lies!

This is our historic land, so recognized by the international community in 1920. And that is an unalterable truth! The Arabs were given their land, and we were given ours. If it bothers them that we live in their general proximity, they can move. We are here to stay! We will not allow some conspirators to divide our land, to make us an easy prey for the Arabs. The unholy "Road Map" and all similar attempts must be buried for good.

As for Gaza, it is tragic and totally unjust that our people were dispossessed from their homes — all Israel shares their pain! But, if it was a majority strategic decision for the IDF to leave Gaza, it follows that it was not possible to leave our people behind to the mercies of the cutthroats of Gaza. As painful as all this is, we will have to see what the Israeli government will do when all manner of missiles — including some which they have not yet tried — attack our towns and villages. The official position was that in such an event we would retaliate severely; we had better do just that.

As Charles Krauthammer said in a TV interview, "If they [the Arabs] should fire missiles on Israel, Israel should fire right back." Israel should no longer be willing to fight terrorism with one hand tied behind its back!

No more sacrifices!

Prime Minister Sharon promised painful sacrifices; Gaza was surely enough of a sacrifice!

We do not owe anybody anything! Not to the Arabs, not to the Europeans, not even to our friends the Americans.

The Arabs living on our land in Judea and Samaria have no rights, other than residency, provided they respect our laws and sovereignty. Any seditious utterances should be treated accordingly! We live in a state of war, declared on us by jihadist terrorists and their assorted sponsors.

Treason, and terrorism during time of war — and this global jihad most certainly is a time of war — must be dealt with as severely as the law allows.

Terrorism and global jihad must be treated seriously and severely. Only that way can it be defeated, and it surely must be defeated. There can be no half measures!

With the Almighty's help, we will be triumphant!

Chapter XXXVIII

Summing Up

This book is nearing completion, and yet, as I look at my table, there are papers and documents lying around that cannot possibly be left out. Headlines and pictures practically scream at me from the pages of the newspapers: on the front page of the July 31, 2005, *Jerusalem Post*, under the headline "PA, Hamas, Jihad to cooperate for smooth Israeli withdrawal," there is a telling subtitle: "Following weeks of fighting among the factions." But the even more disturbing item beneath the headlines is a picture of Abbas looking self-satisfied next to Quartet "disengagement envoy" James Wolfensohn, smiling broadly under a larger-than-life picture of a smiling Arafat!

There is something deeply offensive about this picture. A self-satisfied grinning Abbas, and the equally happy "Quartet envoy," under a smiling picture of Arafat! What are these two so happy about? And why did they choose to take a picture next to Arafat? What are they trying to tell us with all this symbolism? Oh, and the article itself tells us that the PA "has reached an agreement with Hamas and Islamic Jihad to work together to ensure a smooth Israeli withdrawal from the Gaza Strip and to hold joint celebrations marking the 'liberation of Palestinian lands'"!

Elsewhere in the article, they spoke of how "resistance" was responsible for the "victory."

In the August 21, 2005, *Jerusalem Post* (page 3), under a picture of gun-toting masked men was the following caption: "Masked gunmen from the Aksa Martyrs Brigades, the Popular Resistance Committee and the Ahmad Abu-Elreesh Brigades arrive for a press conference in Gaza City on Saturday." The headline reads, "Gaza withdrawal is a defeat for Israel, says PA Foreign Minister."

Also, August 21, 2005, on the front page of the *Jerusalem Post*, is the following headline: "Gaza women join Hamas's armed wing"; alongside the article is a picture of three masked women with guns, in long dresses made of camouflage material, with the following description: "Female recruits are trained by Hamas in the Gaza Strip in a photo from Hamas web site."

Not only are the terrorists not being disarmed by the PA as "promised," but apparently training of new recruits goes on openly!

Gaza has become an armed camp for terrorists even more than before. And there is every reason to believe that since they've been left to themselves, we can expect only more of the same. Only now, after their perceived "victory," the terrorists will be ever bolder. There is already talk of transferring their rockets and other weapons to Judea and Samaria, while at the same time demanding free passage between Gaza and Judea and Samaria. In addition, they demand an airport and a seaport (to better supply their weapons).

Money is flowing in from every direction. The G8 countries have promised three billion dollars. The EU is separately donating — in an ongoing fashion — hundreds of millions of dollars. Canada — which has been involved in this "nation-building" scheme for years — is doing its level best to support the "Palestinians"; even the US is pouring hundreds of millions into the PA-PLO sinkhole.

And what exactly has improved as a result of all of this funding? Certainly not the lives of the average Arabs in Gaza! What has visibly improved is better uniforms and weapons of choice for these thugs, such as shoulder-fired rocket launchers, and shoulder-fired anti-tank and anti-aircraft missiles! Oh, yes, the "official" buildings of the PA-PLO are more impressive, as are the "official" cars for dozens of the "ministers" of the inner circle.

Needless to say, the terrorists are becoming ever bolder in their demands and their propaganda. The recent violence exercised against their "officials," while demanding money and jobs, is to the terrorist as natural as breathing air. They are simply saying that they too are entitled to share in the spoils. After all, they claim it was their "work" — their terrorism — that resulted in the "victory."

The front page of the August 28, 2005, *Jerusalem Post* featured a picture of young recruits — probably fifteen-year-olds — marching in the Gaza Strip in a Hamas rally. The boys — dressed in uniforms consisting of camouflage pants and black shirts with some sort of insignia, and carrying green Hamas flags — look like a commercial for in-your-face terrorism. On the same page of the paper is the headline "Bomb maker Deif calls for Israel's demise"!

Amid all sort of threats and propaganda, Deif declared that the "operations" are being moved to Judea and Samaria. He also issued a threat to the

PA-PLO not to attempt to disarm Hamas, thereby giving Abbas the necessary fig leaf not to disarm the terrorists for fear of a "civil war."

So why is all this money being poured into the PA-PLO, and why is Bush still talking about the "two-state solution?"

Many Americans are calling on the US president to "More than ever... speak up for Israel," As the headline of Gary Bauer's August 18, 2005 article in the *Jerusalem Post* said. Bauer, former contender for the US presidency and a leading American Christian figure, wrote that US Secretary of State Condoleezza Rice's statement on her recent trip to the Middle East, praising PA Chairman Mahmoud Abbas for having taken "important steps" against terrorism, "has produced considerable disquiet among those committed to fighting terror and devoted to the realization of a secure and sovereign Jewish State." He wrote:

> In the past, the Bush administration publicly acknowledged that Israel should not be expected to negotiate with the late PA leader Yasser Arafat because he was duplicitous and remained committed to employing armed violence as a principal vehicle by which to achieve his goals.
>
> [...] Abbas is more diplomatically astute than was Arafat, but in reality they are birds of a feather.
>
> Never at any time has Abbas declared his objection to terror on moral grounds. While he repeats the mantra that terror is counter to Palestinian interests, he at once unequivocally declares that he has no intention of dismantling the terrorist infrastructure, including even elements of Fatah, the terrorist subsidiary of his own organization.
>
> [...] Abbas has pleaded with those who organize suicide bombings — Hamas and Islamic Jihad — to take part in his government, and has even invited Hamas terrorists to join his security forces. Would President George W. Bush authorize his administration to negotiate with a leader who was trying to enroll Osama bin Laden's killers to join his army?.
>
> Following the London terror attacks, Prime Minister Blair himself stated that it was a delusion to believe socioeconomic status alone was responsible for the growth of terror. "It is an evil ideology, [Blair] said, which breeds in the religious, edu-

cational and social structure of certain societies which act as incubators of terror." And the fact of the matter is that the PA today remains one of the world's greatest breeding grounds for transforming human beings into lethal weapons.

It is our understanding that the US provides substantial grants to the PA and recently authorized for it a major portion of the $3 billion annual package being provided by the G8...It is troubling that these grants were not accompanied by a caveat that the PA first be obliged to dismantle the terror infrastructure, end the incitement, and ensure these funds be monitored in a transparent manner to guarantee they will not once more be funneled into terror activities or the secret bank accounts of corrupt Palestinian officials.

He writes that it is therefore "incumbent" upon the US president to "ensure" that "these funds be made conditional on the PA undertaking corrective measures to curtail terror."

He continues that "the creation of what could only be described as a terror state controlled by virtual warlords would only send a message to terrorists the world over that terror does indeed pay."

He makes reference to the Bush letter (of April) in which the US president declared the need for Israel to retain major settlements in Judea and Samaria:

It is critical for the president to voice unqualified support for Israel's retention of these settlement blocs, which are of existential importance to the Jewish state's future.

[...I]t would be highly constructive for the president to forthrightly and explicitly restate that there is no validity to the Palestinian demand for the right of return [of "the descendants of the Arabs who fled the region during the 1948 war"].

[...] Israel needs the moral and political backing the US alone can provide... This would, furthermore, also be a good time to send a message to the world reiterating that the US will never come to terms with those who have still to learn that the appeasement of evil and terror is a prescription for disaster.

The above quotes originally appeared as part of Gary Bauer's open letter to

Mr. Bush, co-signed by Isi Leibler (www.ouramericanvalues.org/israel_letter: php).

The US House Majority leader, Roy Blunt, was interviewed on Israeli TV Channel One, August 27, 2005. He also told the *Jerusalem Post* (August 26, 2005, page 5) that the PA must now prove itself in the Gaza "laboratory."

Blunt, leading a sixteen-member Republican delegation, was visiting Israel for a week. Blunt believes that now, after Israel's withdrawal from Gaza, the PA: "needs to prove to the world that they can govern… This gives the Palestinians the first opportunity to show what will happen with full sovereignty."

As I write these words, the radio reports a suicide bomber detonating himself near a bus in Be'er Sheva! Initial reports refer to over forty people wounded, some critically. Subsequent information reported fifty-one wounded, at least two in critical condition. The two were security guards who prevented an even greater tragedy as they confronted the bomber who allegedly wanted to explode himself at the nearby Soroka Hospital.

I have no doubt that Mr. Blunt means well, in calling for Gaza to be a laboratory for PA leadership. But he ignores — perhaps unwittingly — that Gaza and towns in Judea and Samaria were under PA control for some ten years during the Oslo "process," and those towns were used after the handover (and still are) as terrorist bases. And Jewish civilians were the guinea pigs in that "laboratory." He also should know that 94 percent of the Arab population of Judea, Samaria, and Gaza were under PA control and still are. Considering that terrorism was never curbed, but in fact increased every day, every week for the past decade, Israel had no choice but to re-enter some of the areas where terrorism functioned unhindered (particularly after major terrorist attacks).

Israel attempted to destroy kassam rocket factories, bulldozing buildings where terrorist suicide bombers lived or from where terrorists attacked. Israel did all this while taking every imaginable precaution to avoid civilian casualties. Arab propaganda claimed the opposite; and so Israel, not the evil terrorist, was regarded as the "villain."

Prime Minister Sharon took a calculated risk — some say a very dangerous risk — to disengage from the terrorist hellhole that Gaza is and always was. The disengagement was not part of the Road Map, nor was it part of a "two-state solution." Sharon, realizing that reform was not possible with the current PA-PLO leadership, not now, and likely not in the foreseeable future, took this unilateral step. He reasoned that unfortunately he could not leave behind the Jewish population of the twenty-one different communities in Gaza, and so he ordered the tragic uprooting of a wonderful and dedicated people from their very homes, livelihood and beautiful garden cities, which they created with such single-minded dedication out of arid desert sand dunes.

And yet, despite this dangerous and unilateral step, the Arabs and their supporters insist that Israel must continue with the Road Map.

Meanwhile, as we discover in the *Jerusalem Post* (August 18, 2005, front page) under the heading "Egypt, PA agree on joint control of Gaza entry points," the PA and Egypt had "reached an agreement to jointly control the Palestinian airport in the southern Gaza Strip."

This as-yet nonexistent "international airport" is to be operated by both Mubarak and Abbas. We are also told by "Deputy Prime Minister" Nabil Shaath, that "the two sides are opposed to the presence of Israeli soldiers at the Rafah border crossing"!

The Israeli agreement with the Egyptians dealing with the control of the Philadelphi Route, separating Gaza from the Egyptian border — to prevent weapon smuggling by the PLO and other assorted terrorists — had not yet been ratified by the cabinet or Knesset, and the PA-PLO was already making demands even though they were not even included in that agreement.

Shaath also said "he expected the Egyptian official to urge all Palestinians to preserve the unofficial truce with Israel."

In the same article, we are also told that:

> [T]he PA leadership [the previous day] sent urgent messages to the Quartet members imploring them to exert pressure on Israel to halt settlement construction in the West Bank.
>
> [...Erakat] said the PA has called on the international community to interfere with Israel to halt the settlement activities "that undermine efforts to revive the peace process and prejudice final-status talks with Israel."

As one can gather from the above, there is no prospect for peace; the propaganda war, harassment and terrorism continue.

Again, on August 31, 2005, the front page of the *Jerusalem Post* announces: "Egypt vows to support Palestinians until 1967 borders are restored"!

In the article we read how Egyptian Intelligence Chief Omar Suleiman is working feverishly with the various terrorist factions to maintain "Palestinian unity," and vowed that "Egypt will continue to support the Palestinians until they establish their state on all territories occupied by Israel in 1967"!

He also urged the terrorist factions to maintain the period of "quiet"! I suppose he thought that if they can do it for long enough, they could indeed achieve a "Palestinian" state. This spymaster is providing counsel to the terrorists on how best to achieve their mutual goals.

What could Prime Minister Sharon — who urged his cabinet and the Knesset to entrust to Egypt control of the border with Gaza in order to prevent weapon smuggling — have been thinking?!

During the signing of the peace accords between Israel and Egypt, 1979–80, there was of course no talk of creating yet another Arab state on Israel's historical territory; it was merely a question of allowing the resident Arab population a limited autonomy.

Furthermore, if Israel were to allow the PA-PLO to build an airport and a seaport, the flow of weapons and international terrorists would flow unhindered under Egyptian "supervision."

September 6, 2005: A large gang of Arabs, among them many teenage hoodlums, infiltrated the area of a former Jewish settlement. An IDF tank nearby was pelted with stones by the gang, who attempted to do everything possible to provoke the IDF by coming dangerously close to the tank and throwing stones at the soldier exposed in the turret. The gang infiltrated through a fence. Some reporters were wondering whether the infiltrating stone-throwing gang was a "spontaneous occurrence."

Well, it wasn't! As we have seen on TV, they came with cameras and news reporters. We also noticed an adult male cutting through the wires of the fence.

It's interesting, isn't it, how all these "spontaneous occurrences" are always well planned and accompanied by TV and press crews! This time, as nearly always, there appeared to be an Arab (Khalil Hamra) taking pictures for the AP (*Jerusalem Post*, September 7, 2005, page 1).

September 2005 marked the sixtieth anniversary of the establishment of the United Nations. Prime Minister Sharon, among the leaders of the world nations, was to address the UN General Assembly. Both he and the Israeli Foreign Minister Silvan Shalom were seen meeting with various leaders. President Bush, Prime Minister Blair and Canadian Prime Minister Paul Martin were among several leaders taking advantage of the photo-op, now that Sharon was suddenly declared a "courageous" leader!

Not so courageous were several Arab leaders who met on the sidelines with the Israeli foreign minister, preferring however not to be photographed with the "Zionist enemy." Nonetheless, a few made some "peaceful" overtures — predicated on the condition that Israel must go back to the indefensible pre-1967 borders.

President of Pakistan Pervez Musharraf, went so far as to attend a meeting of leaders of the American Jewish community, and while trying to flatter them, he stressed that only Israel's going back to the pre-1967 borders would bring peace.

One doesn't even have to wonder what kind of peace he had in mind.

Meanwhile Simon Wiesenthal died at the age of 96, and was buried in Israel. This untiring gentleman fought all his life for justice and was responsible for the capture of Adolf Eichmann, the man who carried out the Final Solution. He was also responsible for the capture and trial of another Nazi monster, who sent Anne Frank and her family along with thousands of others to their deaths.

Despite the capture and trial of these two major war criminals, Wiesenthal's lifelong efforts have not shown the results he had a right to expect. Both the US and Canada have done practically nothing to bring to justice Nazi war criminals living in their countries, who were responsible for the mass murder of European Jewry.

It should, however, not have been the responsibility of Simon Wiesenthal and other individuals, including survivors of the Holocaust, to search for and bring to trial Nazi war criminals.

After the initial trial of Nazi leaders at Nuremberg following WWII, no Western country appeared interested in providing even a modicum of justice in response to the greatest crime in world history — the greatest tragedy ever to befall the Jewish people!

I, too, among others, fought to achieve some justice for the innocent victims of Nazi persecution and mass murder. I have spent most of my adult life searching for justice with practically nothing to show for it!

And so, an era is coming to an end — the survivors of the Holocaust will soon be gone. The words *"Never again"* have long since lost any meaning, as Jewish people are once again the designated scapegoats of the world, with precious few friends in a hostile and cruel world.

The chairman of the Knesset's Foreign Affairs and Defense Committee, Dr. Yuval Steinitz, commented to the press following a defense team briefing regarding arms smuggling through the Philadelphi corridor between Gaza and Egypt that the latter is very interested in keeping the PA-PLO well armed.

This is the first time in a long time that an Israeli official openly stated that Egypt, far from being a part of the solution, is part of the problem. This, after Israel's prime minister "entrusted" Egypt with preventing arms smuggling in that very area.

But no one should really have been surprised, since Egypt insisted several months ago on the release of a member of a Hamas rocket squad who had been arrested the previous day by the PA-PLO only minutes after the terrorists fired two rockets toward an Israeli community (*Jerusalem Post*, May 4, 2005, p.3). In addition to the arrested terrorist, there were two others in the car with him. Despite the fact that they opened fire at the PA-PLO police, only one was arrested. All this, while Egypt was negotiating with all the terrorist factions for months to maintain a period of "quiet," quite apparently in anticipation of future "rewards" from Israel.

Predictably, following the chaos and accusation of corruption against the PA-PLO, Hamas, which was always stronger in Gaza, won the election in January 2006. The "Palestinians" who always supported terrorism and suicide bombers by some 70–80 percent (as reported in various polls over the last years), have elected Hamas by a similar margin. In the 120-seat council, Hamas took 76 seats and the PA-PLO-Fatah some 36, with the rest going to other terrorist splinter groups.

Predictably, too, the arrangement of Prime Minister Sharon (who suffered a massive brain hemorrhage in November 2005 and was suddenly and dramatically removed from the political scene) with Egypt regarding the border crossing between Egypt and Gaza, even with the "help" of the EU observers, deteriorated beyond recognition. Israeli officials admitted that they no longer control the border — even in a limited way (Israel was previously forced to accept a limited video hookup, "thanks" to US Secretary of State Condoleezza Rice) — following a total breakdown.

In TV reports, one could see how masses of humanity crossed in both directions as Egyptian border control proved insufficient under the circumstances.

Israeli intelligence reported that a great deal of armament has been smuggled over the border with Egypt since Egypt took responsibility. Many suspected al-Qaeda terrorists have managed to cross the border as well. The armament included shoulder-held ground to air missiles as well as grenade launchers — all very dangerous to Israel.

Hamas claims to be upholding the *hudna* — for now — while "sub-contracting" its kassam missiles to Islamic Jihad.

And kassam missiles keep falling into neighboring towns and villages. Even though they often fall into empty spaces, unfortunately, all too often they injure and sometimes kill; as very recently an infant of four months sustained severe head injuries and was in critical condition for several days.

At about the same time that Hamas in Gaza talked about *hudna* — for now — the Hamas leader in Damascus issued its "Manifesto" declaring total war on Israel and the West.[1]

We can only hope that our leaders will know how to respond.

Our people, both in Israel and the Diaspora, find it difficult to understand how Western leaders fail to see the Arab-Muslim designs against us. And how, in fact, Western leaders continue to support, finance and legitimize the terrorist jihad in spite of their dire pronouncements against us. Any sane person has to ask the most obvious question: how, in view of the Arab-Muslim quest to eliminate us, can our Western "friends" ask us to create a state for these unreconstructed jihadists on our own historic land in the very heart of the country? How can we be asked to give up Judea and Samaria, our patrimony? That is clearly a prescription for national suicide. Our so-called friends cannot be unaware of all this.

The answer may be far more simple and frightening than we dare to admit.

As we have seen at the end of the infamous "Oslo process," the Arabs were not interested in peace, not in autonomy, not even in a state, but rather in continued terrorist jihad. As the PLO "Phased Plan" clearly states: the Arabs will accept any territory ceded to them and proceed to launch jihad — a terrorist war — from that territory.[2]

Western leaders know all that, so why do they continue to support the terrorist jihad?

As already pointed out earlier, the Europe-Arab League pact provides for European support for the "Arab cause" against Israel. The "Palestinians" — the

---

1. See Appendix 13.
2. See Appendix 11.

terrorist PLO — are to be legitimized according to that pact, while Israel is to be demonized and delegitimized!

But why?

Here comes that ugly word again — supersession!

I touched on it briefly in chapter 17: the supersession myth is a fundamental part of Christian dogma. "The cornerstone of Christian Antisemitism is the superseding or displacement myth, which already rings with the genocidal note," writes Franklin Littel, a Christian theologian.[1]

According to this theology, the Jewish people were expected to vanish from history with the coming of Christianity, either through conversion, or suffering and humiliation deliberately inflicted on us. "And this is precisely why Israel is a challenge," continues Littel, "a crisis for much contemporary Christian theology."

The very existence of the Jewish people and the Jewish state — the State of Israel, on its own ancestral soil — poses an impossible "challenge, a crisis" to the Church, and very likely to many Christian leaders.

So, I suppose we shouldn't be surprised if they do all they can to undermine our very existence.

That would certainly explain why the Vatican took some four decades before recognizing the State of Israel, and why Jerusalem is still not recognized as the capital of the Jewish state. And this is why the Vatican apology for the suffering of the Jewish people during the Holocaust and throughout centuries of Christian persecution was no apology at all.

But as we can see, things get even more sinister. The Arab Muslims, who had also claimed to have superseded both Judaism and Christianity (according to their theology), have found a ready ally among many Christian leaders of Europe.

How is that possible — you may well ask — considering that the Muslim supersession myth also includes Christianity? The fact remains that they have signed a pact against Israel,[2] a pact which provides the Europeans with economic benefits, including guaranteed oil supply.

But the Arab Muslims, flushed with the success of their propaganda war against Israel, are now claiming not only supersession, but that Islam "in fact"

---

1. Franklin H. Littel, *The Crucifixion of the Jews*, New York: Harper and Row, 1975, page 2.
2. See Bat Ye'or, *Eurabia*.

preceded Judaism and Christianity. As we have already seen, history has never gotten in the way of Arab-Muslim propaganda, but whatever happened to Christian "claims"?

The Arab supersession myth made it imperative for them to conquer Israel in the seventh century CE and to build a mosque atop the ruins of our First and Second Temples (in addition, one might add, to conquering large parts of Europe).[1]

To see Israel re-established in its own Land is not only a challenge and a crisis to the Church, but also to the Arab Muslims, according to their own supersession myth.

It may be possible therefore for both sides, the Christian and Arab-Muslim leaders, to be "reconciled" under the principle of "the enemy of my enemy is my friend." In a roundabout way, the newest Arab-Muslim propaganda claiming to have "preceded" Judaism, may have even found favor among some Christians, since their supersession theory could then still "triumph."

And so, as we can see, the present and "old" Arab-Israeli "conflict" is not about a "Palestinian state"; it never was!

It certainly was not in 1948, when they declared a genocidal war against the reborn State of Israel. It certainly was not in 1967 or in 1973.

Jews were puzzled in 1967 when the Egyptians openly declared the genocidal war against Israel and sent the UN Peace-Keeping Forces packing; why didn't the Western Christian world protest?

We can now say with greater certainty that they did not protest for the same reason they did not protest during the Holocaust, when the Christian Church remained silent while millions of Jewish people were being murdered in cold blood.

We can now say perhaps with greater certainty that the British leaders never intended to carry out the League of Nations Mandate to help re-establish the Jewish homeland in *Eretz Israel* ("Palestine") despite the Balfour Declaration. That would have been totally incompatible with the Christian supersession theory.

And this is why the British had no mercy on the thousands of Jewish refugees escaping the Nazi inferno, and sent them right back into the hands of their would-be murderers.

---

1. See *Carta's Historical Atlas of Israel: Survey of the Past and Review of the Present*, Jerusalem: Carta, 1983.

And this is certainly why instead of bringing large numbers of Jewish exiles back to Israel as mandated by the League of Nations in 1920, they instead populated the Land with Arabs from the farthest reaches of the Middle East.

And this is why in the 1940s the British Foreign Office and the BBC had no problem agreeing that "saving Jewish lives was not a desirable aim" (*Jerusalem Post*, Sept. 4, 1993, page 20, in reference to BBC archival material 1939–45).

And this is why Nazi war criminals, many of whom eagerly collaborated in the murder of the Jewish people, were never brought to justice in Britain, in Canada and even in the US, but rather lived freely under their own names in these and other countries.

In the words of Franklin Littel:[1]

> The murder of six million Jews by baptized Christians from whom membership in good standing was not (and has not yet been) withdrawn raises the most insistent question about the credibility of Christianity.

This is why Britain has illegally, in contravention of its own Balfour Declaration, twice divided the Land designated as the Jewish homeland, leaving Israel with "Auschwitz borders," as Abba Eban (the Israeli foreign minister at the time of the Six Day War) called them. And this is why Britain, even now, is leading the pack to push Israel back into those indefensible borders.[2]

This is why British academics and clergy call for boycotts of Israel, and this is why the "Road Map to Peace" was designed by Europe and Saudi Arabia to accomplish their nefarious goals.

This is why the British clergy urge the supporters of Israel, the Christian Zionists, to abandon Israel (see *Jerusalem Post*, March 9, 2006, article by Pastor Elwood McQuaid, a leader in the Christian-Zionist movement). And this is why the Arab Muslims urge the United States to abandon Israel to their mercies.

But Christian Zionists, thankfully, reject the replacement theology.

In a recent interview (*Jerusalem Post*, March 21, 2006, editorial page, interview by Editor David Horovitz), Dr. John Hagee expressed his unconditional support of Israel and the Jewish people, saying: "We have a mandate…to be supportive of Israel and the city of Jerusalem…" Dr. Hagee also said, "the

---

1. *The Crucifixion of the Jews*, New York: Harper and Row, 1975.
2. See Appendices 2, 3, 6 & 7.

notion that the Church has 'replaced Israel' is both false and being rejected by more and more evangelical leaders."

Dr. Hagee is also the initiator of a new Christian-style AIPAC, in support of Israel.

And so perhaps, just perhaps, there is a light at the end of the proverbial tunnel. Perhaps the Church will find a way to accommodate itself to the reality of the reborn Israel.

For we are here to stay. We will never again be subjugated to the *dhimmitude* of the Arabs, nor the suffering and humiliation, massacres and genocide perpetrated against our people.

Perhaps, now that the Western world has experienced global jihad first-hand, they too will soon discover who their real enemies are…

Chapter XXXIX

The Indictment

Throughout these pages I have shown the roots of anti-Semitism, I have shown an almost straight line from Nicaea to Auschwitz, with the bloody massacres and persecution all along the way. The many attempts at converting the Jewish people, the burning at the stake, the torture of innocents during the Inquisition, the expulsions from one state to another and often back again, all of which our persecutors explained away by calling us "the wandering Jew." To the Church Fathers, this was "a clear sign" that the Jews were being punished for their "sins."

What a powerful device propaganda can be. You blame the intended victim despite the fact that you inflict upon him the conditions of his suffering.

The Nazis used similar tactics, similar propaganda, inflicting on the Jewish people inhuman suffering, and then saying, "the Jews are our tragedy (loosely translated from *Die Juden sind unser Unglück*)." The Nazis demonized our people until we were equated with vermin; after that, "extermination" was almost logical! (That is why I avoid the term "extermination" — it is denigrating as our enemies intended.)

I have attempted to show how most perpetrators of the Holocaust — the mass murderers of our people and their eager helpers — lived out their lives in several democratic countries free from prosecution.

I have attempted throughout these pages to show the dangers of propaganda, of hate propaganda, and incitement to violence, which has inevitably led to violence throughout history.

During the Holocaust, I watched helplessly the unfolding and inevitable results of propaganda. I am again watching how another set of our enemies are using propaganda and incitement to violence (as well as actual horrific violence) against us, while we, the intended victim, are accused of the very thing our enemies are doing to us!

Our Arab enemies have waged several wars against us, with the declared aim of destroying our people, and our state, Israel.

Our enemies, in a truly Orwellian twist, in the manner of all previous propagandists, are calling Israel and the Jewish people racist, and even "Nazis."

How does the intended victim of genocidal aggression get to be called racist?

We live indeed in a perverted world, where black is white, where war is peace, where a "peace process" is intended to destroy Israel in stages, and where Israel is threatened with total isolation if it does not succumb — to allow itself to be dismembered!

I attempted in these pages to describe how the UN became perverted from an institution originally devoted to promote peace and reconciliation among nation states, and to promote human rights for all peoples, and is, instead, serving the despots and human rights abusers.

I attempted to describe how Israel has become the target of anti-Israel, anti-Semitic abuses, from the very fora of the United Nations, by the coercive power of the Arab-Muslim automatic majority, exercised without shame.

I attempted to describe how the coercive power of Arab-Muslim nations, with the help of OPEC, has turned Europe into a tool of Arab-Muslim propaganda against Israel; how in fact Europe has become a tool to undermine the very existence of Israel.

I attempted to describe how Europe itself has become a victim of Arab-Muslim propaganda, which has in stages perverted its own way of life, turning it into a vassal of Arab-Muslim corrosive power, having invaded its universities, exposing its peoples to perversion of truth.

I attempted to show in these pages how the Arab League created the PLO in 1964 — a terrorist entity which was to become the Arab-Muslim proxy and a tool for the destruction of Israel — the proverbial Trojan horse.

I have attempted to point out that much of Western Christian leadership, still imbued with hatred of the Jewish people, has had no problem promoting the "Arab cause," turning a blind eye to the realities of the Middle East.

Just as most of the Western world turned a blind eye during the centuries of persecution of the Jewish people culminating in the Holocaust, so it is doing now, again.

Western leaders have been pursuing a short-term policy, as diabolic as it was, not realizing that their turn was not long in coming. As Caroline Glick described the message of former Malaysian President Mahmoud Mahathir's speech to the applause of Arab-Muslim leaders: "Not everyone in the hated West hates the Muslims back. Mahathir counseled the Islamic leaders to use those Westerners who support them and who 'see our enemies as their enemies'" ("Malaysian Road Map," *Jerusalem Post*, October 24, 2003). He insinuated that Muslims should use Western leaders to advance their nefarious goals against Israel.

But "the writing on the wall" has been there for a long time already! Muslim preachers in mosques throughout Europe, in the Middle East, and to some extent in the US, have preached holy jihad against the West and Israel. The West was the "Big Satan"; Israel was "merely" the "Little Satan." For a long time no one was listening.

Now, finally, Britain has awakened, having experienced terrorism on its own soil, and has suddenly become aware of the threat from within. Other countries of Europe, too, are realizing that they are not immune to the global jihad.

Is it too late? I hope not. For much depends on what Europe and the US will do next. Now they too realize that they have nurtured an enemy within: sleeper cells of al-Qaeda or other related terrorist groups, all committed to the global jihad. But as long as these terrorists were merely using European states as a staging ground for attacks elsewhere, Europe didn't seem to mind.

Now they are finally waking up to the stark reality that they were the intended victims all along, and that transplanting large numbers of Arabs and other Muslims was part of the nefarious plan.

The US, of course, had its wake-up call on 9/11, 2001. Thankfully, the American population was not as easily brainwashed as its counterpart in Europe. Not that the Arab Muslims haven't tried. In the US, too, the universities are heavily influenced by Arab professors, who occupy chairs of Middle East and Islamic studies, thanks to the Saudi "largesse." These professors use their classrooms as platforms and tools for Arab-Muslim propaganda. Fortunately not all students are swayed by the thinly veiled lies. Also American Christians, many of whom are deeply religious, openly profess an affinity towards the Jewish people. Certainly, in these difficult times for Israel, their friendship is more than appreciated.

Mr. Bush, the US president, who is a deeply religious man, often assures Israel of his friendship. But Mr. Bush has many friendships, among them an apparently personal one with Tony Blair, and Mr. Blair's agenda has interfered dangerously with Mr. Bush's declared commitment to Israel, at least until now.

The coming months and years will certainly tell us who our friends really are. The ongoing anarchy, violence and terrorism emanating from Gaza, the various expressions of fanatical hostility towards Israel by Hamas, Islamic Jihad, the Aqsa terrorists, the Fatah, and other assorted gangs, marching fully armed, masked and in camouflage uniforms, carrying rocket-propelled grenades, anti-tank missiles, and shoulder-held anti-aircraft missiles, do not bode well for any kind of peace. Yet Mr. Bush, as if hypnotized, still repeats the "peace process" mantra.

Our leaders must make it clear to Mr. Bush that talking about creating yet another Arab state on Israel's land is dangerous to Israel. The mantra which Mr. Bush continues to repeat, of "a two-state solution, living side by side in peace" — Israel and "Palestine" — is a pipe dream. Not only because the intentions of the Arabs are anything but "peaceful," but also, and very importantly, there simply is no room for two "viable states" on the already tiny territory of *Eretz Israel.*

Mr. Bush will have to understand that Israeli leaders' primary concern must be the security of their people and Israel's borders.

We remember our tragic past during our exile, and the horrible memory of the Holocaust when no Allied power lifted a finger to prevent the slaughter of our people, even refusing to bomb the railway lines to Auschwitz, which could have prevented the slaughter of tens of thousands, perhaps even more. The Allies had no trouble bombing the rubber factory (Buna) which was practically next door, yet the excuse was that Auschwitz was out of range of the bombers!

We will neither forget, nor forgive the British for their perfidy, for reneging on their commitment to facilitate "close settlement by Jews on the land" according to the League of Nations Mandate, and their betrayal of the Jewish people and the international community which entrusted the British to carry out the Mandate.

Instead of allowing the largest possible numbers of returning Jewish exiles to settle the Land as the Mandate required, they looked for every possible subterfuge to reduce Jewish immigration to a trickle. And instead, they allowed unrestricted inflow of Arabs, mostly illegals, from neighboring Arab states, contrary to the Mandate.

If it weren't for the British betrayal, hundreds of thousands of Jewish people could have been saved from the Nazi mass murder! The Land could have absorbed many hundreds of thousands in 1920–33, before Hitler came to power, and it could have absorbed many hundreds of thousands more in the following ten years, when Jews could still flee Europe. The small, often leaky boats of refugees were mercilessly turned away from the very shores of *Eretz Israel* by the British — often sinking or exploding due to underwater mines within sight of *Eretz Israel*.

That merciless depravity we must never forget!

Mr. Bush, our friend, must understand that we do not trust the British, and we cannot put too much trust in Europe, since it has become Eurabia.

From time to time, an item will appear in the press such as the one on page 5 of the *Jerusalem Post*, August 1, 2005, "Did the Allies bury early intelligence on the Holocaust?" or the one on September 4, 1993 (*Jerusalem Post*, page 20), "BBC Foreign Office hid news of the Holocaust." In the body of this article, we discover that while the BBC was preparing a documentary based on its own archival material, it revealed that senior officials from both the Foreign Office and the BBC "believed that saving Jewish lives was not a desirable aim." This research was based on archival material from 1939 to 1945.

All of the above is an indictment primarily against Britain and the Arab-Muslims, but as many pages of this book testify, there have been many other not-so-minor players. They know who they are…

Our people are resilient and resolute. I hope that the revelations in these pages will help them to understand better the dangers we are up against, and to see clearly that our nation must unite more than ever before. Together we can surmount every obstacle and every danger. We must always be self-reliant. We cannot, as history has proven over and over again, rely on foreign powers for our safety and security. We have to be grateful for faithful friends, but we must not forget that there is a cruel world out there, and that only we must be responsible for our common destiny, for our safe future. We have faced and survived even greater dangers. With the Almighty's help, we will overcome every difficulty and every challenge.

Appendix 1
Preamble to the League of Nations Mandate for Palestine, July 24, 1922

The Council of the League of Nations:

Whereas the Principal Allied Powers have agreed, for the purpose of giving effect to the provisions of Article 22 of the Covenant of the League of Nations, to entrust to a Mandatory selected by the said Powers the administration of the territory of Palestine, which formerly belonged to the Turkish Empire, within such boundaries as may be fixed by them; and

Whereas the Principal Allied Powers have also agreed that the Mandatory should be responsible for putting into effect the declaration originally made on November 2nd, 1917, by the Government of His Britannic Majesty, and adopted by the said Powers, in favor of the establishment in Palestine of a national home for the Jewish people, it being clearly understood that nothing should be done which might prejudice the civil and religious rights of existing non-Jewish communities in Palestine, or the rights and political status enjoyed by Jews in any other country; and

Whereas recognition has thereby been given to the historical connection of the Jewish people with Palestine and to the grounds for reconstituting their national home in the country; and

Whereas the Principal Allied Powers have selected his Britannic Majesty as the Mandatory for Palestine; and

Whereas the mandate in respect of Palestine has been formulated in the following terms and submitted to the Council of the League for approval; and

Whereas his Britannic Majesty has accepted the mandate in respect of Palestine and undertaken to exercise it on behalf of the League of Nations in conformity with the following provisions; and

Whereas by the afore-mentioned Article 22 (paragraph 8), it is provided that the degree of authority, control or administration to be exercised by the Mandatory, not having been previously agreed upon by the Members of the League, shall be explicitly defined by the Council of the League of Nations.

Appendix 2

Map: Palestine According to the 1922 League of Nations Mandate for Palestine

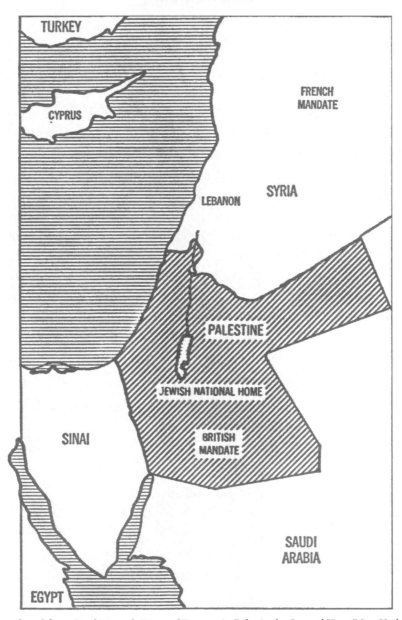

Maps reproduced from *Battleground: Fact and Fantasy in Palestine* by Samuel Katz (New York: Bantam, 1973), by permission of the author.

Appendix 3

Map: Israel in the Armistice Lines 1949 – June 5, 1967

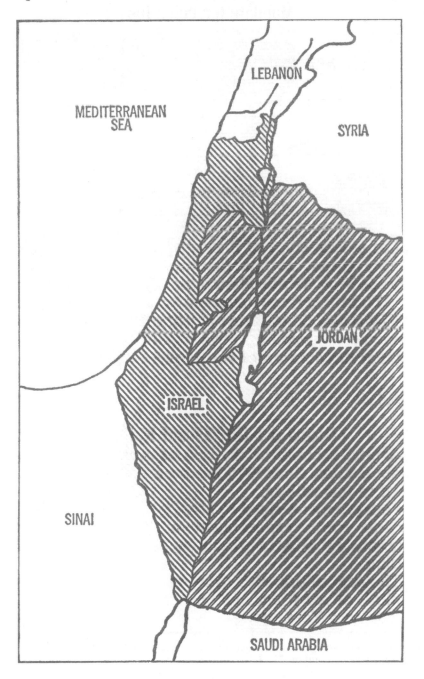

Appendix 4
Map: The Partition Proposed by the United Nations 1947

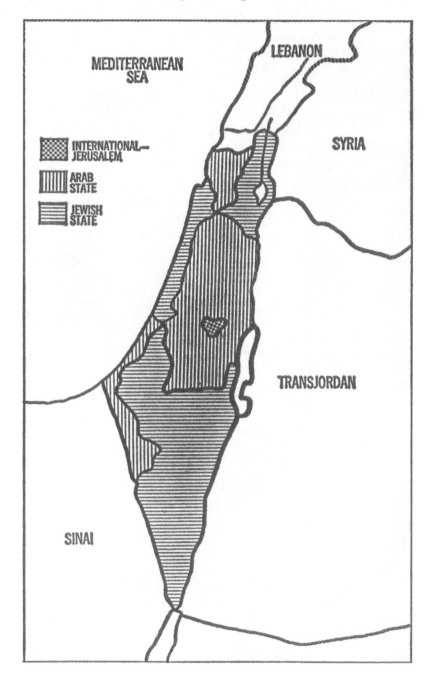

Appendix 5

Map: Proposal of the World Zionist Organization to the Paris Peace Conference (1919)

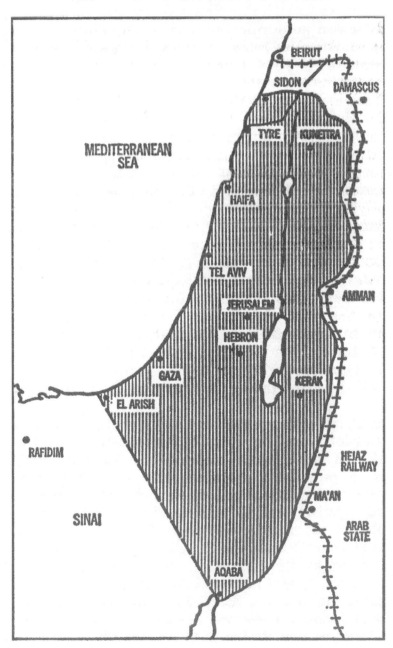

Appendix 6
Map: The First Partition

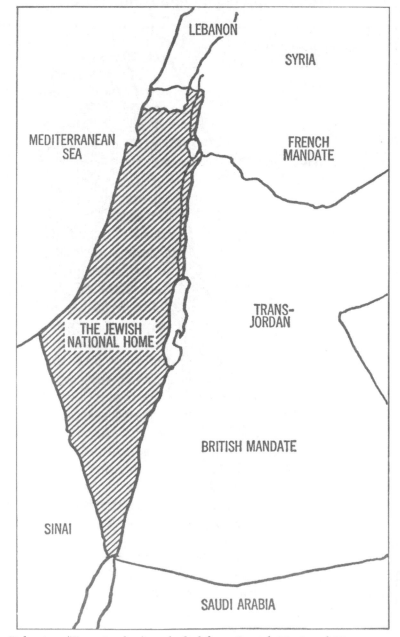

Eastern Palestine (Transjordan) excluded from Jewish National Home 1923–1946

Appendix 7

Map: Peel Commission Partition Plan, 1937

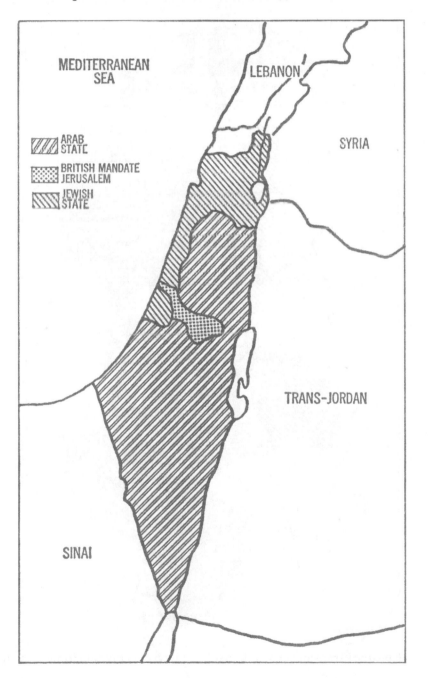

Appendix 8
Map: The Arab States and Israel

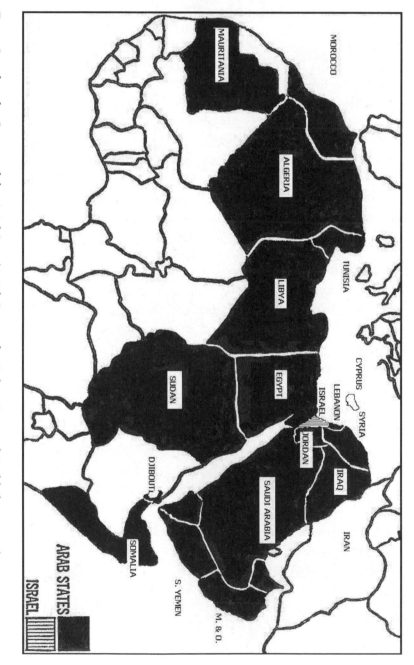

From *Israel at the Crossroads* by Ariel Stav (Ariel Center for Policy Research Publishers, 1997). Reprinted courtesy of the Ariel Center for Policy Research.

Appendix 9
UN Security Council Resolution 242
November 22, 1967

Following the June '67, Six-Day War, the situation in the Middle East was discussed by the UN General Assembly, which referred the issue to the Security Council. After lengthy discussion, a final draft for a Security Council resolution was presented by the British Ambassador, Lord Caradon, on November 22, 1967. It was adopted on the same day.

This resolution, numbered 242, established provisions and principles which, it was hoped, would lead to a solution of the conflict. Resolution 242 was to become the cornerstone of Middle East diplomatic efforts in the coming decades.[1]

The Security Council,

Expressing its continuing concern with the grave situation in the Middle East,

Emphasizing the inadmissibility of the acquisition of territory by war and the need to work for a just and lasting peace in which every State in the area can live in security,

Emphasizing further that all Member States in their acceptance of the Charter of the United Nations have undertaken a commitment to act in accordance with Article 2 of the Charter,

1. *Affirms* that the fulfillment of Charter principles requires the establishment of a just and lasting peace in the Middle East which should include the application of both the following principles:

 i Withdrawal of Israeli armed forces from territories occupied in the recent conflict;

 ii Termination of all claims or states of belligerency and

---

1. From the Israel Ministry of Foreign Affairs web site: http://www.mfa.gov.il/MFA/ Peace+Process/Guide+to+the+Peace+Process/UN+Security+Council+Resolution+ 242.htm

respect for and acknowledgement of the sovereignty, territorial integrity and political independence of every State in the area and their right to live in peace within secure and recognized boundaries free from threats or acts of force;

2. *Affirms further* the necessity

   (a) For guaranteeing freedom of navigation through international waterways in the area;

   (b) For achieving a just settlement of the refugee problem;

   (c) For guaranteeing the territorial inviolability and political independence of every State in the area, through measures including the establishment of demilitarized zones;

3. *Requests* the Secretary-General to designate a Special Representative to proceed to the Middle East to establish and maintain contacts with the States concerned in order to promote agreement and assist efforts to achieve a peaceful and accepted settlement in accordance with the provisions and principles in this resolution;

4. *Requests* the Secretary-General to report to the Security Council on the progress of the efforts of the Special Representative as soon as possible.

Adopted unanimously at the 1382nd meeting.

Appendix 10
The Palestinian National Charter:
Resolutions of the Palestine National Council
July 1–17, 1968

Article 1: Palestine is the homeland of the Arab Palestinian people; it is an indivisible part of the Arab homeland, and the Palestinian people are an integral part of the Arab nation.

Article 2: Palestine, with the boundaries it had during the British Mandate, is an indivisible territorial unit.

Article 3: The Palestinian Arab people possess the legal right to their homeland and have the right to determine their destiny after achieving the liberation of their country in accordance with their wishes and entirely of their own accord and will.

Article 4: The Palestinian identity is a genuine, essential, and inherent characteristic; it is transmitted from parents to children. The Zionist occupation and the dispersal of the Palestinian Arab people, through the disasters which befell them, do not make them lose their Palestinian identity and their membership in the Palestinian community, nor do they negate them.

Article 5: The Palestinians are those Arab nationals who, until 1947, normally resided in Palestine regardless of whether they were evicted from it or have stayed there. Anyone born, after that date, of a Palestinian father — whether inside Palestine or outside it — is also a Palestinian.

Article 6: The Jews who had normally resided in Palestine until the beginning of the Zionist invasion will be considered Palestinians.

Article 7: That there is a Palestinian community and that it has material, spiritual, and historical connection with Palestine are indisputable facts. It is a national duty to bring up individual Palestinians in an Arab revolutionary manner. All means of information and education must be adopted in order to acquaint the Palestinian with his country in the most profound manner, both spiritual and material, that is possible. He must be prepared for the armed struggle and ready to sacrifice his wealth and his life in order to win back his homeland and bring about its liberation.

Article 8: The phase in their history, through which the Palestinian people are now living, is that of national (watani) struggle for the liberation of Palestine. Thus the conflicts among the Palestinian national forces are secondary, and should be ended for the sake of the basic conflict that exists between the forces of Zionism and of imperialism on the one hand, and the Palestinian Arab people on the other. On this basis the Palestinian masses, regardless of whether they are residing in the national homeland or in diaspora (mahajir) constitute — both their organizations and the individuals — one national front working for the retrieval of Palestine and its liberation through armed struggle.

Article 9: Armed struggle is the only way to liberate Palestine. This is the overall strategy, not merely a tactical phase. The Palestinian Arab people assert their absolute determination and firm resolution to continue their armed struggle and to work for an armed popular revolution for the liberation of their country and their return to it . They also assert their right to normal life in Palestine and to exercise their right to self-determination and sovereignty over it.

Article 10: Commando action constitutes the nucleus of the Palestinian popular liberation war. This requires its escalation, comprehensiveness, and the mobilization of all the Palestinian popular and educational efforts and their organization and involvement in the armed Palestinian revolution. It also requires the achieving of unity for the national (watani) struggle among the different groupings of the Palestinian people, and between the Palestinian people and the Arab masses, so as to secure the continuation of the revolution, its escalation, and victory.

Article 11: The Palestinians will have three mottoes: national (wataniyya) unity, national (qawmiyya) mobilization, and liberation.

Article 12: The Palestinian people believe in Arab unity. In order to contribute their share toward the attainment of that objective, however, they must, at the present stage of their struggle, safeguard their Palestinian identity and develop their consciousness of that identity, and oppose any plan that may dissolve or impair it.

Article 13: Arab unity and the liberation of Palestine are two complementary objectives, the attainment of either of which facilitates the attainment of the other. Thus, Arab unity leads to the liberation of Palestine, the liberation of Palestine leads to Arab unity; and work toward the realization of one objective proceeds side by side with work toward the realization of the other.

Article 14: The destiny of the Arab nation, and indeed Arab existence itself, depend upon the destiny of the Palestine cause. From this interdependence springs the Arab nation's pursuit of, and striving for, the liberation of Palestine. The people of Palestine play the role of the vanguard in the realization of this sacred (qawmi) goal.

Article 15: The liberation of Palestine, from an Arab viewpoint, is a national (qawmi) duty and it attempts to repel the Zionist and imperialist aggression against the Arab homeland, and aims at the elimination of Zionism in Palestine. Absolute responsibility for this falls upon the Arab nation — peoples and governments — with the Arab people of Palestine in the vanguard. Accordingly, the Arab nation must mobilize all its military, human, moral, and spiritual capabilities to participate actively with the Palestinian people in the liberation of Palestine. It must, particularly in the phase of the armed Palestinian revolution, offer and furnish the Palestinian people with all possible help, and material and human support, and make available to them the means and opportunities that will enable them to continue to carry out their leading role in the armed revolution, until they liberate their homeland.

Article 16: The liberation of Palestine, from a spiritual point of view, will provide the Holy Land with an atmosphere of safety and tranquility, which in turn will safeguard the country's religious sanctuaries and guarantee freedom of worship and of visit to all, without discrimination of race, color, language, or religion. Accordingly, the people of Palestine look to all spiritual forces in the world for support.

Article 17: The liberation of Palestine, from a human point of view, will restore to the Palestinian individual his dignity, pride, and freedom. Accordingly the Palestinian Arab people look forward to the support of all those who believe in the dignity of man and his freedom in the world.

Article 18: The liberation of Palestine, from an international point of view, is a defensive action necessitated by the demands of self-defense. Accordingly the

Palestinian people, desirous as they are of the friendship of all people, look to freedom-loving, and peace-loving states for support in order to restore their legitimate rights in Palestine, to re-establish peace and security in the country, and to enable its people to exercise national sovereignty and freedom.

Article 19: The partition of Palestine in 1947 and the establishment of the state of Israel are entirely illegal, regardless of the passage of time, because they were contrary to the will of the Palestinian people and to their natural right in their homeland, and inconsistent with the principles embodied in the Charter of the United Nations, particularly the right to self-determination.

Article 20: The Balfour Declaration, the Mandate for Palestine, and everything that has been based upon them, are deemed null and void. Claims of historical or religious ties of Jews with Palestine are incompatible with the facts of history and the true conception of what constitutes statehood. Judaism, being a religion, is not an independent nationality. Nor do Jews constitute a single nation with an identity of its own; they are citizens of the states to which they belong.

Article 21: The Arab Palestinian people, expressing themselves by the armed Palestinian revolution, reject all solutions which are substitutes for the total liberation of Palestine and reject all proposals aiming at the liquidation of the Palestinian problem, or its internationalization.

Article 22: Zionism is a political movement organically associated with international imperialism and antagonistic to all action for liberation and to progressive movements in the world. It is racist and fanatic in its nature, aggressive, expansionist, and colonial in its aims, and fascist in its methods. Israel is the instrument of the Zionist movement, and geographical base for world imperialism placed strategically in the midst of the Arab homeland to combat the hopes of the Arab nation for liberation, unity, and progress. Israel is a constant source of threat vis-a-vis peace in the Middle East and the whole world. Since the liberation of Palestine will destroy the Zionist and imperialist presence and will contribute to the establishment of peace in the Middle East, the Palestinian people look for the support of all the progressive and peaceful forces and urge them all, irrespective of their affiliations and beliefs, to offer the Palestinian people all aid and support in their just struggle for the liberation of their homeland.

Article 23: The demand of security and peace, as well as the demand of right and justice, require all states to consider Zionism an illegitimate movement, to outlaw its existence, and to ban its operations, in order that friendly relations among peoples may be preserved, and the loyalty of citizens to their respective homelands safeguarded.

Article 24: The Palestinian people believe in the principles of justice, freedom, sovereignty, self-determination, human dignity, and in the right of all peoples to exercise them.

Article 25: For the realization of the goals of this Charter and its principles, the Palestine Liberation Organization will perform its role in the liberation of Palestine in accordance with the Constitution of this Organization.

Article 26: The Palestine Liberation Organization, representative of the Palestinian revolutionary forces, is responsible for the Palestinian Arab people's movement in its struggle — to retrieve its homeland, liberate and return to it and exercise the right to self-determination in it — in all military, political, and financial fields and also for whatever may be required by the Palestine case on the inter-Arab and international levels.

Article 27: The Palestine Liberation Organization shall cooperate with all Arab states, each according to its potentialities; and will adopt a neutral policy among them in the light of the requirements of the war of liberation; and on this basis it shall not interfere in the internal affairs of any Arab state.

Article 28: The Palestinian Arab people assert the genuineness and independence of their national (wataniyya) revolution and reject all forms of intervention, trusteeship, and subordination.

Article 29: The Palestinian people possess the fundamental and genuine legal right to liberate and retrieve their homeland. The Palestinian people determine their attitude toward all states and forces on the basis of the stands they adopt vis-à-vis the Palestinian revolution to fulfill the aims of the Palestinian people.

Article 30: Fighters and carriers of arms in the war of liberation are the nucleus of the popular army which will be the protective force for the gains of the Palestinian Arab people.

Article 31: The Organization shall have a flag, an oath of allegiance, and an anthem. All this shall be decided upon in accordance with a special regulation.

Article 32: Regulations, which shall be known as the Constitution of the Palestinian Liberation Organization, shall be annexed to this Charter. It will lay down the manner in which the Organization, and its organs and institutions, shall be constituted; the respective competence of each; and the requirements of its obligation under the Charter.

Article 33: This Charter shall not be amended save by [vote of] a majority of two-thirds of the total membership of the National Congress of the Palestine Liberation Organization [taken] at a special session convened for that purpose.

(Text available online at The Avalon Project at Yale Law School, http://www.yale.edu/lawweb/avalon/mideast/plocov.htm.)

Appendix II
Phased Plan Resolution
Adopted at the 12th Session of the Palestinian National Council
Cairo, June 9, 1974

On the basis of the Palestinian National Charter and the Political Programme drawn up at the eleventh session, held from January 6–12, 1973; and from its belief that it is impossible for a permanent and just peace to be established in the area unless our Palestinian people recover all their national rights and, first and foremost, their rights to return and to self-determination on the whole of the soil of their homeland; and in the light of a study of the new political circumstances that have come into existence in the period between the Council's last and present sessions, resolves the following:

1. To reaffirm the Palestine Liberation Organization's previous attitude to Resolution 242, which obliterates the national right of our people and deals with the cause of our people as a problem of refugees. The Council therefore refuses to have anything to do with this resolution at any level, Arab or international, including the Geneva Conference.

2. The Liberation Organization will employ all means, and first and foremost armed struggle, to liberate Palestinian territory and to establish the independent combatant national authority for the people over every part of Palestinian territory that is liberated. This will require further changes being effected in the balance of power in favour of our people and their struggle.

3. The Liberation Organization will struggle against any proposal for a Palestinian entity the price of which is recognition, peace, secure frontiers, renunciation of national rights and the deprival of our people of their right to return and their right to self-determination on the soil of their homeland.

4. Any step taken towards liberation is a step towards the realization of the Liberation Organization's strategy of establishing the democratic Palestinian state specified in the resolutions of previous Palestinian National Councils.

5. Struggle along with the Jordanian national forces to establish a

Jordanian-Palestinian national front whose aim will be to set up in Jordan a democratic national authority in close contact with the Palestinian entity that is established through the struggle.

6. The Liberation Organization will struggle to establish unity in struggle between the two peoples and between all the forces of the Arab liberation movement that are in agreement on this programme.

7. In the light of this programme, the Liberation Organization will struggle to strengthen national unity and to raise it to the level where it will be able to perform its national duties and tasks.

8. Once it is established, the Palestinian national authority will strive to achieve a union of the confrontation countries, with the aim of completing the liberation of all Palestinian territory, and as a step along the road to comprehensive Arab unity.

9. The Liberation Organization will strive to strengthen its solidarity with the socialist countries, and with forces of liberation and progress throughout the world, with the aim of frustration all the schemes of Zionism, reaction and imperialism.

10. In light of this programme, the leadership of the revolution will determine the tactics which will serve and make possible the realization of these objectives.

The Executive Committee of the Palestine Liberation Organization will make every effort to implement this programme, and should a situation arise affecting the destiny and the future of the Palestinian people, the National Assembly will be convened in extraordinary session.

(Text available at Ariel Center for Policy Research Web site, http://www.acpr.org.il/resources/plophased.html)

Appendix 12
Memorandum of Conversation between Abdul Aziz Al Saud, King of Saudi Arabia and President Roosevelt
February 14, 1945

(*Outpost*, March 2005; reprinted by permission of Americans for a Safe Israel.)

> "Memorandum of Conversation between His Majesty Abdul Aziz al Saud, King of Saudi Arabia and President Roosevelt, February 14, 1945, aboard the U.S.S. Quincy."

(Editor's note: AFSI member David Kirk first discovered this memorandum when he went through the Peter Bergson papers in Yale University library. He has confirmed its authenticity: the document is in the FDR library, President's Map Room Papers, Naval Aid's Files, Crimea Conference A/16. Saudi Arabia's attitude toward Jews comes as no surprise to anyone; Roosevelt's coldness to Jewish survivors of the Holocaust — resettle them in Poland! — and apparent total lack of sympathy for Jewish claims to a homeland in Palestine may come as a surprise to some. It would appear to be fortunate indeed that Harry Truman, not Roosevelt, was President when Ben Gurion declared the birth of Israel and sought international recognition.)

I. The President asked his Majesty for his advice regarding the problem of Jewish refugees driven from their homes in Europe. His Majesty replied that in his opinion the Jews should return to live in the lands from which they were driven. The Jews whose homes were completely destroyed and who have no chance of livelihood in their homelands should be given living space in the Axis countries which oppressed them. The President remarked that Poland might be considered a case in point. The Germans appear to have killed three million Polish Jews, by which count there should be space in Poland for the resettlement of many homeless Jews.

His Majesty then expounded the case of the Arabs and their legitimate rights in their lands and stated that the Arabs and the Jews could never cooperate, neither in Palestine, nor in any other country. His Majesty called attention to the increasing threat to the existence of the Arabs and the crisis which has resulted from continued Jewish immigration and the purchase of land by the Jews. His Majesty further stated that the Arabs would choose to die rather than yield their lands to the Jews.

His Majesty stated that the hope of the Arabs is based upon the word of honor of the Allies and upon the well-known love of justice of the United States, and upon the expectation that the United States will support them.

The President replied that he wished to assure His Majesty that he would do nothing to assist the Jews against the Arabs and would make no move hostile to the Arab people. He reminded His Majesty that it is impossible to prevent speeches and resolutions in Congress or in the press which may be made on any subject. His reassurance concerned his own future policy as Chief Executive of the United States Government.

His Majesty thanked the President for his statement and mentioned the proposal to send an Arab mission to America and England to expound the case of the Arabs and Palestine. The President stated that he thought this was a very good idea because he thought many people in America and England are misinformed. His Majesty said that such a mission to inform the people was useful, but more important to him was what the President had just told him concerning his own policy toward the Arab people.

II. His Majesty stated that the problem of Syria and the Lebanon was of deep concern to him and he asked what would be the attitude of the United States Government in the event that France should continue to press intolerable demands upon Syria and the Lebanon. The President replied that the French Government had given him in writing their guarantee of the independence of Syria and the Lebanon and that he could at any time write to the French Government to insist that they honor their word. In the event that the French should thwart the independence of Syria and the Lebanon, the United States Government would give to Syria and the Lebanon all possible support short of the use of force.

III. The President spoke of his great interest in farming, stating that he himself was a farmer. He emphasized the need for developing water resources, to increase the land under cultivation as well as to turn the wheels which do the country's work. He expressed special interest in irrigation, tree planting and water power which he hoped would be developed after the war in many countries, including the Arab lands. Stating that he liked Arabs, he reminded His Majesty that to increase land under cultivation would decrease the desert and provide living for a larger population of Arabs. His Majesty thanked the President for promoting agriculture so vigorously, but said that he himself could not engage with any enthusiasm in the development of his country's agriculture and public works if this prosperity would be inherited by the Jews.

Appendix 13

The Nation of Islam Will Sit at the Throne of the World

(Address of Hamas Leader Khaled Mash'al at the Al-Murabit Mosque in Damascus, translated by MEMRI.[1] Used by permission.)

We say to this West, which does not act reasonably, and does not learn its lessons: By Allah, you will be defeated. You will be defeated in Palestine, and your defeat there has already begun. True, it is Israel that is being defeated there, but when Israel is defeated, its path is defeated, those who call to support it are defeated, and the cowards who hide behind it and support it are defeated. Israel will be defeated, and so will whoever supported or supports it.

America will be defeated in Iraq. Wherever the [Islamic] nation is targeted, its enemies will be defeated, Allah willing. The nation of Muhammad is gaining victory in Palestine. The nation of Muhammad is gaining victory in Iraq, and it will be victorious in all Arab and Muslim lands.

...They do not understand the Arab or Muslim mentality, which rejects the foreigner... I say to the [European countries]: Hurry up and apologize to our nation, because if you do not, you will regret it. This is because our nation is progressing and is victorious. Do not leave a black mark in the collective memory of the nation, because our nation will not forgive you.

Tomorrow, our nation will sit on the throne of the world. This is not a figment of the imagination, but a fact. Tomorrow we will lead the world, Allah willing. Apologize today, before remorse will do you no good. Our nation is moving forwards, and it is in your interest to respect a victorious nation.

...Israel will be defeated and will be of no use to you. The Arabs will be victorious. The Muslims will be victorious. Palestine will be victorious. Change your policy soon, if you want to protect your interests, and maintain healthy relations with the East.

---

1. Middle East Media Research Institute, Special Dispatch Series, number 1087, February 7, 2006.

Bibliography

Abella, Irving, and Harold Troper. *None Is Too Many: Canada and the Jews of Europe 1933–1948*. Lester and Orpen Dennys, 1982.

Bard, Mitchell G. *Myths and Facts: A Guide to the Arab-Israeli Conflict*. Chevy Chase, MD: American Israeli Cooperative Enterprise, 2001.

Carroll, James. *Constantine's Sword: The Church and the Jews*. Boston: Houghton Mifflin, 2001.

Carta's Historical Atlas of Israel: A Survey of the Past and Review of the Present. Jerusalem: Carta, 1996.

Cornwell, John. *Hitler's Pope: The Secret History of Pius XII*. New York: Viking Penguin, 1999.

Dimont, Max I. *The Indestructible Jews*. New York: Signet, 1973.

— *Jews, God and History*. New York: Signet, 1962.

The Encyclopaedia Americana. Danbury, CT: Grolier, 1986.

The Encyclopaedia Judaica. Jerusalem, Keter Publishing House, 1972.

Fackenheim, Emil L. *The Jewish Return into History: Reflections in the Age of Auschwitz and a New Jerusalem*. New York: Schocken, 1978.

Flannery, Edward H. *The Anguish of the Jews. Twenty-Three Centuries of Anti-Semitism*. New York: Macmillan, 1965.

Gibbon, Edward. *The Decline and Fall of the Roman Empire*. New York: Dell, 1963.

Gold, Dore. *Hatred's Kingdom: How Saudi Arabia Supports the New Global Terrorism*. Washington, DC: Regnery Publishing, 2003.

Goott, Amy Kaufman, and Steven J. Rosen, eds. *The Campaign to Discredit Israel*. Washington, DC: American Israel Public Affairs Committee, 1983.

Grayzel, Solomon. *A History of the Jews*. Toronto, Ont: Mentor Books, 1968.

Herzog, Chaim. *Who Stands Accused?: Israel Answers Its Critics*. New York: Random House, 1978.

Israel Pocket Library: History from 1880. Jerusalem: Keter Publishing House, 1973.

Johnson, Paul. *A History of the Jews*. New York: Harper Collins, 1988.

Josephus: The Essential Writings. Translated and edited by Paul L. Maier. Grand Rapids, MI: Kregel Publications, 1988.

Josephus: The Jewish War. Translated by G. A. Williamson. New York: Penguin, 1959.

Katz, Samuel. *Battleground: Fact and Fantasy in Palestine*. New York: Bantam, 1973.

Kertzer, David I. *The Popes against The Jews: The Vatican's Role in the Rise of Modern Anti-Semitism*. New York: Alfred A. Knopf, 2001.

Littel, Franklin H. *The Crucifixion of the Jews: The Failure of Christians to Understand the Jewish Experience*. New York: Harper and Row, 1975.

Moynihan, Daniel Patrick, with Suzanne Weaver. *A Dangerous Place*. Boston: Little, Brown and Company, 1975.

Netanyahu, Benjamin. *A Place among the Nations: Israel and the World*. New York: Bantam, 1993.

Netanyahu, Benjamin, ed. *Terrorism: How the West Can Win*. New York: Farrar, Straus and Giroux, 1986.

Parkes, James. *The Conflict of the Church and the Synagogue: A Study in the Origins of Antisemitism*. New York: Atheneum, 1969.

Peters, Joan. *From Time Immemorial: The Origins of the Arab-Jewish Conflict over Palestine*. New York: Harper and Row, 1984.

Silver, Abba Hillel. *Where Judaism Differed*. New York: Macmillan, 1956.

Spencer, Robert. *Onward Muslim Soldiers: How Jihad Still Threatens America and the West*. Washington, DC: Regnery Gateway, 2003.

Stav, Arieh, ed. *Israel and a Palestinian State: Zero Sum Game? The "Phased Plan" as adopted by the Palestine National Council*. Tel Aviv:. Zmora-Bitan Publishers for the Ariel Center for Policy Research, 2001.

Stav, Arieh, ed. *Israel at the Crossroads: The Economic Aspects of the Peace Process*. Tel Aviv: Ariel Center for Policy Research, 1997.

Timmerman, Kenneth R. *Preachers of Hate: Islam and the War on America*. New York, Random House, 2003.

Ye'or, Bat. *Eurabia: The Euro-Arab Axis*. Madison, NJ: Fairleigh Dickinson Press, 2005.

Zimler, Richard. *The Last Kabbalist of Lisbon*. London: Arcadia Books, 1998.

Zimmerman, Bennett, Roberta Seid, and Michael L. Wise. *Arab Population in the West Bank and Gaza: The Million Person Gap*. Ramat Gan: Begin-Sadat Center for Strategic Studies, 2006.

General Background Research

UN Conventions: Geneva Convention, The Hague Convention, Genocide Convention.

The Canadian Commission on Hate Propaganda: Prof. Maxwell Cohen, Dean McGill University, Montreal. Pierre Elliot Trudeau, later Prime Minister of Canada. Marc McGuigan, later Minister of Justice in Trudeau government.

Papers by Prof. H. E. Fried, Assistant to Judges at Nuremberg and Advisor to the UN on International Law and War Crimes. Personal meeting and discussions with Prof. Fried.

Participated and helped in research of several trials of Nazi War Criminals: Imre Finta, and Ernst Zundel on Hate Propaganda.

Researched and participated in preparations of briefs and documents to the Canadian government as well as *participated in several delegations to Ministers*, including Minister of Justice, Jean Chretien, later Prime Minister.

Index